Deliberative Democracy, Political Legitimacy, and Self-Determination in Multicultural Societies

Date Due

Deliberative Democracy, Political Legitimacy, and Self-Determination in Multicultural Societies

Jorge M. Valadez

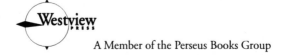

A Member of the Perseus Books Group

To the memory of my mother and father,
Antonia and Manuel Valadez.

Copyright © 2001 by Westview Press, A Member of the Perseus Books Group

Published in 2001 in the United States of America by Westview Press, 5500 Central Avenue, Boulder, Colorado 80301–2877, and in the United Kingdom by Westview Press, 12 Hid's Copse Road, Cumnor Hill, Oxford OX2 9JJ

Find us on the World Wide Web at www.westviewpress.com

Library of Congress Cataloging-in-Publication Data

Valadez, Jorge.
    Deliberative democracy : political legitimacy and self-determination in multicultural societies / by Jorge Valadez.
    p. cm.
    Includes bibliographical references and index
    ISBN 0–8133–9114–8 (pbk.)
    1. Minorities—Civil rights. 2. Representative government and representation. 3. Multiculturalism. 4. Legitimacy of governments. 5. Self-determination, National. I. Title.

JF1061 .V35 2000
321.8—dc21
    00-043785

PERSEUS
POD
ON DEMAND   10 9 8 7 6 5 4 3

Contents

Preface

This book is the first part of a three volume work on the philosophical bases of multiculturalism. My primary concern here is to reconceptualize some of the most fundamental issues in political theory from a perspective that takes into account the culturally pluralistic character of contemporary democracies. As we will observe, many basic themes in political philosophy—such as political obligation, sovereignty, property rights, and democratic deliberation—will be seen in a very different light once we jettison mistaken assumptions concerning the culturally homogeneous nature of the polity. The limitations and deficiencies of traditional theories of the state will become apparent once the implications of the multicultural perspective are articulated.

The second volume will deal primarily with the epistemological and metaphysical issues related to intercultural understanding. A great deal of philosophical research needs to be done on the extent to which it is possible for the adherents of different and incommensurable cultural conceptual frameworks to understand one another. While the history of philosophy offers a plethora of theories about the nature of reality, metaontological theories—that is, theories that provide the conceptual mechanisms for systematically analyzing and comparing the internal structure of conceptual frameworks—are relatively rare. But in a world in which it is essential to learn to coexist peacefully with others who have different visions of the world, it is very important to develop metaontological theories for intercultural understanding. An adequate metaontological theory for multiculturalism would enable us to analyze, compare, and perhaps adjudicate (in some areas and for certain purposes) between different cultural world views. Such a metaontological theory would provide inference rules for reasoning across incommensurable universes of discourse and would explain how to understand statements that articulate various relations of ontological dependence and priority between the members of these domains. Moreover, in developing a theory of intercultural understanding, particular attention will be given to epistemological and metaphysical themes that have been generally neglected by Western philosophers, such as the functions of metaphor and the body in structuring conceptual frameworks, the cognitive structure of the emotions and their role in reasoning, and the special contributions that can be made by minority women (given that they stand at the intersection of multiple forms of oppression) to intercultural understanding.

My principal concern in the third volume will be multicultural political economy. Intercultural economic inequalities often lead to differences in political and social power between cultural groups, which in turn facilitate discrimination and oppression of vulnerable minorities. As long as significant intercultural economic inequalities exist, it is highly unlikely that cultural groups, either at the national or international level, will relate to one another on equal footing and exhibit the social solidarity characteristics of healthy democracies. In addition to addressing intercultural group economic inequalities, an adequate theory of political economy is important for the creation of ecologically sustainable societies. The connections between multiculturalism and ecological consciousness have yet to be explored. Though I make a preliminary attempt to articulate these connections in the final chapter of this first volume, the topic merits more detailed treatment, and I will revisit it in the third book. Among the themes that will be considered are the potential contributions of some minority cultures for the creation of ecologically sustainable economies, the importance of using cultural resources for preserving and defending cultural life-places from environmental degradation, and the role of ecological consciousness in creating social solidarity in multicultural societies and in mobilizing political movements for political and economic self-determination.

The theorization of multiculturalism has been plagued by an unfortunate association with intellectual movements that have undermined its credibility and usefulness. Often, such theorizations have been excessively partisan and poorly argued, and have involved the adoption of highly implausible and even inconsistent positions. As a result, these theoretical justifications have, on the one hand, provided conceptual ammunition to those who are unsympathetic or antagonistic to the rights of minority cultural groups and, on the other, have alienated those individuals who are potentially supportive of the multicultural perspective but have become disenchanted with the inadequacy of these theoretical justifications. This situation underscores the need for a more balanced and rigorous defense of the multicultural perspective.

The impact of multiculturalism, when this perspective is properly articulated and justified, is bound to be far-reaching and revolutionary. When the three-volume work is completed, it should provide a coherent alternative to the political-economic paradigm, which is rapidly attaining global dominance, of individualistic liberal democracy underpinned by neoliberal economics. Note that I said a "coherent" alternative and not a "comprehensive" one. This is because it is not my purpose to develop a universal theory of oppression. There are other important forms of oppression, particularly those afflicting women throughout the world, that I will not consider systematically, even though in the second and third volumes I will examine issues that are of particular relevance to women. In any case, I believe that themes concerning the empowerment of women and other groups can be integrated within the general theory that I will elaborate in the three-volume work. Despite my criticisms of conventional conceptions of liberal democracy, my own perspective is grounded on the normative principle of equal respect for the moral agency and dignity of individuals, and to this extent it falls within the boundaries of liberalism, when the latter is broadly construed. I believe that liberal principles provide the most appropriate framework for defending a theory of ethnocultural self-determination.

To forestall unnecessary objections, a terminological explanation is in order. Sometimes, I will talk about the bases or foundations of multiculturalism. I do not interpret these terms in the (Cartesian) sense of indubitable universal axioms on which multiculturalism is grounded, rather, I understand them as referring to the basic normative and cognitive assumptions made by multiculturalism. I take this interpretation of these terms to be relatively uncontroversial, given that every ideological perspective, whether its adherents admit it or not, makes certain basic presuppositions. Thus, my concern to establish the bases or foundations for multiculturalism simply amounts to the project of articulating the basic normative and theoretical tenets on which multiculturalism, as I define it, is based, as well as elucidating its central principles.

Acknowledgments

I would like to thank those individuals and institutions who supported me in the production of this work as well as those who promoted my development as a person and a philosopher.

The Department of Philosophy at Marquette University granted me several course reductions, which enabled me to spend more time working on the manuscript, while the Philosophy Department at Southwest Texas State University exhibited early confidence in my capacities as a philosopher. Thanks also to the Philosophy Department at Our Lady of the Lake University for its assistance during the last year of writing the manuscript.

The support provided by Robert Solomon and Kathleen Higgins over the years has been very helpful. Their support opened doors that would likely have remained closed. I am particularly grateful to Dave Nowak, who read every word of every draft of the book (sometimes several times). Dave called my attention to numerous books and essays I had overlooked that were relevant to my project. Sometimes it seemed as if he served as my second set of eyes and ears in searching for pertinent material. Jeff Gordon's advice and encouragement were crucial for my attaining my career goals as a philosopher. He was a willing listener for germinating ideas, concerning which he was a sympathetic but perceptive critic. I am also grateful to the encouragement that Tom Anderson, Michael Wreen, Mike McNulty, Mike Vater, Stan Harrison, and Bob Ashmore gave me when I taught at Marquette University. During the last two years of this writing project, Katherine Taylor's moral and material support contributed significantly to its completion. My editor at Westview Press, Sarah Warner, exhibited great patience and flexibility in accommodating changes and extensions in finishing this work. Her suggestions regarding the manuscript were invariably helpful.

There are a number of friends with whom I have had philosophical and eclectic conversations from which I have profited in different ways. Among these are Peter Hutchinson, Vincent Luizzi, Dale McCollough, Patricia Keating-Valadez, Sarita Rodriguez, Lewis Friedland, Sara Stevenson Queen, Danny Goldberg, Kevin Gibson, Rachel Napier, and John Reubartsch. David Montejano, *camarada de corazón*, provided encouragement and support throughout the writing of the manuscript. His friendly, if sometimes persistent, prodding for me to finish this book was helpful, and his suggestions about delimiting its scope made it a manageable project. The intellectual exchanges and experiences I shared with Esther Chavez alerted me to the different forms that oppression can take, and furthered my development as a person and a Chicano. My brothers and sisters—Gregoria, Juanita, Elvira, Hilario, Rogelio, and Paula—gave me the kind of encouragement and inspiration that only family can provide. *Gracias por su apoyo.*

Without doubt, I owe the greatest debt of gratitude to my wife, Tricia, who was the sounding board for many of my ideas and who used her excellent intuitions on many complex issues to give me insightful feedback. Her love and spiritual focus helped me work through several difficult events during the writing of this book. My children, Teresa and Emilio, besides enriching my life immensely, kept me connected to those human experiences that are intrinsically meaningful and that are the ultimate source of what makes life worth living.

1

Introduction

In this first chapter I provide a conceptual road map to the terrain covered in the book. Given the scope and complexity of this project, it is useful for the reader to have a summary of the principal claims and arguments that will be discussed.

Construed broadly, a theory of multicultural democracy addresses the wide range of social and political issues that arise between majority groups and ethnic, religious, linguistic, and national minorities and, less commonly, between dominant minority groups and disempowered majority ethnocultural groups.[1] Such issues include equitable political representation, language rights, social and economic inequality, regional autonomy, and rights to preservation of cultural integrity. Intercultural conflict, ranging from open warfare to interethnic tensions that undermine social solidarity and democratic engagement, is the major source of conflict in the world today.[2] Such conflicts can take the form of religious wars, battles over scarce natural resources, racial hate crimes, military conflicts over disputed territories, struggles for political self-determination, disputes over immigration policies, and "cultural wars" over education and social policies. Since most democratic countries are culturally pluralistic, the resolution of intercultural issues represents perhaps the single most important challenge to contemporary democracies.

In multicultural democratic societies we find some of the clearest illustrations of the shortcomings and dangers of democracy.[3] We need only examine, for example, the history of inequality and political marginalization of Catholics in Northern Ireland, or the lack of equitable political representation at the federal level of African-Americans, Native-Americans, and Latinos in the United States to recognize the capacity of democratic systems to tolerate significant cultural group inequalities and injustices. But the failure of contemporary democracies to deal with cultural pluralism also provides an opportunity to identify the sociopolitical principles, institutions, and practices necessary to create just and sustainable multicultural democratic societies that meet the challenges presented by cultural diversity.

Ironically, authoritarian regimes have often been the most successful at minimizing intercultural conflicts. Their approach has been to eliminate such conflicts by repressing ethnocultural groups. Through coerced incorporation of these groups into a central state, policies outlawing maintenance of cultural identity, forced migration, or outright genocide, authoritarian governments have managed to curtail intercultural conflict. Needless to say, since such "success" has been achieved at the cost of fundamental and sometimes brutal violations of human rights, authoritarian approaches for dealing with intercultural conflict are not viable options. It is instructive to note, however, that liberal democratic governments have sometimes dealt with cultural diversity by adopting policies similar to those used by authoritarian regimes. In the United States, for example, policies of forced schooling have been used to assimilate Native-American children into the mainstream culture, and Mexican-American children in parts of the Southwest have been physically punished in the schools for speaking Spanish. Though these policies may have been paternalistic attempts at assimilating the members of these groups "for their own good," such practices have no place in a democratic society because they violate basic principles of autonomy as they relate to choice of cultural tradition.[4] I will argue that democratic principles of autonomy and pursuit of happiness protect the right to preserve one's cultural tradition, and that the use of coercive policies that suppress cultural identity, whether motivated by authoritarian or paternalistic justifications, is not an acceptable way to deal with cultural differences.

While acceptable answers to intercultural issues will thus have to conform to basic principles of democratic governance, our conception of democracy itself will be transformed by the effort to find a just resolution to intercultural issues. Confronting cultural diversity will ultimately lead to a more profound and comprehensive understanding of what such basic notions as political equality, autonomy, and justice mean in culturally diverse democracies. For instance, in some cases the just treatment of indigenous groups requires recognition of collective territorial rights and rights of cultural integrity, which are rights traditionally unrecognized from the perspective of democratic societies. Likewise, in order to obtain an adequate understanding of the concept of autonomy in a multicultural society, it is necessary to see how it applies to cultural groups and not only to individuals. The impact of multiculturalism on democratic theory is bound to be significant because, despite the fact that most contemporary democracies are culturally pluralistic, most political philosophers in the Western tradition have assumed a culturally homogeneous body politic. Failure to take cultural diversity fully into account has resulted in theoretical perspectives that are inadequate for resolving many of the social and political dilemmas that arise in democratic societies.

What we must do is create just and effective sociopolitical frameworks that give due recognition to cultural group differences while making possible the fair intercultural negotiation of needs and interests. These frameworks should be sufficiently adaptable to deal with the diversity of problems that may arise within multicultural societies. In addition, we must establish societies that conform to the highest democratic ideals of justice, equality, and autonomy, because it is only in such societies that these sociopolitical frameworks can perform their intended functions and resist forces of destabilization. Ultimately, the goal of multiculturalism should be not merely to minimize intercultural conflicts, but to provide an answer to one of the basic dilemmas of the human condition—how to live and flourish in coexistence with others who have fundamentally different conceptions of the world.[5]

Three Dilemmas of Multicultural Democracies

The resurgence of ethnic identity and internal nationalism is among the strongest centrifugal forces straining democratic states. With the decline of centralized authoritarian governments, official policies that suppressed ethnic and national identity have been eliminated or weakened, and this has created the political space for minority groups to seek self-governance. This tendency is clearly discernible in the political events following the disintegration of the Soviet Bloc and the decline of military dictatorships in Latin America and Africa. Another factor contributing to minority group empowerment is a changing global political climate in which greater legitimacy is granted to the rights of indigenous peoples and ethnocultural groups to exercise political self-determination. Supragovernmental organizations like the United Nations now explicitly disavow both external and internal forms of colonialism, and recognize that other collectivities besides states can be legitimate bearers of political rights of self-governance. In addition, countries such as India and Mexico, that have long experienced pervasive and systematic political corruption despite having had formal democratic institutions in place for many years, have recently revitalized these institutions so that they conform better to true democratic ideals. This move towards more genuine democratic governance has introduced new elements of civic tension, as formerly marginalized minorities challenge the status quo and demand fair inclusion in their country's political life.

Contemporary discussions of multiculturalism often fail to distinguish between the different categories of ethnocultural groups seeking self-determination.[6] Indigenous peoples, national minorities, linguistic minorities, and ethnic immigrant groups, for instance, are indiscriminately classified under the general rubric of "racial and ethnic minorities," without noting the important differences between them. Failure to distinguish between these different minority groups is likely to lead to a clouded understanding of the nature and legitimacy of their various claims to empowerment. Ethnic, national, religious, and linguistic minority groups struggling to achieve self-determination can be divided into three categories: those groups seeking greater political representation and socioeconomic empowerment in the majority society's political and socioeconomic institutions; those groups desiring autonomous self-determination but willing to remain part of the country where they live; and those groups demanding secession and either independent statehood or irredentist integration.[7] Thus, intercultural conflict can take a variety of forms, depending on the different political and historical circumstances affecting the ethnocultural groups in question.

Even though there are numerous ways in which intercultural conflicts and tensions manifest themselves, there are discernible sociopolitical and economic structural features which characterize the social settings which give rise to intercultural conflict or peaceful coexistence. Intercultural conflicts tend to occur where there is a history of discrimination and oppression between cultural groups, where discriminatory or oppressive practices (or their effects) are still present, and where there is an absence of just sociopolitical frameworks for the resolution of intercultural conflicts of interest. Sociopolitical settings in which diverse cultural groups can flourish and coexist peacefully are those in which the interests and needs of all cultural groups are mutually understood and respected, in which political rights and obligations reflect the differential circumstances of the cultural groups comprising the body politic, and in which all cultural groups have the opportunity to determine their political and cultural destinies. More precisely, to create fair and sustainable multicultural democracies, it is necessary to adequately address the dilemmas of intercultural understanding and cooperation, the proper political relationship between a culturally diverse citizenry and the state, and minority demands for cultural, political, and economic self-determination. I will systematically examine these dilemmas and propose doctrines on epistemological egalitarianism, the function and justification of political communities, and self-determination that address, respectively, each of these dilemmas. After a description of the general democratic framework within which these doctrines apply, I will briefly discuss these doctrines and provide a preliminary account of the arguments that I will use to support them. I will then comment briefly on the relevance of these sociopolitical doctrines for the philosophical foundations of multicultural democracies.

Deliberative Democracy

The vision of a multicultural democratic society that I advocate recognizes reasoned public deliberation as a means by which citizens can arrive at policy decisions that are collectively binding and generally justifiable.[8] In this conception of democracy, citizens rationally evaluate the reasons for, and the implications of, policy alternatives in open public forums designed to incorporate the perspectives of all members of society. Collective decisions do not result merely by aggregating the pre-existing desires of citizens; rather, members of the polity attempt to influence each others' opinions by engaging in a public dialogue in which they examine and critique, in a civil and considerate manner, each others' positions while explaining the reasons for their own views. In the forums of public deliberation, participants strive to understand the perspectives and needs of others, and through a process of mutual clarification and justification seek solutions that accommodate as far as possible the needs and interests of all. Even the most fundamental and cherished values and beliefs may be challenged in the course of these public deliberations,[9] and citizens are expected to defend underlying assumptions and modes of justification that may not be shared by others. It will also be generally recognized that it is the force of the better argument, and not political power or coercion, that should be the primary legitimizing factor of social policies.

A central aspiration of deliberative democracy is that by participating in and observing these public deliberations, citizens will increase their understanding of policy options, develop their capacities for mutual respect and compromise, and deepen their understanding of the collective good. In contrast to what is advocated by certain theories of discursive democracy, however, public deliberation in a multicultural society need not always aim at consensus; in the more difficult cases of intercultural disagreement, it will suffice that participants believe they have equitably influenced the deliberative process and agree to continue to cooperate in good faith in future deliberations.[10]

An advantage of deliberative democracy is its capacity to enhance reflective, autonomous decision making. It can be plausibly argued that if autonomy is understood, at least in part, as a second-order capacity to critically evaluate first-order desires and choices and revise them on the basis of higher-order preferences[11], deliberative democracy is especially effective in promoting individual and collective autonomy. Individuals and groups will be in a better position to evaluate their first-order desires and options, and thus enhance their autonomy, by subjecting their first-order preferences to critical scrutiny in deliberative public forums. Since political decisions are by nature not purely personal decisions but always have a public dimension ... which the interests of others are involved, through public deliberation citizens will be better able to determine whether their personal preferences accord with individual, group, and general societal interests. In short, deliberative democracy will expand peoples' capacity for self-governance by providing structured public settings for political deliberation and by cultivating the cognitive and civic capacities appropriate for democratic citizenship.

Deliberative democracy is particularly suited for multicultural societies because of the existence of deep and enduring differences in conceptions of the good in these societies. Since deliberative democracy focuses on the collective resolution of common problems on the basis of mutual understanding and cooperation, it provides some of the dialogical mechanisms needed for fruitful democratic engagement in culturally pluralistic contexts. But multicultural societies are beset not only by incommensurable moral visions—and the propensities for cross-cultural misunderstanding that accompany them—but also by significant and persistent cultural group differences in socioeconomic and political power. Such differences can provide more powerful groups with inordinate and unjustified advantages in the deliberative process. Low levels of formal education and lack of access to information technologies, for example, can significantly hinder the capacity of some cultural minorities to compete on equal footing with other cultural groups in public deliberation. Further, long-standing legacies of oppression introduce profound cultural and psychological elements which may hinder the persuasive proficiency of certain cultural minorities in public deliberation. Additionally, entrenched suspicions and resentments, not to mention outright hatred, between cultural groups can distort the dialogical process and make it difficult for them to engage in collective deliberations which presume a high degree of civility and public magnanimity.

Epistemological Egalitarianism

The doctrine of epistemological egalitarianism[12] addresses these problems by placing constraints on the deliberative process which contravene these distorting factors. According to this doctrine, all members of a multicultural society should have equal access to the epistemological resources needed for effective participation in public deliberation. If reasoned public deliberation is recognized as a priority in a multicultural society, then—assuming that we accept the ideal of political equality—providing the resources and competencies that make it possible for the members of all cultural groups to compete on an equal basis should also be a priority. More specifically, all members of a multicultural society should have equal access to information and information technologies, equal educational opportunities to develop the critical thinking abilities for analyzing and evaluating that information, and equal access to the social and material means necessary for the intracultural and intercultural exchange of information. In addition, epistemological egalitarianism advocates the expansion of deliberative forums to include brief biographical and cultural narratives, exercises in empathetic imagination, and other means by which participants can gain greater mutual affective understanding.[13] Public deliberation should not be confined to purely cerebral, disputative discourse aimed at convincing others of one's point of view, it should also enhance mutual sympathy and emotive understanding.

These objectives would not only provide all members of a multicultural society with the epistemological resources and cognitive skills to make as compelling a case as possible for their perspectives, needs, and interests, it would also provide them with a more profound understanding of each other's life circumstances, values, and concerns. Further, implementing epistemological egalitarianism would empower minority groups so that they would be less susceptible to ideological and political manipulation. When people are more knowledgeable and educated, they have a better chance of detecting and negating attempts by others to influence and control their thoughts and behavior. This form of self-protection is important, given that there are cases in which one cultural group has used its greater knowledge and understanding of other groups for the purpose of domination and control.[14]

A corollary to the doctrine of epistemological egalitarianism is that a multicultural democracy should grant priority to the systematic exploration of how racist and prejudiced attitudes affect the ways in which the members of cultural groups perceive one another's values, beliefs, intentions, and sentiments. This task is particularly important in view of the fact that, as recent studies in cognitive science have shown, people employ modes of reasoning and knowledge structures that often lead to false cultural stereotypes.[15] These studies indicate that commonly used judgmental heuristics and knowledge structures are remarkably resistant to change, even when individuals who employ them are confronted with compelling evidence that falsifies the conclusions obtained by using them. Another factor that makes the eradication of negative cultural stereotypes difficult is a high degree of social and economic stratification. Limited interactions with the members of other cultural groups hinders our knowing them as individuals and makes our perceptions of them more susceptible to negative ethnocultural generalizations because we lack an experiential base from which to critically evaluate such generalizations.

Even though a multicultural democracy can significantly diminish inequalities in deliberative influence between cultural groups by embracing and implementing the ideals of epistemological egalitarianism, substantial group differences in political efficacy can remain. This is particularly true in democracies in which group inequalities in socioeconomic and political power are so pronounced or incommensurabilities between cultural perspectives so great that ethnocultural minorities cannot realistically hope to sufficiently influence the political process to attain self-determination. In these situations, the possibility arises that these ethnocultural groups should be granted either the right to secede or rights of regional self-governance.

But even though the elimination of political inequalities is an important desideratum, one could legitimately ask what moral considerations would justify such drastic measures as the partial or total breakup of a political community. In order to obtain an adequate understanding of the moral rationale for secession and autonomous governance, we need to examine one of the fundamental issues in political philosophy, namely, the proper function and legitimation of political societies.

The Function and Justification of Political Communities

Political philosophers have traditionally given a great deal of attention to the issues of the political authority and legitimacy of the state. Much less attention, however, has been given to the issues of political membership and the right of collectivities to form sovereign political communities with powers of territorial control in a world containing limited land and natural resources. These issues are important for a foundational theory of multicultural democracies because, as we shall see, questions concerning the locus of sovereignty, immigration policies, and moral obligations between political communities are of central importance for such democracies. For example, claims for autonomous governance made by ethnocultural groups in multicultural democracies bear directly on questions concerning collective territorial control and the justification for forming autonomous political communities.

Moreover, conventional foundational theories of the state, such as contractarian doctrines, assume undifferentiated citizenship. But the common practice of states' coercively incorporating ethnocultural groups into their boundaries already suggests that traditional conceptions of the social contract—which are based on universalized conceptions of citizenship and consent—may fail to provide a viable philosophical foundation for multicultural democracies. Culturally pluralistic states with ethnocultural groups seeking or already possessing autonomous territorial self-determination, for example, cannot rely on the notion of a social contract which equally binds all of its citizens into a united polity. Justifiable demands by ethnocultural groups for autonomous self-determination undermine the idea that all members of the polity are equally obligated to recognize the political authority of the state because of their consent to its political institutions. By holding the state historically accountable for violating their consent in forcibly incorporating them into the polity, some ethnocultural groups have called attention to an additional require-ment for state legitimacy which goes beyond the normative adequacy of the state's political institutions. That is, in order for a state to rightly de-mand recognition of its legitimacy, it is not enough that its practices, ideals, and institutions at the present time satisfy criteria of justice; it is also necessary that it answer to the injustice of the procedures through which it incorporated the cultural groups within its boundaries. Con-trary to what Kant, Rawls, and other political philosophers have claimed, state legitimacy is not purely a matter of the consent that ideally rational, autonomous beings would give to its political structures.

What is needed is a foundational theory of the multicultural state that adequately articulates the proper political relationship between a cultur-ally diverse citizenry and the state. Such a theory would take due consid-eration of the relevant factors that affect the state's relationship to differ-ent ethnocultural groups. This theory would also provide an account of the primary function of political communities and identify the rights, values, and institutional commitments that a culturally pluralistic politi-cal body must respect if it is to be normatively justified. I will argue that the primary function of a political community is to promote the flourish-ing of its members in the political, economic, and socio-cultural spheres. This flourishing is best understood and accomplished in terms of the self-determination of the political community to which individuals belong. An appropriate political union for human flourishing is one that confers to the citizenry the familiar civil, political, and entitlement rights; that grants public recognition to their cultural membership; and that, when appropriate, provides the cultural rights and institutional support neces-sary for ethnocultural groups to preserve their cultural traditions. When discussing the rights to which the citizens of a multicultural democracy are entitled, I will assume that traditional civil rights, such as freedom of conscience, speech, religion, assembly, and association, as well as politi-cal rights to vote, run for office, organize political parties, and so forth, are already theoretically well-grounded. For this reason, as well as limita-tions of space, my analyses will focus on those rights whose theoretical foundations are particularly controversial, namely, cultural rights and property rights.

Cultural rights are regarded in the international community as "third-generation" rights, which emerged after "first-generation" civil and po-litical rights and "second-generation" social welfare rights. Even though cultural rights which protect aspects of cultural heritage like language and traditional customs are now formally recognized in such documents as the United Nations Declaration on the Rights of Minorities and the Draft United Nations Declaration on the Rights of Indigenous Peoples, there is still some controversy concerning their nature and philosophical justification. Part of the controversy stems from the fact that since cultural rights are group-specific, i.e., granted on the basis of cultural membership, they do not exhibit a purported central characteristic of rights, namely, universal applicability. My position is that certain ethnocultural groups—such as national minorities, i.e., indigenous and nonimmigrant groups whose homelands were coercively incorporated into the larger state through conquest, colonization, or transference of territorial control between imperial powers[16]—are entitled to cultural rights and state institutional support to protect the cultural traditions that are essential for their attainment of a good life. In comparison to ethnic immigrant groups who voluntarily left their home countries under noncoercive conditions, national minorities and immigrant groups who fled their countries because of political oppression or economic or environmental crises have a relatively stronger case for rights protecting their cultural traditions.[17] However, certain ethnic immigrant groups also merit cultural rights under certain conditions.

A great deal of attention will also be given to property rights, primarily because there are serious philosophical problems with their justification, but also because conventional property rights theories do not address the special problems concerning property ownership that arise in multicultural democracies. In particular, traditional theories of property rights do not deal with claims of indigenous groups for collective property ownership, address demands by ethnocultural groups for group-based economic rectification of historical economic injustices, or propose solutions for the practice of biological piracy, in which transnational corporations appropriate the ethnobotanical knowledge and plant varieties of indigenous communities without providing proper compensation.[18] But property rights issues related to ethnocultural diversity cannot be resolved without a correct understanding of the nature and justification of property rights, because only then can we adequately assess the impact of cultural diversity on such rights. Thus my first task will be to critically examine and reconceptualize conventional theories of property rights, in order to obtain an appropriate understanding of property ownership in multicultural societies.

I will argue that land and natural resources, in their unmediated state, belong to all in common, if they belong to anyone at all. Since land and natural resources are not the product of anyone's labor, no one has ever had an exclusive and privileged claim to ownership of parts of nature. Many of the arguments in support of conventional private property rights attempt to justify individual, original unilateral appropriations of land and natural resources. In his *Second Treatise on Government*[19], for example, John Locke maintains that even though in the original state of nature land and natural resources belonged to all, individuals could justifiably appropriate property and its resources without the consent of others by mixing their labor with nature. Other authors have attempted to justify private property rights on the basis of desert, by virtue of their beneficial social consequences, or because of their necessity for the development of agency and autonomy. I will argue that all of these arguments, Locke's included, fail to provide an adequate moral or rational justification for private property rights as restricted rights, that is, as rights that only some people have. Despite the illegitimacy of restricted private property rights, private property ownership can nevertheless be vindicated by appealing to its necessary role in the exercise and development of agency and autonomy, whether the latter are understood in individual or collective terms.[20] Such ownership rights, however, must be universal in the sense that all members of the society or community should have ownership rights to land and essential natural resources (and the technological means to employ the latter). Since everyone has a right to exercise agency and autonomy, they also have a concomitant right to the materials essential for the enjoyment of these capacities, particularly since no one ever had an original, legitimate, exclusive claim to these materials, namely, land and natural resources.

Property rights have a status in contemporary democracies similar to the status that liberty and voting rights had in earlier times, that is, they are restricted and not universal rights. But just as skin color and gender are, respectively, morally arbitrary bases for restricting liberty and voting rights, so possessing the capacity to coercively displace the inhabitants of territories or happening to appear first on the scene are not morally legitimate bases for nonuniversal ownership of parts of nature. The universalization of rights to natural property represents the next fundamental step in the evolution of liberal democracy because it resolves a fundamental inconsistency at its very core. While liberal democracy gives pride of place to the autonomy of individuals, it unjustifiably upholds a system of property rights that limits the autonomy of many members of the citizenry.[21] Unless constitutional liberal democracies resolve this fundamental inconsistency, they will never truly fulfill their promise as just systems of governance.

While universal rights to land and natural resources are eminently defensible, I will maintain that this is not the case with mediated property, that is, with capital goods, technological forms (including intellectual property), and manufactured commodities. These forms of property are mediated in the sense that, in contrast to land and natural resources, their design and construction require capital investments and physical or conceptual labor exerted by specific individuals. The rights of ownership of these forms of property should take into account the labor and economic inputs provided by those individuals responsible for their existence. Economic systems with free markets in labor, capital, and goods and services conform best with individual agency and autonomy, and are the most efficient systems of economic production and exchange in industrial technological societies.²² In these systems individuals are entitled to the economic gains obtained through their labor and transactions involving mediated property. As in the case of property ownership, rights to mediated property will differ in the case of those cultural groups who favor collective ownership of most forms of mediated property and a community economy over a market economy. However, I will argue that there are important constraints on ownership of mediated property, particularly in the areas concerning the satisfaction of basic needs and unrestricted rights to income from mediated property.

Self-Determination for Ethnocultural Groups

Aside from the fact that questions concerning the normative legitimacy of political communities are of central importance for a theory of the state, what prompted our discussion of the proper function and justification of political communities was the expectation that it would provide us with a better understanding of the moral basis for self-governance claims. Earlier we noted that even if we adopted the doctrine of epistemological egalitarianism, the cultural and socioeconomic differences between some ethnocultural groups and the majority society may be so great that these groups may be unable to effectively defend their needs and interests in a multicultural democracy. In these cases, separation or divorce from the existing political community, in the form of autonomous governance or secession, respectively, may be appropriate for these groups. If, as I maintained in the last section, a political community is normatively legitimate when it fulfills its proper function of promoting the flourishing of its members, does this view of the state support the claims for self-governance of ethnocultural groups seeking regional self-rule or secession?

This question should be answered in the affirmative because, to the extent that ethnocultural groups seeking self-governance cannot flourish by being part of a particular political community, the latter is failing to carry out its primary function as a political body. Thus, the formation of a separate autonomous political union is justified so that the members of these groups can achieve human flourishing. But for a particular ethnocultural group to be entitled to self-governance, it must be established that factors such as state-sponsored systematic discrimination, policies of inequitable economic redistribution, or threats to their physical security undermine their capacity to flourish as human beings. Further, they have to show that the particular form of self-governance they desire provides them with a reasonable opportunity to achieve control over their own political, cultural, social, and economic affairs.

There is another important rationale besides the inability to flourish that can support self-government claims. This rationale is based on the historical fact that many ethnocultural groups were forcibly incorporated into the state in which they live. If a group formerly lived in its own autonomous political community and if this self-governing status was violated by the state, they can legitimately argue that they have the right to reclaim their lost political autonomy and the territory that was formerly under its control. To the extent that an ethnocultural group can successfully argue that it was deprived of its territorial control over its homeland and it never consented to becoming part of the existing political community, it can strongly buttress its case for self-governance. Even though my emphasis thus far in discussing self-determination has been on ethnocultural groups seeking autonomous governance or secession, there are cultural groups who strive for self-determination within the institutional structures of the state. As we shall see below, the conditions for these groups to exercise self-determination differ from those for autonomist and secessionist groups.

The doctrine of self-determination that I will defend recognizes that for different ethnocultural groups, self-determination can have different meanings and involve different institutional requirements. This doctrine fills a crucial gap in conventional theories of the state, which fail to account for the exceptional circumstances and obstacles faced by cultural minorities in achieving self-determination. The doctrine of self-determination has three parts: the first relates to accommodationist cultural groups who seek self-determination within the institutional structures of the majority society; the second concerns cultural groups who strive for self-determination through autonomous governance within the boundaries of the state; and the third deals with cultural groups seeking secession and either independent statehood or irredentist integration.

Cultural groups in the first category typically try to attain greater control over their cultural, socioeconomic, and political affairs through more equitable democratic representation, enhanced socioeconomic status, and the elimination of discrimination.[23] In addition, these groups, rather than opting for total assimilation, typically wish to retain aspects of their cultural traditions. Maghrebins in France, Sikhs in Canada, and Latinos and African-Americans in the United States, who have fought for civil rights, greater political participation, and equality of opportunity, would be included in this category.[24] In contrast to the cultural groups in the other categories, rarely have they called for either partial or total autonomy. I will thus refer to these groups as accommodationist, because for the most part they are trying to satisfy their political and sociocultural needs and interests within the general sociopolitical framework of the majority society.[25] According to the doctrine of self-determination I will defend, what justifies the demands of these cultural groups for equal and fair representation is their political equality with the members of the majority society and their status as autonomous moral agents capable of rational self-direction. The justification of their demands for enhanced socioeconomic opportunity is also based on conceptions of equality and, in addition, on the theory of property rights described earlier.

According to the doctrine of self-determination, the aim of democratic governments in culturally pluralistic societies with accommodationist groups should be to ensure that the members of all groups are included in the political process. These societies should adopt electoral systems such as proportional representation and cumulative voting that reflect more accurately the diversity of political perspectives of the citizenry. In proportional representation, officials are elected in multimember districts in accordance with the proportion of the vote their party receives in an election. These systems are more inclusive than majoritarian systems because candidates do not have to obtain a majority of votes to get elected and because almost all voters, including members of minority groups, will get to elect representatives of their choice. In cumulative voting, voters get the same number of votes as there are seats to vote for, and they can aggregate their votes in any way they desire.[26] For example, if there are five seats in a county commission race, minority voters, by aggregating their votes for a minority candidate, could elect that candidate even if they comprise only twenty percent of the voting population. A desirable feature of cumulative voting and most kinds of proportional representation is that they do not rigidly pre-determine cultural group divisions in a society, but allow different groups to organize themselves politically on the basis of self-perceived cultural membership or other shared interests. This flexibility enables multicultural societies to deal with mixed-race groups and shifting cultural group identities and coalitions. Rather than essentializing cultural group identities and priorities, these forms of political representation allow for contestation of these group features. Though no electoral system is perfect, proportional representation and cumulative voting are superior to single-member plurality systems for providing minority groups, and interest groups of other kinds, more equitable representation.

The second part of the doctrine of self-determination deals with cultural groups who seek varying degrees of autonomous self-determination within the boundaries of the state. To distinguish these groups from those in the other categories, I will classify them as autonomist. The groups in this category are further divided into three subgroups. The first of these involves indigenous peoples—such as the Quichuas and Otavalenos of Ecuador, the Saami of Sweden and Norway, the Aboriginal peoples of Australia, the Kunas of Panama, and Native Americans in the U.S.—who want political and territorial autonomy and exclusive control over certain aspects of their economic and social life. Of paramount importance for these groups are the defense or recovery of indigenous land and natural resources, the implementation of their internal forms of sociocultural organization, and the establishment of their own forms of political governance. These groups are seeking not political integration into the mainstream society but cultural and political autonomy, including sustainable material bases for their communities. Where they have succeeded, they have created political units that exist parallel to the state and that exert a considerable degree of control over their people, land, and natural resources. Their members may have dual citizenship and two sets of citizenship rights, corresponding to the indigenous polity and the state.

The second subgroup in this category is constituted of territorially concentrated ethnocultural groups such as the Catalonians, Greenlanders, and Basques, who generally have sought autonomous self-determination through greater control of the state's political apparatus within their territories.[27] On occasion, splinter organizations have fought for independent statehood, but in general the focus of most of these groups has been on obtaining regional self-determination within some kind of federalist or decentralized structure. Unlike indigenous peoples, they typically have not tried to establish distinctive forms of sociopolitical and economic organization, such as tribal councils and collective property ownership, but have sought regional control of forms of sociopolitical organization essentially like those of the state where they reside. I will refer to these groups as ethnonationalists.

The third subgroup in the autonomist category consists of ethnocultural groups who live in culturally pluralistic societies in which political power in the central government is shared by intergroup coalitions. The Sunni Arabs of Iraq, the Mainland Chinese of Taiwan, the Tutsi rulers of Burundi, and the Flemish and Walloons of Belgium, are examples of such ethnocultural groups. These groups maintain their own separate communal identities and organizations, and through a variety of power-sharing arrangements with other ethnocultural groups, participate in the collective governance of the state. I will call these groups communal contenders.[28] In searching for political arrangements that answer to the needs of these ethnocultural groups, it will be useful to examine systems of power-sharing such as those discussed by Arend Lijphart.[29]

But what justifies the stronger claims of groups seeking autonomous self-determination? Unlike calls for equitable political representation and equality of opportunity, demands for autonomous self-governance go beyond the traditional rights of uniform citizenship associated with democratic governments. In the case of the autonomist ethnocultural groups mentioned above, a consideration that could justify their claims is that they have a right to self-governance that derives from their status as distinct cultural communities with their own form of collective life. This argument is sometimes buttressed by the claims of indigenous and ethnonationalist groups that their right to cultural and political self-determination has been endangered by the more powerful majority society and that the only way to safeguard their cultural integrity is through some form of self-governance.[30]

Another rationale that is used by some autonomist groups to justify self-governance is based on their coerced incorporation into the state and their lost territorial autonomy. This rationale can be illustrated by the aboriginal status of many indigenous groups, that is, their status as peoples whose initial forcible incorporation into the state violated their collective agency and autonomy. Before the arrival of European colonizers, these groups lived in sovereign communities with their own sociopolitical institutions and economic forms of life. These indigenous societies were unjustly displaced from their homelands and their members never assented to, and often vigorously resisted, conventional citizenship status. These communities have maintained their distinctive cultural identity and their ancestral connections to the peoples originally displaced by settler societies. The justification for self-governance in this case is a form of rectificatory justice, since they are reclaiming something of which they were unjustly deprived. Moreover, the cultural survival of many of these groups is contingent upon their having control over their homelands and its natural resources. Aboriginals are thus entitled to self-determination free from alien subjugation and retention of the distinctive forms of self-governance and material forms of life of which they were unjustly deprived, and without which they cannot survive or flourish as a people.

The third part of the doctrine of self-determination concerns secessionist cultural groups, that is, those groups seeking secession and either independent statehood or irredentist integration, such as the Palestinians, the Tamils of Sri Lanka, and some Kurdish communities. In some ways, these are the most difficult cases of intercultural conflict to resolve, because national as well as international issues are involved and because of the determination of the international community to maintain the territorial integrity of existing states.[31] Secession may undermine the economic basis of the original state by jeopardizing accessibility to raw materials, ports, roads, or other resources and facilities necessary for economic subsistence and trade. Granting secession may also create a geographical separation of the original state into regions that may then be more susceptible to military aggression by hostile neighbors. In some cases there may be legitimate concerns on the part of the international community regarding the status of "trapped" minorities in the emerging state, especially when there are questions concerning the secessionist's commitment to human rights.[32]

The core normative issues in secessionist movements, however, have to do with the criteria justifying the right to secede. Several arguments for secession will be discussed, the most prominent of which will be arguments based on rectificatory justice, discriminatory redistribution, and cultural or physical survival. Arguments from rectificatory justice apply to those seceding groups whose territory was either unjustly incorporated by an existing state or was unjustly acquired by an earlier state that is the ancestor of the state from which these groups want to secede. Discriminatory redistribution can provide a justification for secession if it can be established that a government implements social or economic policies that systematically and invidiously disadvantage a cultural group while benefiting others in the existing state.[33] Secession is also justified in situations in which the only, or the most viable, way the physical survival of a cultural group can be ensured is by obtaining sovereign control over a territory. Finally, and more controversially, in exceptional cases secession may be justified if a cultural group can exercise the territorial control necessary for its cultural survival only by obtaining sovereignty.

The Significance of These Sociopolitical Doctrines

The three sociopolitical doctrines I have discussed jointly provide a theoretical base for multicultural democracies. Speaking broadly, these three sociopolitical doctrines are grounded on a vision of the human person as a culturally constituted, moral decision making, autonomous agent striving to develop and flourish within a culturally pluralistic society. This vision of the autonomous individual functions as an overarching regulative ideal underpinning these doctrines. There are three objectives that are important for the realization of this conception of integrated autonomy: first, the preservation of the cultural contexts which make life-options meaningful and within which self-identity and collective responsibilities are established; second, the development of the political institutions that allow for individual revision of ends and for genuine collective self-determination; and third, access to the material resources needed for people to take control of their individual and collective destinies. These components elucidate, respectively, the cultural, political, and economic dimensions of autonomy. In my discussion of the three sociopolitical doctrines, I will show how they promote different aspects of this three-fold conception of integrated autonomy.

Far from being an ideal imposed from a Western perspective on multicultural societies, this tripartite conception of autonomy captures some of the deepest aspirations of minority cultural groups around the world. Indeed, it is not possible to understand the strivings of most minority groups without reference to this communally mediated vision of autonomy. In contrast to the Western liberal tradition, autonomy is understood here as a variable notion, mediated and even constituted in important ways by cultural context. Autonomy is also understood as applying not only to individuals and states, but to other collectivities as well, such as ethnocultural groups. This more comprehensive conception of autonomy provides a more adequate basis for understanding justice in multicultural democratic societies, but problems can arise when attempting to realize both group and individual autonomy, particularly when cultural groups who exercise autonomous self-determination appeal to collective autonomy to justify placing internal restrictions on their members. Given our understanding of autonomy as partially involving the capacity to revise choices on the basis of higher-order preferences, members of cultural groups should be granted what Joseph Raz calls the "right of exit," that is, the right to leave their cultural group under nonpunitive conditions.

The extent to which autonomous cultural groups must understand and implement civil, political, and entitlement rights in a way that conforms to liberal interpretations may be difficult to determine in some cases. Extreme transgressions of certain of these rights, such as violating the right of bodily integrity through forms of punishment that involve mutilation, for example, are unacceptable. Similarly, denying women the right of political participation, which is of fundamental importance for political equality and autonomy, should also be proscribed.[34] However, other cases are not so clear cut. For instance, efforts by a cultural group to protect its cultural integrity by denying certain benefits (such as housing benefits) to group members that reject the group's religion should not be proscribed outright, even though they should be subject to external adjudicatory or judicial review.[35] I will maintain that review of such controversial cases should not be conducted by the state's highest court, but by regional or, less ideally, international commissions and tribunals. For example, organizations such as the African Commission on Human and Peoples' Rights, established in 1986 as the regulatory body of the African Charter on Human and Peoples' Rights, can serve as external sources of appeal that are knowledgeable of, and sensitive to, the relevant cultural contexts that affect the cases at hand. Given that many countries have a long history of systematic legal endorsement of oppressive policies against ethnocultural groups, it is understandable why these groups would not trust the institutional forms of judicial review of their conquerors. Moreover, indigenous groups in particular have shown a willingness to abide by the rulings of external adjudicatory bodies and international courts.[36]

The sociopolitical doctrines discussed above also delineate the limits of cultural tolerance in multicultural democratic societies. They provide necessary conditions that all just multicultural democracies should observe. As long as cultural groups respect the right of exit and the external judicial review of their implementation of liberal democratic rights, it is acceptable for them to imprint their own interpretation on civil, political, and entitlement rights by establishing alternative forms of property ownership, implementing their own forms of justice, establishing special requirements for entrance into or residence in tribal territories, determining educational policies, employing consensual procedures for making political decisions, and so forth. Cultural groups should be free to implement these policies even when they differ significantly from those used by the majority society.

Finally, we should note that these sociopolitical doctrines have a complementary character and form a cohesive political basis for the multicultural democratic state. The doctrine of epistemological egalitarianism, and the conception of deliberative democracy within which it is embedded, articulate the general nature of the democratic framework in which political negotiations are to take place. This doctrine also sets the broad framework within which political decisions not predetermined by the other two doctrines are to be reached. The doctrine of self-determination elucidates the normative bases which should guide the intercultural negotiations between the state and cultural groups making claims for political and socioeconomic empowerment. At this point in history, these negotiations represent one of the most important political dilemmas facing multicultural democracies. The doctrine articulating the function and justification of political communities describes the rights of citizens and cultural groups that are not subject to political negotiation. Included among these are those rights that form the basis for economic justice, namely, universal rights to natural property.

Developing Democratic Citizenship
in Multicultural Societies

Contemporary multicultural democracies can flourish only in a civic milieu in which individuals exhibit such qualities as willingness for mutual compromise, trust in democratic institutions, the capacity to understand the perspectives and needs of others, and a sense of social solidarity. A decline in civic character and social trust undermines the effectiveness of democratic institutions and the capacity for democratic self-governance. The problems associated with the erosion of democratic virtues and social cohesion can become especially acute in multicultural societies made up of cultural groups with significantly different worldviews and conceptions of the good. Indeed, one of the most common objections to multiculturalism is that by advocating the primacy of cultural identity and tradition, it sacrifices national unity and sets the stage for cultural fragmentation.[37] When peoples' interests and self-identity are based on cultural membership and not national citizenship, the argument goes, social fault lines are created that reinforce divisions and conflicts within a society.

What these critics have failed to note, however, is that cultural conflict and Balkanization are caused primarily not by preservation of and adherence to cultural traditions, but by historical and existing discrimination and oppression of ethnocultural groups and, most important, by the lack of just sociopolitical institutions for equitable democratic representation and the negotiation of cultural group interests and needs. Identifying with one's cultural tradition in and of itself does not necessarily lead to social divisiveness. There are examples of culturally diverse societies in which cultural groups have maintained a strong sense of national identity while retaining their cultural traditions.[38] In fact, societal respect for cultural identity and tradition can actually lead to an increased identification and pride in one's country, as citizens realize that they live in a society that appreciates the significance of a dimension of their lives that is dear to their hearts and minds.

Nevertheless, even though the critics of multiculturalism overstate the degree of social fragmentation that arises from retention of cultural tradition and misidentify the causes of Balkanization, their concerns are not entirely unjustified. Increased emphasis on cultural identity and tradition can, and sometimes does, weaken citizens' identification with the state. Merely making rhetorical appeals for national unity and social solidarity while accentuating cultural membership is disingenuous. An adequate theory of the foundations of the multicultural democratic state must therefore address in a systematic way the problem of developing and maintaining civic virtue and solidarity in culturally pluralistic societies. In the last chapter, I discuss two ways in which the roots of democratic citizenship can be cultivated in contemporary multicultural democracies, namely, by citizen participation in networks of civic engagement and by the development of ecological consciousness.

The Civic Sphere

In the civic sphere, democratic citizenship is developed by networks of civic engagement, which consist of voluntary associations that individuals form in order to pursue common social projects and goals in a variety of areas.[39] Such associations include neighborhood organizations, cooperatives, parent-teacher associations, charity groups, sports clubs, trade unions, ethnic organizations, religious groups, art alliances, labor unions, and environmental groups. These forms of social organization are civic environments in which people develop communal commitments and learn the civic skills of social cooperation, interest negotiation, and ideological mediation.

An important characteristic of enriching civic voluntary associations is that typically their participants are bound by horizontal relations of cooperation and mutuality. That is, they relate to one another not through hierarchical relations of dependence and authority, but through interactions in which their status as equal fellow citizens is recognized and respected.[40] To function successfully in these networks of civic engagement, individuals must learn to take the needs and interests of others into account and moderate their views accordingly. By engaging in social projects based on shared interests, the members of a community develop a sense of solidarity and trust even when they do not agree on all issues concerning the social project that brought them together. However, in order for our civic engagements to develop civic character they must not be confined exclusively to the circle of individuals in our socio-economic and cultural groups, because then we will miss out on precisely the kind of civic interactions that are the most valuable for expanding our understanding of different people and perspectives. In addition, certain kinds of hierarchically structured voluntary associations can actually entrench parochial attitudes that restrict rather than broaden social vision and civic engagement.[41]

Another noteworthy feature of voluntary associations is that they function as mediating institutions, that is, they constrain the power of the state while enhancing the influence of its citizens and promoting the identification and resolution of problems overlooked or intentionally neglected by formal governmental institutions.[42] This citizen-empowering function of voluntary associations is particularly important for democracies in developing countries, where colonial legacies of institutionalized patronage, limited public funds, and nascent democratic institutions restrict the capacity of governments to adequately respond to important social needs.

Developing Ecological Consciousness

Greater participation in networks of civic engagement is a familiar strategy to develop democratic virtue which has been proposed by other authors.[43] The second strategy I will advocate, however, is one whose implications have yet to be fully explored. The development of ecological consciousness will be examined as a promising strategy for cultivating a democratic political culture for multicultural societies. The underlying idea of this strategy is that by recognizing the potentially devastating effects of our actions on the integrity of the earth's ecosystems, we can foster a sense of common responsibility and shared destiny. Since we all depend on the same biosphere for survival, ecological responsibility can be a powerful force in forging a common perspective in which the interests of all cultural groups converge. Further, ecological consciousness can enrich our collective moral vision by, for example, making us aware of our responsibilities to future generations. The expanded social vision and nonegocentric orientation engendered by ecological consciousness can have salutary civic implications for contemporary societies permeated by the morality of self-interest.

Ecological consciousness also aids in discerning the actual and potential analogical relationships between the interdependencies in nature and those in the social realm. Ecosystems provide paradigmatic examples of complementarity, in which different plant and animal species support one another in complex networks of symbiotic relationships. I will maintain that similar relationships of complementarity can be developed in pluralistic societies, and that ecological consciousness encourages a positive view of human diversity in which cultural differences in such areas as spirituality, affective connectivity, personal validation, and aesthetic orientation broaden our selfhood and freedom by providing diverse models of self-realization. Just as diversity in nature is essential for the viability of ecosystems, so cultural and individual diversity are important for maintaining open and dynamic democratic societies. An enhanced appreciation for diversity is an invaluable asset for a multicultural society seeking to cultivate a democratic political culture characterized by tolerance and a sense of societal interdependence.

In understanding the relevance of ecological consciousness, however, we must be careful to also note the differences between natural ecosystems and social ecologies, the most important of which is the contrast between the intentionality of human agents and the primarily instinctive behavior of nonhuman organisms. I will not advocate that we use natural ecosystems as "models" for human societies, because there are too many differences between natural and social ecologies for this to be a viable project. Nevertheless, there are important similarities between natural and social systems, and the awareness of these can be used as a heuristic strategy for developing vital kinds of cognitive and affective transformations in culturally pluralistic societies.

Chapter Overview

In the next chapter, I examine the basic principles of deliberative democracy, and identify the ways in which this form of democracy is particularly suited for multicultural societies. In the third chapter, I discuss the doctrine of epistemological egalitarianism, placing particular emphasis on how inequities in epistemological resources debase the process of public deliberation in democratic societies. Here I also discuss the prerequisites and procedures for fruitful intercultural dialogue. In the fourth chapter I discuss the function and justification of political communities and argue that the promotion of human flourishing, which is the primary function of a political union, is best understood and accomplished in terms of the self-determination of that political body. The doctrine of self-determination is covered in the fifth and sixth chapters. In Chapter 5, I discuss the nature of self-determination for ethnocultural groups, and defend an integrated and expansive interpretation of self-determination. In the sixth chapter, I examine issues of self-determination confronting accommodationist cultural groups. I focus on the issues of political representation of African-Americans and Latinos in the U.S. to illustrate the kinds of problems that groups in this category typically face in attaining equitable representation. In Chapter 7 I discuss the normative justifications for the claims of autonomist and secessionist groups.

In Chapters 8 and 9, my focus is on rights to the ownership of land, natural resources, mediated property, and intellectual property. My examination of property rights will complete my analysis of self-determination for ethnocultural groups. In these two chapters I examine the territorial rights of states and the impact that cultural group differences have on property rights in a multicultural society, especially with regard to intellectual property and the collective territorial rights of indigenous groups. In Chapter 10 the discussion shifts to the issues pertaining to the cultivation of democratic citizenship in culturally pluralistic societies. In this chapter I focus on the development of civic skills and values that can be obtained through participation in voluntary associations, and also examine the potential of ecological consciousness to develop the sense of collective responsibility, expansion of moral vision, and conception of self-transcendence so important for sustainable democratic societies.

Notes

1. I will use the general phrase "ethnocultural groups" to include racial groups in this broad category. Technically speaking, the concept of race is included in the notion of ethnicity, even though in some contexts the terms "racial" and "ethnic" are used to characterize different groups. When I want to refer to groups identified by dominant societies primarily on the basis of their physical characteristics, I will use the term "race" to emphasize this particular mode of identification.

2. For a general account of existing and potential intercultural conflicts, see Hurst Hannum, *Autonomy, Sovereignty, and Self-Determination: The Accommodation of Conflicting Rights*, rev. ed. (Philadelphia: University of Pennsylvania Press, 1996), Ted Gurr, *Minorities at Risk: A Global View of Ethnopolitical Conflicts* (Washington, DC: United States Institute of Peace Press, 1993), and "Embattled Minorities Around the Globe: Rights, Hopes, Threats," *Dissent*, ed. Michell Cohen, special issue, 43, no. 3 (1996).

3. In making this claim I am using the term "democratic" in a general sense to include any country that grants the universal franchise, provides citizens with the freedom to organize political parties, and holds regular multi-party elections. In this broad sense countries that do not respect some civil liberties would still be considered democratic. At the beginning of the twenty-first century the problem of the proliferation of "illiberal democracies" is becoming increasingly severe. The celebration of the victory of democracy over autocratic forms of governance had barely ended when emerging democratic countries all over the world started to elect officials willing to suspend or repudiate some of the most basic civil rights. For a discussion of the problems of illiberal democracies, see Fareed Zakaria, "The Rise of Illiberal Democracy," *Foreign Affairs* 76, no. 6 (1997): 22–43.

Except where otherwise indicated (as when I use the term "liberal democracy"), I will use the term democracy in the broad sense. Part of my purpose in doing this is to underscore the fact that formally granting democratic rights is not nearly enough to ensure either a just society or fair democratic representation for all members of the polity. One of my primary goals in this book is to delineate the additional conditions that must be in place before the promise of democracy can be realized.

4. Here I will follow Will Kymlicka, Yael Tamir, Joseph Raz, and others in maintaining that for some cultural groups, the preservation of cultural tradition is essential for their conception of the good and for their self-identity, and that adopting social policies to secure these ends is in some cases politically justifiable. I also concur with these authors that a cultural context is presupposed for meaningful choice-making, and thus for the exercise of autonomy itself. For an example of these lines of reasoning, see Will Kymlicka, *Multicultural Citizenship: A Liberal Defense of Minority Rights* (Oxford: Oxford University Press, 1995) and Yael Tamir, *Liberal Nationalism* (Princeton: Princeton University Press, 1993).

An important intellectual precursor to the view that culture is central to our capacity to conceive of meaningful life-options is Alasdair MacIntyre's *After Virtue* (Notre Dame, IN: University of Notre Dame Press, 1981).

5. As one might infer from these comments, my conception of multiculturalism involves a great deal more than issues concerning the "recognition" of cultural groups. Contemporary discussions of the "politics of recognition" were initiated in response to Charles Taylor's influential work, "The Politics of Recognition," in *Multiculturalism and the "Politics of Recognition,"* ed. Amy Gutmann (Princeton: Princeton University Press, 1992). Taylor argued that some of the new political movements in the U.S. and Canada were motivated by cultural group demands for societal recognition of their cultural particularity, and that these movements represent a conception of liberal democracy that is incompatible with traditional liberal democratic principles. While Taylor is correct in saying that multiculturalism challenges conventional views of liberal democracy in important ways, I maintain, with Kymlicka, Tamir, and Raz, that demands by cultural minorities for cultural rights and self-determination are best defended by appeal to traditional principles of agency and autonomy central to liberal democracy. For liberal defenses of cultural minority rights, see Kymlicka, *Multicultural Citizenship* and Tamir, *Liberal Nationalism*.

Furthermore, I contend that there are other fundamental aspects of liberal democracy, such as property rights, that need to be reconceptualized in order to create just and sustainable liberal democratic systems for culturally pluralistic societies.

6. See, for example, Arthur M. Schlesinger's *The Disuniting of America* (New York: W. W. Norton and Company, 1992) and David Hollinger, *Postethnic America: Beyond Multiculturalism* (New York: Basic Books, 1995).

7. My appreciation for the differences between cultural minorities derives from Will Kymlicka's important distinction between national minorities and ethnic groups. Roughly, national minorities are nonimmigrant groups who were incorporated into settler societies through annexation, colonization, or conquest, while ethnic groups are comprised of individuals who immigrated to a society into which, typically, they want to be integrated. My three-part classification of cultural groups (actually it is a five-fold classification, since groups in the autonomist category are further divided into three subgroups) is more nu-

anced that Kymlicka's, because it allows for more precise ethnocultural group distinctions that are relevant for understanding issues of self-determination for these groups. Moreover, my classificatory system is based primarily not on differential historical circumstances (though these are recognized as important), but on the nature of the different political aspirations of the groups involved. In addition, while African-Americans do not fit easily into either of Kymlicka's categories, in my scheme they provide a good example of groups in the accommodationist category.

8. The conception of democracy I have in mind is deliberative democracy. For a discussion of this democratic theory see Amy Gutmann and Dennis Thompson, *Democracy and Disagreement* (Cambridge, MA: Harvard University Press, 1996), John S. Dryzek, *Discursive Democracy* (Cambridge, U.K.: Cambridge University Press, 1990), and James Bohman, *Public Deliberation: Pluralism, Complexity, and Democracy.* (see p. 367) (Cambridge, MA: MIT Press, 1996). The most important contemporary influence in the development of deliberative democracy has been Jurgen Habermas. See, for example, his *Moral Consciousness and Communicative Action*, trans. Christian Lenhardt and Shierry Weber Nicholsen (Cambridge, MA: MIT Press, 1993). However, the foundational ideas of deliberative democracy probably date back to Aristotle. For a brief description of the Aristotelian conception of public political discourse, see Martha Nussbaum and Amartya Sen, "Internal Criticism and Indian Rationalist Traditions," in *Relativism: Interpretation and Confrontation*, ed. Michael Krausz (Notre Dame, IN: University of Notre Dame Press, 1989), pp. 299–325.

9. There will, however, be certain fundamental rights that will be beyond political negotiation. I will discuss this issue in Chapter 4.

10. James Bohman proposes and defends this weaker conception of the aims of political dialogue when deep differences are involved in *Public Deliberation*, pp. 99–101. I discuss Bohman's views in Chapter 2.

11. First-order desires are desires that directly affect my decisions and actions, e.g., my desire for a cigarette directly influences my decision to light and smoke a cigarette. Second-order desires are desires about desires, e.g., my desire to live a long, healthy life may override my first-order desire to smoke. Second-order capacities are those which involve reflective evaluation of first-order desires or preferences. For a discussion of this conception of autonomy, see Gerald Dworkin, *The Theory and Practice of Autonomy* (Cambridge, U.K.: Cambridge University Press, 1988), p. 20.

12. Epistemology is the branch of philosophy that deals with the theory of knowledge. This area of philosophy deals with such issues as the nature of truth, the validity of sensory knowledge, the role of abstract concepts in knowledge acquisition, and the influence of social factors in our understanding of the world. By "epistemological resources" I mean the material and educational resources to which different groups in the society have unequal access.

13. I agree with Iris Marion Young that it is not enough to address economic inequalities in order to create frameworks of public deliberation that are equitable and fair to all concerned, and that we must also try to rectify or equalize more subtle cultural and social factors that tend to disadvantage the members of certain groups in public deliberations. I will discuss these issues in Chapter 3. For a discussion of the considerations that must be taken into account in addressing

these issues, see Marion Young, "Communication and the Other: Beyond Deliberative Democracy," in *Democracy and Difference: Contesting the Boundaries of the Political,* ed. Seyla Benhabib (Princeton: Princeton University Press, 1996).

14. See, for example, Jorge Valadez, "Pre-Columbian and Modern Philosophical Perspectives in Latin America," in *From Africa to Zen: An Invitation to World Philosophy,* eds. Robert Solomon and Kathleen Higgins (Lapham, MD: Rowman and Littlefield, 1993).

15. *Naturalizing Epistemology,* ed. Hilary Kornblith, 2nd ed. (Cambridge, MA: MIT Press, 1994), pp. 261–290.

16. Will Kymlicka, "The Good, the Bad, and the Intolerable: Minority Group Rights," *Dissent* 43, no. 3 (1996): 29. Kymlicka was perhaps the first writer to recognize the importance of distinguishing between national minorities and ethnic immigrant groups for assessing the moral legitimacy of the claims for self-determination of the former.

17. Irish immigrants coming to the U.S. during the potato famine or persecuted Jews seeking refuge in a country are examples of groups who immigrated under exceptional circumstances. In addition, ethnic immigrants who leave their home countries under duress have an even stronger case for cultural protections if the state to which they immigrate is responsible for the political, economic, or environmental disruptions in their home countries. Guatemalan and Salvadoran refugees who fled because of oppression made possible by U.S. military aid to their governments are cases in point. Furthermore, under certain conditions other cultural groups, such as the Quakers and the Amish, also merit special protections.

18. Another reason, not intrinsically connected with property rights *per se,* for paying close attention to property ownership in multicultural societies is that intercultural group inequalities in ownership of land, natural resources, and capital make possible the disfranchisement of ethnocultural groups. There are many ways in which wealth creates the potential for such disfranchisement, including discriminatory hiring practices, differences in the capacity to influence public opinion, inequitable power in setting the terms for economic agreements, and abuse of greater access to political power. While I will not discuss at length the specific impact of property rights on intercultural exploitation, this issue will affect various aspects of my general theory.

19. John Locke, *Two Treatises of Government,* ed. Peter Laslett (Cambridge: Cambridge University Press, 1960).

20. The argument here will be that control rights over private property in an individualistic society is the scheme that best permits the development and exercise of autonomy and agency because it provides control over the material resources needed to carry out one's life projects and enables one to autonomously satisfy at least some basic sustenance needs. I will argue that control rights should be distinguished from income rights to property (a distinction discussed and defended at length by John Cristman in *The Myth of Property: Toward an Egalitarian Theory of Ownership* (New York: Oxford University Press, 1996) and that this distinction allows for a variety of economic systems which can simultaneously answer to autonomy and egalitarian needs. In addition, private ownership of

property promotes ecological sustainability insofar as it encourages people to protect the ecological integrity of their life-place.

In communities that opt for collective property rights, agency and autonomy are still relevant for justifying these property rights. In these cases, it is the agency and autonomy of the group and its continuing ability to live in cohesive communities of interdependent individuals that are of primary importance and not the capacity of individuals to exercise their agency and autonomy through private property ownership.

21. An important qualification to universal private property ownership is that a multicultural democratic society should recognize that for certain cultural groups, agency and autonomy are best developed and exercised in a communal context, and that these groups have the right to determine whether they wish to have collective or private property rights. In the view of some of these cultural communities, private property may actually undermine developed personhood and the proper exercise of agency. The members of these cultural groups will also be entitled to property rights, but these rights will take a communal form.

22. Of course, this is not to say that existing market schemes are the most efficient systems of economic production and exchange. On the contrary, present market systems are unsustainable and ecologically inefficient (in their externalization of ecological costs, for example). In addition, they deprive billions of people throughout the world of a basic level of agency and autonomy. In this book I will not develop a theory of the material base of multicultural societies; this task will be the subject of a future volume on the foundations of multiculturalism.

Another important observation we should make is that even though market systems are important in complex technological societies, they are not necessary for small, decentralized, agrarian community economies with simple divisions of labor. In such communities collective property ownership and the principle of usufruct work quite well in providing basic needs in sustainable ways.

23. Recently there have been some discussions of cultural groups with diasporic or transnational identities. These groups consist of immigrants, such as Dominicans or Peruvians, who retain strong ties with their home countries while obtaining dual citizenship or permanent residence in other countries. To the extent that these groups would seek self-determination, it is likely that they would try to achieve such goals as political equality, socioeconomic empowerment, and cultural rights in their adopted countries. Since it is highly improbable that they would seek autonomous self-determination (given their territorial dispersion and lack of status as national minorities within their adopted home countries) or secession, these groups would fall into the first of the three categories of cultural groups I will discuss here.

24. Given the recent U.S. Supreme Court decisions declaring race-based congressional districts unconstitutional, it is all the more urgent that cumulative voting or some form of proportional representation be adopted to promote fair political representation for minority groups in the U.S.

25. This is not to say, of course, that these groups are necessarily interested in cultural assimilation into the majority society. Also included in this category are those groups with a diasporic identity and mixed-race groups, because their aims are generally accommodationist.

26. In other words, the minority voters, by placing all of their five votes for the candidate of their choice, could elect the representative of their choice. Of course, cumulative voting respects the "one man, one vote" principle because everyone gets the same number of votes that they can aggregate in any way they desire. A prominent defender of this electoral system is Lani Guinier. She defends this system in *The Tyranny of the Majority: Fundamental Fairness in Representative Democracy* (New York: The Free Press, 1994).

27. Guntram F. A. Werther, *Self-Determination in Western Democracies: Aboriginal Politics in a Comparative Perspective* (Westport, CT: Greenwood Press, 1992), pp. 88–89.

28. The term "communal contenders" is from Ted Gurr. See Ted Gurr, *Minorities at Risk: A Global View of Ethnopolitical Conflicts* (Washington, D.C.: United States Institute of Peace Press, 1993).

29. Arend Lijphart, "Self-Determination versus Pre-Determination of Ethnic Minorities in Power-Sharing Systems," in *The Rights of Minority Cultures*, ed. Will Kymlicka (Oxford: Oxford University Press, 1996): 275–287.

30. Of course, at the most basic level what justifies the right of autonomist groups to self-determination through self-governance is, as in the case of accommodationist groups, their status as autonomous agents capable of self-direction. Political equality is emphasized with the latter groups (given their membership in a common political community with the majority society) and autonomous governance with the former, but the moral basis for the right to determine their own affairs is ultimately the same for both groups.

31. For a discussion of the current international perception of the right of self-determination as it relates to secession, see Hannum, *Autonomy, Sovereignty, and Self-Determination*, pp. 27–49.

32. For a discussion of these and kindred concerns related to secession, see Lee C. Buchheit, *Secession: The Legitimacy of Self-Determination* (New Haven: Yale University Press, 1978), pp. 216–245.

33. Allen Buchanan, "The Morality of Secession," in *The Rights of Minority Cultures*, ed. Will Kymlicka (Oxford: Oxford University Press, 1995), pp.355–364.

34. It is important to note here that political participation can take different culturally specific forms. We cannot assume that this right has been violated simply because a cultural group does not use conventional Western methods of political participation. Some cultural groups, for example, use consensual agreement and not majority voting methods for decision making. Even though in some groups participation has traditionally been gender-stratified, many groups (particularly indigenous groups) are moving towards more inclusive forms of participation.

35. The rationale for treating this third case differently from the other two is that religion may be so basic for the distinctive cultural identity of the group that its very cultural survival may very well depend on the continuation of its religion. By contrast, forms of punishment and prohibitions against women's suffrage, though they may be part of a cultural tradition, are not likely to be *essential* for the continuation of the culture. In fact, some cultures have changed attitudes towards the roles of women without ceasing to exist as distinct cultures. But it is difficult to see how an orthodox Jewish group, for example, could continue to exist if its members no longer practiced the religion. Benefit of the doubt concerning

what is essential for cultural integrity should be granted to the cultural group, subject to the external judicial review mentioned earlier.

36. Will Kymlicka, "The Good, the Bad, and the Intolerable: Minority Group Rights," *Dissent* 43, no.3 (1996): 22–30.

37. An influential work that has propagated this fallacious argument against multiculturalism is Arthur M. Schlesinger's *The Disuniting of America* (New York: W.W. Norton and Company, 1992). To be fair to Schlesinger, when he was making this argument he had in mind a more "extreme" form of multiculturalism than the one I advocate here. Nevertheless, he is mistaken in thinking that strong attachments to cultural traditions lead to social fragmentation, for there are examples (such as Belgium and Switzerland) of countries where strong cultural identities do not detract from a solid sense of national unity.

38. Canada recognizes the polyethnicity and multinationality of its citizens (roughly, the former refers to immigrant ethnic groups while the latter denotes national minority groups who were incorporated through conquest, colonization, or federation into settler societies), while Switzerland and Belgium recognize national minorities with language rights and rights of political self-determination. On this issue, see Kymlicka, *Multicultural Citizenship*.

39. The phrase "networks of civic engagement" is from one of the best accounts of the role of voluntary associations in sustaining a democratic culture, namely, Robert D. Putnam's *Making Democracy Work: Civic Traditions in Modern Italy*, (Princeton: Princeton University Press, 1993). In particular, see pp. 167–185. As a caveat against taking voluntary associations as a panacea, we should note that in certain circumstances these associations can have the opposite effect and actually entrench divisions and ideological dogmatism. This can be particularly true of religious organizations.

40. Developing civil societies based on the notion of equal citizenship is particularly important in Third World countries with long histories of political patronage and institutional and informal vestiges of colonial rule. For a discussion of the impact that nongovernmental action groups are having on democratic structures in developing countries, see Jeff Haynes, *Democracy and Civil Society in the Third World: Politics and New Political Movements* (Malden, MA: Polity Press, 1997).

41. See Putnam, *Making Democracy Work*, pp. 107–109 and 175–176.

42. In recent years the number and influence of nongovernmental organizations (NGOs) in developing countries has greatly increased. In some cases these organizations have taken over functions which governments are unable or unwilling to perform due to lack of funds, organization, or political corruption. For an examination of the increasing influence of NGOs in the Third World, see Haynes, *Democracy and Civil Society in the Third World*.

43. For example, see Robert Bellah, et al., *Habits of the Heart* (Berkeley: University of California Press, 1985) and Putnam, *Making Democracy Work*.

2

Deliberative Democracy

My primary objective in this chapter is to discuss the advantages and limitations of deliberative democracy as a form of governance for multicultural societies. As we observed in the first chapter, one of the greatest dangers of multicultural democracies is the potential for civil fragmentation and Balkanization. Deliberative democracy, with its emphasis, *inter alia*, on a commitment to the common good, the promotion of mutual understanding in political discourse, the recognition of all political voices, and the identification of collectively binding policies that take the needs and interests of everyone into account, is a form of democratic governance that has great potential for responding successfully to some of the central problems of intercultural dialogue and understanding in multicultural societies.

Even though there is general agreement among advocates of deliberative democracy on some of the basic principles of this democratic theory, a number of different conceptions of deliberative democracy have been developed.[1] My purpose here is not to provide an exhaustive account of the increasing number of such theories; rather, my goal is to delineate a preliminary version of deliberative democracy which is particularly suitable for making collective decisions in culturally pluralistic societies. In this chapter and the next, I hope to shed some light on some of the most difficult problems facing deliberative democracy, particularly three dilemmas that threaten to derail the whole project of basing democratic decision making in multicultural societies on public deliberation, namely, the absence of unitary political communities, the existence of moral and cognitive incommensurable differences within the polity, and the dilemma of group inequalities. These three problems arise in a strikingly forceful way in multicultural societies, since the latter are often comprised of cultural groups who have deep differences in their conceptions of the good and who are characterized by a significant degree of economic and social stratification. Indeed, it is no exaggeration to say that deliberative democracy faces its greatest challenges in multicultural societies. It is in these societies that we can most clearly identify the limits of deliberative democracy as well as its most fundamental problems.

In this chapter, I begin by providing a general characterization of deliberative democracy, and then identify the principal ways in which this theory promotes normative ideals and sociopolitical conditions which enhance effective democratic governance in multicultural societies. I continue by arguing that despite these advantages, deliberative democracy faces serious problems when it is applied in culturally pluralistic societies, viz., the problems of multiple loci of political loyalty, moral and cognitive incommensurability, and inequalities of epistemic resources between ethnocultural groups. After indicating that the problem of inequality will be dealt with in the next chapter, I conclude by arguing that in spite of its limitations, when appropriately conceived deliberative democracy can significantly mitigate the problems of political loyalty and incommensurability or, in those cases where it cannot deal with these problems, provides us with an argument that strengthens the case for self-governance rights for certain ethnocultural groups.

The Nature of Deliberative Democracy

The notion of public deliberation is at the core of the theory of deliberative democracy. Public deliberation is the process in which the members of a political community participate in public discussion and critical examination of collectively binding public policies. The process of deliberation through which these policies are reached is best understood not on the model of political bargaining or contractual market transactions, but as a procedure guided by the commitment to the common good. The primary goal of public deliberation is not the narrow pursuit of one's self-interest, but rather the use of public reason to find policies that, as far as possible, answer to the concerns of all citizens. By seeking to identify policies that take the needs and interests of all into account, the participants in the deliberative process express their belief in the political equality of all members of the citizenry. The interests of no particular member of the polity have *a priori* precedence over the interests of any other. The systematic consideration of the needs and interests of all citizens is ensured by providing an equal voice to all, removing institutional barriers to participation in public deliberation, and developing accessible forums in which all citizens can freely participate in the deliberative process.

In addition to the commitment to the common good and the procedural fairness characterizing public deliberation, the substantive character of the deliberative process should be based on rationality and aim towards truth. It is the force of the better argument that should carry the most weight, and not manipulative, coercive, or emotive appeals that promote sectarian interests. Participants should be willing to modify their proposals on the basis of the most complete and compelling information available, and should subject their proposals to critical scrutiny. They are also expected to respond to challenges to their proposals by using reasons which others will find compelling. This process of collective critical reflection presupposes that participants will strive to move beyond the limitations of their own points of view and understand each others' perspectives, needs, and interests. Rather than seeking to impose one's perspective on others through whatever persuasive mechanisms are available, a sincere effort should be made to reach agreement through a process of mutual understanding and compromise. In short, the political legitimacy of the outcomes of public deliberation is grounded not only on the comprehensive consideration of the needs and interests of all, but also on the fact that the deliberations are guided by the use of publicly scrutinized reasons.

The process of reasoned public deliberation provides, at least in part, deliberative democracy with its conception of political legitimacy. Since consent is at the center of democratic decision making, public deliberation is the vehicle through which citizens justify the self-imposed laws and policies which are collectively binding. Because the outcomes of the deliberative process arise out of the autonomous and epistemically unrestricted collective reasoning of the polity, its members are obligated to obey these outcomes. Deliberative democracy seeks to refine the process of autonomous self-governance by placing conditions on the deliberative process which ensure that the outcomes of deliberation do not merely aggregate existing desires but reflect a higher degree of collective knowledge and mutual moral responsibility. A democratic process which merely sums up the desires of the members of a political community deprives them of the opportunity to critically assess existing beliefs and preferences and examine the presuppositions and likely consequences of various policy alternatives. In brief, the political legitimacy of deliberative outcomes is based not merely on the will of the majority, but on the results of collective reasoned reflection by political equals engaged in a shared project of identifying policies which respect the moral and practical concerns of all members of the citizenry.

Since individual political decisions are not merely personal decisions but have a social dimension which affects the lives of others, through public deliberation citizens can discursively reflect on the social and economic conditions which can limit or expand their individual autonomy. Fiscal priorities, educational policies, and health care programs, for example, play a significant role in determining the quality of peoples' lives and the kinds of opportunities to which they have access. By obtaining a better understanding of the socioeconomic dimensions of their existence, members of the citizenry can take greater control of the factors which have a great influence on their lives. Rather than narrowly conceiving of political autonomy as a decision-making process involving isolated individuals, deliberative democracy adopts a more inclusive perspective which takes into account the individual as well as the collective social and economic dimensions of autonomy.

Publicity is another important feature characterizing public deliberation. Publicity enables the citizenry to scrutinize the deliberative process. By making the reasons for advocating policies public, people can challenge the assumptions and implications of these policies. They will have the opportunity to review the deliberations and point out possible inconsistencies or factual omissions. The requirement of publicity thus reinforces the idea that everyone has the right to know and critique the rationale for the adoption of collectively binding decisions. Publicity also furthers the general educational function of public deliberation by ensuring that all citizens have access to the procedures by which agreement is reached. By seeing the process of civil disagreement, deliberation, and cooperation modeled by the participants in public deliberation, members of the citizenry are educated in the procedures through which narrow self-interest is transcended for the sake of the common good. Publicity also discourages secret and behind-the-scenes agreements because participants know that they are expected to reveal the reasons and motivations for supporting their positions.

Another important function of publicity is that it makes accountability possible. By knowing the sources of specific proposals and the rationale behind them, citizens will be better able to identify the agents, parties, and organizations who have supported particular policies. Publicity also reveals the connections between ideological orientations and public policies, and makes possible a broader understanding of accountability that involves identifying not merely who advocates which policies, but also which ideologies give rise to particular methodological approaches and social consequences. While in conventional political debates no more than a general connection between ideological positions and policies is discernible, in public deliberation a much fuller and more detailed account of the specific epistemological justification for policies and their likely consequences would be expected from the participants engaged in deliberation. It would not suffice, for example, for individuals or organizations to simply appeal to their traditional support of a certain political position or to provide a justification which depends on accepting assumptions specific to their political ideology. Participants would have to show not only why an ideology commits us to a specific policy alternative, but also why we must accept that ideology, its background assumptions, and the particular interpretation of it that they are advocating. In addition, since public deliberation involves giving reasons that others will find compelling, a full and convincing account of why a particular policy should be adopted must show how it is based on generally accepted principles or how it furthers some fundamental common goal. In short, accountability in deliberative democracy involves not merely identifying sources of political responsibility, but also providing epistemic accountability.

Even though publicity is an important desideratum in deliberative democracy, it is not an unqualified ideal, and it can justifiably be overridden when its implementation would lead to serious negative consequences for the public interest. Even though the occasions on which secrecy is appropriate must themselves be nonpublic in order for the limitation of information to be effective, there should be public scrutiny of the organizations which can exercise the right of withholding information from the public and of the circumstances in which such decisions are appropriate.

Civic Implications of Deliberative Democracy

The adoption of deliberative democracy would likely have important positive effects on a society's political culture. Deliberative democracy develops the civic virtues necessary for sustaining healthy democracies. Character traits associated with democratic citizenship, such as mutual understanding among the members of the political community, are cultivated when pride of place is granted to public deliberation, which promotes political discourse in which people learn to see the world from the perspective of others. When we genuinely comprehend the internal logic of the forms of thought and experiences of our fellow citizens, we learn to understand and respect them as autonomous moral agents who may have normative beliefs and commitments significantly different than our own. By understanding them in the fullness of their distinctive humanity, and appreciating the specific reasons why they hold their moral convictions and follow their normative practices, we can better understand their aspirations, concerns, and needs. In addition, to the extent that we manage to transcend the awkwardness, fear, or hostility with which we might initially approach those who are different from ourselves, we will be expanding our own personhood as we learn to respect them and appreciate the plausibility of seeing the world from a different perspective.

Learning to respect others as autonomous moral agents cultivates the capacity to moderate our own demands without feeling that we were forced to do so by factors over which we have little or no control. That is, members of the polity will see that it is possible to retain their moral integrity and convictions while moderating their policy demands if the compromise results from a genuine appreciation of the needs and moral commitments of others, and not from a sense of being coerced into compromise. This is particularly important in societies in which there is the widespread belief that government decisions interfere with people's autonomy. If moderation of demands results from external forces impinging upon our moral autonomy, we are likely to feel resentful of others and lose faith in the fairness of the deliberative process. Since compromise is an inevitable component of political negotiation, the crucial question is how compromise is achieved, that is, what motivates it, how it affects future prospects for dialogue and cooperation, and how it transforms the perception of the members of the political community. Deliberative democracy, with its emphasis on mutual understanding and reciprocity, cultivates the willingness to compromise and moderate one's demands through understanding and respect for the needs and moral interests of others, and not out of a sense of forced submission to moral claims that are incomprehensible and alien to our own. For instance, by understanding the profound spiritual significance that a certain territory has for an indigenous group, we will be better able to see the rationale for restricting public access to this territory for recreational or commercial purposes.

Another salutary effect of deliberative democracy is that is fosters a sense of collective responsibility. With its commitment to the common good and systematic examination of the ramifications of policy alternatives, public deliberation enables citizens to see the sometimes obscured connections between individual behavior and the good of the larger community. The deliberative processes that are at the center of deliberative democracy serve as much needed correctives to the individualism and the morality of self-interest so prevalent in contemporary liberal democracies. Because individual freedom and autonomy are of central importance to liberal societies, they need to be balanced by an appreciation and understanding of the need for a common concern for the life of the community. Without such a counterbalancing concern, liberal democracies run the risk of being undermined by an insular individualism where people seek to maximize their own well-being without regard to the broader implications of their individual choices. Deliberative democracy, by publicly examining the consequences and assumptions of individual decisions, will make clear how every member of the political community is a part of a larger society whose well-being depends on her willingness to assume her share of collective responsibilities.

Public deliberation on issues of common concern also enhances the capacity of the citizenry to discern the advantages of sacrificing short-term interests for the sake of long-term goals. The political wisdom of the polity is increased when it collectively understands the prohibitive costs of neglecting problems which may be far more manageable if addressed in a timely and systematic fashion. Indeed, there are certain issues, such as those of environmental degradation and overpopulation, which by their very nature can be adequately addressed only through long-term strategic planning. A citizenry that is well informed and capable of discerning the likely consequences of neglecting long-term collective problems will be less vulnerable to manipulation by politicians who seek their support by appealing to their present short-term interests at the expense of problems which if neglected will prove to be more intractable in the future.

Specific Advantages of Deliberative Democracy for Multicultural Societies

In addition to the general positive benefits of deliberative democracy for political culture, there are special advantages that this form of democracy has for culturally pluralistic societies. One of these is the promotion of intercultural understanding. Mutual understanding between the members of ethnocultural groups is important for the civic health and the common life of a multicultural democratic society. This is especially true when a society has a history of intercultural discrimination and oppression, as most democratic societies in the world do. When such discrimination and oppression, or their effects, are still present, it is essential that the groups with a history of conflict understand one another's perspectives, needs, and concerns. Otherwise, intercultural tensions and conflicts are likely to be exacerbated when there is disagreement over sociopolitical and economic policies. The members of groups that have been traditionally marginalized or oppressed are likely to feel that they are still regarded as second-class citizens and that their needs and interests are not of concern to the majority. On the other hand, members of the majority are apt to misconstrue the motivations and reasons behind the perceptions and feelings of the oppressed, or formerly oppressed, ethnocultural groups. Without knowing the history of the minority groups in question, or the varied and sometimes profound ways in which the socioeconomic conditions and the psychic structures of the members of these groups have been affected by the oppression they have experienced, the majority society is unlikely to understand either their points of view or how to best deal with the socioeconomic problems that beset them.[2]

Lack of intercultural understanding is particularly serious in those societies which are residentially segregated or which exhibit a significant degree of socioeconomic stratification along cultural or racial lines. When the latter conditions hold, the members of a society are less likely to engage in intercultural dialogue and interaction. When the members of different ethnocultural groups live, work, play, worship, and are educated in segregated environments, their opportunities for developing the kinds of relationships which enable them to comprehend one another's way of life are severely diminished. The bonds of friendship and the forms of civic interaction that could lessen the personal, cultural, and social distance between the members of ethnocultural groups are more difficult to establish in segregated and stratified societies.

Public deliberation can make a significant contribution to intercultural understanding by candidly examining the effects of discrimination and oppression on existing problems. Since epistemic openness is a central feature of public deliberation, the sources of misunderstanding between cultural groups are potential topics of discussion. Hidden prejudices and unexamined assumptions about the motivations, experiences, and circumstances of other groups would be exposed and analyzed with the intellectual honesty and integrity that such topics demand. By bringing to light suppressed intercultural tensions and their causes, cultural groups would attain a deeper level of mutual understanding that could then serve as the basis for developing the social trust needed to engage in ongoing cooperative behavior. Without the social trust that makes intercultural cooperation possible, it is difficult to see how a multicultural society could successfully address intercultural conflicts and, more generally, problems of common concern. Though it is difficult for cultural groups with a history of conflict to attain social trust and engage in cooperative behavior, they must start by achieving a basic level of mutual understanding.

An additional way in which public deliberation is beneficial in multicultural societies is by drawing attention to the inconsistencies that may exist between social realities and avowed principles of justice and equality. One of the most important reasons why minority groups feel marginalized and alienated from the civic life of the larger society is because they see the gaps between the majority's professed ideals of social justice and equality and the personal and social realities of exclusion and discrimination they continually experience. When a society fails to live up to its own ideals by excluding certain sectors of the citizenry from the enjoyment of these ideals, the members of the excluded groups are likely to develop cynical attitudes towards their fellow citizens and the society's political institutions. Worse yet, this cynicism may extend to areas of associational civic life—which offer some of the best opportunities for ongoing intercultural interaction—and may lead to skepticism regarding the possibility of peaceful intercultural coexistence. Thus, it is extremely important for a culturally pluralistic society to promote dialogue and understanding between ethnocultural groups.

Even on those occasions in which majority and minority group members form mistaken beliefs about the moral legitimacy of one another's decisions or actions, it is still of primary importance that they reach mutual understanding of how and why erroneous judgments were made. In order to understand minority judgments regarding actions of the majority, the latter need to understand the experiences of cultural minorities, as well as the psychological mechanisms of self-protection on which they rely to survive in a society in which they are excluded or oppressed. By doing this, the majority will be better able to comprehend not only the rationale behind the minority's beliefs and behaviors, but also the more subtle consequences of systems of discrimination and oppression which, because the majority is not negatively affected by them, they may have little motivation to understand. Likewise, it is also crucial for minorities to discern how cultural majorities arrived at mistaken beliefs about them. Even though minorities will in general have greater awareness of racist or discriminatory attitudes, given that they bear the brunt of oppressive practices, they need to see the specific reasons and procedures through which the majority arrives at their erroneous beliefs and inaccurate perceptions. They need to discern why majorities see them as threatening, morally deficient, or undeserving of the rights and demands they advocate.

An interesting and distinctive epistemological feature of public deliberation is that, unlike other epistemic procedures, false beliefs or unreasonable proposals should not be considered as irrelevant or unhelpful for achieving the ends of reasoned deliberation. This is because it is instructive for all participants to understand why and how those mistaken beliefs came to be held or why those proposals are considered reasonable. Some of the most revealing insights about how individuals think are those that explain in a systematic way the generation of their false beliefs. What assumptions about, or limited experiences with, the members of other groups account for our propensities to falsely attribute to them certain negative or positive characteristics? Why are we inclined to remember those incidents and situations in which our stereotypes of other groups are reinforced? Why are proposals that some groups deem unreasonable considered fair and rational by other groups? Providing the answers to such questions can be highly illuminating for achieving intercultural understanding.

Finally, deliberative democracy contributes to the political legitimacy of the multicultural state by including in the deliberative process formerly excluded voices of ethnocultural groups and by demonstrating to such groups that the outcomes of public deliberation derive from fair and inclusive procedures. The majority, by demonstrating that they are seriously committed to hearing the concerns of ethnocultural minorities and incorporating these concerns in the formation of public policies, would show that it considers these groups as true political equals. Sustaining the political legitimacy of the state is very important in culturally pluralistic societies because political exclusion can exacerbate the marginalized status of some cultural minorities and lead them to question their allegiance to the political community. This is particularly true of minority groups who are alienated from the civic institutions of the society and who believe that their priorities, aspirations, and needs are not sufficiently taken into account by the social and political institutions of the majority society. In order to establish sound and sustainable multicultural democracies, it is essential that all groups comprising the polity, including such marginalized groups, believe in the fairness of social and democratic institutions and that they believe they have a vested interest in the common civic life of the political community.

Problems with Implementing Deliberative Democracy in Multicultural Societies

As we have observed, the advantages of deliberative democracy for the normative adequacy and effective functioning of culturally pluralistic societies are considerable. However, there are also features of these societies that present significant problems for implementing the ideals of deliberative democracy. More precisely, there are three problems faced by multicultural societies in applying deliberative democracy: (1) the absence of unitary or common political communities, (2) the problem of cognitive and moral incommensurability, and (3) the dilemma of significant inequalities between ethnocultural groups. I will discuss each of these problems in turn.

The Absence of Unitary Political Communities

One of the central presuppositions of deliberative democracy is that participants in the deliberative process will be committed to the common good. This commitment involves the willingness to moderate and in some cases even sacrifice one's self-interest for the sake of the greater good of the political community. This is one of the most important and demanding requirements for the successful implementation of the ideals of deliberative democracy. What makes public deliberation distinct from other forms of negotiation such as bargaining and market behavior is that, while the latter take for granted that participants are primarily motivated by the maximizing of their self-interest, in the former participants have to make a genuine commitment to reach a position that takes into account the needs of the larger political community and that may involve compromise and the overriding of one's self-interest. But the presupposition of having a commitment to the common good invites the question: commitment to which or whose common good? The obvious answer is that the commitment should be to the common good of the particular political community of which one is a part. The assumption is that every member of the political community is equally bound by an obligation to it, and that this obligation involves responsibility and loyalty to their fellow citizens and to the state.

However, some groups in a multicultural society may not, for a variety of plausible reasons, have this sense of commitment to the larger political community. Some ethnocultural minorities were coercively incorporated into the state, have experienced continued discrimination and oppression which has given them *de facto* status as second-class citizens, and have a strong sense of cultural identity that is different from that of the majority society. Indigenous groups in many liberal democracies, for example, were forcibly displaced from their homelands by settlers who formed the existing state. Many of these indigenous groups—such as Tarahumaras in Mexico, Crees in Canada, Navajos in the U.S., and the Saami people in Norway, Finland, and Sweden—have maintained their cultural identity and their ancestral connections to the pre-colonial inhabitants of their homelands, and have often resisted incorporation into the state and the unilateral imposition of citizenship by the federal government. In many cases they have experienced brutal treatment at the hands of settler societies, and at present are often socially, politically, and economically marginalized by the majority society. The primary sense of obligation and loyalty of many of these groups is to their fellow tribal members and tribal institutions, and not to the larger political community. Likewise, non-indigenous ethnocultural groups who, historically and at present, have experienced pervasive discrimination and oppression, may also lack the sense of obligation to the larger political community that is presupposed by deliberative democracy. Israeli Arabs, Catholics in Northern Ireland, Basques in Spain, and Romany (gypsy) populations in various European countries, for instance, have a strong sense of cultural identity, different from that of the majority society, which has been reinforced by discrimination and exclusion.

To the extent that advocates of deliberative democracy presuppose that there is a united political community with a uniform and inclusive commitment to the common good, they assume that existing democratic *states* are also *nations*. That is, they assume that states, understood as sovereign political entities with clearly delineated territorial boundaries and the power to enforce obedience to their legal edicts, coincide with nations, defined as communities bound by a shared culture and history, a sense of solidarity, and an awareness of their collective distinctiveness. Many contemporary multicultural states contain within their boundaries national groups whose historical experiences, cultural distinctiveness, and self-consciousness as a distinct people sets them apart from the majority society.[3] With the exception of a few culturally homogeneous countries such as Iceland, most democratic states in the world contain groups with varying degrees of commitment and obligation to the larger political community. To be sure, not in all multicultural countries is the sense of solidarity of cultural minorities so strong that it seriously undermines the commitment to the common good presupposed by deliberative democracy. However, many of these ethnocultural communities are sufficiently distinct and cohesive to thwart facile assumptions about the political unity and homogeneity of the polity. Most advocates of deliberative democracy have not given enough recognition to the fact that in multicultural societies the high level of civic magnanimity and commitment to the common good required by deliberative democracy may be nonexistent or extremely difficult to achieve. As I argue in what follows, special measures need to be taken to cultivate the commitment to the common good in culturally pluralistic societies.[4]

The Problem of Cognitive and Moral Incommensurability

In addition to the problematic assumption of a polity united by a common sense of belonging, loyalty, and obligation, there is also the problem of deep cultural diversity. Even if we assume that a commitment to the common good of the larger political community could be cultivated in multicultural societies, in some cases the differences between ethnocultural groups may be so profound that it is not clear whether they can engage in the kind of rational deliberation advocated by deliberative democracy. As we observed earlier, public deliberation is characterized by the giving of reasons that others will find compelling. This requirement, however, presupposes that the cognitive and moral frameworks of the participants are sufficiently similar to permit the mediation and adjudication of differences between them. After all, if participants are to provide reasons to one another that they find compelling, there must be a set of shared basic epistemic beliefs and moral convictions in relation to which these reasons make sense. In the absence of such a set of common beliefs and convictions, it is difficult to see how all participants could find these reasons compelling.

Even if we weaken the strong requirement that the reasons participants use must be of a compelling nature, we must at least assume that they will be understandable and plausible to all participants. Such a minimal requirement appears to be necessary so that participants can reach agreement that does not violate their sense of reasonableness and fairness. In the absence of reasons that all participants find at least understandable and plausible, public deliberation will degenerate into political bargaining or manipulation, because there will be no minimal basis of common agreement to which participants can appeal in rationally persuading those with whom they disagree.

But if the differences in perceptions, values, and beliefs between groups are sufficiently deep, even a minimal basis of shared understanding may not be available. In order to see the depth of disagreement that may exist between cultural groups, it would be instructive to delineate the kinds of differences that may hold between the conceptual frame-

works used by ethnocultural groups. Basically, there can be differences
with regard to basic beliefs and assumptions about the nature of reality,
differences concerning normative principles and practices, and differences concerning the epistemic principles through which factual and normative claims are generated and legitimized. Taken together, these differences may give rise to such a degree of incommensurability in the
conceptual frameworks employed by different cultural groups that the
very possibility of fruitful dialogue and reasoned deliberation can be severely undermined. But before seeing how these differences in conceptual frameworks can lead to problems in public deliberation in multicultural societies, we should make sure that we understand each of these
conceptual framework differences.

A conceptual framework can be defined as a set of beliefs, values, and
epistemic procedures which a community of knowers uses to conceptualize the world, relate to one another, and generate and verify knowledge
claims. The set of beliefs and values typically includes empirical and
moral beliefs which are used, respectively, to formulate a description of
the world and to determine the appropriate ways in which one should
act toward others. Epistemic procedures refer to the systematic methods
which we employ to gather information about the world and to determine whether particular knowledge claims are true or false. In practice
these components of a conceptual framework do not function in isolation
from one another but work in conjunction to produce a general outlook
on the social and natural world.

As indicated above, the conceptual frameworks employed by cultural
groups can differ in a number of ways. The first of these involves differences in beliefs about the nature of reality. While most cultural groups in
contemporary societies share many beliefs about the world, in some
cases the differences can be quite profound. The members of some indigenous groups, for example, believe that natural entities such as trees
and mountains possess spirits or souls, or that genuine communication is
possible between the persons in dreams and persons in the waking
world. These beliefs about the world are not idiosyncratic components of
their conceptual frameworks that are disconnected from their other beliefs, but are often at the core of their orientations towards reality. For
many indigenous groups, beliefs about the spirituality of natural entities
structure their basic attitudes towards the natural world, including animals, plants, and inorganic entities. As a result, their conception of the sacredness of nature is wholly different from the predominant view in contemporary technological societies that nature consists of physical
resources to be used for human profit and consumption.

The second way in which conceptual frameworks can differ is with regard to normative principles and practices. At the most general level, normative principles express fundamental beliefs about value, the entities

that possess value, and the appropriate behavior towards valued entities. Most normative principles involve moral prohibitions or articulate the obligations and responsibilities that we have to entities possessing value. Such principles are based, either explicitly or implicitly, on what we deem intrinsically valuable, and therefore worthy of respect and moral consideration for its own sake, or on what we consider instrumentally valuable and subject to protection or care because of its usefulness for some ulterior purpose or end. Normative principles, however, need not take the form of general moral claims, but can involve statements of cognitive or epistemic value. Representational accuracy, ontological economy[5], and predictive power, for example, are cognitive values which are highly prized by certain cultural traditions, such as Western philosophical and scientific disciplines. Generally speaking, there is less awareness of our commitment to normative principles involving cognitive values than awareness of normative principles involving moral claims. Though more deeply embedded within conceptual frameworks and less apparent to consciousness, cognitive values can be no less important than moral values in understanding a cultural group's orientation to reality.

Cultural traditions can vary significantly regarding normative principles. In contrast to contemporary Americans from Western European backgrounds, for example, some U.S. minority cultural groups, such as those from Latin American and Chinese traditions, generally grant greater value to loyalty and responsibility to one's family and community than to individual liberty and autonomy. Islamic traditions typically ascribe different strict rules of ethical conduct for men and for women, unlike Western traditions which generally conceive of ethical rules as essentially universal and applying equally to everyone. Navajo conceptions of justice focus primarily on restoring the communal bonds severed by moral transgressions, unlike cultures influenced by Christian, Jewish, and Islamic traditions, which focus more on punishment and retribution to "balance the scales of justice." Normative differences such as these can greatly influence the judgments of different cultural groups concerning the appropriateness and fairness of particular actions and social policies and institutions. Differences in cognitive values can also have a great impact on judgments regarding the adequacy of knowledge claims. Since indigenous groups generally place greater value on perspectives that incorporate holistic orientations towards nature and society, they are more likely to consider as inadequate perspectives that do not, for example, take into account the long-term ecological and cultural impact of policies of economic development.

The third way in which the conceptual frameworks of cultural groups can differ concerns the nature of knowledge structures, that is, the epistemic principles and methods that are used to generate and validate claims about the world. For instance, according to the prevailing conceptions of natural and social scientific knowledge in technologically advanced Western countries, legitimate knowledge is instrumental, impersonal, decomposable, replicable, and universal. This conception of knowledge, which Stephen Marglin calls *episteme*[6], is theoretical and taught in formal institutional settings. Its primary purpose is to provide a cognitive, analytical account of reality based on universally applicable principles. *Episteme* is the theoretical base for Western scientific and technological knowledge, and is a kind of knowledge that is unattached to social or ecological contexts and can be applied anywhere. In contrast to *episteme*, some traditional non-Western cultures employ systems of knowledge that are implicit, embodied, practical, and grounded in local contexts. These localized systems of knowledge, which Marglin calls *techne*, are intrinsically connected to the cultural practices of the people who employ them. *Techne* is thoroughly infused with cultural meaningfulness and is a part of the daily lives of the members of these groups. In addition, *techne* is implicit knowledge and often not capable of being explicitly articulated by its practitioners. *Techne* involves knowing how to weave or farm or heal, but not knowing how to write an instructions manual or provide a theoretical account of these skills. Thus, with *techne* "one knows with and through one's hands and eyes and heart as well as with one's head."[7]

The difficulties for public deliberation raised by these three conceptual framework differences are profound and far-reaching. These differences can undermine reasoned deliberation by making it impossible to justify particular beliefs, values, or policies in a way which the adherents of different frameworks find mutually acceptable. When the incommensurability between conceptual frameworks concerns fundamental differences in normative or epistemic principles, there may be no common basis for resolving disagreements. Consider, for instance, public deliberation regarding the right of indigenous groups to use hallucinatory substances in religious practices or the determination of appropriate compensation for Indian communities displaced from their homelands. In the former case, there are radical cultural differences concerning the role that mind-altering substances can play in bringing about higher states of spiritual awareness. Western cultures generally consider hallucinogens as distorting our perceptions of reality rather than as opening avenues of extrasensory perception that can lead to religious enlightenment. In the latter case, indigenous groups may not believe that monetary remuneration to individuals is appropriate compensation, since they may maintain that the original transgression was against them as a people and not as individuals. That is, while in the Western perspective intercultural moral transgressions are primarily understood as violations against the interests or rights of individuals, in many indigenous worldviews it is the community or group that is the proper unit of analysis for understanding violations by majority societies against indigenous minorities. Appropriate rectification would accordingly have to take into account the impact on the community as a whole (e.g., whether it promotes or undermines the cultural survival of the community). Thus, because in these two cases the disagreements concern fundamental differences in cognitive and empirical convictions, it is unlikely that a common basis of agreement can be found to resolve these controversies in a mutually acceptable way.

Cultural Group Inequalities

A third major problem that we encounter in implementing deliberative democracy in multicultural societies is the existence of significant socioeconomic differences between cultural groups. Socioeconomic differences usually entail inequalities in epistemological resources, such as level of education, access to information technologies, and influence in media organizations that gather and disseminate information. Since deliberative democracy grants a central role to public deliberation, differences in epistemic resources between cultural groups can severely hinder the capacity of some of these groups to participate effectively in deliberative processes and equitably defend their needs and interests. Even if all cultural groups are guaranteed formal rights of participation in public deliberation, inequalities in epistemic resources create significant asymmetries in their capacity for functioning effectively in forums of public deliberation. I will postpone a detailed treatment of epistemological inequalities and related issues until the next chapter; for now it will suffice to note the centrality of the problem of cultural group inequalities for multicultural societies that want to implement the ideals of deliberative democracy.

Deliberative Democracy Reconsidered

What measures can a multicultural democracy take to resolve the problems of the lack of unitary political communities and the existence of cognitive and moral incommensurability? Beginning with the first of these dilemmas, it is necessary to understand the historical and existing social, political, and economic factors that have led to the creation of the multiple ethnocultural communities that exist in multicultural democracies. On the basis of this understanding, we must then differentiate between: (i) those cases in which an intercultural sense of civic loyalty can be realistically cultivated so as to create unitary[8] and inclusive political communities and (ii) those situations in which the differences between cultural groups are sufficiently great to justify the establishment of separate public spheres in which ethnocultural minorities can give institutional expression to their cultural forms of life. Distinguishing between these two types of situations involves recognizing the wide diversity of intercultural scenarios that can exist in pluralistic societies. What must be strenuously avoided is the imposition of one model of intercultural relations on all multicultural democracies.

A useful first step in achieving the understanding needed to address the problem of promoting political solidarity in multicultural societies is to develop a classificatory scheme for ethnocultural groups that allows us to make the above-mentioned differentiations. With this purpose in mind, I would propose that ethnocultural minorities be divided into accommodationist, autonomist, and secessionist groups.[9] In the accommodationist category are those groups that seek to integrate successfully into the socioeconomic and political institutions of the majority society. Their desire for institutional integration, however, does not necessarily mean that they want full cultural assimilation into the mainstream culture. Many of these groups—such as Turks in Germany, Maghrebins in France, Sikhs in Canada, and African-Americans and some Latinos in the U.S.—want to retain features of their cultural heritage, and generally also desire to have their cultural distinctiveness publicly recognized and respected by the majority. With some notable exceptions, the members of accommodationist groups (or their predecessors) have immigrated to the countries where they live with the intention of adapting to the public institutions of their newly adopted country.[10] Assuming that they did not leave their country of origin under coercive conditions—such as fleeing ethnic cleansing, environmental devastation, or political persecution—their immigration signals an implicit willingness to integrate into the institutional frameworks of their adopted country, but not necessarily to forsake their cultural identity.[11] The members of these groups want to prosper by functioning successfully within mainstream political, economic, and social institutions while retaining their cultural identity or choosing for themselves the degree to which they will assimilate into the majority culture.[12]

The autonomist category is comprised of three ethnocultural groups: indigenous peoples, ethnonationalists, and communal contenders. Indigenous groups, such as the Kunas of Panama, the Mapuches of Chile, and the Aboriginal peoples of Australia, desire political and sociocultural autonomy and significant control of their territorial homeland and its natural resources. Many indigenous groups, before the arrival of the settler societies into which they were forcibly incorporated, lived in self-governing communities with their own social and political institutions and distinctive material forms of life.

Also included in the autonomist category are territorially concentrated ethnonationalist minorities, such as the Basques in Spain, the Quebequois in Canada, and the Scots in Great Britain, who have struggled for greater regional control of the state's social and political institutions. Unlike indigenous groups, the sociopolitical and material forms of life of these ethnocultural minorities are not radically different from those of the majority culture, and their cultural survival is not as closely tied to autonomous control of their land and natural resources. Nevertheless, these ethnocultural groups often have a strong nationalist consciousness, and they want to organize their public institutions so that they reflect their cultural history and heritage. They see themselves as culturally distinctive and as needing some degree of autonomous control over their public life in order to protect their cultural heritage and identity, even though, like indigenous groups, they are willing to remain part of the larger political community that constitutes the state.

The third group within the autonomist category comprises ethnocultural groups living in culturally pluralistic societies deeply divided along religious, linguistic, cultural, racial or ethnic lines. I will call these groups, following Ted Gurr,[13] communal contenders. These ethnocultural groups have their own subsocieties with their own media of communication, political parties, civil associations, neighborhoods, and schools. These groups exercise a fairly high degree of social and cultural autonomy (hence their classification as autonomist groups) within the larger political community. Unlike ethnonationalists, however, communal contenders do not seek autonomous political governance separate from the central government's political institutions; rather, they have established, in conjunction with other ethnocultural groups, power-sharing arrangements in which they vie for influence in the political institutions of the central government. The ethnocultural groups participating in power-sharing arrangements in such countries as Belgium, Malaysia, Lebanon, Kenya, and Nigeria are examples of communal contenders.

In the third category are secessionist groups, whose principal goals are secession from the state and either independent statehood or irredentist integration. These groups maintain that secession represents the only or most viable way of achieving self-determination. Secessionist groups, such as the Palestinians and the Tamils of Sri Lanka, not only appeal to the right to self-determination to justify their secessionist demands, they generally maintain that power-sharing or political autonomy arrangements in which they would be granted limited powers of self-government are either not feasible or insufficient to satisfy their needs and interests. Arguments centered on their refugee status or the need to have a state to ensure their physical security can sometimes play an important role in justifying the demands of these ethnocultural groups.

Creating Unitary Political Communities
with Accommodationist Groups and Communal Contenders

Since this classificatory schema for ethnocultural groups is based on a broad range of considerations, such as their present needs and aspirations and the manner in which they were incorporated into the state, through its use we can gauge the varying prospects for creating the uni-

tary political communities required for the effective functioning of deliberative democracy. We will then be able to identify more precisely the
ways in which deliberative democracy can function in the context of different pluralistic societies.

Multicultural societies comprised of accommodationist groups present
the most promising possibilities for creating inclusive civil societies in
which all of the members of the polity have a commitment to the common good. The cultural identities and loyalties of the individuals in these
societies are generally not as deeply entrenched as the cultural identities
and loyalties of individuals in other pluralistic societies. The members of
accommodationist groups do not have separatist aims, but want to be integrated successfully into the economic, political, and social institutions
of the larger, common political community. Their struggles for civil rights
and full socioeconomic participation in the political and economic life of
the majority society clearly attest to this.

Communal contenders also have a high stake in building a common
political community in which deliberative democracy functions best.
Since ethnocultural groups in these societies share power in the political
institutions of the central government, it is to their mutual advantage to
build among ethnocultural group members the intercultural understanding and willingness to cooperate that can sustain power-sharing arrangements. The stability of the governing coalitions which are common in
these democracies would be enhanced by achieving a higher degree of
cohesiveness in the political community. Accomplishing civic solidarity
in power-sharing societies, however, is more difficult than in multicultural societies with accommodationist groups, because the social and political institutions in power-sharing societies tend to reinforce cultural
identities and loyalties. In addition, the most powerful groups in these
societies sometimes use a combination of co-optation, concessions, and
coercion to attain dominance over the other groups in the power-sharing
political institutions,[14] and this clearly militates against building civic
solidarity. Despite these difficulties, however, the intercultural understanding and expansion of civil vision promoted by deliberative democracy would provide important advantages to multicultural societies consisting of communal contenders.

There are also general factors that undermine the creation of common
political communities. In multicultural societies with accommodationist
groups, as well as those constituted by communal contenders, there can
exist deep social, political, and economic divisions between ethnocultural groups.[15] In societies with significant intercultural socioeconomic
stratification and political inequalities, it is of primary importance that
disadvantaged ethnocultural groups believe that their needs and interests receive the same consideration as those of dominant groups. A
merely formal or rhetorical recognition of their concerns is not enough,

there has to be tangible evidence that disfranchised cultural groups are indeed regarded as equal members of the polity. One of the major causes of civic fragmentation, political alienation, and lack of commitment to the common good in multicultural societies with either accommodationist minorities or communal contenders is the realization by some of these groups that they are treated as second-class citizens. On the other hand, when the members of these groups see that equitable participation in the society's political institutions provides them with the opportunity to control their own destinies, they will have a vested interest in developing and maintaining civic loyalty to the state's democratic institutions as well as making the commitment to the common good necessary for the effective functioning of deliberative democracy. It is therefore of primary importance for a society to foster political inclusion and participation by all groups, and to address discriminatory and oppressive practices that undermine ethnocultural self-determination.[16]

Creating the unitary (though not necessarily homogenous) political communities appropriate for deliberative democracy, however, requires more than eliminating discrimination and oppression and ensuring that the needs and interests of all members of the polity are heard. To understand why this is so, it would be useful to discuss the proposals David Miller makes in his book, *On Nationality*.[17] In this work, Miller argues that developing civic solidarity and political cohesiveness in multicultural societies requires the systematic cultivation of a sense of national identity that can unite all cultural groups. This conception of national identity, according to Miller, will articulate the meaning of citizenship in the national community, and serve as a template for everyone to follow in acquiring the attitudes, knowledge, and dispositions appropriate for civic membership. Miller contends that this overarching conception of common citizenship, which must transcend the particularistic ties between the members of the cultural groups constituting the society, is necessary to make meaningful the common language that members of the polity will employ in public deliberation to articulate their needs and interests. That is, the set of principles and values underpinning the common conception of citizenship will provide the shared understanding necessary for meaningful political dialogue in the civic community.

In addition, Miller maintains that a sense of membership in the larger national community is necessary for the appeals to justice made by ethnocultural groups to have a realistic chance of being acted upon. He argues that the intercultural trust that grounds support for social justice depends on the possession of a common sense of national identity. He states:

> . . . if we believe in social justice and are concerned about winning democratic support for socially just policies, then we must pay attention to the

conditions under which different groups will trust one another, so that I can trust your just demand on this occasion knowing that you will support my just demand at some future moment. Trust requires solidarity not merely within groups but across them, and this in turn depends upon a common identification of the kind that nationality alone can provide.[18]

Miller's suggestions concerning the need for a unitary sense of citizenship initially seem sound, but what conception of common national identity is the most appropriate for contemporary multicultural democracies? Relying solely on traditional conceptions of national identity may not be feasible, because of the presence of culturally different new immigrant groups or the demographic increase of long-standing ethnocultural groups in the society. Not only would a narrowly conceived conception of common citizenship that is too culturally specific alienate culturally different members of the society, it would also undermine their cultural autonomy by marginalizing them in response to the cultural choices they have made.

Miller suggests that an inclusive national identity should adapt to incorporate new cultural groups, and that these groups should be willing to leave behind aspects of their culture that do not conform to the political ideals and beliefs underpinning common citizenship. He states:

> What must happen in general is that existing national identities must be stripped of elements that are repugnant to the self-understanding of one or more component groups, while members of these groups must themselves be willing to embrace an inclusive nationality, and in the process to shed elements of *their* values which are at odds with its principles.[19]

In defending the plausibility of his recommendation, Miller points out that nations do not have an intrinsic and unalterable character, but are "imagined communities"[20] that rely on such elements as symbols, historical narratives, customs, and institutional structures to create and reinforce a sense of a national identity characterized by distinctive ethical beliefs and a special collective social character. These national identities are not fixed and uniform, but can be transformed over time as a result of a variety of factors, such as changing political circumstances or alterations in the demographic composition of the polity. Given the alterable nature of national identities, it is therefore possible that they can be transformed to conform better with the realities of cultural pluralism. Miller contends that the new sense of national identity should be articulated within a context of deliberative democracy which incorporates the perspectives of all cultural groups in the society. The voice of no cultural group should be privileged in this dialogue, and no one should feel afraid of retaliation for expressing her beliefs and suggestions, even if they run counter to traditional conceptions of what it means to be a member of that national community. Once articulated, education would play a crucial role in disseminating the shared conception of multicultural citizenship. Schools, both public and private, would contribute to the cultivation of citizens who understand the public language of citizenship and for whom membership in the national community carries important civic duties and responsibilities to all fellow members of the polity.

Miller recognizes that in some countries it will be difficult to develop a common sense of national identity that is nonalienating to groups who differ from the mainstream culture. He indicates that, generally speaking, the closer the connection between the public culture of a society and the culture of the groups who established it, the harder it will be to develop an inclusive conception of citizenship. For instance, he notes that it will be comparatively more difficult to develop a common national identity in some countries of Western Europe, where the culture of the majority groups is intimately connected to the civic traditions of their countries, than in the U.S., where nationality is more closely associated with allegiance to a set of civic institutions and political ideals. Even though in no country will we find a complete dissociation between political ideology and cultural tradition, the point is that we must recognize the various factors that must be dealt with in developing and implementing a common national identity in different countries.

All told, Miller makes a number of helpful suggestions for developing the unitary political communities in which deliberative democracy can function best. Of particular importance is his insistence that a common national identity is necessary to promote mutual trust between ethnocultural groups and to develop a public language of citizenship to facilitate civic understanding. But despite the usefulness of this suggestion, it is not clear to what extent the articulation of a common sense of national identity would by itself develop the intercultural solidarity and mutual trust necessary for the effective implementation of deliberative democracy. After all, the very idea of a sense of common national identity could be used to exclude groups who are culturally different from the mainstream society. The idea that a country has the right to protect its culturally distinctive character by excluding or marginalizing those groups whose culture is "essentially" different is bound to have great persuasive power to those already predisposed to discriminate against them. Nationalist politicians could easily exploit the fears of mainstream cultural groups by arguing that nothing will remain of their traditional national identity if it is watered down in the effort to incorporate culturally distinct groups. These repressive tactics would likely be more effective against culturally distinct new immigrant groups, but they might also be successfully used against groups, such as Hispanics in the U.S., whose increased numbers generate mainstream fears of "cultural dilution" and cultural fragmentation.

Even though repressive ideologies would be somewhat restrained by Miller's suggestion that the public discussion on a shared national identity should occur within the framework of deliberative democracy, it is nevertheless uncertain whether ethnocultural minorities would not be marginalized in this discursive process. This is because, as we have noted, deliberative democracy works best when unitary political communities with a high degree of solidarity already exist, and we cannot assume that multicultural societies will exhibit such social solidarity. Thus, there is an element of circularity in Miller's position, because he wants to create a unifying sense of national identity by employing a dialogical framework, namely deliberative democracy, whose effectiveness assumes precisely the kind of solidarity he wants to create. Even though, to be fair to Miller, initiating the practice of public deliberation would in itself have beneficial consequences for building civic consciousness, as citizens learn to appreciate the advantages of reasoned public discourse, it is doubtful whether this would take us very far in building the common sense of citizenship he advocates.

To be effective in creating unitary political communities, it seems that a common conception of national identity will have to be underpinned by a set of shared egalitarian civic, social, and economic practices. Egalitarian social and economic policies and civil intercultural interaction must be maximized at a number of levels to combat divisive forms of socioeconomic stratification that, on the one hand, fuel racism, ethnocultural prejudice, and lack of understanding between cultural groups and, on the other, induce some disfranchised ethnocultural minorities to behavior that reinforces negative cultural stereotypes. And unless the structural conditions reinforcing socioeconomic stratification and ethnocultural prejudice are addressed, it is questionable whether the articulation of an inclusive conception of national identity would by itself lead to unitary political communities.[21] Eliminating socioeconomic and political group inequalities is particularly important in multicultural societies with communal contenders, because power-sharing arrangements work best when there is rough parity between the ethnocultural partners. When there are significant differences in power between communal contenders, the powerful groups tend to abuse their power and use it to obtain unfair advantages.

Furthermore, it is also important to cultivate a more expansive moral vision within the polity. There are other factors besides the bonds of nationalism that can hold a political community together. I will revisit these important issues in some of the following chapters and discuss measures to cultivate intercultural solidarity, egalitarian material autonomy, and an ecological communal vision. What we must note here is that there is no simple set of steps to take in resolving the difficult problem of creating unitary political communities in multicultural societies, and that this dilemma must be addressed simultaneously at a number of levels, with a view toward systematically addressing the interconnected factors that account for its intractability.

To summarize, creating common political communities in multicultural societies containing either accommodationist groups or communal contenders is, though by no means easy (particularly in the case of communal contenders), at least feasible under certain circumstances. In the case of societies with accommodationist groups, the mitigating of socioeconomic and political group inequalities would certainly be a positive factor in creating a common political community. The commitment of accommodationist groups to integrate into mainstream institutions would be strengthened by egalitarian commitments and practices. In communal contender societies, the elimination of significant group differences in socioeconomic and political power would also be a propitious development for building a common political community. Empirical evidence indicates that stable, power-sharing political institutions are much more likely to succeed, as has occurred in Belgium and Switzerland, where none of the ethnocultural groups involved have decisive advantages over the others.[22] But even when one of the groups is relatively advantaged, it is still possible for the society to develop non-coercive and stable (if not ideally just) power-sharing arrangements, as in the case of Kenya, Zambia, and Malaysia.[23]

It is important to emphasize that neither the elimination of political and socioeconomic group inequalities nor the willingness to integrate into the institutions of the majority society (in the case of accommodationist groups) or the commitment to share power with other ethnocultural groups (in the case of communal contenders) are sufficient conditions for creating the common political communities that are most suitable for deliberative democracy. My purpose here has been to identify some of the most important necessary conditions—which have been almost totally neglected by advocates for deliberative democracy—for the creation of unitary political communities in multicultural societies containing accommodationist groups or communal contenders.

Indigenous Peoples, Ethnonationalist Groups, and the Limits of Deliberative Democracy

In comparison with societies with accommodationist groups or communal contenders, multicultural societies with indigenous and ethnonationalist groups face additional problems in creating the civic milieu in which deliberative democracy can best be practiced. These groups seek self-government rights which will enable them to create a separate public sphere to give institutional expression to their distinct cultural forms of life. Their educational institutions, criminal justice systems, modes of material existence, and forms of political organization, for example, can differ significantly from those of the majority society. In order to appreciate the difficulty in creating political solidarity with these autonomist groups, it is important to understand the bases for their claims to self-government rights. Indigenous groups and ethnonationalist groups claim that, before their forced incorporation into the state, they were self-governing communities with their own forms of social, political, and economic organization. They point out that they never gave up their rights to govern their own affairs, and that they often resisted becoming part of state. These groups would likely also emphasize the coerced appropriation by the state of their homelands and natural resources. Given the centrality of consent in democracies and the almost universal recognition by the international community of self-determination as a fundamental human right, the refusal of indigenous peoples and ethnonationalist groups to be assimilated into the larger political community is understandable and in many cases morally justifiable.[24]

Several considerations must be kept in mind in assessing the prospects for creating unitary political communities in multicultural societies with indigenous or ethnonationalist groups. First, it must be recognized that the civic bonds uniting a political community cannot be coercively created by destroying the sense of national identity and solidarity that exists among the members of these communities. In many cases, attempts to strengthen loyalty to the state by suppressing the cultural identity of indigenous and ethnonationalist groups have not only failed, they have often reinforced the very sense of cultural identity and solidarity that they were intending to destroy. For instance, efforts by the Spanish government to ban the use of the Catalan language to promote a greater sense of Spanish unity lead to the covert maintenance of the language by Catalonians and strengthened their sense of ethnic solidarity. Furthermore, pragmatic considerations aside, there are moral reasons for granting some ethnocultural groups the right to cultural and political self-determination. As we shall see in the fifth and seventh chapters, cultural and self-government rights—such as, respectively, the right of some ethnocultural minorities to employ their language in public institutions and the right to adopt forms of political organization that conform to their cultural perspective—can be justified by reference to basic principles of liberal democracy.

Second, majority cultures need to realize that the basis of solidarity in most ethnocultural political communities rests on such factors as a sense of shared history, a common language and culture, a common ancestry, an experience of shared oppression, and perhaps most important, a subjective sense of collective identity as a distinct people. Even though, as a number of authors have pointed out, the sense of national identity of many groups is not an objectively definable, "natural" property of such groups, but has been constructed and reinforced through a variety of mechanisms[25], it is nevertheless vital to acknowledge that in the sociopolitical realm it is how people think of themselves that is of crucial importance, and that the reality of cultural identity and allegiance has proven to be remarkably persistent.

Given that the source of political solidarity is often based on such factors as the existence (or perceived existence) of the particularistic ties of shared culture and heritage, and that the suppression of ethnocultural identity is not a viable option, what measures can a multicultural society take to create unitary political communities with indigenous and ethnonationalist groups? To a large extent, the degree of political cohesiveness that can be reasonably developed and sustained depends on the kind of power-devolving political system that is eventually adopted by the multicultural society in question. Since there are a number of such political systems, the degree of civic unity of the resulting greater political communities will vary accordingly. A political system in which Catalonia exercises regional autonomy, for example, will likely give rise to a different civic community, as well as a different political environment for public deliberation, than a reservation-based system of self-governance for Native Americans in the U.S.

In any case, since indigenous and ethnonationalist groups will remain part of the state, political deliberations between the majority society and these groups will still take place, and it is instructive to look at the contexts of these deliberations to assess the kinds of political communities that could feasibly be created. Such deliberations can take two forms: those that take place prior to the devolution of power (if such devolution has not already taken place) and those that occur after the self-government rights warranted by these groups have been decided. The structure and process of the pre-autonomy public deliberations will be more difficult to determine, because the very legitimacy of the power of the state to legislate over the affairs of the autonomist group will be in question. That is, since the autonomist groups will be challenging the fundamental assumption that the sole locus of sovereignty lies in the state, the usual assumptions of deliberative democracy regarding a stable, unified political community making collectively binding decisions will not be operational. Moreover, the forums of deliberation will be provisional in character, because the character of future forums will depend on the degree of autonomy that the indigenous and ethnonationalist groups achieve as the result of the negotiations. The role of supra-national bodies may be more prominent than in conventional domestic deliberations, as autonomist groups appeal to the international community for political and material support. The use of international documents concerning rights of self-determination may play an important role in the negotiations, and these groups may question conventional ideas regarding national unity and the historical origins of the state. The net impact of these factors is that the assumption of a united national political community will be hard to sustain, since indigenous and ethnonationalist groups will be appealing to universalistic conceptions of normative legitimacy in challenging the claims of the state.

One of the most important steps that a majority society can take to evaluate justly the claims of these groups is to remain open to the diverse and culturally specific modes of cognitive and moral justification that they may employ. An example of this is the recent ruling by Canadian courts that previously unrecognized indigenous oral traditions could legitimately be used as evidence in legal proceedings to decide questions regarding land claims.[26] By its willingness to consider alternative conceptions of epistemic and normative legitimacy, the majority society can demonstrate that it is treating indigenous and ethnonationalist groups as equal agents capable of rational and moral self-direction. Of course, this does not mean that the majority society should uncritically accept all of the autonomist group's epistemic and moral standards, it just means that it should be willing to suspend the assumption of the legitimacy of its own standards while acceding to stand on equal footing with the ethnocultural minority community. This mutual respect is very important for both parties to exhibit, because in order for the agreements concerning the devolution of power to be acceptable to indigenous and ethnonationalist groups, they must believe that they were treated fairly by the majority. This may be particularly difficult given the oppressive and sometimes brutal treatment that many of these ethnocultural groups have received in the past. There are cases around the world, however, that show that mutually agreeable negotiations and agreements can be reached.[27]

On the other hand, autonomist groups must themselves treat majorities justly. In some cases this might mean that despite the fact that indigenous communities, for example, have a just claim to large territories from which they were displaced, they will have to realize that it is unrealistic and unjust to displace the present inhabitants of these areas. These indigenous groups have to recognize the needs and interests of majority groups, and moderate their demands so that they receive what is needed for them to thrive, but not so much (even though they may have an ostensibly plausible moral claim to it) that the basic well-being of the majority is seriously compromised. In short, evidence of mutual respect for the well-being of other groups will be important in pre-autonomy deliberations, and some of the principles of deliberative democracy will still be useful for carrying the negotiations forward in a way that furthers the interests of all of the parties involved.

What form will post-autonomy public deliberations have? The lines demarcating the boundaries of self-governance will determine to a large extent the scope and content of post-autonomy public deliberations. The

degree of political autonomy that a particular group attains and the social, cultural, and economic areas over which it can autonomously legislate will determine which issues of common concern need to be decided
through collective deliberation with the majority society. In the areas
over which indigenous and ethnonationalist groups have jurisdiction,
they will in effect create their own political community to arrive at decisions in these areas. Regarding issues of common concern with the majority, or issues over which it is unclear where the locus of sovereignty
lies, forums of deliberation will have to be developed which reflect and
are constrained by the specific forms of self-government rights that the
autonomist group in question enjoys. In brief, the greater degree of clarity regarding jurisdictional control in post-autonomy deliberations will
entail greater clarity in the structure of forums of public deliberation.

It is in multicultural societies with indigenous and ethnonationalist
groups that some of the greatest limitations of deliberative democracy
will emerge. The structural conditions of self-governance for these
groups will significantly restrict the development of unitary political
communities in which there is a high degree of social solidarity and a
shared commitment to a common good. Claims of mutual responsibility
between these autonomist groups and the majority society, for example,
cannot possibly have the same meaning in a political community with
differential jurisdictional control as in a unitary state. The granting of
self-government rights will in effect formalize the idea that a single unitary political community no longer exists. Abandoning the hope of creating common political communities with indigenous and ethnonationalist
groups, however, may ultimately be a small price for the state to pay to
ensure fairness and stability. When we consider that the alternative to
granting self-government rights to these groups is the suppression of the
right to self-determination and the conflicts that arise as a result, a bifurcated but structurally stable polity in which the autonomy of all cultural
groups is respected is to be preferred.

Secessionist Groups and Deliberative Democracy

Needless to say, when we consider secessionist groups, the possibility of
creating unitary political communities is even further diminished. While
autonomist groups are at least willing to remain part of the state, secessionist groups claim the right to form their own sovereign state, or in the
case of irredentist integration, to become part of another political community. When a large majority of the members of secessionist groups
support secession, it is highly unlikely that many of the demanding civic
assumptions of deliberative democracy can be met. The situation is further complicated by the fact that other states or the international community may play a role in negotiations concerning secession. But perhaps

the most damaging factor for the prospect of employing deliberative democracy with secessionist groups is that by the time a secessionist movement has gathered momentum, the political relations between the secessionist groups and the majority society have been so damaged that the civic environment for public deliberation has been seriously and perhaps irreparably undermined. However, a mitigating consideration in secessionist conflicts is that, as I will argue in Chapter 7, they can sometimes be resolved through the judicious use of self-government rights, so that in practice power-devolving arrangements can in some cases satisfy secessionist demands. If satisfying a secessionist demand can be feasibly accomplished through the devolution of power, that case will in effect become an autonomist conflict. But in those cases in which secessionist conflicts cannot be resolved through the devolution of power, the possibilities of creating the unitary political communities in which deliberative democracy functions best are practically nil.

Cognitive and Moral Incommensurability

Another problem faced by multicultural societies committed to deliberative democracy arises from the existence of incommensurable cognitive and moral differences in the conceptual frameworks used by different ethnocultural groups. As we observed earlier, incommensurable differences undermine the possibility of finding a common ground for resolving intercultural disagreements. Incommensurable differences, whether cognitive or moral, arise when conceptual frameworks are so distinct that there is no shared set of beliefs or principles of epistemic validation on which the participants in public deliberation can rely to reach agreement. Since participants try to persuade one another by giving reasons which they find mutually acceptable, without a shared set of beliefs or principles of adjudication they will not be able to provide such reasons. The most serious cases of cognitive and moral incommensurability can be expected to arise between those groups with the greatest cultural or political differences, namely, indigenous peoples and majority societies, and secessionist groups and the political community from which they seek complete separation.

We noted earlier that there are three basic kinds of incommensurable conceptual framework differences: (1) those dealing with fundamental claims concerning the nature of reality, (2) those dealing with normative principles and practices, and (3) those concerning epistemic principles used to generate and validate factual and normative claims. When confronted with incommensurable framework differences, participants in public deliberation may not only be without a common basis for agreement, they may also lack shared epistemic procedures for adjudicating between their competing claims. For instance, suppose that there is a disagreement between an indigenous group and the majority society concerning the appropriateness of extracting natural resources from a mountain site that the former regards as sacred. In this situation, not only is there a difference of opinion concerning the sacredness of the site, there is also disagreement regarding how their disagreement is to be resolved. The evidence that would be cited by each group would likely not be acceptable to the other, because their conceptual frameworks differ with regards to what counts as evidence.[28] In situations such as these, it is difficult to see how each side could provide reasons that the other finds compelling or even plausible. The net result of incommensurable differences is that participants in deliberative democracy will be unable to achieve reasoned agreement, because they will not share a basic epistemic common ground. This will undermine in a fundamental way the whole process of reasoned deliberation on which deliberative democracy is based.

One possible strategy for dealing with the problem of deep incommensurable differences between conceptual frameworks is to eliminate the requirement that participants in public deliberation must always provide one another with reasons that they find mutually compelling or convincing. Perhaps there is some other way to reach agreement that is not based on the mutual acceptance of identical reasons for the position reached. James Bohman, in *Public Deliberation*[29], argues that deliberation should be seen as a joint social activity which succeeds not when all participants agree with the reasons for a deliberative outcome, but when they are willing to continue their ongoing cooperation. More precisely, a deliberative outcome is successful when agents believe they "have contributed to and influenced the outcome, even when they disagree with it."[30] Bohman contends that in the more difficult cases involving incommensurable differences, this is all that we can realistically expect, and all that is required to maintain democratic deliberation in a diverse political community.

In articulating his position, Bohman contrasts his views with those of two prominent writers on democratic deliberation, John Rawls and Jurgen Habermas, and shows how they fail to resolve the problem of incommensurability. According to Bohman, Rawls appeals to the notion of public reason—which involves the capacity to draw logical inferences, evaluate evidence, and balance competing considerations—as a universal cognitive capacity on which participants can rely in public deliberation. Rawls contrasts public reason with nonpublic reason—which assumes a particular cognitive and moral standpoint—and he associates nonpublic reason with the various sectors of civil society, such as cultural groups, civic associations, and interest groups, that comprise a political community. Public reason not only involves universal epistemic capacities, it also incorporates an expansive capacity for deliberating and judging from the perspective of others. That is, public reason enables us to evaluate in an impartial way the competing claims made by different participants in the deliberative process. Thus, public reason allows us to resolve our differences by relying on universal cognitive capacities for objectively evaluating the respective adequacy of our claims.

In response to Rawls's use of public reason to deal with the problem of incommensurability, Bohman argues that in a culturally pluralistic society there are a number of conceptions of public reason, that is, there is a multiplicity of public standpoints from which claims can be evaluated. Bohman maintains that cultural communities within the state may have different conceptions of what counts as reasonable, and may have different procedures for evaluating the rationality of empirical and normative beliefs. According to Bohman there is no universal, impartial standpoint of public reason that the agents in a multicultural political community can use to resolve their disagreements. Bohman points out that even if participants have the capacity to put aside their own interests in evaluating the claims of others, in a diverse society cultural groups may have different standards of impartiality. In the case mentioned above concerning the disagreement between an Indian community and the state over the appropriateness of extracting resources from a sacred mountain site, the state's conception of an objective, impartial judgment might be based on an economic assessment of the value of the natural resources. For the indigenous community, an impartial judgment grounded on the facts of the situation would likely be based on respect for the spiritual integrity of the religious site.

Bohman also argues that Rawls's notion of "overlapping consensus" is inadequate for dealing with the problem of incommensurability. A consensus is overlapping when it is based on common moral values that participants recognize as parts of their conceptual frameworks. Such a consensus could be used to determine a political context of deliberation that all participants agree with. Since the moral values underpinning the overlapping consensus are accepted by each agent in public deliberation, relying on these values would respect the participants' moral convictions. That is, compromise based on the shared values of an overlapping consensus respects the moral autonomy of all participants while allowing them to reach an agreement uncoerced by external circumstances. While other features of the participants' conceptual frameworks may differ, the overlapping consensus can be used as a common basis for defending their respective claims in a way that is mutually understandable and acceptable.

Despite its initial appeal, Bohman points out that the notion of overlapping consensus is inadequate for dealing with the dilemma of incommensurability because it is a minimal condition that, in the most difficult cases, will be insufficiently robust to allow participants to resolve their disagreements. That is, even though there may be a consensus among the participants regarding certain moral convictions, their divergence on other beliefs and values may still give rise to disagreements concerning how to resolve the issues at hand. Just because they agree on certain values, it does not follow that participants may not disagree on other beliefs and values where consensus is needed to resolve the more difficult cases created by incommensurability. Even though Bohman concedes that in the less difficult cases overlapping consensus may suffice for participants to reach a mutually acceptable compromise, this method will not necessarily succeed in all cases.

Bohman also contends that Rawls's "method of avoidance" is not helpful for resolving the incommensurability dilemma. According to this method, participants should exclude from public deliberation conflicts on which no agreement is possible, such as religious differences. Deliberation can then proceed without being hindered by unbridgeable differences between the participants. In response to the "method of avoidance," Bohman contends that it cannot resolve deep incommensurable differences, because it merely sets them outside of the boundaries of public deliberation. He points out that even though this method might be useful in certain circumstances, as often as not it will obstruct democratic deliberation by setting limits on the discussion of issues that may be important to examine. As Bohman points out, one of the most interesting features about deep incommensurable disagreements is that they challenge the accepted modes of public justification. It is in attempting to resolve these disagreements that a pluralistic political community can become more inclusive by expanding the scope of public justification.

Bohman indicates that Habermas has a more open and dynamic conception of democratic deliberation than Rawls, because Habermas recognizes that there is no single, universally accepted "public reason." Habermas also contends that we cannot determine in advance which reasons are public or nonpublic. He maintains that the range of acceptable reasons may be broadened by the inclusion of more diverse perspectives, and that the interpretive perspectives of the participants themselves will be enlarged by including more voices in the dialogue. Habermas believes that as deliberators exercise plural public reason, conventional as well as minority conceptions of justification will be challenged, and as a result both majority and minority groups will expansively transform their conceptual frameworks. He thus emphasizes the changing, dynamic character of public deliberation in which participants achieve mutual respect and greater understanding as they reflexively interpret and accommodate different perspectives.

Bohman believes that Habermas is right to recognize the existence of diverse conceptions of public reason and to advocate an open and dynamic approach to public deliberation. However, he points out that Habermas does not provide much guidance regarding how the potentially greater number of conflicts arising from the use of plural public reason are to be normatively resolved. Bohman indicates that in explaining how such conflicts are to be settled, Habermas relies almost exclusively on our capacity for abstraction, which involves impartiality and neutrality in evaluating reasons and proposals. When we deliberate from the standpoint of impartiality, we are to objectively assess the relative adequacy of alternative positions.

For Habermas, deliberating from the standpoint of impartiality provides reasons with "their consensus producing force."[31] That is, the outcomes which result from neutral and impartial deliberation have normative legitimacy because all perspectives were given due consideration and no perspective was arbitrarily privileged in the process of deliberation. This normative legitimacy in turn prompts general agreement, as participants recognize that their perspectives and moral autonomy were respected. Deliberative outcomes reached through impartiality and neutrality are thus not the result of mere compromise based on strategic bargaining or pragmatic considerations, but are justified by mutually acceptable reasons. As Habermas states, "Whereas parties can agree to a negotiated compromise for different reasons, the consensus brought about through argument must rest on *identical reasons* that are able to convince the parties in the same way."[32]

Bohman points out, however, that no neutral or impartial standpoint is possible in cases of deep incommensurable differences. In the latter cases, we cannot assume that we can identify a neutral standpoint from which we can impartially judge conceptual frameworks that are fundamentally different. What we find in situations of deep cultural diversity is that the conflicting perspectives differ not only with regard to basic beliefs about the world, but also with regard to modes of justification. Thus, there can be no neutral appeal to a common procedure of adjudication for resolving the disagreements. Because in many frameworks basic beliefs and methods of claim validation are indissociably linked, we cannot isolate a shared and impartial procedure to establish the truth of disputed claims that is not imbued with conceptual features of the rest of the framework. In the dilemma mentioned above involving the indigenous group and the sacred mountain site, for example, there is no shared procedure of claim validation because the scientific, materialist framework employed by the majority society is fundamentally incompatible with the holistic, spiritual ecological framework of the indigenous group. While in the former framework the verification of claims is based on quantitative, standardized measurement techniques, in the latter the relevant claims are verified through nonstandardized experiential criteria.

How do we find a way around the problem of disagreements based on incommensurable conceptual frameworks? According to Bohman, the fundamental limitation of Rawls's and Habermas's approaches is that they depend on a consensus building standpoint of impartial neutrality to identify legitimizing reasons with which all participants agree. Because Rawls and Habermas believe that a legitimate deliberative outcome can be reached only if all participants accept identical reasons for it, they are committed to excessively strong and unrealistic assumptions regarding public deliberation. Bohman argues that we need to give up the stipulation regarding the existence of an impartial standpoint leading to universally accepted reasons. We should realize that public deliberation is first and foremost a social cooperative activity that aims at resolving concrete problematic situations, and not a form of theoretical or argumentative discourse in which disagreements are amenable to theoretically ideal solutions. A deliberative outcome is successful, Bohman contends, when "agents are sufficiently convinced to continue their ongoing cooperation. An outcome of an actual decision is acceptable when the reasons behind it are sufficient to motivate the cooperation of all those deliberating."[33] More precisely, participants must believe that "they have contributed to and influenced the outcome, even when they disagree with it."[34] It is not necessary, Bohman maintains, that the legitimizing reasons for the outcome be the same, or that a neutral, impartial standpoint be found from which to arbitrate the disagreement.

Bohman calls this weaker form of compromise in public deliberation moral compromise. In this form of compromise, participants broaden the common framework of democratic deliberation in the process of dialogical give and take. Each participant incorporates the standpoint of others in his or her deliberations by taking systematic account of their beliefs, concerns, and modes of justification. Bohman states:

> In distinctly moral compromise, the parties do not modify the framework to achieve unanimity, although they may when conflicts are not so deep. Rather, they modify their conflicting interpretations of the framework so that each can recognize the other's moral values and standards as part of it. The framework is then common enough for each party to continue to cooperate and deliberate with the other. Nonetheless, it is still not already assumed to be the *same* framework, as would be true for an impartial agreement; in this way it remains plural.[35]

Moral compromises thus occur within a framework that includes the conflicting beliefs and values of the participants; it will not consist of a single set of consistent or coherent principles. Bohman points out that as the concerns of each party as well as their beliefs and principles of justification are incorporated into the common framework of negotiation, new rules of cooperation and new modes of justification emerge.[36] At each stage of the deliberative process, the common framework is sufficiently modified to bring about continued cooperation among the parties involved. What motivates the continued cooperation is the acknowledgement by all sides that their concerns and views are being taken into account by all participants in the deliberative process. The participants' reasoning concerning the issues is transformed as they try to accommodate the concerns and views of others.

Moreover, as Bohman indicates, a new framework emerges as a result of the deliberations that fuses the original frameworks of the participants even as these frameworks themselves are modified. That is, as new reasons and different forms of justification are incorporated into the common deliberative framework, critical reflection on the cultural perspectives of the participants is likely to occur. In the new framework, fair comparison of competing claims becomes possible through the use of an expanded vocabulary that employs the resources of the original frameworks. In this way, this third framework does justice to the concerns and perspectives of each side of the debate. Bohman mentions the Federalist and Anti-Federalist compromise that lead to the creation of a Constitutional Assembly exemplifying "dual democracy" as an example of moral compromise.

How adequate is Bohman's solution to the problem of deep cultural disagreements arising from conceptual framework incommensurability? Bohman's solution is ingenious, and provides a realistic account of how some of these disagreements might be resolved. Because it rejects idealized assumptions concerning the degree of overlap between cultural frameworks, it is more useful than Rawls's and Habermas's accounts for understanding the dilemmas that are likely to arise in a multicultural society where deep divisions exist between ethnocultural groups. Moreover, Bohman's account is also realistic in the sense that participants need not give up their values and perspectives and adopt a neutral stance; rather, they try to understand and accommodate the needs and perspectives of others even as they remain faithful to their moral convictions. Moral compromises thus respect the moral autonomy and standpoints of all deliberators. Even when participants do not agree with a deliberative outcome, they are willing to accept it because they realize that their viewpoints have been taken into account and have affected the process by which the outcome was reached. Their acceptance of the outcome is not tantamount to agreement with its truth, rather it indicates their willingness to continue to cooperate with the other members of the political community.

Despite the strengths of Bohman's approach for dealing with the incommensurability problem, it is not entirely satisfactory. According to Bohman, moral compromises are fair if they satisfy two criteria: (1) if they take deliberative inequalities into account and (2) if they promote the ongoing participation of all groups in a common deliberative political community. The problem is that Bohman is ultimately unable to provide support for either one of these criteria for the fairness of moral compromises. Let us consider each of these criteria in turn.

Taking deliberative inequalities into account is important, Bohman points out, because in cases of extreme economic and political inequalities between majority and minority cultural groups, the latter will be unable to effectively influence deliberative outcomes. As a result, minority groups such as Native Americans will not be able to adequately defend their needs and interests in public deliberation. Bohman recommends that these groups be granted powers of local jurisdiction—such as controlling property ownership and restricting voting rights of non-Natives in Indian reservations—so that they may be able to achieve greater parity with the majority society through local self-governance and speak with a more effective and cohesive voice in public deliberations with the larger political community. In making this recommendation, however, Bohman does not realize that despite powers of local self-government, severely disadvantaged minorities such as Native Americans may still be unable to effectively influence deliberative outcomes at the national level, including those outcomes that affect their interests. If the socioeconomic and political disadvantages of these groups are great enough to hinder their capacity for self-determination at the local level, why should we suppose that these inequalities will not hinder their effectiveness in public deliberation at the national level? Bohman does not provide sufficient evidence to support his claim that economic and political deliberative disadvantages at all levels of democratic deliberation would be rectified merely by granting severely disadvantaged cultural minorities powers of local jurisdiction.

But there is another more enduring kind of deliberative disadvantage, which has nothing to do with familiar economic and political inequalities, that would continue to afflict some cultural minorities even if they had powers of local self-governance. I am referring to deliberative disadvantages created by incommensurable differences between the conceptual frameworks of minority and majority cultural groups.[37] When deep cultural disagreements are involved, a minority group may find itself constantly losing out in public deliberation, since their way of looking at the world will be fundamentally at odds with that of the majority society. What makes the continued rejection of minority policy alternatives likely is the logical cohesiveness of conceptual frameworks, which are cognitive structures consisting of systematically interconnected beliefs, values, and principles of justification. That is, conceptual frameworks do not consist of miscellaneous components randomly associated with one another. Rather, their components give rise to meaningful wholes which enable individuals to make sense of their experience of the world. For example, the normative conviction of some Native Americans that nature should be treated with moral respect is underpinned by certain beliefs concerning the spiritual character of natural entities. Their fundamentally different view of nature will likely affect their position on many social and economic issues.

The relevance of the interconnectedness of the elements of conceptual frameworks for the continued marginalization of some cultural minorities is that the fundamental incompatibility of minority and majority frameworks will give rise to deep disagreements over a wide range of issues. When the conceptual framework of a minority cultural group represents a fundamentally distinct way of perceiving reality, it is probable that the disagreements between majority and minority groups will not be sporadic, but systematic and continual. Minority groups may thus constantly find themselves at the losing end in public deliberation. Some indigenous groups, for instance, are likely to disagree with the decisions of the majority society covering a broad spectrum of ecological, social, and economic issues. The deliberative disadvantages arising from deep incommensurable differences will not be remedied by obtaining powers of local jurisdiction.

Bohman does not fare much better in providing support for the second criterion determining the fairness of moral compromises. There are two problems with his arguments for the second criterion, which stipulates that a just moral compromise is one that promotes the ongoing participation of all cultural groups in a common deliberative political community. First, Bohman simply begs the question regarding the normative priority of maintaining unitary political communities. Even though the maintenance of such communities is certainly a desirable goal in many multicultural democracies, particularly those comprised of accommodationist cultural groups, we cannot simply rule out of court the claims of indigenous peoples, ethnonationalists, communal contenders, and secessionist minorities who challenge the assumption that the sole locus of sovereignty lies in the central government. It may well turn out that the claims for self-governance of a particular ethnocultural group are unwarranted, but we are surely unjustified in prejudging the issue. In some cases, the arguments presented by these groups for creating their own separate political community—such as claims that they constitute a distinct nation or that their fundamentally different worldview will condemn them to perpetual marginalization—may be compelling enough to override the desirability of retaining a unitary political community for democratic deliberation.

Second, the suggestions that Bohman makes to promote ongoing deliberation of all groups in a common political community are inadequate. As we observed earlier, at the national level the deliberative disadvantages of some cultural minorities created by their extreme economic and political inequality are unlikely to be remedied by powers of local jurisdiction. As a result, they may find that they consistently lose out in deliberative outcomes. In addition, deep incommensurable cultural differences will most likely also put some minority groups in the position of pervasive and persistent marginalization. As a consequence of unremedied deliberative disadvantages and incommensurable differences, some cultural minorities will find that they are unable to effectively influence deliberative outcomes. But, according to Bohman, what motivates participants in public deliberation to continue to cooperate in future deliberations is the reasonable expectation that on another occasion the roles will be reversed and their position will prevail. When a cultural group constantly loses out in public deliberation, however, it will not be reasonable for them to maintain this expectation, and this will in turn undermine their willingness for continued cooperation.

What should we conclude from Bohman's failure to provide adequate support for the criteria determining the fairness of moral compromises involving certain cultural minorities? Despite its shortcomings, I believe that Bohman's moral compromise approach for dealing with the dilemma of incommensurable differences is plausible and useful for many multicultural contexts. It is a feasible approach which does not force us to make unrealistic assumptions about the ideological flexibility of participants or the degree of overlap between the conceptual frameworks employed by different cultural groups. We must be mindful, however, of the limitations of Bohman's solution. Even though it may work relatively well when dealing with disagreements between accommodationist and majority groups (and even here caution is advised when accommodationist minorities constantly lose out in deliberation), it may not, as we have seen, resolve in a fair manner disputes between majority groups and indigenous, ethnonationalist, or secessionist groups. It may also fall short when adjudicating between competing differences of perspectives among communal contenders or even accommodationist groups and majority societies deeply divided by religion or race. In examining the shortcomings of Bohman's theory of moral compromise, we can also see the limits of deliberative democracy. Some autonomist and secessionist groups, by questioning the assumptions of deliberative democracy concerning unitary political communities and the possibility of intercultural understanding, pose a challenge that deliberative democracy ultimately cannot answer. It is at this point that we should consider the possibility of granting these groups rights of self-government, so that they can create separate public spheres in which they can achieve self-determination. To be sure, recognizing the limitations of deliberative democracy for treating these groups fairly may not be a sufficient reason to justify granting them such rights; a detailed discussion of the justification of self-government rights will be provided in the fifth and seventh chapters. Before examining rationales for self-governance, however, we must first attend more closely to an important dilemma that we barely touched in this chapter, namely, the rectification of political inequalities between cultural groups in multicultural democracies.

Notes

1. See, for example, Joshua Cohen, "Deliberation and Democratic Legitimacy," in *The Good Polity: Normative Analysis of the State*, eds. Alan Hamlin and Philip Pettit (Oxford: Basil Blackwell, 1989), Amy Gutmann and Dennis Thompson, *Democracy and Disagreement* (Cambridge, MA.: Harvard University Press, 1996), and James Bohman, *Public Deliberation: Pluralism, Complexity, and Democracy* (Cambridge, MA: MIT Press, 1996). In my summary of some of the basic concepts of deliberative democracy, I borrow liberally from these sources.

2. One often hears that the best policy for a multicultural society is to disregard ethnic and racial differences and treat people simply as human beings. As well intentioned as this suggestion may be, it makes the fallacious assumption that cultural differences are unimportant both for the ways in which people perceive and treat one another and for the ways in which people see themselves. As Charles Taylor has pointed out, because cultural heritage is for many cultural group members an integral part of who they are, one of the most important demands of ethnocultural minorities is for their cultural distinctiveness to be recognized. By neglecting cultural differences, we may be failing to take into account factors which are important for understanding the self-conceptions and behavior of others, as well as denying them the recognition of a cultural identity they consider as important. To be sure, the matter is complicated by the fact that the members of some ethnocultural groups may resent the assumption that they necessarily have the characteristics and experiences considered as typical of their group. Even given this fact, however, it is still essential to be knowledgeable of the distinctive cultural characteristics and experiences of different groups, since we may have to resort to these in understanding those cultural group members for whom cultural identity is important. For a fuller discussion of this point, see Charles Taylor, "The Politics of Recognition," in *Multiculturalism and the Politics of Recognition*, ed. Amy Gutmann (Princeton: Princeton University Press, 1992), pp. 25–73. It is also significant to note that in arguing for the importance of cultural membership, we do not have to assume that it is equally crucial for all ethnocultural groups. We need only suppose that it is important for those groups demanding cultural rights or self-governance.

3. I am not assuming here that these national groups are themselves entirely homogeneous or united in their political orientations and sense of cultural identity. There are significant differences within many minority communities regarding these factors. However, it is certainly the case that there are many ethnocultural groups who are part of multicultural states who are culturally different from the majorities, and who, most important, have a self-consciousness of being a distinct cultural and, in some cases, political community. As Walter Conner has stated, despite differences within ethnocultural groups, political developments throughout the world have shown that, when the chips are down, ethnocultural or national identity emerges as a, or even the, most important form of group identity.

4. It is important to note that it is unlikely that the willingness to override one's self-interest for the good of the larger political community can be attained by a commitment to abstract general principles of liberty and equality. One of the greatest disappointments of liberal democracy is that the commitment to general principles of justice and equal citizenship has proven to be insufficient to carry

the weight of civic solidarity in many contemporary democracies. It appears that civic solidarity—and certainly the high level of civic magnanimity presupposed by deliberative democracy—requires membership in a political community grounded on a shared collective identity that includes cultural, historical, and political elements. For a discussion of the factors needed for having a sense of belonging to a distinctive political community, see Yael Tamir, *Liberal Nationalism* (Princeton: Princeton University Press, 1993), Chapter 6.

5. Ontological economy refers to the idea that where there are a number of alternative theories with equal explanatory or predictive power, the one that posits the existence of the fewest entities or categories of entities is the true or most acceptable theory.

6. For a summary of Marglin's distinction between *episteme* and *techne*, see Stephen Marglin "Farmers, Seedsmen, and Scientists: Systems of Agriculture and Systems of Knowledge," in *Decolonizing Knowledge: From Development to Dialogue*, eds. Frederique Apffel-Marglin and Stephen A. Marglin (Oxford: Clarendon Press, 1996). Even though Marglin's account of *episteme* is not entirely accurate, his distinction between these two kinds of knowledge is generally sound and is useful for our purposes here. In this section I will basically follow his understanding of these two concepts.

7. Ibid., p. 230.

8. By unitary communities I mean political communities that are sufficiently cohesive to embody the civic requirements that we have identified as implicit in deliberative democracy. These unitary communities would have a concern for the common good, even when they disagree about the precise meaning of that common good. By unitary communities I do not mean political communities that are united in terms of their cultural ideals, practices, and beliefs.

9. I will discuss these groups more fully in later chapters. My purpose here is to differentiate roughly between these groups to assess the prospects for deliberative democracy in different multicultural societies.

10. Obviously, a notable exception is African-Americans, who were brought as slaves to the U.S. I classify them as accommodationist, despite this notable difference with immigrant groups, because on the whole (movements like those lead by Marcus Garvey aside) their primary political goals, like those of other accommodationist groups, have focused on obtaining equal civic rights, removing barriers to socioeconomic progress, and fighting discrimination.

11. Also, some non-indigenous groups, such as the Amish, want to create separate institutions that are different from those of the majority society. In the U.S., the fact that the cultural distinctiveness of these groups is religion-based and the fact that they are small and do not represent a threat to the institutional arrangements of the majority society affects the dynamic of acceptance of these groups by the state. They are more readily tolerated than larger groups that may pose a threat to the cultural dominance of the majority society.

12. Included in the accommodationist category are groups with transnational identities who, unlike traditional immigrants, maintain a high degree of connection with their country of origin, such as dual citizenship or continued involvement in its political affairs (e.g., Dominicans who travel to the Dominican Republic to vote in political elections). Also included in this category are "mixed-race"

groups for whom recognition of their autonomously determined ethnic or racial self-ascription is important.

13. Ted Robert Gurr, *Minorities at Risk: A Global View of Ethnopolitical Conflicts* (Washington, DC: United States Institute of Peace Press, 1993), p. 15.

14. Ibid., p. 22.

15. In some countries racial differences are of particular significance in accounting for divisions between groups. Even when the minority groups involved are accommodationist, the majority society can refuse to allow them to fully integrate into the society's social, political, and economic institutions if they are perceived as racially distinct. This is one salient difference between accommodationist groups that I will discuss in Chapter 6, where I examine issues of empowerment for these groups.

16. These crucial issues will be addressed more fully in later chapters.

17. David Miller, *On Nationality* (Oxford: Clarendon Press, 1995). Note that Miller is using the term "nation" to refer not to ethnocultural groups, but to states.

18. Ibid., p. 140.

19. Ibid., p. 142.

20. The phrase is from Benedict Anderson, *Imagined Communities: Reflections on the Origin and Spread of Nationalism* (London: Verso, 1983). In this influential text, Anderson argues that national groups are constructed through a variety of symbolic and narrative mechanisms.

21. These issues will be discussed further in Chapters 3, 8, and 9.

22. Gurr, *Minorities at Risk*, p. 311.

23. Ibid., p. 23.

24. The justification of self-governance rights will be provided in the fifth and seventh chapters.

25. On this point, see Margaret Canovan, *Nationhood and Political Theory* (Cheltenham, UK: Edward Elgar Publishing limited, 1996), chapters 6 and 7, and Anderson, *Imagined Communities*.

26. See Anthony De Palma, "Canada Pact Gives Tribe Self-Rule for First Time," *New York Times*, August 5, p. A2, 1998.

27. Gurr, *Minorities at Risk*, pp. 300–305.

28. The indigenous group may consider certain experiential evidence of the spiritual essence of the mountain as evidence.

29. Bohman, *Public Deliberation*.

30. Ibid., p. 33.

31. Jurgen Habermas, *Faktizitat und Geltung* (Suhrkamp, 1992), p. 411.

32. Ibid., p. 344.

33. Bohman, *Public Deliberation*, p. 33.

34. Ibid., p. 33.

35. Ibid., p. 91.

36. Ibid., p. 92.

37. Even though Bohman mentions in passing that deep cultural differences could be a deliberative disadvantage, he does not appreciate the depth of this problem.

3

Epistemological Egalitarianism

The problem of political inequality has been much discussed by writers on deliberative democracy. The amount of attention given to this problem is understandable, given that deliberative democracy requires a particularly demanding conception of political equality. Unlike conceptions of democracy in which legitimacy is based on aggregating existing preferences through such rudimentary mechanisms as voting, deliberative democracy involves far more complex procedures of political participation in which equality of political functioning can be undermined in a variety of ways. Among the most important of these is the monopolization of public deliberation by intellectual elites and those with advantages in epistemological resources. In recent years, there has been an increased appreciation for the many factors that need to be taken into account in arriving at an adequate understanding of political equality in deliberative democracies. Less attention, however, has been given to the specific problems of political equality that arise in multicultural societies. As we shall see, certain features of culturally pluralistic democracies make it very difficult to arrive at a satisfactory resolution of these problems. But the fact that practically all contemporary democracies are culturally pluralistic makes it imperative that these special problems be addressed.

In this chapter, I begin by discussing how the understanding of political equality has evolved from approaches that focus on equalization of resources for political participation to approaches that also take into account capabilities for using such resources effectively. I then argue that in order to adequately understand political equality in deliberative democracies, we must go beyond equality of resources and capabilities and consider motivation for political engagement, for without motivation, resources and capabilities do not lead to equitable political functioning. Far from being a purely subjective, individual matter, motivation for political participation can be systematically reinforced or undermined by a variety of sociocultural, economic, and political factors. Cultivating motivation for participation is particularly important for ethnocultural minorities, who are often marginalized from political processes in which advantaged groups have an inordinate degree of influence. In the final section of the chapter, I contend that there is yet another level of understanding political equality beyond resources, capabilities, and motivation, namely, one that is centered on equitable effectiveness in inducing social cooperation to accomplish one's goals in the political sphere. Even though such unequally distributed effectiveness cannot be fully equalized without unacceptable losses in liberty, its tendency to create asymmetries in political power in multicultural societies can be minimized by promoting intercultural understanding. I conclude by noting what is involved in intercultural understanding, as well as identifying the most prominent measures that can be taken to achieve understanding between cultural groups.

Resources, Capabilities, and Political Equality

A prominent account of the requirements for equal political functioning is provided by John Rawls. He maintains that primary goods—which include income and wealth, basic liberties, "freedom of movement and choice of occupation," "powers and prerogative of offices and positions of responsibility," and "the social bases of self-respect"[1]—are things that we can reasonably suppose everyone wants. According to Rawls, members of the polity should be guaranteed a minimum threshold of these primary goods so that they can attain the economic and political goals that they deem desirable.

Ensuring a minimal threshold of primary goods is important not only because such goods are valuable in themselves, but also because they are the resources which provide individuals with the wherewithal to attain their conceptions of the good, which is a goal that is a central desideratum of liberal democracies. We should note that Rawls's conception of primary goods is broad enough to include resources and capabilities that are important for deliberative democracy. A reasonable income, for instance, facilitates access to information and information technologies, which play an increasingly crucial role in effective political advocacy in contemporary democracies. Similarly, positions of responsibility and autonomous decision making are conducive to the development of skills and dispositions, such as self-direction, initiative, and a sense of strategic thinking, that are useful in public deliberation.[2] Rawls is undoubtedly correct to emphasize the importance of guaranteeing this broadly defined range of primary goods as necessary conditions for political equality. It is highly unlikely that individuals can advocate effectively for their political interests, particularly in a deliberative democracy, without possessing the resources included in his conception of primary goods.

According to Rawls, however, a just society need not require anything beyond this minimal threshold for political equality. Regarding the effective use of these primary goods, Rawls assumes that agents will have the moral, intellectual, and physical capacities necessary to use their resources effectively. Even though he maintains that the worth of political liberty for all citizens should be roughly equal—in the sense that all should have the opportunity to hold public office and influence political decisions—ultimately he merely assumes that approximate equality of capacities to make effective use of resources will be in place.

In contrast to Rawls's conception of political equality, Amartya Sen points out that a minimal threshold of primary goods is not sufficient for political equality, because there are great differences in individuals' capacities to use a given threshold of resources.[3] A person with a parasitic disease that prevents her from assimilating nutrients in an efficient manner, for example, may be unable to fulfill her nutritional needs with the threshold income level, while a healthy individual would not face this problem.[4] Likewise, a person who failed to develop his cognitive capacities due to poor education or malnutrition would be less effective in using the base level of resources for political participation than someone with access to a good education and adequate nutrition. According to Sen, because significant variations exist between the ability of different people to use the resources at their disposal to attain their goals, we cannot assume that guaranteeing a minimal amount of primary goods will result in equality of political functioning.

Sen distinguishes between the *means* and the *extent* of freedom, that is, between the means that one may have to accomplish the goals which one deems desirable and the extent or range of goals that one can feasibly accomplish.[5] Sen believes that to attain an adequate understanding of the freedom an individual actually possesses, we should focus on the "alternative sets of accomplishments" that the individual has the power to achieve. By looking at the number of accomplishments that the individual can realistically attain, we will obtain a better understanding of the extent of her freedom than by looking merely at the resources (which can be construed as means to accomplish goals) that she possesses. Because there are limitations in our capacities to employ resources effectively, focusing solely on resources or means does not provide an accurate measure of the achievements the individual can attain in the political (or other) realm. Despite the fact that Rawls includes in his list of primary goods factors (such as positions of responsibility) which would cultivate capacities useful for political deliberation, as a whole his resource-based approach for understanding political equality is inadequate, because he pays insufficient attention to the role of capabilities in effective political functioning.

Capabilities to employ resources effectively thus emerge as being of central importance for determining the political efficacy of individuals. When we compare people with regard to their political equality, we should concentrate not merely on the resources they possess, but also on their capabilities for their effective use. Recognizing the relevance of capabilities for political equality, Jack Knight and James Johnson make three recommendations to rectify capacity-based political inequities.[6] The first and most important of these is the provision of material resources to ensure the appropriate development of cognitive capacities. These material resources would include government support of education to ensure a basic level of development of cognitive skills, as well as government aid to eliminate childhood malnutrition and poverty. Knight and Johnson indicate that substantial scientific research reveals that diet and environment play a crucial role in cognitive development not only in the early formative years but well beyond childhood.[7] They correctly point out that without adequately developed cognitive capacities, individuals cannot effectively articulate and defend their needs and interests in a deliberative democracy. It is important to realize, even though Knight and Johnson do not point this out, that rectifying nutritional deficiencies early in children's lives is particularly important because of the permanence of their negative effects. Deficiencies in cognitive development caused by malnutrition are often irreversible, so that there is little, if anything, that a society can later do to remedy this capacities-based kind of political inequality.

The second recommendation that Knight and Johnson make to bring about political equality in deliberative democracies involves the capacity to formulate autonomous preferences. Nonautonomous preferences are those that are reflexively formulated in response to unfair background conditions.[8] These inauthentic preferences constitute a form of political inequality insofar as they reflect socially induced (though ostensibly self-imposed) constraints that can limit agents in public deliberation. Under conditions of economic and social deprivation, an individual may adapt to the limitations of her restricted and unjust circumstances by lowering her self-esteem and expectations of what she is realistically capable of accomplishing. For instance, nonautonomous preferences can be formulated in response to ethnocultural prejudice. As a result of suffering lifelong prejudice, individuals can internalize negative social attitudes towards themselves and members of their ethnocultural group, and limit the range of achievements they believe they are capable of accomplishing. These self-imposed limitations can in turn hinder them when they engage in public deliberation. They may believe that they are incapable of making worthwhile contributions to their political community, or may avoid participating in public deliberation altogether. Similarly, agents with nonautonomous, prejudice-induced preferences may lower their demands excessively, in the belief that they do not deserve that to which in all fairness they are entitled.[9]

Nonautonomous preferences can also arise from the effort to reduce cognitive dissonance in socioeconomic circumstances characterized by dire need or insufficient opportunities. For instance, there is evidence that workers sometimes underestimate the dangers of labor tasks in order to minimize the cognitive dissonance that would result from a correct assessment of hazardous working conditions.[10] When living in poverty, the need to obtain work may be so great that disempowered workers may find ways to justify taking risks that they would not find acceptable if they had other employment options. The decision of these workers to accept inordinately hazardous work could therefore be considered as a nonautonomous preference, since it was made under conditions of extreme need and excessive limitation of opportunity. Their capacity to advocate in forums of public deliberation for safer working conditions or better wages, for example, could be compromised by their nonautonomous preferences. These workers may consider dangerous working conditions acceptable, not because these working conditions are actually safe, but because under their circumstances of dire need, they have convinced themselves (against their best interests) that these conditions are satisfactory.

Other instances in which nonautonomous preferences can function as dissonance-reducing strategies involve situations in which individuals living in conditions of material deprivation or social constraint blame themselves for their lack of achievement. By shifting the source of failure on themselves, they are better able to maintain a belief in the general fairness of the world. In some cases it may be preferable to believe that one's suffering and deprivation are justified than to believe that they are the result of injustice on the part of others.[11] Of course, not in all cases are the preferences of people living in materially and socially disadvantaged circumstances inauthentic and nonautonomous. The point is that we cannot simply assume that in all social contexts peoples' preferences always reflect their best interests, that is, the interests they would articulate under noncoercive, autonomy-enhancing circumstances. Under social circumstances that unfairly compromise their capacity to formulate autonomous preferences, the political functioning of these participants in public deliberation will be significantly restricted and hindered relative to that of individuals living under material and sociocultural conditions conducive to greater autonomy and freedom.

The third capacity-related recommendation made by Knight and Johnson to establish political equality in deliberative democracies entails the effective use of cultural resources. They cite with approval Iris Young's argument that cultural minorities are in a position of great disadvantage relative to dominant cultural majorities when the former are required to employ the terminology, values, and modes of discourse and argumentation of the majority.[12] Since minorities are likely to be less familiar, and therefore less adept, at expressing their ideas in the language of the majority or dominant society, they will be less effective in public deliberation. Their reduced capacity to influence other participants in forums of public deliberation will place them at a disadvantage relative to the members of the majority culture. Knight and Johnson do not elaborate on this third recommendation, they merely mention it in passing and move on to discuss other issues. I will return to the issue of the cultural advantages that are imbedded in the general structure of the majority or dominant society—including *inter alia,* prevailing ideas, forms of social organization, and modes of discourse—which collectively confer cultural privileges to the members of the majority society in public deliberation. These cultural privileges, I will maintain, represent a significant and intractable form of political inequality in deliberative democracies. In the final section of this chapter I will show why intercultural understanding is important for constraining the deliberative advantages conferred by cultural privileges of this kind. For now it will suffice to note that differences in the capacity to make effective use of cultural resources related to public deliberation represent a form of political inequality that needs to be addressed.

All told, the recommendations made by Knight and Johnson to rectify capacity-based inequalities are valuable and important. Taken together, they would minimize not only general inequalities among the citizenry, but also inequalities between ethnocultural groups and majority or dominant groups. The third recommendation they make is explicitly culture-based, while the other two are clearly relevant for political situations in which ethnocultural groups are burdened by social and economic disadvantages. Concerning the second recommendation, which deals with the capacity to formulate autonomous preferences as a condition for political equality, it is important to note that its implementation would require a thorough understanding of the conditions that might hinder the exercise of agency and autonomy of the members of ethnocultural groups. This requirement would in turn presuppose a high level of reflective self-knowledge among the members of these groups, so that they can accurately identify and collectively examine the ways in which their choices are conditioned and hindered by the limitations and disadvantages they face. It would also be necessary for these disadvantaged groups to have the means to convey effectively to the majority the socially imposed restrictions on their preferences, so that in forums of public deliberation policies could be formulated to eliminate these hindrances to autonomous decision making. The principal objectives of self-understanding, and the capacity to publicly convey the disadvantages of failing to achieve this epistemic condition, would be for ethnocultural groups to attain a higher degree of autonomy, and to raise the general level of intercultural understanding of the society.

We should also point out certain limitations of the first recommendation that Knight and Johnson make, which involves a general government guarantee of a basic level of education and nutrition to ensure the proper development of everyone's cognitive capabilities. The second part of their recommendation could be readily specified by reference to medical facts concerning the level of nutrition required for proper mental development. However, the first part of their proposal is vague, because it does not specify in a clear manner what is involved in a base level of educational attainment. If the threshold is set at a fairly low level, it will remedy only extreme forms of education-based inequalities caused by economic impoverishment or social disadvantage. But even if the guaranteed threshold level of educational proficiency is set at a fairly high point, not all epistemological resources and capabilities would be equalized. Their recommendation would certainly not suffice to create parity with regard to other epistemological resources which can have a significant impact on the relative ability of ethnocultural groups to effectively defend their needs and interests in a deliberative democracy.

To achieve even approximate parity in epistemological resources and capabilities, it would also be necessary to ensure equal access to sources of information, to information technologies, and to the development of the capabilities needed for their proficient use. Given the increasing complexity of contemporary democratic societies, information and the critical thinking and technical capabilities for its effective use play a critical role in political advocacy. In deliberative democracies, which grant central importance to public deliberation, the role of specialized information and cognitive capacities attains even greater prominence. There are numerous private data bases, for instance, that only individuals with financial means can use to strengthen their policy proposals in public deliberation. Individuals who are economically impoverished would not only be unable to access such data bases, they would also be denied an equal opportunity to develop the capabilities to use diverse and interconnected sources of information to fortify and defend their policy recommendations in public deliberation. Unless we address the various kinds of epistemological inequality that can exist in multicultural deliberative democracies, we will be unable to successfully rectify capacity-based forms of political inequality. The proposal of Knight and Johnson to ensure a basic level of education and the satisfaction of basic nutritional needs is certainly a step in the right direction, but it merely touches the surface of capability- and resource-based forms of political inequality.

Motivations and Political Equality

We have observed how the understanding of political equality in deliberative democracies has evolved from accounts based on equality of resources to accounts that also include equality of capabilities for political functioning. The rationale for including capabilities in an adequate conception of political equality is that differences in capacities to use available resources could lead to inequalities in the ability to defend one's needs and interests in public deliberation. Approaches to political equality that incorporate resources and capabilities have garnered a wide consensus among authors who have examined these issues.[13] It is not clear, however, whether resources and capabilities, despite being equitably distributed, are in themselves sufficient for political equality. The reason is simply that another important factor, namely, motivation, is necessary for individuals to employ their resources and capabilities for political engagement. Social agents need to have the motivation to participate in political activities before their resources and capabilities can be politically relevant. Since political leaders and democratic institutions are more likely to respond to those messages that are communicated to them, those who have the motivation to participate will have a more prominent political voice.[14] Cultivating motivation for political participation is particularly important in deliberative democracies because participation in forums of public deliberation generally requires more commitment, time, and preparation than other forms of participation, such as voting or making nominal financial campaign contributions.

Perhaps writers on deliberative democracy have not given sufficient attention to motivation for political participation because it is tempting to construe motivation as a purely individual, subjective disposition that cannot be explained in terms of social, economic, or political structural factors. Or perhaps they believe that there are so many different and varied factors responsible for the motivation to participate that they cannot be systematically analyzed. Despite the apparently nonsystematic character of motivation, there are a number of identifiable factors that can promote or undermine political participation. Chief among these are level of formal education, social networks in which one is asked or encouraged to participate, exposure to successful forms of political engagement, and a sense of social responsibility. Either singly or jointly, factors such as these can affect in significant ways motivation for political participation, and differences in motivation can in turn lead to differential employment of politically relevant resources and capabilities. Even though, as we shall see below, resources and capabilities relevant for political equality sometimes coincide with factors which strengthen motivation for political participation, in some cases what prompts motivation goes beyond resources and capabilities.

One of the factors that can create motivation for political participation is level of formal education.[15] Those that are better educated are, for example, more likely to read newspapers, to keep up with political developments, and in general to be more psychologically engaged with politics. Education tends to widen one's awareness of the ways in which political developments affect individual and collective life. To the extent that motivation to participate presupposes an understanding of the issues in which one may be engaged, education is a contributing factor in motivation for political participation. In a deliberative democracy the supportive effects of formal education for political participation are likely to be even greater than in democratic systems that do not grant pride of place to public deliberation, because understanding disputative discourse, especially when complex issues are involved, is facilitated by education. Since education is an important component of socioeconomic status, in the absence of intervening factors, differences in socioeconomic status between ethnocultural and dominant groups will represent an important form of motivational inequality.[16]

Social networks are also positively connected to the creation of motivation for political engagement, because they can function as sources for recruitment for political participation.[17] One of the primary reasons why people participate in political activity is because they are asked or encouraged to do so. In the workplace, in civic associations, and at church, for example, people may receive requests for political participation, and they are more likely to engage in political activity as a result of such requests. In those democratic societies in which social networks for political recruitment are more horizontally distributed than level of formal education, these networks tend to promote motivational equality. That is, in some societies individuals who may not have access to educational opportunities that promote engagement with politics might nevertheless have access to voluntary organizations which encourage political participation. In Austria, Japan, and Nigeria, for example, affiliations with civic organizations play a significant role in equalizing participatory motivation despite differences is socioeconomic status.[18] Thus, to the extent that participation in civic associations or organized religious worship declines in societies in which such institutions motivate political activity, opportunities for members of disfranchised groups, including ethnocultural minorities, to be exposed to sources of stimulation for political participation also decline. Impoverished minority communities whose members do not have equitable access to educational opportunities are particularly vulnerable to declines in civic associational life, since they must often deal with the effects not only of poverty, but also of political marginalization.

Another factor that is conducive to creating motivation for political engagement is a sense of social responsibility. When individuals believe and feel that they have a moral responsibility to resolve a social problem or rectify an injustice, for example, they are more likely to be motivated for political activity. Social responsibility can arise from a variety of sources, ranging from narrowly conceived group interests to more widely generalized concerns for the common good. On its own, social responsibility does not necessarily lead to political participation. Typically, other conditions must also be in place before actual political participation occurs, such as a sense of one's efficacy as an agent of social change, structured opportunities for participation, and exposure to fruitful cases of political engagement. These conditions can vary widely depending on an individual's economic status, type of employment performed, and degree of cultural integration into the majority society. Nonetheless, social responsibility is a contributing factor in a set of social conditions, which are sometimes mutually reinforcing, that are conducive to political engagement.

In this section we have observed that simply because citizens have resources and capabilities for participation does not mean that they will use them, and that there are a number of cultural, economic, and political factors that can serve as sources of motivation for political participation. Crucial questions arise here concerning the impact of differences in motivational sources for the political participation of ethnocultural minorities in multicultural democracies. It is to these differences that we now turn.

Motivational Sources and Ethnocultural Groups

It is important to understand the ways in which sources of motivation for political engagement affect the political equality of ethnocultural groups. It may appear at first sight that some motivational inequalities can be straightforwardly remedied by equalizing the resources and capabilities that are relevant for political participation. As we noted above, when cultural minorities are economically disadvantaged relative to the cultural majority, their level of formal educational attainment will tend to be lower, and thus they will experience motivational inequalities *vis-a-vis* the majority. These differences in motivation for political engagement generated by differences in educational opportunities could be rectified, it would seem, by ensuring that the members of all cultural groups in the polity have the material resources and opportunities necessary to attain parity in educational capabilities.[19] However, with some ethnocultural groups it may not be enough to equalize resources and opportunities for developing educational capabilities.

Due to past and continuing discrimination and marginalization, ethnocultural minorities may have developed dysfunctional ways of dealing with such important goals as educational achievement. It is well known, for example, that in some African-American impoverished communities young people stigmatize educational attainment as "white" behavior, and exert social pressure on their black peers to avoid educational dedication and achievement.[20] Studious black youth may thus feel ostracized for allegedly rejecting their black identity, and as a result of this ostracism may come to see educational achievement in a negative light. For these communities it would not be enough to merely equalize material resources and opportunities for attaining parity in educational capabilities. Remedial measures that take into account the specific circumstances and problems faced by these disfranchised ethnocultural minorities would be necessary to remedy the educational inequalities that in turn give rise to differences in motivation for political participation. A multicultural deliberative democracy that wants to rectify motivational inequalities will thus have to seriously address such questions as: What processes and influences, past and present, have contributed to the development of these dysfunctional ways of looking at educational achievement? What sociocultural and psychological dimensions of ethnocultural prejudice must be carefully examined in order to adequately resolve the problems arising from dysfunctional ways of looking at educational capabilities? As we can see from the case of disfranchised African-Americans, a straightforward resource and capabilities approach to rectifying political inequalities may not always be adequate to the task of addressing motivational inequalities caused by the individual and social destructive effects of long-term disfranchisement. It may very well be the case that other ethnocultural groups have internalized similar attitudes regarding educational achievement.

Consider now social networks that function as sources of motivation for political participation. Ethnocultural minorities will be disadvantaged relative to the majority unless they have the wherewithal to develop their own civic associational networks. Here again it may not be enough for disadvantaged minorities to have the same resources and opportunities as other cultural groups to form their own voluntary civic organizations. Due to past discrimination, internalized racist attitudes, or lack of employment involving a high level of autonomous decision making, for example, they may not have the sense of social agency and efficacy needed to develop effective civic associational networks. Of course, many ethnocultural groups who have long experienced discrimination and oppression may exhibit exceptional capacities for civic organization and mobilization. Indeed, the experience of shared oppression can be a powerful factor engendering a sense of ethnic or racial solidarity among the members of these groups. We cannot, however, assume that this is the case with all ethnocultural groups. In some cases the particular forms of oppression experienced by certain groups has undermined their capacities for civic organization and mobilization. For ethnocultural communities struggling with drugs, gang violence, poverty, and a breakdown in familial cohesion, for example, the effort to achieve self-determination through associational civic life can be very difficult. In these cases it might be necessary to go beyond the equalization of resources and opportunities for development of capabilities for civic organization, and special policies may have to be adopted to address the specific factors, both social-structural and psychological, that would enable ethnocultural minorities to remedy motivational inequalities arising from the absence of social networks that promote political engagement.

Michael Walzer has advocated state support for civic organizations that promote mutual aid, further the pursuit of communal goals, and teach groups civic and political skills. He argues that these civic organizations—which include day-care centers, ethnic associations, homeless shelters, old-age homes, and environmental organizations—are powerful sources of revitalization for civil society and for civic/political participation. He points out that some of the strongest civic associations are organized by ethnic/religious groups, such as Irish Catholics, German Lutherans, and Jews. However, Walzer indicates that there are great differences in proficiency of organizational skills, political access, and financial and educational resources between civic ethnic organizations. Given the important role that associational organizations play in encouraging participation in civil society, Walzer maintains that it is important that there be greater parity in the capacity to engage in and form effective voluntary civic associations. To this end, he proposes that government play a central role in supporting these associations by offering subsistence wages and basic benefits so that individuals can volunteer their services to these organizations, on a full-time basis, for several years at a time. By having individuals work full-time for extended periods of time, rather than intermittently and on a short-term basis, the continuity and effectiveness of these civic voluntary associations would be greatly increased. And perhaps more important, providing government support would reduce some of the inequalities in resources and capabilities that now exist between different ethnic civic organizations.

Walzer's proposal is a good one, particularly if it is expanded to include consideration of the special problems mentioned above that beset certain ethnocultural communities. This additional attention might entail, for the most impoverished and civilly damaged communities, economic revitalization, intensive support for education, and social services aimed at promoting self-reliance for the members of these communities. By providing state support for self-help ethnocultural civic organizations, a traditionally very effective mechanism of minority group organization and mobilization could be strengthened. These organizations could then function as social environments for teaching the members of cultural minorities civic and political skills that would be instrumental in encouraging political participation. By increasing the sense of social agency and efficacy of their members, and by developing organizational and communication skills, these voluntary associations could play a significant role in equalizing existing sources of motivation for political engagement. I will return to Walzer's proposal in the last chapter, where I will discuss it in more detail.

Social responsibility as a source of political motivation presents an interesting dilemma for ethnocultural groups. Historically, a sense of social responsibility for the well-being of the members of one's ethnic group has been a major factor in promoting ethnocultural political mobilization. Ironically, however, in some cases the upward socioeconomic mobility of some members of ethnocultural groups can undermine group solidarity and coordinated political activity in defense of ethnocultural interests. When some members of an ethnocultural group achieve a high level of formal education and improve their occupational status and income, they may leave the community where they were raised. As a result of changes in income, lifestyle, residential community, friends, and associational networks, their political priorities and orientations may change so that their preferences no longer coincide with, and may actually be antagonistic to, the political interests of the members of the disfranchised communities from which they departed. When this occurs, fractures can arise within the ethnocultural community, as its most educated, resourceful, and economically successful members acquire different political interests (which are usually class-based) that make it difficult for the group as a whole to advocate effectively for the needs of its most disempowered members. In brief, as a result of the upward mobility of some of its members, the sense of social responsibility that formerly mobilized and united the minority community may diminish to the point where its capacity for the kind of political participation that empowers the group as a whole may be seriously impaired. Even though not all ethnocultural group members of high socioeconomic status will have political orientations different from those of disempowered minority communities, we cannot simply assume that there is a straightforward connection between individual socioeconomic success and collective empowerment.

Thus, reinforcing a sense of mutual social responsibility among the members of ethnocultural minorities is of major importance in equalizing *group-based* motivational sources for political participation. While upward socioeconomic mobility may provide some group members with *individual-based* resources, capabilities, and motivation to participate, this does not necessarily translate into greater empowerment of ethnocultural minority communities. The needs and interests of these communities may go unheeded by political leaders and democratic institutions, even as some of their members achieve gains in socioeconomic status and political influence. Indeed, the greater political visibility and economic well-being of the upwardly mobile minority group members may actually diminish, in the eyes of the majority, the urgency of the social, economic, and political needs of disfranchised minority communities. Since ethnic and racial membership has a "high social profile," successful minorities are likely to be prominently noticeable in public consciousness, and the majority could acquire a false picture of the progress that ethnocultural minorities have actually made. It may, for example, be difficult for some members of the majority society to take seriously the claim that minorities are disempowered when the city mayor or the chief of police are minorities, despite the fact that as a whole ethnocultural minorities may be burdened by socioeconomic disadvantages and inequitable political representation.

In view of these considerations, the proposal discussed above to provide public funding to ethnic civic associations—particularly those rooted in impoverished communities—becomes all the more important. Since many of these civic associations are organized around common, group-based goals, they are social environments not only for the teaching of civic and organizational skills, but also for the reinforcement of a sense of mutual social responsibility among their members. This sense of social responsibility can encourage political activity in which the interests of the most disadvantaged members of minority communities are not overlooked. Moreover, when members of ethnocultural minorities engage in cooperative projects that answer to communal needs and interests, they are more likely to acquire a sense of social agency and efficacy that can turn social responsibility into motivation for actual political participation. Finally, civic organizations can provide forums for public deliberation that can train members to be effective participants in broader public forums in which general political issues are discussed and resolved. Even though civic organizations are not sufficient to equalize differences in sources of motivation for political participation, they are important mechanisms for providing resources, developing capabilities, and motivating ethnocultural minorities for group-based political advocacy.

Equality of Political Efficacy

Going beyond resources and capabilities by taking account of motivation for political participation deepened our understanding of political equality, while considering the specific factors that are important for motivating ethnocultural minorities extended our understanding of political equality in multicultural democracies. There is, however, another level of examining political equality that goes beyond resources, capabilities, and motivation, namely, one that considers political efficacy, that is, the capacity to induce social cooperation necessary for the attainment of one's political goals. Political efficacy can be implemented in a variety of ways, such as through the use of threats or monetary inducements. If someone has enough physical or economic power to make credible threats on a sufficiently large number of members of a political community, for example, she may induce them to cooperate with her to implement her political objectives. Of course, in a truly democratic society, and certainly in a deliberative democracy, such methods of inducing social cooperation are considered illegitimate. In a deliberative democracy legitimate political efficacy should be based on the fairness, reasonableness, and effectiveness of one's proposals.

The notion of equitable political efficacy as a form of political equality is a component of Bohman's conception of equality of political functioning, and is also implicit in Young's notion of cultural privilege. Bohman is concerned with identifying and examining the factors that are necessary to bring about equality of political functioning in deliberative democracies, and in this connection he considers the social dimensions of political effectiveness. He correctly points out that looking from an individualistic perspective at the capabilities that an agent possesses to bring about certain goals overlooks the social factors that are relevant for achieving political objectives. Bohman indicates that political influence in a deliberative democracy involves social cooperation, and therefore cannot be adequately understood as a capacity of isolated individuals. One must be able to convince others of the reasonableness of one's policy objectives, and thus induce them to undertake actions which will accomplish these objectives.

Bohman goes on to articulate a conception of political equality based in part on a minimum threshold of public functioning that all citizens should have. He advocates the establishment of a "floor" level of effective political influence that is necessary to protect political equality. This threshold, which involves the capacity to initiate deliberative engagement to protect one's interests, would be consistent with the fact that the political effectiveness of citizens could still be affected by factors beyond their control, such as "undetected cultural biases" and the effects of division of labor, which may involve unequal distributions of information and expertise relevant for public deliberation. Bohman believes that some inequalities in the distribution of relevant knowledge and expertise are inevitable in any complex society, and should be regarded as consistent with political equality. Thus, Bohman is willing to accept epistemological inequalities as a necessary, *albeit* undesirable, consequence of the size and complexity of technological societies.

Bohman is correct regarding the need to have a minimum threshold of political functioning if the ideal of political equality in deliberative democracies is to be respected. He is also on solid ground in claiming that it is practically impossible to completely eliminate all differences in epistemological resources, even though, as I have already observed, there is more that could be done to equalize epistemological resources and capabilities than he indicates. Bohman fails to realize, however, that the un-

equal distribution of knowledge and expertise is not the only form of uneven distribution of epistemic factors that gives rise to differences in political efficacy. He also does not take notice of the fact that intercultural
understanding can play a major role in remedying an important kind of
uneven distribution of beliefs and values that creates inequalities of political efficacy in multicultural societies. To clarify the latter two statements,
it would be instructive to first briefly examine Iris Young's notion of cultural privilege.

Young's conception of cultural privilege is particularly useful for examining the issue of equality of political efficacy in multicultural societies. According to Young, members of the majority culture will have an
advantage in public deliberation because it is more likely that their policy
proposals will seem more plausible and reasonable than those presented
by members of cultural minorities. When minorities have to articulate
and defend their proposals using the terminology, normative assumptions, and modes of justification of the majority, they will be at a relative
disadvantage on those occasions in which they differ from the majority
with regards to these discursive factors. Due to less familiarity and mastery of the ideology and modes of discourse employed by the majority,
the defense of their policy proposals will in general seem less persuasive
and rationally justified than the proposals presented by members of the
majority culture. The relative unpersuasiveness of their presentations
need not have anything to do with the intrinsic value or plausibility of
their proposals, but may be more a function of their being compelled to
make their case using the resources of an unfamiliar cultural conceptual
framework. But even more important, even if members of the minority
culture were to master the ideology and discursive methods of the majority, to the extent that their values, terms, and affective orientations differ
from those of the majority society, they would still be at a disadvantage
when persuading the majority in public deliberation. This is because the
persuasiveness of reasons given for proposals will depend on whether
fellow deliberators find these reasons, and the background assumptions
on which they depend, plausible.

Like Bohman's notion of political functioning, Young's conception of
cultural privilege takes into account the collective dimensions of political
efficacy. That is, she realizes that an important part of the persuasiveness
and effectiveness of one's reasons in public deliberation may be due to
the fact that others share one's convictions, values, affective orientations,
and cultural background assumptions. When others share one's basic
empirical and normative beliefs, they are more likely to see one's policy
recommendations as plausible, and not regard them as questionable from
the outset. Of course, this does not mean that the majority in a democratic society shares a unified vision of how to analyze and resolve issues
of common concern. Particularly in contemporary cosmopolitan democ-

racies, a wide variety of opinion exists regarding many socioeconomic and political issues.

Nevertheless, it is also the case that there are some basic factual and normative beliefs that most members of the majority society share, and that ethnocultural minorities may not generally hold these beliefs. For instance, a fundamental assumption of deliberative democracy is that knowledge that is relevant for the examination and resolution of social problems should be free and publicly accessible to all[21], and it is safe to assume that most people in contemporary democracies would see this as a reasonable assumption that should be adopted to facilitate the fair resolution of collective problems. Some ethnocultural groups, however, believe that there are certain kinds of knowledge that should be divulged only in special, spiritually appropriate circumstances. From the perspective of these groups, such forms of knowledge should not be freely accessible in public deliberation, which is an inappropriate context for the discussion of this spiritual knowledge. In cases in which such sacred knowledge is relevant to the issues at hand, an ethnocultural group will be unable to use this information in the deliberative process, and as a result will be at a deliberative disadvantage relative to the cultural majority. This conception of protected knowledge, which is held by some indigenous groups, will diminish their political efficacy by rendering inaccessible information they could use to induce others to understand their proposals and cooperate with them to achieve their political objectives.

Inequalities in political efficacy are extremely intractable and perhaps the most difficult to rectify, because attempts to completely equalize this form of political functioning will almost invariably violate the autonomy of members of either the majority or minority. For instance, since this form of political inequality arises from the degree of agreement that exists among the citizenry regarding certain beliefs, values, affective orientations, and modes of justification, one way this inequality could be remedied is by compelling some members of the majority to change their minds so that their political convictions coincide with those of the minority. By getting a suitable number of members of the majority to alter their convictions so that a more even distribution of similar beliefs across the society is attained, minority proposals would receive a more sympathetic hearing, since now a greater number of people would share the minority's point of view. Needless to say, this suggestion is absurd, not only because its implementation would involve a clear violation of the autonomy of those citizens who were compelled to change their political convictions, but also because it is not clear whether we could devise a workable procedure for bringing about the required belief transformations. Like cultural minorities, members of the majority society have the right to pursue their conception of the good and preserve their cultural identity and traditions by transmitting and reinforcing their values, beliefs, and practices, even if this means that those individuals from a minority cultural tradition will not enjoy the same degree of political efficacy. In a similar manner, violations of autonomy would also occur if, for the sake of obtaining a more ideologically homogeneous society, members of ethnocultural minority groups were coerced into abandoning their respective cultural perspectives and adopting one that more closely coincided with the views of the majority.

But if differences in political efficacy that derive from inequalities in inducing social cooperation cannot be eliminated without infringing on the autonomy of either majority or minority groups, what measures can be taken to minimize this particular form of political inequality? An important way in which inequality of political efficacy could be minimized, though not completely eliminated, is through intercultural understanding. For what is the source of the difference in political efficacy here, that is, why are the proposals of members of the minority culture—assuming fundamental differences exist between the conceptual frameworks of majority and minority groups—less likely to be regarded as plausible, reasonable, or convincing to the majority society? As we observed above, this is because in multicultural societies: (i) there will be less familiarity and proficiency on the part of cultural minorities with the components of the majority's conceptual framework and (ii) there will be a comparatively higher degree of understanding and agreement among the majority with socially predominant terminology, values, practices, affective orientations, and beliefs that the minority cultural groups may not share.

Intercultural understanding can mitigate the inequalities in political efficacy that arise from these epistemic discrepancies. Through intercultural understanding, ethnocultural minorities can increase their comprehension and mastery of the majority's worldview and vice versa. This mutual understanding will in turn make it more likely that the majority will appreciate and respect the rationale behind minority proposals. In other words, to the extent that intercultural understanding diminishes the cognitive and affective distance between majority and minority group members, both the comprehensibility and plausibility of minority proposals will increase. When the majority obtains a more adequate understanding of the minority culture, they will be in a better epistemic position from which to appreciate the needs and interests that underlie minority policy recommendations. Likewise, when the members of minority groups understand the concerns, beliefs, and traditions of the majority, they will be better able to dialogue with them in a way that is conducive to mutual understanding. In short, intercultural understanding can be a powerful mechanism to increase the fruitfulness, as well as the fairness, of public dialogue in a multicultural society.

But how is intercultural understanding achieved, especially when the cultural groups in question hold incommensurable conceptual frameworks? Since the problem of intercultural understanding is not so severe when the cognitive and affective differences between cultural groups are not so great, our main concern is with the dilemma that arises when there are very significant or seemingly unbridgeable gulfs between the conceptual frameworks employed by majority and minority cultural groups. In order to deal adequately with this important dilemma, it is necessary to first dispel a widely held misconception concerning the nature of intercultural understanding. Examining this misconception will accomplish two purposes. First, it will reveal how misleading and dangerous it is to succumb to this mistake, and second, it will provide important clues concerning how we should conceptualize and promote intercultural understanding.

For ease of reference I will refer to this fundamental epistemological error as the "iron-cage thesis." This thesis is held, in slightly different versions, by such prominent philosophers as Richard Rorty, W.V.O. Quine and, with some qualifications, Donald Davidson. The plausible but mistaken core idea underlying the iron-cage thesis is that when we try to understand a fundamentally different culture, we must rely exclusively on the conceptual resources of our own worldview. Since our own conceptual framework is all that we have to work with, the argument goes, we must employ its resources to translate and explain the language, thoughts, and behavior of those foreign cultural groups we are trying to understand. According to this view, in trying to understand others we are in effect confined or "trapped" by the cognitive boundaries of our own conceptual framework. In defending the iron-cage thesis, use is often made of the principle of charity, according to which when we try to understand a foreign cultural group with whom we have never had any contact we must simultaneously do two things: translate the meaning of their words and interpret their beliefs about the world. We need to accomplish these two tasks if we have any hope of understanding them because we cannot know what they believe about the world unless we know what they mean by their words and, conversely, we cannot decipher the meaning of their terms unless we know what they believe about the world. For example, if the members of an alien group utter the words "Tomba chaka" when a cougar is approaching we cannot determine whether they believe that a cougar is in fact approaching unless we know what these two words mean. On the other hand, we cannot determine the meaning of these two words unless we know what they believe about the world, that is, unless we determine what they believe is happening when they utter these words.

The only way we can simultaneously accomplish the tasks of figuring out what their words mean and what they believe about the world, according to the principle of charity, is by assuming that their beliefs and claims about reality are essentially like our own. That is, we cannot decipher their conceptual framework unless we make the important assumption that both of us for the most part agree on our beliefs about the world and, in particular, that they are correct in most of their beliefs, when the latter are evaluated by our own standards of what is correct or true. It is only by assuming that they, like us, believe that a cougar is approaching, and have an interest in alerting others to this fact, that we can determine that "Tomba chaka" means "A cougar is coming" and not something totally different like "I feel tired today." In other words, without being "charitable" regarding the truth of most of their beliefs—again, where truth is determined by what we believe is true—we would never be able to translate or understand the meaning of the terms they use to talk about the world.

Advocates of the iron-cage thesis maintain that the need for us to rely on the principle of charity in attempting to understand a foreign cultural group implies that, whether we like it or not, we must depend exclusively on our own conceptual framework in attempting to comprehend other cultures. According to the defenders of the thesis, we have no choice in the matter: We are limited by the resources of our own worldview in trying to understand others. Even though they do not put the matter in this way, they believe that we are imprisoned by our own conceptual cages. Moreover, we are destined to understand only those groups with whom we share most fundamental beliefs about the world. If we ever met a cultural group with whom we did not agree on most of our beliefs, we would never be able to understand them, since we would have no common basis of agreement concerning our beliefs about the world on which we could rely to even begin to translate or interpret their language. Thus, according to the principle of charity, we can only understand those who (for the most part) agree with us; those who hold visions of the world radically different from our own we are destined never to understand.

Primarily on the basis of these considerations, Rorty arrives at his "ethnocentrism" thesis. According to this view, we have no choice but to be ethnocentric when it comes to dealing with other cultural groups. Rorty maintains that since we can understand and evaluate the reasonableness of others' beliefs, practices, and values only if we "weave them together with beliefs we already have,"[22] we will inevitably judge them using our own standards and beliefs. Like other thinkers who accept the iron-cage thesis, Rorty agrees with the principle of charity, which is a primary rationale for his ethnocentrism. If it is a necessary epistemic precondition of understanding others that we impose our own belief system on them, there is nothing to regret or be apologetic about concerning ethnocentrism, it is merely the appropriate attitude that arises from a correct analysis of what is involved in trying to understand others.

I believe the iron-cage thesis is an important and fundamental episte-mological error. We can begin to dissect this thesis by noting that it de-pends on a conception of inter-framework understanding which is based on translation. That is, advocates of the thesis believe that the only way in which the adherents of a conceptual framework can understand an-other framework is by translating the terms and claims of that frame-work into their own. They take as the paradigmatic case of inter-frame-work understanding the scenario in which someone encounters a wholly unknown cultural group and attempts to decipher their language and worldview. This, of course, is a misleading picture of the vast majority of cases of intercultural interaction and dialogue. In fact, in this excessively abstracted, make-believe scenario there is no real intercultural dialogue, there is only a philosophical anthropologist taking notes of the natives' linguistic and physical behavior from which he then constructs an inter-pretation of their language and worldview. Thus, in this "philosophically pure" scenario of intercultural interaction, understanding of another cul-ture is achieved by rendering their language and beliefs comprehensible in terms of our own conceptual framework. In other words, understand-ing proceeds through the *translation* of their conceptual framework into the terms of our own conceptual scheme.

But the understanding of another conceptual framework, particularly one that is radically different from our own, is achieved not through translation but through *familiarization*. That is, we comprehend frame-works that are radically different from our own not by finding terms and claims in our framework that isomorphically correspond to the terms and claims of theirs; rather, we gradually achieve greater and greater fa-miliarity with the ways they use the words in their language, with the range of situations in which they use them, with the kinds of claims they make, and so forth. To be sure, we start this process of familiarization by translating simple words in their language into our own, but as the process continues we eventually discover that as we learn more and more about their language and worldview, certain terms and ideas in their framework may have no correlates in our own.[23] We may start by relying on translation, but we are not limited by this procedure in under-standing another framework. Eventually, by familiarizing and immers-ing ourselves in their framework, we progress to the point where we real-ize that we can "think in their language" or "see the world from their perspective." What we have managed at this point, should we ever achieve this level of mastery of their language and framework, is to ex-pand our conceptual horizons by moving beyond our original world-view and enriching it with new knowledge of their culture. But it would be highly misleading to describe this enrichment of our conceptual hori-zons as a translation of their worldview into our own. Rather, what has happened is a transformation, an enlargement, of our cognitive, and in some cases affective, capabilities.

To see more clearly that it is familiarization and not translation that makes possible the understanding of incommensurable conceptual frameworks, consider the case of a Bantu tribesman who, as a young man, begins an education in Western schools. He travels to London, progresses through the English educational system, and eventually undertakes graduate studies in physics. He becomes quite proficient in his mastery of English and in understanding the worldview of modern physics. He periodically returns to his village and spends time with his family, and retains the capacity to communicate with them in his native Bantu language. Now, how did this young man manage to learn English and to master modern physics? According to the proponents of the iron-cage thesis, he must have translated the vocabulary of English and of modern physics into the Bantu language. For every new term he learned, he found either a corresponding word, phrase, sentence, or set of sentences[24] in Bantu that enabled him to understand the new term since, according to this thesis, our own conceptual framework is all we have to work with. But surely this account of how he came to understand English and modern physics is highly implausible. There is no reason to think that there is a word, phrase, or even a sentence or set of sentences in Bantu that corresponds, for example, to the terms "uncouth," "quark," or "muon." It is far more probable that he learned the vocabulary of English and modern physics by enlarging his conceptual horizons, that is, by familiarizing himself with a foreign language and a specialized scientific terminology radically different from the Bantu language. Moreover, he not only learned new terms with no correlates in his native language, he also learned a new way of looking at the world. In learning modern physics, he managed to comprehend a worldview radically different from the one he learned in his native village. Again, there is little reason to suppose that the principles, methodologies, and singular terms of modern physics could all be translated with any reasonable sense of accuracy into Bantu.

Besides relying on a dubious conception of understanding as translation, the advocates of the iron-cage thesis have a faulty understanding of conceptual frameworks. They apparently see such frameworks as monolithic, homogeneous, sealed conceptual structures. As David Wong has pointed out, when advocates of the thesis argue that we must attribute to others' beliefs that are true by our lights, they are assuming that there is agreement among us regarding what is true.[25] Wong indicates that there is no unified perspective that English speakers have of the world. Instead, the worldview of contemporary speakers of English encompasses more diversity, including fragments from different cultural traditions, than defenders of the thesis acknowledge. We can succeed in understanding other cultural groups, Wong argues, because we can draw from the richness and complexity of our conceptual framework. He believes that the speakers of most modern cosmopolitan languages such as English, French, Spanish, and Russian have a large number of conceptual resources for making sense of a variety of worldviews.[26] The insight that we have many resources to draw from in understanding other cultural groups is important, because it shows that we have a greater range of cognitive flexibility than the advocates of the iron-cage thesis suppose. Acknowledging this cognitive flexibility is not tantamount to maintaining that there are no significant differences between our conceptual frameworks and those of other cultural groups; the point is that our conceptual frameworks are not nearly as restricted and uniform as the advocates of the iron-cage thesis presume. In short, not only are we capable of expanding our conceptual horizons by learning new terms and concepts from other cultural groups, we already possess within our conceptual frameworks resources that can facilitate the understanding of their worldviews even when they are radically different from our own.[27]

Intercultural Understanding and Public Deliberation

I have carefully examined the problems with the iron-cage thesis because, as indicated earlier, it is an epistemological error with serious detrimental consequences for intercultural understanding. Rorty's ethnocentrism, which denies the potentially enriching and transformative effects of intercultural engagement and understanding, is but one example of the pernicious consequences to which the thesis can lead. On the positive side, our critique of the thesis revealed that the understanding of other conceptual frameworks proceeds through our familiarization of those frameworks. As we will recall, the motivation for examining intercultural understanding was its potential for mitigating inequalities in political efficacy that arise from the fact that minority proposals are less likely to be regarded as reasonable than proposals by members of the majority. What then are the consequences—for rectifying inequalities in political efficacy—of the insight that intercultural understanding is achieved through familiarization?

The implications of this insight are, I believe, far-reaching. If it is important for the sake of justice to eliminate political inequalities in deliberative democracies, then obtaining substantive knowledge of other cultures emerges as an essential condition for just democratic societies. Intercultural understanding should no longer be relegated to the status of a fringe demand by disenchanted minorities; it should have a central place in multicultural democracies that value public deliberation and social justice. Achieving intercultural understanding through familiarization entails: (i) a wide-ranging and systematic social commitment to multicultural education and (ii) an expansion of our conception of public deliberation to include procedures that move beyond the purely discursive methods usually associated with deliberative democracy. In what follows, I discuss each of these commitments.

Multicultural Education

If our familiarization with other cultural perspectives is to fulfill the function of mitigating inequalities in political efficacy, it must be substantial enough to enable us to understand the historical experiences and present needs, interests, and affective orientations of other cultural groups. Obtaining such an understanding is possible only if systematic efforts are made at different levels of our educational institutions to educate the citizenry in these areas. While it may be tempting to try to achieve intercultural understanding merely by expanding forums of public deliberation to include procedures conducive to understanding the perspectives of other cultural groups, it is unlikely that such a complex educational objective as intercultural understanding could be attained in this manner. Given the intermittent and short-term occasions in which most people would participate in public deliberation, the opportunities to obtain in-depth knowledge of other cultures and participate in fruitful intercultural engagement would not have sufficient regularity, duration, or structure to bring about the necessary mutually expansive transformation of peoples' perspectives.

Multicultural education should include both informative and affective dimensions. The function of these components of multicultural education would be to create empathy between the members of different cultural groups. Empathy can be understood as having cognitive and emotive components, and the informative and affective dimensions of multicultural education could be seen as promoting, respectively, each of these components of empathy. By developing cognitive and emotive empathy towards the members of other cultural groups, individuals would attain greater insight into the reasons why members of other groups think and feel the way they do.

The informative dimension of multicultural education would include knowledge of the history of the cultural group in question, with particular emphasis given to their mode of incorporation into the state. Since some of the most divisive intercultural conflicts often involve minority groups who were coercively incorporated into the existing political community, it is important for majority groups (and minority groups themselves) to understand the circumstances, sometimes unjust and brutal, of this incorporation. Part of this historical understanding should include the role that the respective group's forced incorporation may play in their present economic, political, and social disempowerment. Knowledge of minority group history would also provide the majority society with a better understanding of the rationale behind minority claims for self-government rights, reparations for past wrongs, or cultural rights. Moreover, if all of the groups involved obtained knowledge of each other's history, they would attain mutual understanding of the factors that have engendered intercultural suspicion, resentment, and hatred. Historical knowledge would also enable each group to understand the reasons why the other group may regard certain historical events or territories as particularly significant or certain symbols, stereotypes, or linguistic terms as derogatory.

The empirical dimension of multicultural education should also include knowledge of the values and practices of cultural groups. Both descriptive accounts and aesthetic modes of expression would be useful for conveying the significance and implications of a group's values and practices. Descriptive social scientific accounts of other cultures would go a long way for providing those outside the culture with crucial information regarding how the different features of a culture are interconnected and give rise to a broad narrative context that provides a sense of meaning and self-identity to cultural group members. It is only by having factual information concerning the concrete features of a culture that others outside of it can have an accurately informed vision of why members of that culture see the world the way they do. Further, aesthetic works such as novels, poems, songs, plays, dances, and rituals would play a central role in providing insight into the concrete significance of a group's values and practices. Such aesthetic works would convey the emotive dimensions of group experience, which can be very important for revealing the sources of a group's values and practices.

The greatest role of aesthetic works, however, would be to develop the affective aspects of empathy. In order to understand the worldview of other cultural groups, it is not sufficient to understand the rationale behind their beliefs, values, and patterns of behavior; it is also necessary to attain some insight into the structure of their affective group experience. Thus, one of the primary functions of multicultural education should be to develop the *empathetic imagination*. Only then can we see others in the fullness of their humanity and begin to understand the nature of the experiences that are the source of their collective identity and solidarity. By reading novels depicting the slave experience or seeing films that thematize the experience of displacement or exodus, for example, the members of the polity would understand members of other groups not merely with their minds but with their hearts as well. That is, experiencing the suffering of the members of other cultural groups can play a central role in helping us to recognize that the harm done to them is as morally repugnant as harm done to us. The powerful affective effects of aesthetic works could thus strengthen the capacity of individuals to affectively perceive the harm done to others as a form of self-harm, and counteract the dehumanization and denigration of minority groups that can result from racist or prejudicial attitudes.

However, aesthetic works depicting the suffering of other groups are not the only form of art that can have transformative effects. Works of art by members of other cultures can, by their sheer beauty and joyful effects, change the way in which we see the members of these cultures. Music, theater, dance, crafts, and visual works of art can help us appreciate the creative spirit of other cultural groups, as well as the manner in which they relate aesthetically to the world. Such works of art express the ways in which the members of a culture celebrate life, love, sexuality, triumph, and closeness to God. By participating in their artistic, joyful celebration of life, we can join them in their celebration of life. By its very nature, art is an externalized expression of affective experience. It is an invitation for those who see and feel artistic creations to participate in that affective experience. Through aesthetic participation, members of the majority society can experience a proximity and even intimacy with minority and majority group artists and, to the extent that the artistic creations convey a collective sense of joy or suffering, with the structure of the affective experiences of cultural groups themselves. Such participatory artistic experiences can play an important role in creating non-threatening affective channels through which members of different cultural groups can feel and understand both their common humanity and cultural particularity.

In short, developing the cognitive and affective dimensions of empathy is important not only for enhancing general intercultural understanding, but also for increasing the sympathetic reception of proposals that address the needs and interests of marginalized and oppressed ethnocultural minorities. By enhancing the capacity of members of the majority to understand the beliefs, values, practices, and affective experiences of ethnocultural minorities, cognitive and affective empathy would narrow differences in comprehensibility and plausibility between majority and minority proposals. And because the members of the polity are not cerebral automatons persuaded by reason only, but human beings motivated by affective and emotive considerations, the acceptability of minority proposals will depend not merely on their intrinsic cognitive plausibility, but also on the willingness of members of the majority to moderate their demands for the sake of minority needs and interests. To the extent that empathy increases the compassion and concern of dominant groups for minorities, it will motivate the majority society to give a more sympathetic hearing to the latter's policy objectives and proposals. This will in turn mollify inequalities in political functioning that derive from differences in the conceptual frameworks of minority and majority groups.

Expanding Forums of Public Deliberation

Another way to promote intercultural understanding besides multicultural education is by transforming forums of public deliberation so that features of these forums which disadvantage cultural minorities are eliminated, while the capacity for members of all groups to understand one another is enhanced. Of course, forums of public deliberation are presumably already structured so as to increase mutual understanding among the members of the citizenry. But when the structure of these forums incorporates features which reflect the culturally specific discursive practices and styles of the majority society, the members of ethnocultural minorities are at a disadvantage insofar as their modes of communication may be excluded or considered as inappropriate for forums of public deliberation.

Iris Young has argued that existing models of public deliberation are not culturally neutral, but derive from a Western, male-dominated cultural tradition that is elitist and excludes other cultures.[28] Such models of deliberation, Young contends, are based on forms of debate characteristic of scientific disputation and modern parliaments. These historically and culturally specific conceptions of public dialogue are grounded on confrontation and are not open to culturally different modes of presenting claims and giving reasons. Young states:

> Deliberation is competition. Parties to dispute aim to win the argument, not to achieve mutual understanding. Consenting because of the "force of the better argument" means being unable to think of further counterargument, that is, to concede defeat. The agonistic norms of deliberation reveal ways that power reenters this arena, even though deliberative theorists may claim to have bracketed it.[29]

Young also points out that in conventional conceptions of public deliberation, calm and dispassionate styles of expression are privileged over emotive and physically demonstrative modes of expression. The former, which are associated with greater objectivity and rationality, are often the styles of expression used by middle- and upper-class white men, while the latter, which are associated with lack of control and weakness, are often the modes of expression employed by cultural minorities and women. As a result of identifying the characteristic expressive styles of elite men with greater rationality, and those of minorities and women with lack of objectivity and control, the latter are placed at a disadvantage as far as their effectiveness in public deliberation is concerned.

To rectify the ways in which models of public deliberation marginalize minorities and women, she proposes that we transform our conceptions of deliberation to make them more fair and receptive to these groups. Two particularly useful recommendations that Young makes involve greeting and storytelling. Greeting involves preliminaries to discussion which are intended to establish mutual respect and trust, and may include extolling and recognizing the values and achievements of others and engaging in mild flattery and the stroking of egos. Greeting may also involve nonlinguistic gestures of amicability, such as handshakes, hugs, and the sharing of food and drink. The idea is that when participants in deliberations have significant differences in interests and perspectives, it is important to appeal to each other's human side so as to cultivate their receptivity to each other's needs and interests. If the point of deliberation is to reach agreement on issues of common concern, participants should approach and recognize the multidimensional aspects of their common humanity, including cognitive and affective features.

Storytelling involves relating narratives which inform participants of the experiences, understandings, and perspectives of the other deliberators with whom they are engaged in dialogue. Narratives, Young contends, can be an effective way in which the particular social locations of participants can be conveyed to others. Understanding the social experiences of people from a different socioeconomic, ethnic, or racial background, for example, is important for knowing how to treat them justly, because we will perceive more clearly the specific forms of injustice or marginalization to which they have been subjected or, in the case of members of the majority, the concerns and misgivings they might have of minority separatism or empowerment. Young maintains that narratives also reveal and make meaningful the practices, symbols, and cultural meanings of other groups, and can serve to justify the values of other groups by exhibiting the emergence of these values from the group's situated history. Outsiders will then be better able to appreciate the rationale for the preferences and priorities of the subjects of the narratives. Finally, narratives increase general social understanding by informing participants of one another's socially situated experiences. Young states:

> Each social perspective has an account not only of its own life and history but of every other position that affects its experience. Thus listeners can learn about how their own position, actions, and values appear to others from the stories they tell. Narrative thus exhibits the situated knowledge available of the collective from each perspective, and the combination of narratives from different perspectives produces the collective social wisdom not available from any one position.[30]

Young's proposals for reforming forums of deliberation so that they are more accommodating of other cultural groups are well taken. It is certainly important, as she claims, to acknowledge cultural differences in expressive styles and modes of communication, particularly since certain modes of expression of cultural minorities are sometimes seen as lacking in objectivity, rationality, or effectiveness. She is also correct to point out that prevailing models of deliberation place excessive emphasis on disputation, and do not give sufficient credence to the fact that the expression of emotion and other affective attitudes may be sometimes appropriate to promote mutual understanding. However, there are certain problems with her suggestions. There is a serious difficulty in her questioning of the important role that the "force of the better argument" plays in public deliberation. She does not convincingly establish why the search for the strongest argument or rationale for policy alternatives should not be a central part of public deliberation, that is, she does not show what is wrong with searching for reasons for which no counterargument is available. She suggests that this procedure is excessively argumentative and confrontational, but does not recognize that when decisions must be made and when competing interests are involved, it may be appropriate and even necessary to engage in offering decisive arguments and counterarguments for policy alternatives. And perhaps more important, she does not provide an alternative guiding principle for public deliberation to take the place of the search for the strongest reasons supporting policy proposals. Once we expand deliberative forums to include other cultural modes of expression and justification, what criteria should we employ to adjudicate between competing claims?

Her objections against conventional models of deliberation because they are Western and male-dominated are also unconvincing. If the dominant modes of dialogue and argumentation are of male Western origin, and therefore inadequate because they are culturally specific, so are the modes and styles of minority groups, since they also arise from specific cultural traditions.[31] In other words, if cultural specificity is sufficient to establish the inadequacy of a particular mode of expression and argumentation, then all cultural modes are illegitimate. Perhaps her argument is that conventional models of deliberation are inadequate for multicultural societies because they do not give equal standing to the different discursive and affective modes of expression of other cultural groups. However, her position is still problematic even if we take this interpretation of her argument, because it does not follow from the fact that a model or theory for dealing with a given issue does not give equal standing to other cultural approaches that it is therefore inadequate for dealing successfully with that issue. For instance, an indigenous perspective on the environment that emphasizes ecological sustainability cannot be judged as inadequate simply because it does not give equal standing to Western environmental perspectives that focus on profit and high levels of consumption. This is because there may be features of the indigenous perspective that may be particularly suitable for dealing with environmental issues. Likewise, there may be features of Western-style modes of persuasion and expression that may be more suitable than those of other cultural traditions (which may, for example, involve excessive deference to authority) for resolving issues of common concern in public deliberation.

Even though the predominant deliberative models may have arisen from an exclusivist cultural tradition, it does not follow that they are not appropriate for the purposes of public deliberation, particularly if the latter is understood as a process intended to achieve mutual understanding and the persuasion of others by giving reasons which they will find compelling by their own lights. In fact, some advocates of public deliberation, such as Thompson, Gutmann, and Joshua Cohen, propose this kind of principle of argumentation for deliberative democracy.[32] Young does not give an accurate or fair characterization of conventional models of democratic deliberation, nor does she appreciate the extent to which some of its proponents have tried to incorporate diversity of perspectives among the citizenry. In brief, it is not at all clear that existing models of deliberation do not aim at mutual understanding or that they are illegitimate merely because they are culturally specific or emerged from an exclusivist, racist, or sexist tradition. To be sure, we should be especially vigilant with cultural traditions that have a history of exclusion and oppression against other groups, but the latter fact in itself is not sufficient to disqualify their potential contributions to public deliberation.

As Young indicates, storytelling is an important mechanism for enhancing not only general social understanding but intercultural understanding as well. Her proposal concerning the potentially valuable function of storytelling is well-taken, but here too there is a problem with her suggestion. As I indicated earlier, it is unlikely that participation in forums of public deliberation will be extensive enough to provide participants with the time and opportunities to convey and interpret narratives that would provide the extensive information needed to achieve real cognitive and affective intercultural understanding. For most citizens, participation in forums of deliberation is likely to be intermittent and short-term. It is more appropriate to maintain that brief narratives would have a limited role in public deliberation, and that the proper place of narratives is in educational institutions directed towards multicultural education.

Perhaps the most significant problem with Young's position, however, is that she does not propose criteria of rationality or persuasion in public deliberation. Should we accept the modes of justification and persuasion of any cultural group as legitimate simply because they are practiced by that group? Are there any standards to the reasonableness of modes of persuasion and argumentation? It is clear that at least certain logical principles will have to be accepted in order for public deliberation to be effective and rational. The principle of non-contradiction, for example, will have to be accepted. Deliberators cannot simply contradict themselves at will or employ inconsistent epistemic standards without justification and retain their credibility. Moreover, a mutually acceptable proposition logic will have to be employed for public deliberation to be workable. Thus, if a participant commits herself to the proposition that P & Q, she will also have to commit herself to the proposition P and to the proposition Q. If not, she has to justify why commitment to the latter does not follow logically from a commitment to the former, as well as provide an alternative logic of propositions which is preferable for the purposes of reaching mutual understanding and rational agreement in public deliberation. Much work in epistemology has to be done to clarify conceptions of public reason in pluralistic contexts in which incommensurable cultural traditions meet.[33] But it is doubtful that an uncritical acceptance of all cultural forms of justification is the appropriate attitude to take regarding intercultural discourse.

The Limits of Deliberative Democracy

In the last part of this chapter, I have argued that intercultural understanding can lessen inequalities in political efficacy in multicultural societies that arise from differences in the plausibility of majority and minority proposals in public deliberation. It is important to emphasize, however, that mutual understanding between cultural groups can only mitigate but not eliminate inequalities in political efficacy. Differences in worldview or disagreements in needs and interests between cultural groups can be so deep that the disadvantages of cultural minorities to induce social cooperation to attain their political objectives can remain very significant. When the animosity between cultural groups is very great, when disputes over limited resources make compromise very difficult, or when the cognitive and affective differences between groups are unbridgeable, for example, not even the equalization of epistemic resources and the capabilities for their effective use, equality of motivational sources, multicultural education, or reforms in forums of public deliberation, may suffice to create a deliberative milieu in which the proposals of ethnocultural minorities will receive a fair hearing. This unfortunate scenario is more likely to occur with autonomist and secessionist groups than with accommodationist groups, since the latter are typically more willing to adopt majority values and institutional practices, as well as see themselves as belonging to a common political community.

In situations in which significant inequalities in political efficacy are incapable of rectification, we have once again reached the limits of public deliberation. Thus, we end this chapter in the same way we concluded the last, namely, by recognizing that even in the most egalitarian deliberative

democracies, significant political inequalities may still burden certain ethnocultural minorities. This raises the question of whether these minorities
can be treated justly and achieve self-determination only by obtaining
rights of self-government or forming a sovereign political community. As
we have noted before, the failure to eliminate all forms of political inequality in deliberative democracies may not by itself be a sufficient reason for granting these groups sovereignty or rights of autonomous governance. In order to arrive at a reasoned position with regard to these issues
we need to discuss two of the most fundamental themes in political philosophy, namely, the proper function and justification of political communities. It is to these themes, and their connection to questions of self-determination for ethnocultural groups, that we now turn.

Notes

1. John Rawls, *A Theory of Justice* (Cambridge, MA: Harvard University Press,
1971), pp. 60–65.
2. The point here is that Rawls's conception of basic goods is a bit more complex than some of his critics have maintained. It deals not merely with resources
but also with factors that could be reasonably construed as conducive to developing capabilities for the effective use of resources. Nevertheless, despite this qualification, and as we shall see in what follows, the criticism that Rawls's approach
places insufficient emphasis on capabilities for the effective use of resources is
well grounded.
3. Amartya Sen, *Inequality Reexamined* (Cambridge, MA: Harvard University
Press, 1992), chapters 1–3.
4. Ibid., p. 111.
5. Ibid., p. 26–28.
6. Jack Knight and James Johnson, "What Sort of Equality does Deliberative
Democracy Require?" in *Deliberative Democracy: Essays on Reason and Politics*, eds.
James Bohman and William Rehg (Cambridge, MA: MIT Press, 1997), pp.
298–309.
7. Ibid., p. 306. Knight and Johnson cite J. Larry Brown and Ernesto Pollitt,
"Malnutrition, Poverty and Intellectual Development," *Scientific American*
(February, 1996): 38–43.
8. Cass R. Sunstein, "Democracy and Shifting Preferences," in *The Idea Of Democracy* (Cambridge, UK: Cambridge University Press, 1993), p. 213.
9. It might be pointed out here that many people who have not suffered ethnocultural prejudice and who do not come from impoverished backgrounds can
nevertheless arrive at nonautonomous preferences for a wide variety of reasons,
such as inferiority complexes arising from physical unattractiveness or unsupportive parents. Thus, the argument might continue, we should not single out the
members of discriminated ethnocultural groups as being particularly disadvantaged in the political sphere, since many, if not most, people have had experiences that lead to nonautonomous preferences. The problem with this argument

is that, since there is no reason to suppose that factors such as socially perceived physical unattractiveness, or unsupportive or alcoholic parents are not randomly distributed, it does not show that ethnocultural minorites are not also burdened to the same extent as others by these disadvantages. Since ethnocultural minorities are in addition faced by burdens based on their ethnicity, they are doubly burdened, and therefore are particularly disadvantaged. The general point, however, that many people are disadvantaged in different ways is well taken.

10. Cass Sunstein, "Preferences and Politics," *Philosophy and Public Affairs* 20, 1991, p. 21.

11. Ibid., p. 22.

12. Knight and Johnson, "What Sort of Equality?," p. 298. Knight and Johnson cite Iris Marion Young, "Justice and Communicative Discourse," in *Tradition, Counter-Tradition, Politics: Dimensions of Radical Philosophy*, ed. R. Gottlieb (Philadelphia, PA: Temple University Press, 1994).

13. See, for instance, the essays in *Deliberative Democracy*, Bohman and Rehg.

14. Note that we should resist the inclination to think that in those political systems in which a "leadership by referendum" approach is taken, lack of motivation to participate will be negated by the egalitarianism of statistical methods by which popular opinions are measured. That is, we should not conclude that in political systems in which political leaders formulate their policies largely on the basis of public opinion polls, the motivation to participate politically becomes, for the most part, irrelevant. Even in these systems, political lobbies, financial contributions, access to the media, and so forth have a major impact on policy formation, i.e., motivation for political participation is still crucial for having a political voice. In any case, since we are concerned here with deliberative democracies (in which participation is surely of central importance for effectiveness of political influence), the motivation to participate is still crucially relevant.

15. For an account of formal education as a motivational factor, see Sidney Verba, Kay Lehman Schlozman, and Henry E. Brady, *Voice and Equality* (Cambridge, MA: Harvard University Press, 1995). In what follows I draw from their discussion of motivation for political involvement.

16. An excellent study of the relationship between socioeconomic status, politically relevant institutional affiliations, and political participation is provided by Sidney Verba, Norman H. Nie, and Jae-On Kim in *Participation and Political Equality: A Seven-Nation Comparison* (Cambridge, UK: Cambridge University Press, 1978). In particular, see chapters 4 and 5.

17. Verba, Schlozman, and Brady, *Voice and Equality*, pp. 139–149.

18. Verba, Nie, and Kim, *Participation and Political Equality*, p. 64.

19. When the material inequalities of ethnocultural minorities are caused primarily by discrimination on the part of the majority, these inequalities represent a particularly important form of injustice that a fair multicultural democracy should try to rectify. In later chapters I will address the issue of rectification for present and historical ethnocultural discrimination. Even when no systematic discrimination exists that is the cause of material differences that lead to political inequalities, however, a just deliberative democracy should nevertheless strive to rectify resources for political participation. This is because a just deliberative democracy should ensure that all members of the polity have the resources, capa-

bilities, and sources of motivation that enable them to effectively advocate for their needs and interests.

20. For a discussion of this issue, see, for example, Jawanza Kunjufu, *To Be Popular or Smart: The Black Peer Group* (Chicago: African American Images, 1988).

21. It may seem that there is a parallel case in which the majority society may decide that it cannot make certain information public for the sake of the general good or for compelling security reasons. However, there are crucial differences between these two cases. When people in positions of power in majority institutions justifiably determine that certain information cannot be made public, it would be for reasons of public safety or to protect the well-being of a particular individual or group. In the case of sacred knowledge of indigenous groups, on the other hand, keeping the information secret would result in a deliberative disadvantage to that particular group only. It is much less likely that the majority would withhold dissemination of information that would result in disadvantaging only the majority group.

22. Richard Rorty, "Solidarity or Objectivity?," in *Relativism: Interpretation and Confrontation*, ed. Michael Krausz (Notre Dame, IN: University Of Notre Dame Press, 1989), p. 40.

23. This lack of correspondence between their concepts and beliefs and our own is what Alasdair MacIntryre has in mind when he says that the most interesting cases of incommensurability are recognized precisely at the point at which we attain a fairly high level of mastery of their conceptual framework. On this point, see Alasdair MacIntryre, "Relativism, Power, and Philosophy," in *Relativism*, Krausz, pp. 197–98.0

24. Note that I am using a broad, and charitable, interpretation of translation. I could just as easily have adopted a stricter definition of translation according to which for every term in the English language and in the terminology of physics there has to correspond a word in Bantu. I adopt the broad definition to provide defenders of the iron-cage thesis the best opportunity to make their case.

25. David Wong, "Three Kinds of Incommensurability," in *Relativism*, Krausz, p. 145.

26. This does not mean that there aren't certain dominant beliefs that most speakers of these languages have, such as beliefs in enduring physical objects with perceptible sensory qualities, the existence of minds, and the existence of a supreme, infinite being. Neither does this mean that the speakers of these languages have the resources to translate radically different conceptual frameworks. Despite the complexity of our conceptual frameworks, our worldviews can still be greatly enriched by learning about other cultures.

27. Some defenders of the iron-cage thesis, such as Donald Davidson, argue that we could not understand a radically different framework because we would have no common basis of beliefs on which we could rely to translate their language. This claim is questionable, however, because there could be a set of entities which we and the holders of radically different frameworks could identify by using common identificatory criteria even though we could differ radically regarding the way those entities are constituted. For instance, we could both use the same criteria to identify midsize physical objects (such as trees and rocks) and still metaphysically construe these objects in very different ways. They might re-

gard these objects as being alive and containing spirits, while we might regard them as consisting of subatomic physical particles. The common criteria of identification could be used as a basis to understand their language to a degree sufficient to generate a mastery of it without supposing, as Davidson would argue, that we agree regarding the metaphysical nature of these objects. In other words, defenders of the thesis, such as Davidson, confuse criteria of *identification* with criteria of *constitution*. To understand a radically different language, it is sufficient to share criteria of identification. Thus, we could differ in very significant ways with another cultural group concerning the nature of entities in the world and yet understand our differences on the basis of shared standards for identifying these entities. In fact, there is empirical evidence that shows that probably all cultural groups share certain basic identificatory criteria despite possible radical variations in the metaphysical structure of the world. For an account of basic-level categories that seem to be culturally universal, see George Lakoff, *Women, Fire, and Dangerous Things: What Categories Reveal about the Mind* (Chicago: University of Chicago Press, 1987), pp. 46–48 and Chapter 18. For an account of Davidson's views on conceptual schemes, see Donald Davidson, "On the Very Idea of a Conceptual Scheme," in *Inquiries into Truth and Interpretation* (Oxford: Clarendon Press, 1984).

28. Iris Marion Young, "Communication and the Other: Beyond Deliberative Democracy," in *Democracy and Difference: Contesting the Boundaries of the Political*, ed. Seyla Benhabib (Princeton: Princeton University Press, 1996).

29. Ibid., p. 123.

30. Ibid., p. 132.

31. In fact, a plausible case could be made that other cultural traditions are even more sexist and exclusivist than the Western tradition. Certain Islamic and Hispanic traditions, for example, place even stronger restrictions on the public roles that are socially acceptable for women to fulfill.

32. Thompson and Gutmann advocate what they call the principle of reciprocity, according to which participants in public deliberation should strive to justify proposals by giving one another reasons which they find mutually acceptable. Likewise, Joshua Cohen maintains that participants in deliberative democracy are committed to giving other participants reasons which they will find persuasive. Providing such reasons presupposes mutual understanding, for we cannot give other individuals reasons which they will find acceptable unless we understand them sufficiently to identify the reasons which will satisfy this condition. See Amy Gutmann and Dennis Thompson, *Democracy and Disagreement* (Cambridge, MA: Harvard University Press, 1996) and Joshua Cohen, "Deliberation and Democratic Legitimacy," in *The Good Polity: Normative Analyis of the State*, eds. Alan Hamil and Philip Pettit (Oxford: Basil Blackwell, 1989).

33. This is one of the subjects that I will deal with in future work on the philosophical foundations of multiculturalism.

4

The Function and Justification
of Political Communities

As we observed in the last chapter, the general democratic framework that I advocate for multicultural democracies, namely, deliberative democracy, can face serious difficulties in eliminating certain forms of political inequality that burden autonomist and secessionist ethnocultural groups. Some of these difficulties arise because there are fundamental cultural differences between the majority society and these groups. When these differences are so deep that the political inequalities to which they give rise cannot be eliminated or significantly alleviated, the possibility must be considered that the existing political body should be divided in such a way that autonomist and secessionist groups can exercise self-governance. Besides the issue of irremovable intercultural differences in political efficacy, the broader question that arises here is whether a political community with a public sphere that reflects only the culture of the majority, that adopts a conception of undifferentiated citizenship, and that does not provide institutional recognition to the cultural distinctiveness of autonomist or secessionist ethnocultural groups, can be a suitable civil environment in which these groups can flourish. Ethnocultural groups who have an identity as a distinct people maintain that they have the right to collectively determine the direction of their lives by developing their own cultural, political, and economic institutions and forms of social organization. That is, they claim the right—which is already exercised and taken for granted by members of the majority society—to develop their own distinctive political and cultural communities.

Because the claims for self-determination of indigenous peoples, ethnonationalists, and secessionist groups involve either autonomous governance or secession, questions concerning the proper function of political communities and the justification of their formation are relevant for the evaluation of these claims. Whether the objectives of self-governance or secession that these groups desire are justified depends on whether these objectives conform better than the status quo with criteria for the justifiable formation and proper function of political communities. Regarding the self-determination claims of communal contenders, the fairness and adequacy of the power-sharing arrangements in which they participate depends on the extent to which these arrangements fulfill the proper function of a political community and whether they satisfy the criteria of a legitimate political union. For example, institutional frameworks in which one of these groups enjoys unfair systematic advantages over other communal contenders will violate normative standards for the legitimacy of a political community.

Issues regarding the state's function and legitimacy are also relevant for evaluating calls for self-determination made by accommodationist groups. Despite the fact that these groups want to integrate into the institutional frameworks of the majority society, they seek to retain aspects of their cultural traditions, and want public recognition and support (for example, through the use of public funds for bilingual programs) of their culture. The point could be made that, to the extent that public institutional support for the cultural practices of particular ethnocultural groups weakens social solidarity and the sense of national identity of the society as a whole, the proper function of the political community would be undermined or weakened by acceding to accommodationist demands. In brief, questions concerning the legitimacy and proper function of political communities are relevant for determining the justification of claims to self-determination of all three categories of ethnocultural groups.

In examining the normative justification of a political community, it is important to distinguish between three questions: (1) what grounds the political authority a particular political community has for a given individual?; (2) what justifies the establishment by a group of individuals of an autonomous political body with powers of territorial control (and what external responsibilities are thereby incurred by the resulting political body)?; and (3) what grounds the moral adequacy or legitimacy of a political community? Even though all of these questions relate in one way or another to the central issue of the normative foundations of political communities, they are distinct questions. For instance, a state can satisfy the criteria involved in answering question (3) by granting its citizens the appropriate civil, social, and democratic rights, and yet its political authority—an issue which question (1) deals with—may not be binding on an individual who is not a citizen of that state. Similarly, a collectivity, even if it adopts or is willing to adopt normatively adequate democratic principles and institutions—and thereby fulfills criteria used in answering question (3)—may not be justified in forming a sovereign state (e.g., through secession) because in doing so it may jeopardize the well-being or rights of another political community and its members, and would therefore violate constraints on the formation of a political body specified in answering question (2). Finally, question (1) deals with the relation between an individual and a particular political community, while question (2) concerns the rationale for forming an autonomous political body and the moral constraints placed on that body by the needs and rights of other political communities and their members. To be sure, the issues that must be considered to answer these three questions will sometimes overlap, but this does not diminish the importance of distinguishing between the normative issues dealing, respectively, with the authority, formation, and justness of political societies.

Keeping these questions distinct will also facilitate a better evaluation of conventional normative theories of the state, and will help us identify the ways in which these theories are incomplete or inadequate for dealing with the dilemmas faced by multicultural democracies. As we shall see, most philosophical theories of the state give a great deal of attention to questions (1) and (3) but generally neglect question (2), even though the latter is crucial for understanding such issues as the nature of political membership, powers of exclusion and territorial control, and moral obligations between political communities. And more important for our purposes, focusing on these distinct questions will prepare us to deal with the subject of the next three chapters, namely, the meaning and justification of self-determination for ethnocultural groups. In order to obtain an adequate conceptual grip on the complex issues involved in ethnocultural self-determination—as well as in self-determination in general—it is necessary to be clear about the various questions that arise in connection with the authority, formation, and moral adequacy of political communities.

In what follows I will take an empirically informed approach to the normative justification of political bodies. When examining philosophical theories of the state, what is being justified is not always identified precisely. Philosophers typically articulate a theoretical conception of the state and present arguments to show that their theory can ground the normative legitimacy of the state as an abstractly characterized civil society. But it is not always clear what such theoretical conceptions have to do with the moral justification of actual states. Even if one constructs a theoretically coherent and compelling account of the moral foundations of a hypothetical state, such an account cannot be employed to justify existing states, unless it can be shown that these states conform to, or at least approximate, the normative criteria set out in the theory. Carrying out the latter task requires empirical analyses that philosophers often neglect to provide.

Even when philosophers acknowledge that normative theories of the state merely articulate moral ideals that actual states should strive to satisfy or approximate, failure to consider historical circumstances or the global context in which the needs of other political communities arise makes it difficult to recognize all of the normative issues relevant for understanding the moral legitimacy and appropriate function of actual states. For instance, if we neglect the fact that many states at some point in their history engaged in a process of nation-building which involved the coerced incorporation or displacement of ethnocultural groups, we will fail to identify the additional criteria that a state must fulfill to be considered a just political body. That is to say, even when a state satisfies conventional criteria of moral legitimacy by providing appropriate democratic, civil, and social welfare rights, it does not follow that it is a just state, because it may be unwilling to deal justly with the historical legacy of its oppressive treatment of ethnocultural groups within its boundaries. Contrary to what most philosophical theorists of the state have assumed, standards of normative legitimacy of a state should not be based solely on the character of its present political principles, practices, and institutions, but should also take into account the moral claims made by the ethnocultural groups the state may have forced into its political domain during, or subsequent to, its formation.

And more generally, by neglecting such factors as ethnocultural diversity and global obligations, we will miss some of the most important and interesting normative issues involving conflict and legitimacy in contemporary states. As it turns out, the examination of these often neglected factors is not just an interesting aside, but goes to the heart of what constitutes the normative legitimacy of existing states and emerging political communities. Given the detrimental consequences of overlooking historical and global factors, my concern here will be to provide an account of the moral legitimacy and function of political bodies that does not abstract from historical background and the current global conditions affecting actual states and substate political communities. To understand the function and legitimacy of political communities, and the democratic polities with which we are particularly concerned, it would be instructive to first examine some of the most prominent normative theories of the state, so that we can identify their limitations for adequately addressing foundational issues confronting contemporary multicultural democracies.

Consent-Based Normative Theories of the State

Perhaps the most prominent theoretical approach that has been used to justify and articulate the normative basis of the state is the theory of the social contract. As several commentators have noted, the notion of the social contract actually involves a wide variety of conceptions of mutual agreement in the formation or justification of the state.[1] These conceptions range from the Socratic notion found in the *Crito* that by consenting to live in a political body from which one has obtained numerous benefits one is obligated to respect its laws, to the recent Kantian-inspired conception of the social contract developed by Rawls. Also included in consent-based theories are Hobbes's and Pufendorf's conceptions of the social contract as giving rise to a powerful sovereign enforcer to whom members of the polity grant almost unconditioned obedience. The notion of consensual agreement has even been used in a more general way as a ground for morality itself, as in Gauthier's theory of rational agreement.[2] Obvious limitations of space foreclose the possibility of making a detailed analysis of the many different guises in which contractarianism has appeared. Since my interest here is to examine questions of the normative legitimacy of existing and emerging political societies, I will focus on the adequacy of consent as a theoretical device for establishing and explaining the legitimacy and function of contemporary political bodies. I will attempt to accomplish this by examining some prominent representative cases of philosophical strategies that have used consent as a basis for the moral legitimation of the state. As we shall see, consent is important in the justification and maintenance of political communities, but not in the way that contractarians have supposed.

Some social contract theorists of the seventeenth and eighteenth centuries used the notion of consent as a justificatory basis for the state. The strategy here was fairly straightforward: to use the device of consent to establish both the moral legitimacy of the state and the reason why we are obligated to defer to its political authority. Roughly speaking, according to this approach the state is a legitimate political entity because it has been created through a process of collective voluntary agreement by free and equal individuals, who are bound to obey it because they have promised or consented to do so. The doctrine of the social contract denies that there are any individuals, such as monarchs, inherently possessing qualities which justify their authority over others or that it is possible for some individuals with privileged vision into transcendent Truth, such as philosopher-kings, to justifiably rule over others. The only legitimate political body, according to this doctrine of the social contract, is one based on the agreement of all of those subject to its rule, who are bound to obey it because they have consented to do so. Thus, this strategy in one stroke succinctly answers questions (1) and (3), which deal, respectively, with the authority and moral legitimacy of the state. The background assumptions under which the contract is made, however, as well as the terms of the contract itself, have differed significantly.

In Hobbes, for example, the state of nature prior to the formation of civil society or government was one in which all individuals were free and essentially equal in body and mind.[3] In the state of nature no central authority existed to adjudicate between competing interests, and so people possessed the natural right, concomitant to their original freedom, to determine for themselves the ends that would best contribute to their preservation. Given the universal freedom and equality of all individuals, however, the right of each person to achieve his self-determined ends inevitably came into conflict with the identical right of others to do the same. The fact that humans are passionate creatures with a desire for power exacerbated conflicts in the state of nature. Both the effort to achieve ends that sometimes conflicted with the ends of others and the desire for power created an environment of competition and mutual fear between people in the state of nature. These developments gave rise to a state of war in which each individual tried to secure for himself as much as possible, for in an environment in which no one can be trusted and in which no authority exists to restrain them, Hobbes believed that each person had total liberty and the right to obtain everything he could get.

However, individuals are also rational creatures and have a desire for peace. Through reason they discover the "laws of nature" which include the striving for peace, the willingness to give up their right to all things and impose restrictions on their liberty, and the obligation to keep their promises. In effect, these laws of nature give rise to the agreement to leave the state of nature—and thereby alienate the liberty and the rights enjoyed therein—and create a body politic in which peace and security can be obtained. In order for this peace and security to be achieved, however, individuals must authorize a sovereign, or Leviathan, to govern them that has sufficient power to inspire enough fear to ensure that peace is actually secured. Only such a powerful sovereign would have enough influence to realistically prevent the ever-present danger of war between competing wills.

The natural laws, which for Hobbes were God-given and discovered by reason, were the only true "morality." They prescribed the conditions under which peace and social coexistence could be achieved. He believed that the decision to form a commonwealth was guided not merely by simple unreflective self-interest, but also by the constraints imposed by the laws of nature, which rationally compelled individuals to give up the unrestricted rights they had in the state of nature for the sake of averting the state of war. That is to say, the natural laws themselves have normative implications, in the sense that they impose the rationally discernible obligation to seek a situation of peace in which security can be sustainably enjoyed. The obligatory force of the laws of nature, however, did not derive from the inherent moral dignity and worth of every individual; rather, it flowed from the equal physical and mental capacities and vulnerabilities of individuals, that rationally and self-interestedly compelled them to establish a political society in which everyone could enjoy peace and security. Thus, the decision to leave the state of nature to form a commonwealth ruled by a nearly all-powerful sovereign is for Hobbes a result of our inclination to seek our self-interest and our capacity to rationally discern the conditions under which peace and security can best be achieved.

The contract to create the powerful sovereign is not, however, one between the members of the polity and this powerful authority. Rather, the contract is among the citizenry, and the Leviathan itself is under no obligation to them. The asymmetrical character of the political relations between the members of the polity and the Leviathan makes possible the investment of almost unlimited power in the latter. Moreover, because the right we have in the state of nature to determine for ourselves what is needed for our own preservation is such a strong, comprehensive, and far-reaching right, it becomes necessary to alienate this right in order for a political society to work at all. Unless individuals wholly give up the powerful right to appropriate whatever they judge necessary to preserve themselves, no organized society is likely to function.

Like Hobbes, Locke also makes a distinction between the state of nature and civil society or the commonwealth. For Locke, however, the state of nature is a very different place. In it individuals have inalienable natural rights to life, liberty, and property, and there is a mutual, general understanding that everyone is a child of God with God-given natural rights that should be respected. Unlike Hobbes's characterization of the state of nature as one of constant war, in Locke's state of nature there is peace, good will, and even mutual aid. Locke also maintains that individuals are free and equal in the original state of nature, but in contrast to Hobbes, he emphasizes that their equality is an equality of moral status, and not an equality of physical and mental capacity to harm and to be harmed. Locke's belief that the moral order that exists in the state of nature is ultimately grounded on a divine foundation is significant, because it constrains the possibility that these rights can be alienated in the civil sphere. Contra Hobbes, for Locke the state functions in part as a organizational mechanism for the preservation of our natural rights to life, liberty, and property.

Even though the moral order in the state of nature should be acknowledged and respected by all, the fact that no impartial judge exists to adjudicate between conflicts of interest leads to a state of war. When someone violates my rights to life, liberty, and property, she declares herself in a state of war with me. Locke believes that people in the state of nature have the right to judge and punish those who violate their rights. But people are often biased in their own favor and are likely to punish violators excessively. Moreover, people will often lack the power to appropriately punish transgressors of the natural law. Thus, the right that everyone has to judge and punish violators cannot be applied in a way that is consistent with an orderly and peaceful society. In order to avoid the problems and instability that arise from the absence of an impartial judge, individuals decide to form a civil society and give up their right to judge and punish offenders against the natural moral order. Unlike Hobbes, however, Locke does not believe that we are under the obligation to alienate our rights to a political body. For Locke, it is through consent that people give up the "executive power" to judge and punish offenders and agree to form a political society. An important consequence of Locke's position is that there are strong limits to the authority of government, since our natural rights to life, liberty, and property are inalienable. Indeed, it would not make sense to Locke to give up our claim to these rights in forming a civil society, since the whole point of such a political body is to facilitate the safeguarding of our natural rights.

Though motivated by different considerations, the strategy of using agreement as a basis for the legitimate existence of the state and our obligation to obey it is prominent in the approaches of both Hobbes and Locke. In their theories, there are dimensions of obligation as well as self-interest in the decision to form a political society. Since the decision to establish a commonwealth is constrained and motivated by normative and rational considerations, to this extent it is by no means merely an arbitrary act of volition. Nevertheless, despite the existence of a broader moral context within which the decision to form a commonwealth is made, for both of these thinkers willful consent is still of central importance in grounding the legitimacy of the resulting political society.

How adequate are the attempts of these contractarians to ground state legitimacy on consent? Perhaps the most familiar objection that has been made against the sort of contractarianism we find in Hobbes and Locke is that it is historically inaccurate. It is highly doubtful whether there ever was a state of nature in which people made a collective decision to establish a civil society with the features that either Hobbes or Locke describes. If their theories of state legitimacy are taken as literal descriptions of the origins of the state, the objection that they are historically false is, I believe, a fatal objection. Empirical evidence clearly indicates that most states were founded, not through a collective voluntary agreement involving all members of the polity, but through conquest, invasive settlement, territorial transfer between colonial powers, or some form of coerced incorporation. In some cases, the founding documents of states served to formalize relations of domination between majority societies and ethnocultural groups.[4]

Another problem with using consent as a device for the legitimation of the state is that it is not clear what the source of the moral force of consent is. As is often pointed out, the notion of consent does not by itself provide an answer to the question of why we are obligated to keep our promises. This is because for a promise to be binding, it must be underpinned by a prior moral commitment to keep our promises or by enforcement constraints that ensure compliance. But if the normative force of consent depends on additional considerations which extend beyond the act of consent itself, the central importance of the latter is called into question.

For Hobbes and Locke there are, respectively, a naturalistic and a religious context within which the decision to form a political society is not only explained but justified. For Hobbes it is self-interest constrained by the obligations of natural law that compel us to grant our consent, while for Locke it is the duty to preserve ourselves as creatures of God. But if these pre-existing naturalistic or moral constraints are what account for and justify the granting of consent, then consent loses its independent justificatory force as the basis of legitimacy of the state. Strictly speaking, consent is not even a necessary condition for the normative legitimacy of the state, because we can bypass consent and instead examine directly the political society whose justification is in question. If that political society satisfies the pre-existing dictates of natural law (for Hobbes) or the divine-based requirements for our earthly preservation (for Locke), then it is normatively justified. This point is consistent with Hanna Pitkin's observation that the crucial matter in justifying a particular government is not whether we formed it through our consent, but whether it is the type of government to which we *should* consent.[5]

This last observation that the crucial question is whether the political body in question is one which is morally justified leads us to consider recent, more refined attempts to provide contractarian justifications of the state. The most prominent of these is without doubt the contractarian theory defended by John Rawls in *A Theory of Justice*.[6] Rawls does not use the doctrine of the social contract as a historical justification of the origin of the state. For Rawls, what legitimates a political society is not the fact that it originated through an act of collective consent, or that those bound to its authority consented to give up the rights they enjoyed in the state of nature for the sake of the protections it provides; rather, a normatively legitimate political body is one which embraces the correct principles of justice. He uses the social contract as a conceptual mechanism to articulate the principles that a just state would adopt. For Rawls, justice should be understood primarily as impartiality, and a just state is one which adopts principles and institutional structures which grant each person equal consideration. The fundamental moral tenet underlying his approach is the Kantian notion that every person should be treated as an end in itself, that is, as an individual worthy of equal dignity and respect for her own sake.

The social contract for Rawls functions as a theoretical procedure for implementing socioeconomic and political principles of impartiality in which the needs and interests of all are taken into account. Structuring a society so that it exhibits impartiality, however, is difficult to do, since individuals are prone to be influenced by their interests and position in society in selecting the rights to which individuals are entitled and the principles of distribution of the goods produced through social cooperation. To resolve this problem, Rawls proposes an innovative theoretical device designed to ensure that the rights and distributional principles arrived at will embody principles of impartiality. Rawls calls this theoretical device the original position, which is the scenario in which the normative precepts to be adopted by the political community are negotiated by agents who are free and morally equal. Roughly speaking, the original position is for Rawls the analog of the state of nature discussed by Hobbes and Locke.

In the original position, participants will negotiate under a "veil of ignorance" in which they do not know their socially relevant characteristics, such as their level of intelligence, physical capacities, or social position. The reason for depriving negotiators of this knowledge is that it will prevent them from selecting guiding normative precepts that will further their particular interests. Without knowing, for instance, whether one is intellectually average or gifted, or whether one is physically handicapped or healthy, one will not be able to structure the society in such a way that those individuals with the characteristics one possesses will be advantaged relative to others in the society. Because anyone could be among those who are disadvantaged, everyone will strive to adopt and understand the position of others, including the most vulnerable, so that they can carefully consider their needs and interests. That is, every negotiator in the original position will be forced to negotiate guided by the principle of impartiality, according to which the good of everyone is equally taken into account. The rights and principles that the participants agree to in the original position will therefore reflect the notion of justice as impartiality.

What will actually result from the negotiations, according to Rawls, is that participants will be unwilling to risk being one of the disadvantaged, and will therefore select organizing principles for the society which allow inequalities only if they benefit the most disadvantaged. Thus, differences in income, social status, positions of power, and so forth will be allowed only if they benefit the least well-endowed members of the society. In particular, Rawls argues that the contractors would agree with principles of justice that (i) would grant every individual the maximum degree of liberty possible that was consistent with an equal degree of liberty for everyone else, and that (ii) would allow positions which reward individuals differentially if everyone had an equal opportunity to compete for such positions and if those positions had the effect of maximizing the well-being of the worst-off group in the society. A political society structured by these principles would be morally justified, Rawls argues, because these principles were arrived at by agents who negotiated from a position of freedom and equality and who were guided by the principle of fairness. It is not necessary to suppose that such negotiations actually occurred at the time the political body in question was founded, it is enough to show that the normative precepts accepted would be the ones which agents in the original position would have consented to. Thus the notion of consent is still operative in Rawls's theory, not in the simplistic sense that the legitimation of the state is based on an act of consent, but in the sense that free, rational, and morally equal agents situated in a contractual scenario structurally characterized by fairness would voluntarily agree to the moral principles that underpin the state's basic political and social institutions.

Rawls's theory has several advantages over the positions of Hobbes and Locke. It is not vulnerable to the objection that it is historically false, and it does not rely on moral obligations that are dubiously based, respectively, on a naturalistic or a divine order. The normative basis of Rawls's theory conforms closely with our moral intuitions that we should express equal concern for others and respect their moral dignity and worth. Moreover, his use of the social contract leads to substantive consequences regarding the structure of a society's socioeconomic and political institutions. In contrast to the theories of Hobbes and Locke, Rawls's theory of the state provides more specific guidelines regarding the political, social, and economic priorities that a just political society should embrace.

Despite these advantages, however, there are serious problems with Rawls's theory. Interestingly, a problem similar to the one that confronted Hobbes's and Locke's theories also afflicts Rawls's position, namely, that consent ultimately turns out to be theoretically superfluous. Negotiators in the original position are supposed to agree rationally on the principles of justice that Rawls describes because they are unwilling to take the chance that they will be among the disadvantaged members of society. But as Rawls himself admits, it is possible that the participants in the original position would not be as adverse to risk as he supposes. If we assume that negotiators could be guided by different dispositions, such as a greater willingness to gamble on the capacities and talents the "lottery of nature" might endow them with, then they would arrive at a different set of organizational principles for the political society. These alternative principles, rather than prioritizing the welfare of the most disadvantaged, might permit greater degrees of socioeconomic inequalities by rewarding, for example, economic productivity and initiative.

It is significant to note that Rawls cannot rule out descriptions of the original position that give rise to normative principles different from his own without begging the issue in favor of his own description of the original position and the principles to which it gives rise. Because alternative descriptions of the original position lead to different principles, the device of the original position cannot perform the function it was intended to perform, namely, normatively ground a specific set of moral principles. Unless we assume beforehand that only certain moral principles are acceptable, we cannot rule out descriptions of the original position that lead to moral principles that are inconsistent with those we favor. In short, since the substantive issues concerning justice must be decided prior to the selection of a particular description of the original position, the contract that emerges from the original position becomes redundant, because that agreement merely reflects moral principles that were independently arrived at.[7] As with Hobbes and Locke, in determining whether a political society is just, we could simply bypass the contract and look directly at the society to see whether it exemplifies the principles of justice we have pre-determined as the correct ones. Whether the society is a just political body will depend on whether or not it embraces these principles of justice; in either case, the device of the social contract, as a foundation for the normative legitimacy of the state, drops out of the picture.

In his more recent work, Rawls attempts to rectify the problems with his theory of the social contract by reformulating the role that the contract plays in the justification of the state. He maintains in *Political Liberalism*[8] that the original position should no longer be seen as a scenario in which contractors agree on a comprehensive set of moral principles for a political society, but as a device of representation in which individuals with different comprehensive moral perspectives[9] identify an overlapping consensus of values which serve as the basis for a pluralistic political society. Rawls concedes that a diversity of moral doctrines exists in contemporary societies, and that the notions of the social contract and the original position as he construed them in *A Theory of Justice* cannot lead to a set of moral principles of universal validity. He proposes that we recognize the existence of "reasonable pluralism," that is, the pluralism of moral doctrines which fall within the range of moral perspectives that can be plausibly adopted in societies that embrace constitutional democracy. Given the reasonable pluralism that exists in contemporary societies, Rawls maintains that a theory of the state should articulate a normative basis that permits orderly and peaceful coexistence among individuals holding different comprehensive moral perspectives. The goal is no longer to develop a complete moral foundation which will command universal assent among the citizenry. The normative theory of the state which Rawls is now after is a *political* and not a *metaphysical* theory of the state, in the sense that his theory is designed to resolve the political dilemma of living with moral diversity under terms of fair agreement, rather than to derive a comprehensive and universal moral foundation which transcends the particularity of specific moral doctrines.

But from where does Rawls's political theory obtain its normative force? To answer this question, Rawls resorts to his conception of overlapping consensus. According to this notion, there are points on which the holders of different comprehensive moral doctrines will agree. Since we are assuming that the diversity of the moral pespectives is situated within the boundaries of constitutional democracy, certain values and principles will be agreed upon, such as the importance of tolerance, the conviction that only democratic representation can justify a government, and the categorical indefensibility of slavery. These values and principles, which according to Rawls are beyond the reach of political negotiation, will be accepted and justified by the members of democratic constitutional regimes even while they uphold their own comprehensive moral doctrines.

Rawls emphasizes that the overlapping consensus is not the result of mere political bargaining, which is susceptible to annulment based on changing political circumstances. Rather, the agreement is morally based, in the sense that it is grounded on the comprehensive moral perspectives held by the members of the democratic polity. Rawls argues that the adherents of different moral perspectives will justify the overlapping consensus differently, depending on the values and principles of their own perspective. Those who hold a comprehensive religious moral perspective and who accept freedom of religious belief, for example, will recognize that religious tolerance and the other principles of constitutional democracies are normatively justifiable political principles for a pluralistic society. Similarly, advocates of the kind of liberalism defended by Mill and Kant will see the values and principles of the overlapping consensus as reasonable entailments of their liberal convictions, while utilitarians will regard the consensus as a satisfactory and realistic approximation to what the principle of utility would recommend given limitations in our knowledge of social institutions and the required simplicity of rules for public reason.[10] But even though the rationale for accepting the overlapping consensus will differ, in every case it will be based on the moral convictions held by members of the polity, and it will therefore provide a moral justification for the consensus, and not merely be a compromise reached for reasons of political expediency.

Thus, according to Rawls there is no need to construct a moral basis for the overlapping consensus that is external to the actual moral doctrines that individuals already accept; it suffices to establish that the political values forming the consensus are latent in these doctrines. Moreover, individuals in a pluralistic democratic society will realize that, unless they are willing to resort to force and coercion, in order to have a orderly society they need to cooperate with one another under terms that are fair to everyone. Members of the polity will thus recognize that they have good grounds for accepting Rawls's conception of justice as fairness in pluralistic democracies. And since his political theory serves everyone's interest in living in an orderly society, it does not favor any specific doctrine, and is therefore neutral relative to the particular comprehensive moral perspectives that individuals hold. In this way Rawls's theory can serve as a normative basis for the society as a whole while recognizing and respecting the integrity of existing moral perspectives. The ingenuity of Rawls's conception of political liberalism is that it evidently legitimizes liberal principles on the basis of reasoned and morally grounded common consent despite lack of agreement regarding the nature of the good.

Despite its sagacity, however, Rawls's theory of political liberalism faces serious objections. As Ronald Dworkin has argued, the justification of liberal principles should not be based on mere overlapping agreement, because the consensus might simply be a manifestation of the existing power relations in the society.[11] Even though Rawls maintains that the overlapping consensus should not be determined by existing distributions of political power, in practice it is questionable whether we can rule out the possibility that the overlapping consensus will simply reflect not merely the convictions of the most powerful, but deeply entrenched though morally unjustified assumptions concerning rights and liberties in constitutional regimes. An example of a politically fundamental concept over which there is an overlapping consensus in some constitutional democracies, despite (as I will argue in Chapters 8 and 9) its lack of moral justification, is the conventional idea of restricted private property rights.[12] In general, given that in many contemporary democracies there are significant asymmetries in socioeconomic and political power, we cannot assume that an overlapping consensus on a particular set of values and principles will necessarily serve as a justifiable normative basis for a democratic society. It might very well be the case that these values and principles need to be challenged rather than accepted as normatively legitimate simply because people agree with them. As Dworkin points out, a liberal theory of the state should provide a normative basis for evaluating and, if necessary, reforming existing societies, and in order to do this it must be willing to make moral claims which may contravene the values the society currently holds.

In addition, Dworkin argues that the acceptance of liberal principles commits us to reforming society now, rather than waiting until members of the polity reach the point (if they ever do) when they agree with those principles. The problem with basing liberal morality on a consensual overlapping agreement is that, contrary to what Rawls holds, such morality should have priority over the process of consensual agreement itself. Rawls is in effect reversing the priority of the justificatory force of liberal principles and consensual agreement on them; that is, the moral legitimacy of these principles should ground the contractual decision to accept them, rather than the other way around. Once we recognize the normative priority of liberal principles, we should advocate for them now, and use their moral legitimacy to bring about general agreement on them.

There is also a problem with the conception of reasonable pluralism which Rawls uses as a starting point to reach the overlapping consensus.

The difficulty is that the differences between the perspectives found in democratic societies are significantly greater than he supposes. Some indigenous groups in states that are constitutional democracies, for instance, may have conceptions of democratic governance which differ from the "constitutional essentials" which Rawls thinks everyone will agree with. Such essential principles, which include conceptions of representative government and private property rights, may be rejected by indigenous groups who employ a consensus form of democratic decision making and who believe in collective property ownership. Rawls does not establish why such indigenous perspectives are unreasonable. In fact, it seems that the only way he can rule out these perspectives is by regarding them as outside of the limits of constitutional democracy and therefore illegitimate. This, however, would beg the question regarding their political legitimacy. Indeed, at times Rawls's characterization of reasonable pluralism comes dangerously close to being outrightly circular; he defines perspectives as reasonable if they conform to the basic principles of constitutional democracies as he defines them. Given this characterization, it is not surprising that doctrines that are not consistent with democratic regimes of the type he has in mind will by definition be unreasonable. Finally, we should note that the retort that indigenous groups, given their small size, can be easily accommodated without changing the basic structure of constitutional democracies is of no help for emerging democracies such as Ecuador and Guatemala, where indigenous groups comprise a large part, or a majority, of the citizenry.

Assessing Consent-Based Theories

From our analysis of Hobbes's, Locke's, and Rawls's theories of the social contract, we can see that a fundamental problem confronting consent-based theories of the normative foundations of the state is that the notion of consent ends up being ineffective or redundant. In order for the act of consent to have normative force, it is necessary to rely on a description of the contracting situation which is itself imbued with moral significance, that is, the contracting scenario has to be morally structured. Hobbes appealed to the rational obligations of the natural law, Locke relied on our duty to maintain a specific divine order, and Rawls appealed first to an original position of free and morally equal negotiators characterized by determinate dispositions and, in his later theory, on a pluralism of moral doctrines bounded by the normative principles of constitutional democracies. Without presupposing some background moral framework, it is questionable whether contractual agreements will have normative force, for surely not just any agreement will be morally justified. But if the justificatory force of the act of consent depends on some predetermined normative background, then consent itself is not what really provides the moral foundations for the state. If the legitimacy of the consensual agreement itself depends on other moral considerations, why the emphasis on consent? Why not simply examine the civil society in question to see whether it conforms to the normative criteria provided by the moral framework? In brief, either the social contract by itself has no normative force to legitimize the state or, if the contract is embedded within a larger normative scheme from which it derives its moral legitimacy, there is something besides the contract itself which provides the state with its moral justification. The contract thus turns out to be either ineffective or redundant. Moreover, since any contractual scenario will either be normatively structured or not, it is very difficult to see how consent-based foundational theories of the state could ever overcome this dilemma.[13]

The argument could be made here by contractarians that consent is still essential for justifying a political society because, even if there is an overarching moral framework within which the contract is made, the terms of the contract concretize and operationalize the moral implications of this framework, and for this reason are necessary for evaluating the principles, decisions, and institutions of the political society. General moral constraints, such as respect for the autonomy of the individual, can be interpreted differently, and consent is necessary for specifying which interpretation of these moral constraints a particular civil society adopts and for determining whether the institutional structures of the society actually conform to them. Constitutional arrangements, for example, can be seen as contractual agreements that give concrete meaning to moral visions of the human person and that provide substantive and procedural standards by which to judge on a continuing basis the justness of the political practices and institutions of particular societies.

Two points need to be made regarding this argument. First, claiming that consent plays an important role in articulating how a particular society understands given moral constraints and in determining whether it implements them faithfully is very different from claiming that contractual agreements constitute the moral foundation for the state. Consent in itself still has no independent moral force, even though it may legitimately function as a device for specifying how a particular political society interprets independently articulated and defended basic moral principles. It is instructive to note that even in Rawls's notion of overlapping consensus, what grounds the justificatory moral basis of the consensus is not the mere act of agreement itself, but the *complementarity* of the comprehensive moral perspectives held by members of the polity and the values comprising the overlapping consensus. Second, even if consent is important for concretizing moral constraints and evaluating faithfulness to them, contractarians have been looking in the wrong place for the normative factors that qualify and constrain contractual agreements concerning the state. We should focus our attention not on the abstract or hypothetical conditions which structure a theoretical contractual scenario, but on the factors that have affected and currently affect the formation and powers of political societies in the actual world. As pointed out earlier, and as we shall see more clearly in what follows, the moral legitimacy of a political society is not solely a matter of the principles that an isolated group of individuals (much less a philosopher constructing hypothetical scenarios which neglect historical and empirical factors) decide are normatively acceptable.

These critical remarks concerning consent-based theories of the state are not intended to show that consent plays no role in matters related to political societies. Particularly when dealing with issues concerning political membership, internal mutual commitments, and the maintenance of political bodies, individual and collective consent are important. The point is that consent per se cannot bear the weight of providing the moral foundations of civil societies.

It is also crucial to note that traditional normative theories of the state have placed a great deal of emphasis on questions (1) and (3)—which deal, respectively, with issues of political authority and moral legitimacy of the state—while neglecting issues related to question (2), which deal with the right of a group of individuals to establish a self-governing political body with sovereign powers of territorial control, such as exclusion of foreigners, which in a bounded world necessarily affect the members of other political societies. Failure to examine the issues connected with question (2) has led to a neglect of the external obligations and moral constraints that political societies should bear in their present Westphalian form. In the sections that follow I turn my attention to the justification a collectivity has for establishing an autonomous political society and the obligations and external responsibilities thereby incurred. Having attained an understanding of the issues connected with question (2), we will be in a better position to address questions (1) and (3), which assume that a group of individuals has already legitimately come together to form a political union.

Moral Constraints on the Formation of Political Bodies

Michael Walzer has discussed at some length the rationale for establishing political societies and the moral responsibilities they have to other political bodies and their members. In *Spheres of Justice: A Defense of Pluralism and Equality*[14], he notes that membership in a political community is one of the most important goods that we provide to one another, because such membership determines the context within which we exercise our rights and assume our civic responsibilities. Walzer considers the moral bases on which states should decide policies in such areas as immigration, aid to necessitous foreigners, the granting of full citizenship, and the control of land and natural resources. In contrast to most political philosophers past and present, Walzer recognizes the importance of question (2) as a central question in a normative theory of the state. He correctly points out that since membership in a political body determines many other issues, it is perhaps the central question in a normative political theory, and therefore merits detailed attention.

Walzer starts by considering existing states, and asks what normative considerations should guide their decisions concerning their present and future populations, and what responsibilities they have to individuals who are not members of their political community. Before discussing these normative guidelines, Walzer considers the possibility that states should have no other function than that of maintaining order, and that there should be global freedom of movement and unrestricted immigration. In such a world individuals would be free to move across national borders at will, guided by their desire to maximize their self-interest. He argues that living in such a world would not be desirable, because states would lack the communal cohesion which makes mutual obligations and shared meanings possible in a political society. The existence of constantly shifting heterogeneous populations would undermine the moral and intellectual culture of communities and the efficient functioning of their political institutions. In other words, the shared ways of life through which people give meaning to their lives and in which the loyalty, security, and welfare of a society's individual members are secured would be jeopardized by uncontrolled movement of individuals in and out of political societies. Walzer argues that the cultural distinctiveness of communities is a desirable feature which should be protected, and that such protection is possible only if states have the power of closure, that is, the power to regulate political membership. He states, "At some level of political organization, something like the sovereign state must take shape and claim the authority to make its own admissions policy, to control and sometimes to restrain the flow of immigrants."[15] A world without boundaries, by depriving the members of political communities of the means to decide whom to share obligations and commitments with, denies them the capacity to protect their common way of life.

Even though at first sight the notion of regulating membership and implementing policies of exclusion may sound reactionary, Walzer maintains that, on the contrary, it is when borders are completely unregulated that local neighborhoods and communities tend to become parochial and closed. He notes that in different countries and in different eras, when the state has followed a policy of openness towards foreigners, local communities have sought to exclude newcomers who are different from themselves.[16] Whether in New York during the early twentieth century or in ancient Alexandria (where diverse groups were allowed to develop their own institutional structures), communities and neighborhoods tried to regulate their membership, often in ways that were exclusivist and intolerant of strangers. Walzer argues that these negative consequences of unregulated state borders reinforce his belief in the correctness of recognizing a right of closure for political bodies. He strongly emphasizes, however, that the right of closure has a different moral status than the right to control emigration. While the former is meant to safeguard the welfare and way of life of communities, the latter is a form of coercion that should not be tolerated by democratic governments.[17]

Walzer then proceeds to describe the kinds of obligations that political societies have to foreigners. He notes that the question of who should be admitted is ultimately a political question to be decided by the members of the state, but that there are normative constraints that delimit the range of generally acceptable state policies. Among these constraints is the "kinship principle" which refers to the policy of granting preference to outsiders who are considered national or ethnic relatives. He points out that in this regard, states are like families whose members have unchosen special moral obligations to one another. The state-as-family metaphor also helps us understand the common perception that in times of trouble the home country is a refuge for individuals and their descendants who have ancestral connections to the home country. If they are persecuted in the country where they live, these foreign nationals turn to the home country for shelter and protection. For instance, Greeks and Turks living outside of Greece and Turkey who were driven from their countries of residence after wars of the early twentieth century were taken in by their respective countries of origin. Walzer points out that the kinship principle illustrates that states are not merely random collections of individuals living in a parcel of land, but consist of national groups or peoples who to some extent consider ethnically related individuals and their descendants, when they live in another country, as members in absentia.[18] The obligations and commitments that the home country has to absent kinfolk, although often attenuated by time and distance, are nevertheless markedly different from the commitments and bonds it has to outsiders.

Walzer next considers the powers of territorial control exercised by states, and argues that ethnocultural minority groups have a right to coexist with the majority group in the territory controlled by the state. He maintains that there is a universal territorial right to have a place to live which should restrain governments from driving out "alien elements" to achieve an ethnic cleansing of the state. He justifies this right on the ground that access to a living space is a fundamental human need, as basic as the right to air and water. Further, people require not only a living space, but also need to sustain themselves economically by having access to land and natural resources. The most natural place in which people are entitled to live, Walzer points out, is where they have already made a life for themselves. He argues that the attachments and expectations people have formed by living in a certain area provide reasons against expulsion or forced relocation by the state. The right to a living space within the state is also necessary, Walzer maintains, because it provides a place of physical security from persecution and violence. The security afforded by living within the bounded and protected territory of a sovereign state is particularly important for those groups who are susceptible to persecution and violence.

Walzer also discusses the issue of whether a political society has the responsibility to share its territory with necessitous foreigners. He considers the situation in which a country like Australia, which has large expanses of unoccupied land and a low population density, is confronted with claims to share its land by members of a densely populated state who are driven by famine to relocate to another country. Walzer argues that we must weigh the territorial claims of Australia with the basic needs of the necessitous foreigners, and that it is reasonable to maintain that the satisfaction of survival needs has greater moral weight than state property rights which were obtained through forced displacement of Australian Aboriginal populations. In general, Walzer maintains that as long as members of a country with large expanses of unoccupied land are able to maintain their present way of life, they should be willing to share their territory with outsiders if the economic plight of the latter is great enough to endanger their capacity to satisfy their basic needs. In the case of Australia, Walzer's argument is no doubt strengthened by the dubious moral legitimacy of the method by which Australians acquired their land. In any case, Australians would be confronted with a radical choice: either cede land to the outsiders and retain their relative cultural homogeneity, or retain their present boundaries but create a multicultural society by incorporating the necessitous foreigners.

But as Walzer indicates, there are limits to the moral responsibilities that states can be expected to shoulder. It would not do, for example, to divide all available land equally among every inhabitant of the earth, because this would undermine the right of political societies to stake a claim to a territory. Walzer maintains that connection to a particular place is an important part of national identity, and that the territorial rights of a political society should be respected. Moreover, communal wealth should be recognized as an achievement of a political society, and for this reason continual redistribution of resources across national boundaries would be unjustified. After all, political societies must take some responsibility, as well as credit, for decisions they make that affect their general political and economic well-being. To demand simple equality of land and natural resources would undermine the collective autonomy of political societies. The right to collective autonomy of a particular state would be nullified, for example, by high birthrates in nearby countries, because this would create the need to redistribute land once again.

Refugees from religious, political, or ethnic persecution, according to Walzer, constitute a category of needy outsiders that places particularly strong moral obligations on political societies. When such refugees face mass murder or brutal oppression if they do not receive admission to another country, their appeals will be very morally compelling. In those cases in which a state has been indirectly responsible for the persecution of the refugees, the appeals of the latter for protection will have special significance for that state. U.S. responsibilities toward South Vietnamese refugees fleeing the new Communist government after the U.S. war against Vietnam is a case in point. Walzer also maintains that a country may have special obligations to protect refugees when they are persecuted for upholding ideological principles which that country has encouraged them to defend. Ideological affinities can be a source of special moral responsibilities for a state when individuals in another country have jeopardized their safety by adopting an ideological stance which that state upholds and which it has an interest in disseminating.

An issue faced by many contemporary democratic societies involves articulating standards for granting citizenship to immigrants and other outsiders who have obtained legal admission into the state. Walzer argues that the criteria governing the process of naturalization should be guided by the principle of political equality and mutual commitment which unites members of a democratic polity. Unlike immigration policies, with regards to which political societies are free to adopt a variety of morally acceptable options, naturalization is entirely morally constrained. He maintains that unless noncitizens (such as resident aliens) are offered the opportunity to attain full political equality by achieving citizenship, a democracy will become "a little tyranny." This is because if the individuals who have gained legal residence in the state are deprived of those fundamental political rights that enable individuals to protect their needs and interests in a democracy, they will be relegated to the vulnerable status of political nonpersonhood. By being deprived of the capacity for full participation in the political life of the community, they will be subject to binding political decisions which they have no legitimate way of contesting and which were implemented without their consent. For Walzer, the decision to admit individuals from other countries into a political society carries with it the further obligation to recognize them as political equals. Failure to grant them citizenship institutionalizes their second-class status and ultimately undermines the society's commitment to democratic principles.

Walzer maintains that even guest workers should be given the choice of becoming citizens, because by living and working within the state they are members of the democratic community. Guest workers often perform jobs at low pay which members of the majority society do not want, and they typically live under strict rules regulating, *inter alia*, their employment, the time they can legally reside in the host country, and the family members they can bring with them. In some ways they are even more vulnerable than other resident aliens, because they are likely to be deported if they fail to keep their jobs or if economic circumstances in the host state change so they are no longer needed.

Because guest workers, like other resident aliens, are in effect tyrannically ruled by citizens of the state (even when the latter are well-intentioned and benevolent), Walzer believes that guest workers should be "set on the road to citizenship." Even if they voluntarily decided to become guest workers, subjecting them to political decisions to which they do not consent is fundamentally at odds with democratic principles. Walzer believes that they may choose to return to their home countries or retain their resident alien status, but they should have the opportunity to stay on as permanent members of the political community. In short, if a society has a sufficiently strong need to use the services of guest workers, that political body should be willing to treat them as political equals and prevent them from being subject to the kind of tyranny that is implied by the denial of basic political rights.

Evaluating Walzer's Position on the Moral Responsibilities of Political Communities

Walzer raises some important points for developing a cohesive response to questions concerning the normative basis of political communities. As we have observed, he believes that in the real world, membership in a political society carries with it moral responsibilities to the members of other political bodies. In contrast to most political philosophers, Walzer recognizes that the moral status of a political community is not merely a matter of how it deals with its own citizens. Even though the principle of noninterference—that is, the "negative" principle that a state should not interfere with the sovereignty of another state—has been widely recognized by political philosophers, what is distinctive about Walzer's contribution is the emphasis he places on the positive moral responsibilities of political societies to other political communities. Walzer argues that for a political community to act in a morally responsible way, it is not enough that it provide its citizens with the appropriate rights of democratic citizenship and refrain from interfering with the sovereignty of other political bodies; in addition, it must exhibit external moral considerability in a range of areas, including immigration, its treatment of refugees and guest workers, and even in its willingness in certain situations to share its land and natural resources.

While arguing for a broad set of external responsibilities for political bodies, Walzer is careful to emphasize that such bodies have the right to determine their own destinies by regulating membership. He states:

> Admission and exclusion are at the core of communal independence. They suggest the deepest meaning of self-determination. Without them, there could not be *communities of character*, historically stable, ongoing associations of men and women with some special commitment to one another and some special sense of their common life.[19]

This conception of communal independence and self-determination suggests that the civil relationship between the members of a political society is deeper and more extensive than is generally supposed in liberal democracies. By recognizing that collectivities have the right to form political communities in which individuals can maintain special mutual commitments and obligations, Walzer balances the external responsibilities of political societies with their collective right of cultural and political closure. He believes that for human beings to flourish, not just any political community will do; rather, it has to be an appropriate political community, namely, one in which they can enjoy the distinctive bonds of cultural membership which are an essential part of their particular cultural self-identity.

Even though some of his arguments could benefit from further theoretical development, I believe that Walzer's views are for the most part sound.[20] He correctly realizes that our moral responsibilities extend beyond those that we have explicitly contracted. Indeed, it is difficult to make sense of many of our commonly recognized moral obligations, including those to family members, to neighbors and members of our communities, and even to strangers in desperate need, without maintaining that morality cannot be properly understood if confined to the realm of contractual relations. He is also aware that political societies are not isolated collectivities, but exist in an interconnected world in which decisions made by political communities often affect the well-being and life opportunities of the members of other political bodies. Moreover, while respecting the right of a political body to determine the constitution of its membership, he insists that a democratic society should be consistent in its application of liberal democratic principles, and apply the latter not merely to a selected number of citizens of a particular ethnic heritage, but to all people who live within the territory under its control. His arguments that a political community should eventually extend rights of citizenship to immigrants and guest workers are persuasive.

I introduced Walzer into the discussion because his expansive conception of the moral considerability that political societies owe to the members of other political communities might provide us with some leads concerning a more comprehensive and adequate response to the three questions with which we are concerned, particularly question (2). Because he examines issues commonly neglected by other political philosophers, such as questions concerning the basis for political membership and the external positive responsibilities to the members of other political societies, Walzer's insights are important to keep in mind as we attempt to answer these questions. Before embarking on the latter task, however, a few comments on Walzer's position are in order.

It is rather surprising that Walzer starts his discussion of membership in political societies by taking for granted the legitimacy of existing states. By doing so, he pushes to the background an issue concerning political membership which is of fundamental importance to many indigenous, ethnonationalist, and secessionist ethnocultural minorities, namely, the historical fact of their coerced incorporation into the state. By taking as his point of departure the legitimacy of the present global configuration of political bodies, Walzer de-emphasizes the view that states in certain cases must, in order to justify their present political boundaries, take corrective action in response to their past oppressive treatment of ethnocultural minorities. Even though, in fairness to Walzer, in his later work he recognizes the problem of national minorities and evidently condones self-determination for these groups[21], the issue of coerced political incorporation of autonomist and secessionist ethnocultural minorities should be at the center of any discussion of membership in political societies. Perhaps Walzer's thoughts on these issues had not crystallized at the time of the writing of *Spheres of Justice*. In any case, criteria for determining the political boundaries of just multicultural democracies should consider seriously the challenge of some ethnocultural minorities that the state is not the sole locus of sovereignty.

A more significant moral constraint on membership in political societies that Walzer does not take into account stems from his position on property rights. Walzer, like most political philosophers, evidently takes the normative legitimacy of conventional property rights for granted. He assumes that individuals as well as collectivities have the right to unilaterally appropriate territory (and the natural resources found therein) and enforce the corresponding set of powers implied in conventional individual and state property rights. Putting aside issues related to individual private property rights, with which I will deal later, what grounds the right of a collectivity to appropriate and have sovereign control over parts of nature in forming a political society? And what moral obligations are incurred in this process of such unilateral appropriation? Walzer's answers to these questions are insufficiently developed.

In responding to these questions, he would probably say that a group of individuals has a right to exclusive control of a certain territory because in order for them to form a self-determining political society they

have to obtain a living space over which they can exercise the right of closure. The right of political societies to regulate immigration, we will recall, is according to Walzer essential for communal independence, that is,
essential for preserving the cultural character of a political community
and the special mutual commitments between its members. In addition,
Walzer would likely argue that nations or peoples have special connections to specific territories, or homelands, and that these connections,
which are vital for national self-identity, should be respected. In short, according to Walzer collectivities have the right of self-determination, that
is, the right to determine the political, cultural, and economic character of
their community and to decide criteria for membership in that community. Since self-determination cannot be realized without territorial control, collectivities have the concomitant right to establish political communities which will regulate and enforce sovereign powers over
property, or more precisely, over that territory to which they have a special or exclusive connection.

The problem with Walzer's rationale for the right of collectivities to appropriate natural property, that is, land and its natural resources, is that
in most cases political societies acquired such property by morally illegitimate means, such as conquest, invasive settlement, and coerced annexation. The vast majority of contemporary states did not come into existence through a process of negotiation in which they attained the
permission of other political communities to appropriate natural property. Rather, the process of collective territorial acquisition was unilateral
and in most cases coercive. Furthermore, since in a bounded world there
is a limited supply of natural property, in coercively acquiring territory a
political society restricted the capacity of other political communities to
acquire the natural property necessary for them to exercise self-determination. That is, in at least some cases unilateral territorial appropriation
delimited the natural property necessary for the members of other political societies to collectively determine the course of their own future and
to flourish in community with others with whom they share special
moral obligations.

Though Walzer discusses immigration in general terms, there is an important issue that he does not explicitly discuss, namely, illegal immigration. Since Walzer believes in a political community's right of closure, he
would presumably agree with its right to employ the necessary measures, including coercive means, to control the influx of illegal immigrants. However, as we have observed, for Walzer the right of a political
community to turn away necessitous strangers (and most contemporary
illegal immigration is generated by economic exigency) is limited by
moral considerations, so that the control of borders is not an unconditional right. But are there other moral constraints on a state's right of closure that Walzer does not consider? I believe that there are, and that, as I

will argue later, there are indirect but significant ways in which a political community can interfere with the capacity of another political body to achieve self-determination and enable its members to flourish. In particular, given existing global inequalities and interdependencies, the present institutions and systems of capital financing and economic production and exchange can impair the ability of some political communities to flourish. To the extent that a political community supports and maintains such institutions and systems, it undermines its sovereign territorial powers.

In brief, the mode of territorial acquisition of political communities, its possibly restrictive effect on the self-determination of the members of other political bodies, and economic interdependencies and inequalities suggest that Walzer's position needs to be modified, and that the right of political societies to sovereign territorial control should be more strongly qualified than he supposes. Assuming that all human beings have the right to participate in communal self-determination (an assumption that Walzer would surely agree with) these considerations suggest that the external, positive moral obligations of political communities are stronger and more extensive than those proposed by Walzer. These considerations are also especially problematic for liberal constitutional democracies which grant pride of place to individual autonomy, since material self-reliance is essential for autonomous existence. If, as I will argue later, a compelling case can be made for the universal right to natural property (i.e., land and natural resources), a more systematic basis than that provided by Walzer for articulating and justifying the moral obligations of political societies to other political bodies and their members will have been established.

It is interesting to note that Walzer comes remarkably close to recognizing a universal human right to natural property with his conception of a right to a living space and his view of the obligations that countries with vast unoccupied spaces and a low population density have to certain political communities. But though he moves in this direction, he never quite gets there. Thus, as it stands Walzer's conception of the moral obligations of political communities to other political bodies and their members is limited and unsystematic. His view that we have obligations to take in refugees, for example, is very restricted in its implications for balancing the egregious inequalities in (illegitimately appropriated) natural resources that exist between states. Even the impact of his more radical proposal that countries with large tracts of unoccupied land should share them with overcrowded countries experiencing famine is greatly diminished by his qualification that the members of the land-rich country should not experience a change in their way of life.

At this point I will not draw out the implications of universal rights to natural property. My objective here has been to suggest that the moral obligations between political societies are much more extensive than Walzer and other political philosophers have supposed. As we shall see later, this has important implications for our conception of the moral foundations of political societies.

Another aspect of Walzer's position that we should keep in mind in articulating the normative basis of political communities is his notion that civil societies are also cultural and economic communities in which we collectively cast our lot with others with whom we share a sense of national and cultural membership. A political society not only establishes political institutions that order civil life, it also structures and regulates a whole range of important human activities which reflect the sense of that society's conception of cultural community and human flourishing. This is an important insight, because it calls our attention to the various functions that a political society should perform in promoting human flourishing in all of its varied dimensions. Moreover, this insight also reveals that an adequate moral justification of a political body must take into account the multiple powers and institutional functions of that body, because only then can we determine whether the justification provided covers all of the powers possessed and functions performed by the relevant political union. The normative justification of a political community is neither adequate nor complete if it fails to justify all of the important roles performed by the institutions of that political society. For instance, since states are not only political but also cultural communities which provide institutional support for particular cultural practices, we have to take cultural rights into account in the justification of the state. In other words, does the state guarantee the appropriate cultural rights needed for the human flourishing of all of the groups comprising the society? This integrated and expansive conception of the functions of a political community provides a more realistic and adequate basis for understanding the various issues that are involved in the normative justification of existing political societies.

The Proper Function and Justification
of Political Communities

The remainder of this chapter is devoted to sketching out my position concerning the normative foundations of political communities. Aspects of this position will then be more fully developed in the following chapters. My goal here is not to develop a full-blown normative theory of the state. Rather, I have the more limited, though important, objective of expanding the moral criteria that should be taken into account in formulating such a theory, especially when the political community in question is a culturally pluralistic polity. The multicultural character of contemporary political communities challenges in significant ways conventional normative theories of the state.

Briefly stated, on the basis of the discussion thus far and the analysis to be provided below, my position regarding the three questions with which we started this chapter is as follows. Regarding the second question, which concerns the justifiability of establishing an autonomous political community with territorial powers, we will see (in our discussion of property rights) that such political communities have significant responsibilities, concerning the sharing of natural resources, to other political communities. These responsibilities will be grounded on a stronger normative basis than that provided by Walzer. Moreover, issues concerning the moral justification of secession and autonomous governance, which would involve at least partial territorial control by aspiring political communities, will also be given careful consideration. The issues of secession and autonomous governance, which are often neglected by traditional theories of the state, are particularly important in the contemporary world, in which numerous conflicts arise from ethnocultural group claims to self-determination. Finally, the justification of the powers of political communities to control territory and unilaterally determine immigration policies will be placed within a transnational context in which some political bodies can systematically undermine the capacity of other political communities to provide their citizens with the wherewithal for human flourishing. This broader understanding of state powers of territorial control and the mutual responsibilities between political bodies is particularly relevant in an increasingly interconnected world characterized by egregious inequalities in the life opportunities of the members of different political communities.

Concerning the third question, which deals with the moral legitimacy of a political community, we shall see that such normative legitimacy depends on granting the citizenry not only the familiar civil and democratic rights, but also cultural rights and universal rights to natural property. The latter rights have traditionally been neglected in assessing the moral legitimacy or adequacy of political communities. As we noted in our discussion of Walzer—and shall see more clearly in Chapter 5—the development and preservation of cultural traditions occurs within the context of political communities, and a just state is one that protects the right to cultural self-determination of all of the citizenry. With regard to property rights, while the right to acquire private property is generally guaranteed in democratic societies, property ownership is not considered as a universal right, despite its importance for autonomy. I will argue for the universalization of rights to natural (though not to mediated) property.

Regarding the first question, which deals with the binding authority of a political community on an individual, we will see that political obligation depends in part on whether the political community in question recognizes and respects the possible prior membership of that individual in a pre-existing autonomous political community. As we have noted, some ethnocultural communities were involuntarily incorporated into the state during or subsequent to its formation. In order to justify its political authority to the members of these ethnocultural groups, the state must be willing to deal justly with their claims concerning self-determination and lost autonomy. If these claims are disregarded or inadequately addressed, the members of these groups can justifiably challenge the presumption that they are bound to recognize the political authority of the state.[22]

Returning now to the main theme of this section, the basic stance I want to defend is that the primary function and purpose of a political community is to promote human flourishing in all of its principal dimensions, including the political, the sociocultural, and the economic spheres. In a multicultural society, however, there are a variety of conceptions of human flourishing, and allowance should be made for accommodating this multiplicity. Accommodating diverse visions of the good life in effect means that culturally pluralistic societies should provide individuals with the rights and means for attaining self-determination in accordance with their conceptions of the good. This might entail granting cultural rights to accommodationist groups, devolving powers of self-governance to indigenous and ethnonationalist groups, developing just systems of power-sharing for communal contenders, or even, in the case of secessionist groups, dividing the political community into two or more sovereign political bodies. In all cases, however, a just multicultural democracy should provide individuals and communities with the rights and access to resources necessary to control their life-circumstances, that is, provide them with the wherewithal to exercise self-determination. In my theory of the normative justification of political communities, self-determination is of central importance for human flourishing.

In the following chapters, self-determination will be understood from a communal perspective. More precisely, the unit of analysis for articulating the meaning of self-determination will be the political community. There are persuasive reasons why self-determination should be understood in this way. Self-determination has three principal dimensions: the political, the cultural/social, and the economic. In each of these dimensions, it is the community that is the most theoretically adequate and concrete locus of analysis. At the political level, it is state and substate political bodies that grant and enforce the civil and political rights that make it possible for people to determine their life circumstances and pursue their conception of the good. It is not isolated individuals but individuals qua members of political communities who seek mutual recognition as political equals, justify collectively binding decisions, and create and maintain the institutions that regulate civic life. Even though in recent decades the sovereign powers of the state and substate political communities have been compromised by global forces, these communities still remain the principal centers of organizational and regulative power in a wide variety of areas.

At the cultural and social level, political communities shape and sustain cultural life. By using a particular language (or in some cases languages) as the medium for official state transactions, for example, a political community reinforces the preservation of specific cultural traditions. Similarly, through the selection of state holidays and symbols, or the regulation of mandatory historical material to be learned in the schools, a political community strives to create and maintain a cultural community of memory and character. As we shall see when we discuss Will Kymlicka's views in the next chapter, a political community cannot be neutral concerning its institutional support of a specific culture or cultures. At the cultural and social level it is not the individual in isolation who sustains cultural life or cultural self-determination; rather this is a function of a collectivity which preserves and transmits a cultural tradition through public recognition and institutional support of shared practices and values. Moreover, since an essential component of culture is intersubjective recognition of specific individuals as members of a cultural group, cultural self-determination must occur within a communal context.

Finally, within the economic sphere it is once again the political community that structures and regulates the economic framework within which individuals can attain material well-being. For example, by safeguarding property rights (including increasingly complex intellectual property rights) or enforcing economic agreements through a system of legal penalties, a political community provides individuals with the long-term security of expectation necessary to engage in ongoing economic transactions that further their economic welfare. This is particularly true for large, complex, and globally interconnected economies, which cannot be properly regulated solely by informal agreements and local communal sanctions. It is practically impossible, even for the wealthiest individuals, to develop and maintain the necessary legal and economic infrastructures that permit their own material self-determination. Thus, the extent to which individuals can achieve the latter depends on collective concerted action by a political community. From these observations we can conclude that political, cultural/social, and economic self-determination are best understood and achieved within the context of political communities.

Communal Self-Determination and Autonomy of the Individual

There is wide agreement among political philosophers that one of the cornerstones of liberal democracies is respect for the autonomy of the individual. Respect for individual autonomy is of central importance for liberal democratic societies not simply because it embodies recognition of peoples' moral agency and intrinsic dignity and worth, but also because it serves instrumentally as a means for individuals to attain a satisfying life in accordance with their conception of the good. Adopting the view that individual autonomy has both intrinsic and instrumental value is important for culturally pluralistic liberal democracies, because such societies want to retain their character as liberal democracies while accommodating the multicultural character of the polity. In such democracies, commitment to the liberal principle of the intrinsic moral worth and dignity of the individual restrains the demands and limitations imposed by particular cultural communities on their members, while recognition of autonomy's instrumental value protects the space that the state provides for members of cultural communities to live their lives according to their own cultural values. The possibility of establishing healthy multicultural liberal democracies depends to a great extent on finding a workable balance between these dual aspects of individual autonomy.

Given the importance of respect for the autonomy of the individual in constitutional liberal democracies, the question naturally arises: What is the relation between individual autonomy and communal self-determination? This question is relevant for establishing the compatibility of my position with liberal principles. I will maintain that the autonomy of individuals is best understood within the context of the self-determination of the political community to which they belong. As we have observed, the rights and resources that make it possible for individuals to determine their affairs and control their fates are provided by a political community. The capacity of the latter to provide and safeguard these rights and resources, however, depends in turn on its ability to control its own destiny, that is, on its capacity to make its own collective decisions, to support and protect its cultural resources, and to be economically self-reliant. The extent to which individuals can enjoy autonomy thus depends on the capacity of their political community to make autonomous choices which promote their well-being. Once we realize that autonomy for individuals can be secured only within the framework of a political community and that the latter cannot guarantee such autonomy without self-determination, then communal self-determination can be seen as a necessary moral corollary to one of the basic normative principles on which liberal constitutional democracies are founded, namely, respect for the autonomy and moral agency of individuals. Thus, from the viewpoint of moral justification, it is the autonomy of individuals that provides the normative rationale for communal self-determination. However, from an epistemological and institutional perspective, the self-determination of the political community has priority, because we can understand neither the concrete meaning of individual autonomy nor the forms of social organization necessary to achieve it without focusing on communal self-determination.

In addition to the argument that it is necessary for political communities to enjoy self-determination in order for individuals to exercise autonomy, there is a deeper connection between individual autonomy and communal self-determination, one that reaches to the very nature of individual autonomy itself. To see this, consider the question: What is the metaphysical category into which autonomy should be placed? Is it an object, a property, a process, a fact, or an entity of some other sort? It is tempting to say that autonomy is an ability or capacity possessed by individuals, that is, that it is a dispositional property which individual human beings exhibit. To be an autonomous person, so this answer goes, involves the capacity to critically reflect upon one's choices and preferences, and to be capable of accepting or changing them on the basis of higher-order preferences and values.[23] Thus, an autonomous individual is one who has developed the necessary cognitive and affective capacities[24] to scrutinize her existing preferences and has the wherewithal to transform them on the basis of rational or affective criteria that she has noncoercively chosen. This definition of autonomy seems to conform to our ordinary understanding of this notion, since we usually associate autonomy with the capacity for self-direction and the liberty required for making and implementing our choices.

However, this definition of autonomy is not entirely satisfactory. In the first place, in most situations critical scrutiny of one's preferences assumes the exercise of capacities that cannot be developed by an isolated individual, as well as access to information which does reside wholly in the individual. Just as critical cognitive capacities must be developed in intersubjective contexts, most of the knowledge on the basis of which an individual makes decisions is not gathered and verified by the person who uses that knowledge. Rather, people depend on the capacities of others to learn the skills of critical reflection, just as they rely on the testimony and data-gathering capacity of other individuals and of institutions to make reliable decisions. Even if a person could somehow develop in isolation a capacity for critical reflection, without information relevant to the case at hand she would be unable to make reasoned, sound decisions. Thus, even though autonomy may be a capacity exercised by individuals, it cannot be understood entirely in terms of the characteristics of disconnected individuals, since it incorporates a set of capacities and external conditions which, at least in the vast majority of cases, transcend the individual.

Second, not all choices noncoercively made, even if they involve reflective scrutiny of pre-existing preferences, count as autonomous choices. Decisions made in extremely extenuating circumstances, or on the basis of propaganda, coercive persuasion, internalized self-limitations, and so forth, are not, strictly speaking, autonomous decisions. For instance, as we observed in our discussion of political inequality in the last chapter, a decision made by a person who has lived under imposed servitude may not be autonomous, because his conception of what is possible for him to accomplish has been severely and arbitrarily limited by his life-circumstances. Because his position of servitude has shaped his self-identity and greatly delimited the range of objectives he believes he is capable of accomplishing, his decision to follow a certain option is not made from a position conducive to the making of autonomous decisions. Even if his decision was noncoercively made from a position of new-found freedom, to the extent that it was arbitrarily delimited by his former circumstances, we should be reluctant to call it an autonomous choice.

Similarly, if available information crucial for making a sound decision in an important area of life is made inaccessible to an individual, or if he is lead to rely on false information, it is questionable whether that decision was made autonomously. Here we can recall the familiar example from Locke involving the person placed in a cell who is lead to believe that all of the doors of the cell are locked, when in fact one of them is left unlocked. This individual, even though he is actually free to leave the cell and is thus not being forced to stay, cannot exercise this option given his information. One of the reasons that deception is regarded as a violation of a person's autonomy is that it deprives him of the opportunity to make a decision that is based on an accurate understanding of the situation in which he actually finds himself. What these examples show is that the capacity to exercise autonomy presupposes, *inter alia*, a certain epistemic environment in which an agent can cultivate and exercise the cognitive and affective capacities which enable him to openly consider and implement the choices that are actually open to him.

Because an adequate understanding of autonomy involves a number of factors external to the individual, it is best to construe autonomy not merely as a capacity of individuals, but as a set of life-circumstances or state-of-affairs, extended over time, in which both the cognitive and affective capacities of agents and the nature of their political, cultural, and economic life-world are taken into account. This expansive and integrated conception of autonomy is more adequate for analyzing issues concerning ethnocultural group empowerment, as well as for recognizing the limitations of epistemic closure of some cultural communities. That is, it is important to conceive of autonomy as inhering in a temporally extended framework so that we can take into account the historical circumstances in which the autonomy of the members of political communities may have been systematically undermined by discriminatory and oppressive institutions designed and maintained by dominant groups. Understanding autonomy in this way also permits the identification of excessively restrictive ethnocultural communities that, by not allowing their members to acquire knowledge of the outside world, interfere with their autonomy. This conception of autonomy is consistent with the view that an autonomous individual can voluntarily accept restrictions in her behavior by being a member of a cultural community in which special obligations and commitments are mutually recognized among its members. But it is not consistent with cultural contexts in which individuals are induced to live according to highly restrictive values and practices without ever having had the opportunity to place such values and practices in a reflective perspective by acquiring knowledge of alternative cultural traditions. Cultural traditions in which women are denied an education, for example, and induced to accept narrowly construed social roles without being allowed to develop the capacity for self-reflection are not consistent with the view of autonomy that I advocate.

In fundamentalist cultures which rigidly control behavior and severely restrict access to knowledge, we find some of the most unjust and oppressive internal practices against the members of cultural communities, particularly women. Such cultural traditions not only violate central tenets of the doctrine of epistemological egalitarianism and make intercultural understanding and cooperation difficult, they are ill equipped to survive in a world in which the cultural isolation needed to sustain their values and practices is becoming practically impossible to attain. It is ultimately in the interest of these cultural groups to adopt more egalitarian values and practices in order to maintain the loyalty of their members and insure cultural preservation, rather than use increasingly coercive measures to sustain their restrictive and ultimately unjust beliefs and patterns of behavior. It is critical that the members of these cultural groups realize that most cultural traditions have undergone significant changes in the past and retained their cultural identity, so that abolishing oppressive internal practices is not tantamount to destroying the cultural integrity of their communities.

In employing the more comprehensive conception of autonomy I advocate, we should be careful not to trivialize it by demanding excessively strong conditions regarding agent capacities, epistemic resources, options, and the means to implement them. Since in practice the latter factors are always limited, restrictions must be placed on how much these factors can vary and a decision can still be regarded as autonomous. Unless such restrictions are introduced, practically all of our decisions will turn out to be non-autonomous, since they are always made under non-ideal conditions. Here it would be reasonable to work with a contextualized conception of autonomy, in which what counts as an autonomous choice depends on such factors as the present state of knowledge, available resources, distributions of social power, internalized personal limitations, and the presence or absence of arbitrarily restrictive social barriers. In this view, the capacities and conditions relevant for autonomy cannot be identified in an absolute way, independent of social context, but will depend on the characteristics of the total environment in which agents and communities are situated.[25] Autonomy will thus have an evaluative function, that is, it will be used for determining, given a set of actual conditions and limitations: (i) to what extent individual decisions actually reflect the agency of the people involved and (ii) whether a particular set of life-circumstances limit or promote the capacity of individuals to determine the course of their lives.

It is important to emphasize that even though the primary environment relevant for determining whether individuals can exercise autonomy is the political community to which they belong, attention should also be paid to the distribution of power and resources between political communities, because the latter can obviously affect the capacity of political bodies to attain self-determination and provide an environment for their citizens to exercise individual autonomy. This is certainly true in the contemporary world, in which globalization has undermined the capacity of political communities to make sovereign decisions. At the economic level, capital mobility, currency markets, and the internationalization of labor forces, for example, are making it increasingly difficult for political communities to implement decisions which benefit their members. Culturally, the control of production and dissemination of cultural products by corporate conglomerates, technological and economic changes that dislocate traditional communities, and the internalizing of the values of commercial culture, pose problems for political communities that try to employ their cultural resources for self-determination. Globalization has also affected the political sphere, as supranational organizations such as the United Nations and NATO have adopted a more assertive role in the internal affairs of political bodies. Another way in which the traditional political functions of the state have been attenuated is due to the increasingly prominent role of nongovernmental organizations in a variety of political areas. None of this implies that the state is likely to disappear in the near future, or that it is no longer the major center of organizational and coercive power. It does mean, however, that conceptions of autonomy and self-determination which are entirely state-centered cannot be considered as adequate.

Is Autonomy Exclusively a "Western" Concept?

It could be argued here that the conception of individual autonomy on which I place such great emphasis is not adequate as a foundational notion in a theory of multicultural democracy. According to this argument, since individual autonomy is a value of Western European culture, which is a specific cultural tradition, it is not representative of other cultural traditions that may not grant individual autonomy the central place it has in

Western European culture. By adopting individual autonomy as a foundation stone of our theory, we have unjustifiably privileged a specific cultural tradition, and thereby devalued other ways of life. Moreover, in taking this approach we unfairly evaluate all other traditions using Western European standards, and judge them as inadequate if they do not measure up to these standards, rather than using criteria that evaluate their cultural practices using their own values and ideals. By imposing Western cultural criteria that may be alien or even hostile to the traditions of some of the other groups in a multicultural society, we assume the universal validity of the values of the Western tradition, and thereby marginalize and disrespect these other groups.

In answering these objections, it is first of all important to indicate that the cultural specificity of the values of a particular cultural tradition in itself neither privileges nor disqualifies them for serving particular theoretical or pragmatic purposes. Simply because a value or perspective derives from a specific cultural tradition, it does not follow that it is either more or less suitable for resolving a given dilemma or underpinning a particular theory. It is the reasons that can be adduced in favor of, or against, the value or perspective, and not its origin, that should determine its adequacy for given theoretical or practical purposes. The value of living in a relatively harmonious relationship with nature, for example, is a normative tenet of some indigenous groups. If the cultural specificity of a normative viewpoint disqualifies it from being used to address social problems, we would be unable to employ the indigenous ecological perspective to develop alternatives to the environmental problems that we collectively face. But surely it is unjustified to disqualify this perspective from consideration simply because it derives from a particular cultural tradition. It might very well be the case that we all have much to learn from an indigenous ecological perspective, or even that some aspects of this perspective should be universally accepted.

Furthermore, many ethnocultural groups that are not Western European have appealed to principles of autonomy and self-determination to defend their claims for cultural rights, autonomous governance, or secession. Some of the most impressive political and cultural cases favoring ethnocultural (particularly indigenous) empowerment have been based on "Western" liberal principles of autonomy.[26] Indeed, we cannot make sense of the claims of many ethnocultural groups unless we take autonomy as a central value in their perspectives. Moreover, one of the greatest mistakes that advocates of multiculturalism can make is to romanticize ethnocultural groups and think of them as devoid of internal discrimination and oppression. The truth of the matter is that in many ethnocultural groups, individuals are discriminated against and oppressed on the basis of gender, class, sexual orientation, skin color, religion, and other characteristics. Ethnocultural groups are non-homogeneous, and this internal diversity on many occasions gives rise to marginalization within the groups themselves. One of the best safeguards against this kind of internal discrimination and oppression are Western conceptions of individual rights and respect for the autonomy and moral agency of individuals. The pervasive and sometimes brutal oppression of women in countries like India, Pakistan, and some African, Asian, and Middle Eastern countries also underscores the importance of defending individual autonomy and moral agency. As I discuss below, certain rights protecting the autonomy of individuals should be regarded as basic to any political community. By upholding these rights as fundamental, a political community can arrest the tendency for some of its members to discriminate against and oppress other members on the basis of such characteristics as skin color, sexual orientation, or gender.

Adopting respect for the autonomy of the individual as a fundamental value in multicultural democracies is compatible with a wide range of more specific cultural norms and practices. Simply because autonomy is considered as a basic value does not rule out all, or even a significant number, of forms of cultural diversity. A democratic society can adopt the autonomy of the individual as a bedrock notion while allowing a broad spectrum of religious, linguistic, philosophical, and cultural practices and beliefs. In fact, one of the strongest rationales that we can provide for respecting such diversity is by granting the autonomy of the individual a central place in culturally pluralistic political communities. Rather than undermining cultural diversity, a communally mediated conception of individual autonomy makes it possible to articulate the political, cultural, and economic institutional structures which are necessary for individuals to flourish in self-governing political communities.

Finally, recognizing autonomy as a central value in multicultural democracies is the theoretically and morally appropriate response to the epistemic indeterminacy of alternative visions of the good. That is, assuming that we cannot provide decisive empirical or theoretical arguments to establish the superiority of one or another comprehensive moral vision, when we are confronted with the existence of diverse cultural traditions in a society, the most reasonable position is to grant individuals and communities the freedom and the wherewithal to pursue their conception of the good life. Of course, this does not mean that the political framework of a culturally pluralistic society will be value-neutral; rather, the political institutions of a multicultural democracy will themselves be underpinned by certain overarching values and practices, such as tolerance, intercultural understanding, democratic rights, and freedom of religion. A multicultural democracy should exclude those cultural practices that do not permit individuals and communities to live their lives according to their own moral vision, assuming that this vision falls within the broad boundaries set by the overarching values and practices of liberal democracy that I have articulated. In brief, since there is no question that one or another political framework must be adopted in response to this cultural and moral diversity, granting autonomy pride of place would seem to be the most adequate moral, theoretical, and pragmatic response.

To be sure, it is possible to construe autonomy in an excessively individualistic manner which does not take into account the importance of its communal dimensions. Such conceptions of autonomy will be inadequate as a basis for multicultural constitutional democracies. However, as I have argued, it is possible to construe autonomy in an expansive and communal manner which takes into account the role played by such factors as culture and the self-determination of political communities.

Respect for the autonomy of the individual receives formal recognition in my theory in many ways, including the right of exit, civil rights, democratic rights, and property rights. Since I maintain, in contrast to communitarians, that it is possible for individuals to revise even their most fundamental culturally grounded ends, a just multicultural society should recognize the freedom of individuals to leave their cultural communities. A just culturally pluralistic society should also restrict the obligations and limitations imposed by cultural communities on their members by requiring these communities to conform to the most basic liberal rights. These rights include protection of the physical integrity of individuals, the right of political participation and representation, and (unless an individual willingly and noncoercively chooses to forfeit this right, such as by freely joining a monastery or other religious institution that restricts such rights) freedom of expression.

The rights that a political community should guarantee its members are those that enable them to exercise their moral agency and autonomy, namely, the familiar civil, democratic, and entitlement rights. These rights, some of which are communally mediated, enable individuals to flourish as human beings by exercising their capacity for self-direction and by developing their abilities and potentialities. The category of civil rights includes, among others, the rights of equality before the law, nondiscrimination, freedom of conscience, expression, and religion, while democratic rights include the right to vote, to run for office, to organize political parties, and so forth. Entitlement rights include rights to property, some form of social welfare, and in some cases, support for the preservation of cultural traditions. I take it that the normative justification of civil and democratic rights is well established, and that any democratic society that claims to respect fundamental human rights and the autonomy of individuals will formally, even if not always concretely and consistently, grant these rights to members of the polity. Thus, I will not spend much time in elaborating the justification of the rights in these categories.[27]

The moral basis of entitlement rights, however, is far more controversial. Only recently have cultural rights emerged as rights that liberal constitutional democracies should recognize. Rights to social welfare, on the other hand, have proven to be remarkably vulnerable to political trends and the ideological mood of the citizenry. And even though the moral basis of private property rights is regarded as normatively secure, this is only the case for restricted, not universal, property rights. Even though rights to own private property are some of the most deeply entrenched rights in liberal democracies, they are contingent on their bearer satisfying some criteria for ownership, such as having the financial means for buying property, and, unlike other basic rights, are not granted to individuals solely on the basis of their having status as human beings. In brief, while restricted property rights are widely regarded as well grounded, universal or general rights to property are highly controversial. Given their contested status, I will spend a great deal of time examining cultural and property rights. Another reason that my treatment of property rights will be fairly extensive is that the failure to universalize rights to natural property (i.e., land and natural resources) represents by far the greatest single moral flaw of liberal constitutional democracies. Indeed, I will maintain that this flaw is of such great moral significance that it undermines the very legitimacy of democratic constitutional regimes. Further, conventional views of property ownership in liberal democracies are ill equipped to provide an adequate moral justification of collective property ownership, which is of great importance for the cultural viability of indigenous groups.

My position on economic empowerment, which is necessary for individual autonomy, will be greatly affected by my views of property rights. A major error of advocates of distributive justice is that they take conventional, restricted private property rights for granted. Once they make this move, their enterprise is an uphill struggle, because now they have to introduce moral considerations to limit, and in some cases override, the fundamental normative legitimacy they have already granted to individual rights to property. I will approach the issue of economic empowerment from a more basic level, namely, by challenging conventional conceptions of property ownership. A more secure foundation for economic welfare is needed than that provided by distributive justice. At a theoretical level, it is very difficult to specify in a rigorous manner what justice requires concerning redistribution, while at a practical level the recent experience of countries all over the world has shown how vulnerable welfare rights and policies of redistribution are to political negotiation and ideological shifts. The economic self-reliance required for individual autonomy needs to be protected by the most powerful mechanism available to liberal democracies, namely, the concept of constitutionally protected human rights. This does not mean that distributive justice has no role to play in just multicultural democracies. Its role, however, must be of a supplementary nature; the primary vehicle to economic self-determination should be the recognition that all human beings have a right to natural property and the technological resources needed for its useful employment.

Finally, given that my focus will be on self-determination for ethnocultural groups and their members, to what extent will the theoretical results achieved be generalized to majority societies? While it may appear that focusing on the empowerment of ethnocultural groups and their members rather than on the majority society or the polity as a whole is theoretically limiting, the opposite is actually the case. Examining theories of democratic deliberation, political representation, self-determination, and so forth from the perspective of ethnocultural minorities introduces more demanding standards of theoretical and pragmatic adequacy than examining these theories from the undifferentiated general point of view of the whole society. This is because focusing on the most marginalized, oppressed, or vulnerable groups exposes more clearly and forcefully the weaknesses of the theories under examination. Moreover, since most democracies are culturally pluralistic, the theoretical results we will achieve will be generalizable to most democratic regimes.

In the third chapter we saw how analyzing public deliberation from the perspective of ethnocultural minorities revealed weaknesses and limitations of deliberative democracy that were difficult to identify if we confined our attention to the cultural majority. Similar observations could be made for a wide range of issues in democratic theory. For example, in what follows we will see that standards of adequacy for models of democratic representation can be identified more clearly by examining how ethnocultural groups would fare under such models. Likewise, when examining self-determination, it is more probable that we will arrive at a generally adequate theory of empowerment by analyzing the more serious and numerous obstacles faced by discriminated ethnocultural minorities than by focusing on the situation of the relatively privileged members of the majority or dominant society. This is because whatever problems may confront the latter in attaining self-determination, these same difficulties are likely to be faced by ethnocultural minorities. The reverse, however, is not true, since minorities usually confront obstacles that the majority or dominant group may not even be aware of. In short, examining the fundamental philosophical issues in democratic theory from the multicultural point of view, far from being a disadvantage, introduces higher and more rigorous standards of theoretical adequacy.

My primary purpose at the end of this chapter has been to establish that human flourishing, which I have contended is the central function of political communities and a crucial factor in their justification, is to be basically understood in terms of communal self-determination. This position has important implications for the justification of ethnocultural group claims for autonomous governance, secession, or, in the case of accommodationist groups, for empowerment within mainstream institutions. The justification of these claims now depends on whether the institutional arrangements that these groups seek or possess can reasonably be seen as leading to their self-determination, and therefore to their flourishing as human beings. But before deciding this issue, we need to obtain a more precise understanding of the meaning of self-determination. What, in specific terms, is involved in self-determination? In the chapter that follows I will develop a doctrine for self-determination in multicultural democracies, and in the subsequent chapters I will draw out its implications for accommodationist, autonomist, and secessionist groups.

Notes

1. On this point, see David Boucher and Paul Kelly, "The Social Contract and Its Critics: An Overview," in *The Social Contract From Hobbes to Rawls*, eds. David Boucher and Paul Kelly (London: Routledge, 1994).

2. David Gauthier, *Morals by Agreement* (Oxford: Oxford University Press, 1986).

3. Thomas Hobbes, *Leviathan*, ed. Richard Tuck (Cambridge, UK: Cambridge University Press, 1991), chapter 13.

4. For a detailed account of the ways in which constitutions and other founding documents served to legitimize and formalize relations of domination, see Charles Mills, *The Racial Contract* (Ithaca: Cornell University Press, 1997).

5. Hanna F. Pitkin, "Obligation and Consent, II," in *Readings in Social and Political Philosophy*, ed. Robert Steward (New York: Oxford University Press, 1986), pp. 42–58. See in particular p. 42.

6. John Rawls, *A Theory of Justice* (Cambridge, MA: Harvard University Press, 1971).

7. L. W. Sumner presents this argument against the contractarian position in Chapter 5 of *The Moral Foundation of Rights* (Oxford: Clarendon Press, 1987).

8. John Rawls, *Political Liberalism* (New York: Columbia University Press, 1996).

9. In this context, comprehensive moral doctrines are those that inclusively integrate the numerous components important for living a meaningful life, such as a shared set of values and patterns of behavior, a conception of worthwhile life-options, and a religious perspective.

10. Rawls, *Political Liberalism*, pp. 169–170.

11. Ronald Dworkin, "Foundations of Liberal Equality," in *The Tanner Lectures on Human Values*, vol. XI, ed. Grethe B. Peterson (Salt Lake City: University of Utah Press, 1990), pp. 3–119.

12. In those chapters I will argue that the right to natural property, i.e., to land and natural resources, should be recognized as a fundamental human right. In contemporary constitutional democracies the right to natural property is a *restricted* right, that is, a right that is contingent on economic resources or other factors. I maintain that the manner in which existing property rights were acquired is morally illegitimate, and that the right to natural property (though not to property mediated by human labor) should be universal.

13. Versions of the argument I have presented against contractarian theories are given by Sumner in *The Moral Foundation of Rights*, pp. 151–162 and by Will Kymlicka, "The Social Contract Tradition," in *A Companion to Ethics*, ed. Peter Singer (Oxford: Blackwell Publishers, 1997).

14. Michael Walzer, *Spheres of Justice: A Defense of Pluralism and Equality* (New York: Basic Books, 1983), chapter 2.

15. Ibid., p. 39.

16. Ibid., p. 38.

17. Ibid., p. 38–39.

18. This does not mean that all, or even most, states coincide with nations. As we have already indicated, many contemporary states contain groups who are national minorities. States often accept moral obligations and commitments to individuals in other countries who are similar ethnically to members of the majority society, but neglect or refuse to recognize the same obligations and commitments if those individuals are ethnically related to their national minorities.

19. Walzer, *Spheres of Justice*, p. 62. The position that Walzer defends here clearly assumes that cultural membership, and the existence of cultural communities in which such membership can be sustained, have great value. We will discuss the importance of cultural membership and communities for individual well-being in the next chapter.

20. His position on property rights, for example, could use further development. He makes assumptions regarding access to property that are not clearly justified. This does not mean that his intuitions on these matters are not correct, only that they could stand to be substantiated better.

21. See, for example, Michael Walzer, *On Toleration* (New Haven: Yale University Press, 1997), pp. 27–28.

22. And more generally, concerning the recognition by the members of the majority society of the state's political authority, the realization that political communities are also in important respects cultural communities has important consequences for understanding the basis of political obligation. In contemporary discussions of the latter issue, rationales for our duty to obey the state fall into two broad categories. Volitional theories contend that we acquire or accept our political obligations, while natural duty theories maintain that we have a natural duty to obey the state. Theories in the former category are divided into consent theories and theories based on the principle of fair play. According to consent theories, we acquire political obligations to a political community through an act of consent, while according to fair play theories political obligations are generated by our willing acceptance of benefits made possible by the efforts and sacrifices that others in our political community have made. Natural duty accounts, on the other hand, maintain that, since in general we have a natural duty to promote justice, we are obligated to obey the political institutions of just political communities.

Can consent serve as a basis for justifying political obligations to a particular political community? Or, more precisely—since consent can straightforwardly commit one to accept the legitimacy of a political community through oaths of allegiance like those that occur in a naturalization ceremony—can consent serve as a *general* rationale for the obligation to obey the edicts of a political body even when there has been no willful act of consent? I believe that, in the absence of explicit acts of consent (which are rarely given by most members of the polity), theories based on consent are unlikely to work. As is often pointed out, an act of hypothetical consent is not an act of consent at all, and appeals to the notoriously problematic notion of tacit consent, to the extent that they are plausible at all, will collapse into either fair play accounts, which depend not on an agreement to obey but on a willful acceptance of benefits, or into natural duty accounts, which do not rely on any form of consent to bind one to political authority.

Natural duties, in contrast to obligations, are seen as holding generally for all individuals, regardless of their actions or their special relationship to the individuals, groups, or institutions to which they have the natural duty in question. From a normative standpoint, natural duties, such as throwing a life-preserver to a drowning person or not harming others, are broader in scope but weaker than obligations, in the sense that they are moral requirements only if fulfilling them does not involve great costs to the agent. But construing obedience to the state as a natural duty is problematic because such obedience can have very great costs, such as mandatory military conscription which can lead one to lose one's life. Thus, natural duty accounts face the difficult task of establishing that such strong forms of obedience are morally justified on broad-based but relatively weak natural duties. In addition, the natural duties account has to explain why an individual is bound to obey not all just states, but her own particular state. Since natural duties are generally understood as holding equally for all individuals, what explains my particular special obligations to my country or political community?

It seems that the most promising moral rationale for obedience to a particular political community is the one based on the principle of fair play. The familiar objection to this rationale is that since the goods provided by a political community are public goods, i.e., goods from which everyone benefits, they cannot be understood as being *accepted* (even though they are received) by the citizens. Without willful acceptance, it is argued, an individual cannot be said to be obligated to reciprocate by obeying the state. But once we realize that a political community, insofar as it is also a cultural community, does much more than simply provide services to the citizenry, the whole context of obligation to the state and our fellow citizens changes. If a political community has shaped our very identity and made possible the preservation of the cultural traditions that are crucial for creating the contexts within which our moral agency makes sense, it is misleading to portray what we have received from our political communities merely as services which we were free to reject. While it is possible for an individual to decide to divorce herself from a political/cultural community, in general, evaluating the principle of fair play in terms of the receiving/accepting dichotomy is an inadequate way of understanding the moral obligations involved. Moreover, as George Klosco has argued, it is reasonable to maintain that members of the polity have benefited greatly from goods provided by the state, such as physical security, that can be regarded as essential, so that the argument that the individual did not willingly "accept" the benefits loses its force.

For a discussion of the complex issues involved here, see Jeremy Waldron, "Special Ties and Natural Duties," *Philosophy and Public Affairs*, Volume 22, No.1 (Winter 1993): 3–30, John Rawls, *A Theory of Justice* (Cambridge, MA: Harvard

University Press, 1971), pp. 111–117, and George Klosko, *The Principle of Fairness and Political Obligation* (Savage, MD: Rowman and Littlefield, 1992).

23. For a discussion of this view of autonomy, see Gerald Dworkin, *The Theory and Practice of Autonomy* (Cambridge, UK: Cambridge University Press, 1988), Chapter 1. A higher-order preference is a preference about preferences. For example, I may have a preference or desire to smoke, but may also have a higher-order preference or desire to be healthy. In this case I have a higher-order preference (to be healthy) that contravenes my first-order preference to smoke.

24. I include affective capacities in the definition of autonomy because an individual may have the required intellectual capacities to critically evaluate her first order preferences and yet not have the emotive fortitude to actually carry out and act upon her critical analysis.

25. According to this understanding of autonomy, non-slave, property owning males in ancient Greece had a fairly high degree of autonomy, even though the limitations in their empirical and theoretical knowledge, measured by contemporary standards, would significantly restrict their capacity to arrive at correct decisions in a wide range of areas.

26. See, for example, James Anaya, *Indigenous People in International Law* (Oxford: Oxford University Press, 1993), and Grand Council of the Crees, *Sovereign Injustice: Forcible Inclusion of the James Bay Crees and Cree Territory Into A Sovereign Quebec* (1995).

27. Several good accounts of the normative foundations of these rights, particularly as they relate to democracy, are available. See, for example, David Beetham, *Democracy and Human Rights* (Malden, MA: Polity Press, 1999) and Carlos Nino, *The Ethics of Human Rights* (Oxford: Oxford University Press, 1991) and *The Constitution of Deliberative Democracy* (New Haven: Yale University Press, 1996).

5

The Nature of Self-Determination

Self-determination is a multifaceted notion that involves constraints on institutional orders as well as recognition of various individual, though sometimes collectively mediated, rights. As a normative principle, it is ultimately grounded on conceptions of autonomy and equality. More precisely, self-determination respects human agency and the capacity for self-direction within a universalistic context that acknowledges the equality of all human beings. There are numerous international documents—such as the United Nations Charter, the International Covenant on Economic, Social and Cultural Rights, and the Declaration on the Granting of Independence to Colonial Countries and Peoples[1]—that recognize self-determination as a foundational principle. Indeed, it would be difficult to identify a broad normative principle that commands greater assent (if only formally) across national borders as a fundamental human right.

Despite general formal recognition of the principle of self-determination, there are distinct interpretations of this foundational principle. In the initial sections of this chapter I critically examine some of these interpretations. In the course of criticizing them, I maintain that self-determination for ethnocultural groups should be understood as an integrated, overarching principle, or cluster of rights and resources, which links a number of important human rights with certain social and political institutional patterns. I argue that the different components of self-determination, such as preservation of cultural integrity and economic empowerment, are mutually reinforcing and that, in order to understand self-determination in multicultural societies, we should focus on the complex dynamics between its components. In other words, we should resist reductionist tendencies which isolate one aspect of self-determination and identify it as the core concept needed for understanding this right.

A second insight that will guide my account of self-determination is that an adequate understanding of this notion must take into account the diverse forms that it can take in relation to different ethnocultural groups. For some groups, equitable political representation and control of policies protecting their cultural traditions may be crucial for self-determination, while for other groups territorial control of their ancestral homelands and differentiated citizenship rights may be necessary. I will argue that in determining the meaning of self-determination for a particular enthocultural group, it is of upmost importance that we take into account, *inter alia*, the manner in which it was incorporated into the state, the special factors that may be necessary for that group to exercise self-determination, and its present priorities and aspirations. Thus, at a theoretical level we must make sure that we recognize the relevant historical, cultural, sociopolitical, and material differences between these groups. Conceptually, this involves employing a classificatory scheme that, on the one hand, is sufficiently comprehensive to encompass all of the relevant ethnocultural groups and that, on the other hand, is suitably fine-grained to identify significant differences between them.

The third general stance that I will take regarding ethnocultural group self-determination concerns the impact of globalization on the exercise of this right. Most discussions of self-determination proceed under the assumption that only individuals and states can be the bearers of this right, and that individuals exercise this right within a state-centered context. That is, these discussions assume that ethnocultural self-determination is largely or wholly a matter of minority individuals attaining concessions from the state. I will argue that this view of self-determination neglects not only ethnocultural minorities and other substate groups whose status as distinctive cultural and political collectivities is denied or unrecognized, but also the multiple and overlapping forms of interdependence and association that exist in the contemporary world.[2] Existing states are beset by opposing centripetal and centrifugal forces: on the one hand, by ethnocultural and other substate groups seeking greater self-governance and local control of land and natural resources and, on the other, by regional and global transnational associations and interdependencies. Of particular importance is the entrenchment of the neoliberal economic paradigm on a global level, which is undermining the capacity of states and substate collectivities to practice economic, political, and even cultural self-determination. In order to adequately understand self-determination for ethnocultural groups (as well as for other groups) we need a conception of self-determination that takes into account the increasing number of intra- and international level associations that states and substate communities are forming with one another.

Tamir on National Self-Determination

In order to understand the reasons for adopting the expansive and integrated conception of self-determination for ethnocultural groups I have just outlined, it would be useful to begin by examining Yael Tamir's important discussion of national self-determination in *Liberal Nationalism*.[3] Tamir's principal contention in this book is that nationalist principles of self-governance and cultural self-determination for ethnocultural groups are compatible with liberal principles of freedom and autonomy. She argues that we need not embrace a tribalistic, illiberal conception of nationalism, and that membership in a nation, construed as a collectivity bound by cultural ties, can contribute to the sense of mutual recognition and responsibility necessary for civic participation and the realization of liberal principles of justice.

Tamir distinguishes between two interpretations of the right to self-determination. According to the political interpretation of this right, self-determination involves the right of individuals to participate in the democratic governing of their lives. The rationale underpinning this political right of self-determination is the liberal democratic notion that people have the right to form political associations and to govern themselves in a manner that is free from external dictates, that is, from political directives which are not collectively self-imposed. The bonds that unite the members of the collectivities that bear this political right are the civic bonds characteristic of a political community. The political rights that constitute this conception of political self-determination include the familiar democratic rights of political participation and civil liberties such as rights to freedom of speech and the press.

The other way of understanding self-determination, according to Tamir, is as a cultural right, that is, as a right of cultural groups to create institutions which reflect their distinctive cultural identity and common form of life. In this cultural interpretation of self-determination, individuals are seen as forming collectivities bound by membership in a cultural tradition involving a shared history, values, and practices. Thus, the term "nation" in the cultural view of national self-determination refers not to a nation as a self-governing political body, but to a nation as a group of individuals linked by the enduring, primordial ties of ethnicity, race, religion, language, or national origin. In the cultural view, a nation is not necessarily a state. Tamir maintains that claims for national self-determination are demands for recognition of cultural distinctiveness and for the right to create and maintain a distinct public sphere in which a cultural group can give institutional expression to its traditions, language, norms of behavior, and other forms of cultural identity.

Tamir points out that political and cultural rights of self-determination are distinct rights that are not reducible to one another. Most notably, their rationales are different: The political right of self-determination is justified by reference to liberal democratic tenets of human freedom and self-governance, while the cultural right to national self-determination is a corollary of the right to preservation of cultural tradition. Since the cultural interpretation of the right to self-determination is less familiar, as well as more controversial, than the political interpretation of this right, it is important to be clear about its meaning and justification.

Tamir contends that membership in a cultural or "national" community is a central constitutive factor of personal identity. Seeing oneself as a member of a worthy cultural community grounds self-respect and is crucial for living a satisfying life. Furthermore, choosing to live as a member of a cultural community is not just one more choice among the many choices we make in our lives; rather, it defines who we are in a profound and expansive manner. Culture provides a context of choice which gives meaning to our decisions and life-goals. Without a cultural context of choice, Tamir contends, our life decisions would be arbitrary and devoid of a broader narrative context. Given the role that culture plays in constructing our identity, grounding our sense of self-respect, and providing us with direction in life, it is crucial for well being. A society should therefore respect cultural membership as a fundamental expression of one's agency and autonomy.

According to Tamir, the collective dimension of cultural membership is of crucial importance. The benefits of membership in a culture, such as self-respect and recognition of the value of one's life choices, derive from the collective public expression and shared enjoyment of cultural values, traditions, and practices. It is in the public sphere that people can create the sociopolitical institutions that reflect and maintain their communal forms of life. The enjoyment, sharing, and preservation of the benefits provided by a cultural tradition take place within the context of public institutions. An ethnocultural group's control of the public sphere, Tamir believes, is a necessary condition for the "preservation of a nation as a vital and active community."[4] Thus, the right to preservation of culture involves granting cultural groups the collective wherewithal to develop and maintain their cultural forms of life within social and political institutional settings over which they have effective control.

Tamir's sharp separation between the political and cultural rights of self-determination serves to show that the latter has an independent justification which protects a fundamental interest of individuals, and that this interest is distinct from the political interests, basic as they are, associated with liberal democracy. She states:

> The right to national self-determination cannot be reduced to other human rights, and more particularly, is not synonymous with rights to political participation or with freedoms of speech, press, assembly, and association. . . . Members of national minorities who live in liberal democracies, like the Quebecois and the Indians in Canada, the Aborigines in Australia, or the Basques in France, are not deprived of their freedoms and civil liberties, yet

feel marginalized and dispossessed because they are governed by a political
culture and political institutions imprinted by a culture not their own.[5]

Thus, for Tamir self-determination for cultural groups is not complete
without the right to preservation of cultural tradition. This right, as we
have seen, involves not merely the personal freedom to practice and pass
on one's cultural tradition, but also the rights and means for developing
and maintaining the public institutions where one's communal forms of
life can find collective expression.

For the most part, Tamir's claims regarding self-determination are
sound, but there are several problems with her position. First, it is doubtful whether her account of self-determination is adequate for understanding the struggles for empowerment of certain ethnocultural groups
in multicultural societies. Her account is particularly problematic for understanding groups who seek self-determination but do not want to create a separate and distinct public sphere that stands outside the sociopolitical institutions of the majority society. African-Americans, Latinos,
and mixed-race groups in the U.S., Afro-Asian immigrants in Britain, and
Afro-Arab immigrants in France, for example, by and large have not
tried to create separatist political and social institutions which are different from those of the mainstream society. While they have sought to retain their cultural distinctiveness, their primary concerns have been to secure civil rights, fight racial discrimination, attain equitable political
representation, and remove class obstacles to economic advancement.[6]
Unlike ethnocultural groups with autonomist or separatist aspirations,
these cultural groups have for the most part fought for greater inclusion
in the social and political institutions of the majority society. They have
generally adopted an accommodationist strategy that couples retention
of cultural identity with greater inclusion and participation, rather than a
separatist approach involving the creation of a distinct public sphere
with separate political institutions and a different political culture. To
draw more clearly the distinction between accommodationist and autonomist groups, I will discuss briefly the situation of accommodationist
groups in the U.S., such as African-Americans, Latinos, and mixed-race
groups.

Even though at different historical periods blacks and Latino groups
have established their own organizations and institutions—such as
schools, churches, and civic organizations—they have often done so to
address problems of disempowerment created by official or *de facto* policies of discrimination and exclusion by the majority. During the Jim
Crow period of segregation in the South, for example, blacks formed a
vast network of separate social and political organizations to fulfill needs
that were not met by the institutions of the mainstream society from
which they were excluded. Likewise, from the beginning of the twentieth

century to the 1960s, Mexican-Americans in parts of the Southwest responded to the pervasive segregation they experienced by developing their own social and political organizations and institutions. As the social and political structures that sustained extensive exclusion and segregation were dismantled or diminished in importance, however, these cultural groups shifted their focus to accommodationist strategies involving greater participation and inclusion in mainstream institutions. And, these historical epochs aside, at the present time it is certainly true to say that the primary goals of these groups are essentially accommodationist and not separatist or autonomist.

It is interesting to note that the black and Latino institutions that have retained their separate and distinctive cultural character, such as churches and ethnic civic organizations, are paradigmatic examples of institutions that embody the traditional civil liberties of freedom of religion and association guaranteed by liberal democracy. Such institutions are best understood either as attempts to retain cultural distinctiveness within the parameters of a culturally diverse society or as collective efforts to address socioeconomic and political dilemmas faced by minority ethnocultural communities. They are not attempts to create a separate public sphere that stands outside the political and social institutions of the mainstream society. In fact, black and Latino civic organizations have often functioned as *mediating* institutions designed to attain such goals as greater political representation in mainstream governing bodies and greater inclusion in the economic structures of the majority society.

Tamir's framework for understanding the struggles for self-determination of cultural groups is also inadequate for understanding the goals and aspirations of increasingly prominent mixed-race and mixed-ethnic groups. The rate of inter-marriage, particularly for Latinos and Japanese-Americans, has greatly increased in recent decades, and the size of mixed-race and mixed-ethnic groups is likely to increase in the future. While some of the members of these groups are concerned that their cultural distinctiveness be publicly recognized and respected, their orientations are primarily accommodationist and not separatist or autonomist. This is also the case for those cultural groups who exhibit transnational identities. Dominicans and Peruvians living in the U.S., for example, who retain strong ties with their home countries and with family members who live there, typically do not try to create the separate and alternative public spheres described by Tamir. To be sure, like many Latinos and blacks, cultural groups with transnational identities generally do not want total assimilation into American society, and they do create and maintain their own civil associations. However, as noted above, from the perspective of liberal democracy there is nothing exceptional about these institutions, since they merely exemplify the traditional liberal democratic rights of freedom of association and assembly.

In brief, accommodationist groups like blacks, Latinos, and mixed-race, mixed-ethnic, and transnational-identity groups, do not fit easily into Tamir's framework for understanding cultural self-determination. Tamir's framework works fairly well for ethnocultural groups with autonomist or separatist aspirations, such as the Chechens, the Palestinians, the Scots, and many indigenous groups, but it is likely to distort our understanding of the goals and struggles for self-determination of accommodationist groups who seek a combination of cultural, socioeconomic, and political forms of empowerment within the framework of the majority society.

And there is a second way in which Tamir's account of self-determination is not entirely adequate. By drawing such a sharp distinction between the political and cultural interpretations of the right to self-determination, Tamir makes it difficult to understand the complex dynamics between politics and culture in multicultural democracies. She fails to see that political representation in multicultural democracies—a major component of self-determination—is often deeply affected by cultural factors such as racial discrimination and by judicial decisions that are unfavorable to ethnocultural minorities.

A case in point is the recent trend in U.S. Supreme Court decisions to declare unconstitutional the drawing of congressional districts on the basis of race. In *Shaw vs. Reno*, the U.S. Supreme Court ruled that geographically odd-shaped congressional districts are suspect if they are established for the purpose of grouping racial minorities into the same district. Geographically odd-shaped districts, however, are deemed acceptable if they bring together other interest groups such as tobacco farmers or religious sects. While the court considers being a tobacco farmer or member of a religious sect a legitimate reason for membership in a community of interest whose concerns should be protected, it refuses to grant membership in a cultural group the same consideration. The practice of drawing congressional districts for the purpose of protecting communities of interest has long been recognized as a judicially legitimate practice, yet the court denied this protection to some of the most vulnerable groups in U.S. society.[7]

By sharply dichotomizing cultural and political self-determination, and by maintaining that formal democratic rights of political participation are sufficient for obtaining self-rule, Tamir oversimplifies the complexity of the dynamics between cultural and political issues. In order to understand political and cultural empowerment for ethnocultural minorities, it is necessary to incorporate cultural and political factors within a more expansive conception of self-determination which elucidates the interconnections between them. In the following section I examine the views of an author who analyzes cultural and political rights within a more comprehensive framework for understanding self-determination of ethnocultural minorities in multicultural societies.

Kymlicka on Cultural and Political Self-Determination

In *Multicultral Citizenship: A Liberal Theory of Minority Rights*[8], Will Kym-licka develops an extended defense of the rights of ethnocultural groups based on the foundational values and ideals of liberal democracy. He wants to show that rights that promote the preservation of cultural tradi-tions and that ensure self-governance for cultural minorities are not only compatible with principles of liberalism, but actually promote liberal ideals of freedom and equality. Because Kymlicka's theory of minority rights is the most extensive and plausible treatment of this topic avail-able, it merits our detailed attention.

Even though Kymlicka does not often use the language of self-determi-nation, it is clear that he is concerned with articulating and justifying the rights and institutional structures that would enable ethnocultural mi-norities to control their cultural and political destinies. To this end, he in-troduces three kinds of group-differentiated rights: self-government rights, polyethnic rights, and special representation rights.[9] Self-govern-ment rights may include regional political autonomy, regulation of immi-gration policies in tribal homelands, control of criminal justice institu-tions, and management of land and natural resources. Rights to self-government typically involve a devolution of power to territorially concentrated ethnocultural groups. These rights are seen as permanent rights that are an inherent corollary to self-determination, and not as temporary measures to eliminate inequitable representation or socio-economic disadvantage. Polyethnic rights involve formal protections that ensure that cultural groups can maintain their cultural practices and pre-serve their cultural norms and beliefs without limiting their successful functioning in the social and economic institutions of the majority soci-ety. Such rights may include language policies in the schools to help pre-serve minority cultural traditions, exemptions to school dress-codes to allow the wearing of religious attire, and state funding for minority arts and cultural events. Special representation rights are intended to rectify minority group political under-representation in governing bodies. These rights may include guaranteed minority seats in legislatures, veto power on policies that directly affect ethnocultural minorities, and the formation of power-sharing arrangements in which ethnocultural mi-norities are provided equitable political partnership.

Kymlicka notes that at first sight group-differentiated rights seem to violate principles of equal treatment because they grant special privileges to ethnocultural groups, sometimes at the expense of the majority society. Moreover, since such rights are based on cultural membership, they vio-late the liberal principle of state neutrality regarding individual choice of cultural tradition. In liberal democracies, individuals can associate freely among themselves to support and practice any cultural tradition of their choosing, and it is not the business of the state to support any particular cultural tradition. Like adopting a religion, following a cultural tradition should be an individual private decision, and the state should not interfere in the cultural marketplace by promoting or prohibiting the preservation of any particular culture. Any culture worthy of preservation will find voluntary adherents, while a decaying culture will wither away as a result of a lack of willing followers.

Despite the apparent illiberal nature of group-differentiated rights, Kymlicka makes a convincing case for the view that these rights, rather than violating principles of liberal democracy, are actually consistent with the conceptions of justice that underpin this political perspective. He evaluates three types of argument that could be used to justify group-differentiated rights—arguments based on equality, historical agreements, and the value of cultural diversity—and concludes that each of these arguments, particularly the equality argument, can contribute to the justification of group-differentiated rights. Jointly, these rights comprise an essential part of the structural guarantees that enable cultural minorities to attain self-determination.

In addition to group-differentiated rights, Kymlicka discusses a variety of electoral systems designed to provide group representation for cultural minorities. He correctly recognizes that the institutional guarantees granted by formal democratic rights are not always sufficient to ensure that minority groups are represented fairly in the state's governing bodies. Thus Kymlicka's approach for cultural and political self-determination involves both group-differentiated rights and special electoral systems which allow for equitable minority political representation. Given the seemingly comprehensive nature of Kymlicka's dual strategy of group-differentiated rights and special electoral systems for achieving cultural and political self-determination for ethnocultural groups, it is important to break down the different phases of his argument and evaluate its overall adequacy.

The Value of Cultural Membership

Before we can understand the rationale for rights that safeguard the preservation of culture and that grant cultural groups the wherewithal to maintain their existence as distinctive peoples, it is necessary to appreciate the value of cultural membership. Kymlicka's strategy for justifying group-differentiated rights depends on establishing that cultural membership is sufficiently important to warrant protection by the mechanism of formal rights. He argues that in multicultural societies the exercise of freedom and the promotion of equality, which are fundamental ideals of liberal democracies, can be achieved only by protecting the right of ethnocultural minorities to maintain their cultures and control their political destinies. His conception of group-differentiated rights is intended to be broad enough to protect the fundamental interests of the different groups that may comprise a multicultural society.

Kymlicka begins his defense of group-differentiated rights by explaining that by the term "culture" he means societal culture, which he defines in the following way:

> ... the term 'culture' has been used to cover all manner of groups, from teenage gangs to global civilizations. The sort of culture that I will focus on, however, is a *societal* culture—that is, a culture which provides its members with meaningful ways of life across the full range of human activities, including social, educational, religious, recreational, and economic life, encompassing both public and private spheres. These cultures tend to be territorially concentrated, and based on a shared language.
>
> I have called these 'societal cultures' to emphasize that they involve not just shared memories or values, but also common institutions and practices. . . . in the modern world, for a culture to be embodied in social life means that it must be institutionally embodied—in schools, media, economy, government, etc.[10]

Kymlicka maintains that societal cultures are of central importance for the exercise of freedom, and that liberals should take an interest in protecting them. In order to make his case, he examines the conception of freedom as understood in the liberal tradition. He points out that a defining feature of liberalism is that it grants individuals a wide range of freedoms for leading their lives. Liberalism allows people to lead their lives "from the inside," that is, according to values and beliefs they endorse. In addition, individuals are allowed to rationally assess their conceptions of the good on the basis of new experiences and information, and revise their views of the good life accordingly. This rational assessment is made possible through such means as a liberal education and such liberties as freedom of association and expression.[11] Thus, the capacity to pursue one's conception of the good requires, in the liberal tradition, not only certain liberties, but also the capacities that enable individuals to critically assess and revise their values and life-goals.

Kymlicka then argues that the exercise of freedom involves making choices between options that are provided and made meaningful by our societal culture. The meaningfulness of alternative ends derives from the significance that our culture attaches to them. The shared vocabulary comprised of the language, conventions, and history of our societal culture provide the context within which life-options make sense. By understanding the cultural narratives created by the resources of our cultural traditions, we are able to make intelligent judgments concerning the import of our life-experiences and the value of life-options.[12] Without a cultural framework for identifying and evaluating our life-options, our choices would be arbitrary and devoid of broader import. In brief, our societal culture provides the institutionally embodied cultural resources for meaningfully exercising our freedom and moral agency.

Kymlicka continues by arguing that merely having access to some societal culture or other does not suffice to preserve our capacity for freedom and meaningful choice-making, because of the deep connections we have to our *own* culture. He maintains that membership in our particular culture shapes our self-identity in profound and comprehensive ways. For instance, our primary sense of identification and belonging depends on cultural membership because, unlike the sense of identification we develop as the result of our personal accomplishments, cultural belonging is more secure insofar as it is simply based on who we are. Even though the sense of self-worth derived from our endeavors is important, cultural membership is less vulnerable to the vicissitudes of success and failure that necessarily accompany such endeavors.[13] Cultural membership is primordial and provides a safe social haven for "effortless belonging."[14] This secure form of belonging, Kymlicka points out, is important for an individual's well-being.

Furthermore, cultural membership has a "high social profile" because it affects how others perceive and respond to us. This is particularly true in hierarchically stratified societies in which membership in a particular cultural group is associated with a certain social status. Kymlicka maintains that the public nature of cultural group membership means that our self-respect is affected by the esteem which others have for our cultural group. If a cultural group is not respected, the dignity and self-respect of its members will be negatively affected. Finally, Kymlicka calls our attention to James Nickel's observation that retaining one's culture is important for intergenerational continuity.[15] According to Nickel, many people value the bonds that are created when cultural traditions are transmitted between grandparents, parents, and their children. Such bonds strengthen familial solidarity and provide a deep sense of acceptance and belonging.

From these observations on cultural membership, Kymlicka concludes that because a societal culture provides a context for meaningful choice and supports self-identity, it is very important for people to maintain their societal culture and their connection to it. But is the preservation of societal cultures purely a private matter or does the state play a role in the maintenance of these cultures? As observed earlier, conventional wisdom holds that it is not a legitimate function of the liberal state to support or hinder any societal culture, and that the proper role of the state is to maintain neutrality while providing the liberties needed for individuals to make their own choices regarding cultural membership.

Kymlicka here makes a point of decisive importance, namely, that state neutrality concerning the preservation of societal cultures is not possible. The state, he argues, cannot avoid making decisions concerning which language to use in official state transactions, which public holidays to observe, which state symbols to use, and so forth. In making these decisions, the state directly affects the capacity of cultural groups within its boundaries to preserve their culture. Since a societal culture is one whose language, traditions, and conventions are institutionally embodied, the state's decisions regarding, for example, which language will be used in such institutions as the schools and the courts will strengthen the societal culture of a particular group while marginalizing the societal cultures of other groups. As Kymlicka points out, a cultural tradition is much less likely to survive if it is not institutionally embodied.[16] The unavoidability of state involvement in the maintenance or marginalization of cultures within its boundaries raises an important dilemma: What institutional guarantees, if any, should the state provide cultural groups to protect their fundamental interest in preserving their cultural tradition?

Justifying Group-Differentiated Rights

Kymlicka maintains that given the importance of retaining one's cultural tradition for exercising freedom and supporting self-identity, the state should grant cultural groups the necessary group-differentiated rights to enable them to maintain their culture. Without such state support, minority groups will not have the same opportunities as majority members to preserve their culture. The three kinds of group-differentiated rights he introduces—self-government, polyethnic, and special representation rights—safeguard the needs and interests of vulnerable cultural groups by eliminating the arbitrary and systematic disadvantages they face in the cultural and political spheres. It is important to note that from the outset Kymlicka realizes the interconnectedness of cultural and political issues, and that the group-differentiated rights he proposes are designed to protect cultural as well as political interests.

In order to determine which ethnocultural groups merit which rights, and to understand how these rights are justified by reference to the varying circumstances of these groups, it is helpful to attend to Kymlicka's distinction between national minorities and ethnic groups. National minorities are formerly self-governing groups which were incorporated by settler societies through conquest, annexation, or federation. Ethnic groups consist of immigrant groups who left their countries of origin to integrate into a new society.[17] Self-government rights are relevant for national minorities, while polyethnic rights generally apply to ethnic groups. Special representation rights can apply to either ethnic groups or national minorities. When applied to the latter, these rights are generally understood as a corollary to self-government rights.

As mentioned earlier, Kymlicka believes that group-differentiated rights can be justified on the basis of considerations of equality, historical agreements, and the value of cultural diversity. The most important of these is the equality argument, which I examine first.

The underlying norm for the equality argument is a powerful one indeed, namely, that the state should treat all of its citizens with equal respect and consideration. For national minorities, the relevant conception of equality concerns equal access to one's societal culture. Without group-differentiated rights, the societal cultures of national minorities are vulnerable to economic and political decisions by the majority. For instance, by breaking up a territory which had historically been held in common by an indigenous group, a majority society can make it easier for that group to lose its collective hold on the land. One of the principal ways in which indigenous people have lost their homelands has been through the strategy of granting tribal members individual land titles which were then bought by wealthy members of the dominant society. Because indigenous peoples have profound spiritual, material, and social connections to the land, their capacity to preserve their cultural traditions is greatly undermined by the loss of their communally owned territory. Similarly, state policies that forced Indian children to be educated in schools where only English was used threatened the ability of indigenous groups to maintain their societal culture. Since most indigenous groups rely on oral traditions to transmit their knowledge, songs, rituals, and historical narratives, the loss of their language represents a serious impediment to the preservation of their cultural traditions.

Group-differentiated rights—such as collective property rights to tribal homelands or rights to control educational policies—ensure that national minorities have the same opportunity as the majority society to preserve their societal culture. Given the importance of maintaining one's culture, to deny national minorities the right to preserve and enjoy their own cultural traditions represents a serious injustice. Often the members of the dominant society have difficulty appreciating the need for group-differentiated rights because, as members of the majority, they can simply take for granted that their culture will be institutionally protected by the state. However, the situation is different for national minorities because the state, even without intending to, can undermine the viability of minority societal cultures through its decisions to provide institutional support to the majority culture only.

Kymlicka indicates that the majority cannot justifiably demand that national minorities give up their culture and assimilate into the majority society, not only because of the deep bonds they have to their own culture, but also because national minorities were not voluntarily incorporated into the state. Unlike immigrants who voluntarily left their home countries to integrate into a new society, national minorities—such as the Maori of New Zealand, Aboriginals in Australia, and Native Americans and Puerto Ricans in the U.S.—lived in their own self-governing communities with their own socioeconomic and political institutions before their involuntary incorporation into their respective states. A national minority, as much as the majority society, has a right to preserve the societal culture that it never relinquished and that is essential for its attainment of the good life.

For ethnic groups, the equality argument justifying group-differentiated rights takes a different form. Group-differentiated rights equalize their opportunities to integrate into the mainstream society without discrimination or prejudice. Many of these groups want to become an integral part of the majority society while retaining a measure of their traditional cultures. This is why they seek polyethnic rights that would enable them to exercise their cultural practices and beliefs without hindering their ability to function in the socioeconomic and political institutions and organizations of the mainstream society. For instance, when Sikhs in Canada request that they be exempt from dress-codes in police departments so they can wear their turbans or when Jews in Britain seek exemptions from Sunday closing legislation, they are demanding that their religious needs be taken into account to the same extent as the religious needs of the Christian majority.[18] In predominantly Christian countries, state holidays and official dress codes for many organizations and institutions implicitly follow Christian customs. Such practices can place religious minorities at a disadvantage relative to the members of the majority society. Group-differentiated rights can rectify this inequality by making adjustments in official state policies that were designed with the needs and interests of the majority in mind. As Kymlicka astutely notes, these rights, rather than having a Balkanizing effect, promote the social integration of ethnic groups by equalizing their capacity to function effectively within the institutions of the majority society. This latter point is important, because it is an effective reply to the greatly exaggerated fears that are sometimes expressed in response to the advocacy of polyethnic rights.

Kymlicka believes that arguments based on historical agreements and the value of cultural diversity can also be used, *albeit* to a lesser extent than equality arguments, to justify group-differentiated rights. Historical agreements sometimes articulate the terms under which national minorities came under the legitimate authority of a given state. Treaties and confederation agreements, for example, may specify the jurisdiction that the federal government and the states, provinces, cantons, or other subnational bodies have over a variety of areas, such as language, education, taxation, and criminal justice. Legal and moral considerations would indicate that such agreements should be respected, assuming that they were not made under coercion or conditions of substantial inequality in bargaining power.

Of course, in many instances agreements were not made under equitable conditions and this, according to Kymlicka, creates problems concerning their interpretation. It is difficult to determine how to adjust for conditions of inequitable bargaining power, duress, ignorance, or differences in the meanings of terms. In addition, some agreements may now be unfair due to changing circumstances. According to Kymlicka:

> The land claims recognized in various treaties may be too much, or too little, given changes in the size and lifestyle of indigenous communities. The powers given to Quebec in 1867 may no longer be appropriate in an age of telecommunications. To stick to the letter of historical agreements when they no longer meet the needs of minorities seems wrong.[19]

Because of these difficulties with historical agreements, Kymlicka believes that we should not rely solely on such agreements to defend group-differentiated rights. But even though by themselves historical agreements cannot bear the burden of providing a normative justification for group-differentiated rights, they sometimes have an important role to play in justifying these rights.

The final argument that Kymlicka considers for the justification of group-differentiated rights appeals to the value of cultural diversity. According to this argument, cultural diversity is important because it increases the cultural resources and ways of life available to the members of society. Different cultural groups embody alternative ways of making life meaningful and provide different approaches for adapting to unforeseen circumstances. Indigenous peoples, for example, can provide us with living, workable models of environmentally sustainable living. Indigenous ways of life can be used to critique and transform Western conceptions of nature which are increasingly recognized as environmentally destructive and unsustainable. Likewise, non-Western religions can provide us with alternative ways of conceptualizing our relationship to the transcendent. Religious diversity can expand the range of options for living a spiritually fulfilling life, particularly for individuals who may find the religious perspectives of the majority society restrictive or spiritually alienating.

Kymlicka believes that the benefits of cultural diversity have limited potential for justifying group-differentiated rights. He points out that the benefits of cultural diversity "to the majority are spread out thinly and widely, whereas the costs for particular members of the majority are sometimes quite high."[20] That is, while some members of the majority may benefit from the availability of diverse cultural resources, the preservation of particular cultural groups through the use of group-differentiated rights may restrict in important ways the freedom of other members of the majority. Granting control of language policies to French speakers in Quebec, for instance, can disadvantage unilingual anglophones by making it difficult for them to obtain publicly funded education in English. Likewise, non-Indians living on Indian controlled land may be unable to vote in local elections. Kymlicka maintains that group-differentiated rights that restrict the freedoms of members of the majority society are justifiable only if they are necessary to prevent the even greater sacrifices to which minority group members would be subjected if they were denied such rights.[21]

Furthermore, the cultural diversity argument is questionable as a justification for group-differentiated rights for national minorities, because preserving the culture of these groups does not necessarily expand the range of cultural resources for majority group members. Kymlicka points out that moving from one societal culture to another is a difficult and uncommon practice, and that cultural diversity is easier to take advantage of if it exists *within* a culture. That is, when ethnic groups integrate into the majority society and thereby enrich it through their cultural resources, it is much easier for members of the majority to access and benefit from these cultural contributions. Maintaining the cultures of national minorities, however, is a different matter because national minority cultures are less likely to enrich the lives of majority group members due to the distinct public spheres in which such cultures will be expressed. Thus, Kymlicka argues, the cultural diversity argument is ineffective as a general defense of group-differentiated rights because, while it may be plausible as a defense for polyethnic rights, it is not convincing as a justification for national minority rights.

For these reasons, Kymlicka believes that arguments for group-differentiated rights based on the value of cultural diversity are not sufficient, by themselves, to justify these rights. Nevertheless, he believes that there are important benefits to cultural diversity, but that these are best seen as desirable consequences derived from protecting the cultural rights of minority groups, rather than as providing the primary justification for group-differentiated rights.

Kymlicka on Group Representation

As noted earlier, Kymlicka realizes that the formal guarantees provided by group-differentiated rights are not sufficient for bringing about self-determination for ethnocultural groups. He is aware of the fact that group-differentiated rights need to be interpreted before being institutionally implemented, and that, more generally, majority and minority cultural groups need to engage in ongoing political negotiations to resolve differences in needs and interests. In order for the outcomes of these political processes to be fair, however, it is essential that cultural minorities be equitably represented in governing bodies and judicial institutions. Political under-representation of cultural minorities is a fact of life in many liberal democracies.[22] This lack of equitable political representation often means that minority concerns do not receive a fair hearing or commensurately influence political decisions and policies.

Kymlicka maintains that numerous differences in the political cultures of countries, the voting patterns of electorates, and the needs and interests of cultural minorities make it very difficult to develop a general theory of group representation. He notes that "the results of particular electoral mechanisms are notoriously context-specific,"[23] and that electoral reforms can have very different consequences in different countries. For these reasons, rather than proposing a general theory of minority representation, he focuses on the more modest tasks of establishing that group representation is not necessarily undemocratic or illiberal and on examining some of the problems that arise in connection with group representation.

Kymlicka begins by arguing that the notion of group representation is not as foreign to liberal democratic ideas of political representation as one might suppose. He points to the long-standing tradition in many liberal democracies, including Canada and the U.S., of drawing the boundaries of constituencies so that they reflect communities of interest consisting of, for example, rural residents, workers, or religious groups. In Canada there is explicit legal recognition of the idea that boundary-drawing procedures should be employed so that territorially concentrated communities of interest can be adequately represented. The reality of voting procedures, he states, indicates that people vote as members of communities of interest, and the *de jure* or *de facto* recognition by democratic governments of this fact shows that political representation in these governments has never been understood as a purely individualistic process. In determining the fairness of political representation, it is the interests of groups that is of primary importance, and not the interests of particular individuals.

In fact, argues Kymlicka, protecting the interests of disadvantaged groups can be seen as a logical extension of the rationale underpinning the idea used in some countries of special Senate representation for smaller regions. The Australian and the U.S. Senate, for example, grant states an equal number of representatives regardless of population. He states:

> The argument for special regional representation in the Senate assumes that the significant economic and cultural diversity between regions leads to different and sometimes conflicting interests; that the interests of smaller or poorer regions might not be effectively represented under a pure system of

majority rule. . . . But each of these claims can also be made for various social groups; the diverse conditions and experiences of men and women, anglophones and Hispanics, whites and blacks, immigrants and indigenous
peoples, . . . give rise to different and sometimes conflicting interests; and
the interests of smaller or poorer groups might not be represented under a
system of majority rule.[24]

The allowances made for the fair representation of minority interests
show that the idea of group representation has a long history and is of
central importance in liberal democracies such as Canada, Australia, and
the U.S.

Kymlicka believes that the most plausible defense of group representation for ethnocultural groups is based on "contextual arguments," that is,
arguments based on the particular historical and present circumstances
of specific cultural groups. These contextual arguments are divided into
two categories: those based on systematic discrimination and those based
on self-government rights. According to the systematic discrimination argument, the discrimination and oppression that some groups have experienced have seriously hindered their capacity to participate effectively
in the political process.[25] The legacy of discrimination experienced by
some cultural groups includes formal institutional barriers to political
participation, lack of access to education and other forms of human resource development, and non-institutionalized cultural practices of exclusion and marginalization. Kymlicka maintains that justifications of
group representation based on systematic discrimination, insofar as they
are measures to rectify existing barriers to political participation, are best
understood as temporary measures, and not as permanent rights granted
to cultural minorities. The Voting Rights Act in the U.S., for example,
which endorses the drawing of congressional districts to increase the representation of Blacks and Latinos, depends for its periodic renewal on the
continued existence of obstacles hindering the political empowerment of
Blacks and Latinos.

Group representation based on the right to self-government is different
in several ways from group representation based on systematic discrimination. First, when rights to self-governance are used by national minorities to justify special policies of group representation, these policies are
seen not as temporary measures to remove barriers created by past discrimination, but as permanent entitlements that are corollaries of self-
governance. Since national minorities claim that they are distinct peoples
with a right to self-determination, they maintain that, for example, guaranteed representation in federal bodies that legislate in areas affecting
them is a logical consequence of their right to govern their own affairs.
Such guaranteed representation is important for safeguarding their political and cultural autonomy.

Second, group representation based on self-government rights will sometimes involve *reduced* influence or representation (at the federal level) of national minorities in bodies that legislate in areas not affecting them. This restriction in political participation in the passage of policies that do not directly apply to them is the other side of the partial autonomy coin. Just as rights to self-government restrict potentially unjust federal jurisdiction over national minorities, it would be unfair, for instance, for the Quebecois to cast votes on immigration legislation that does not apply to Quebec. As Kymlicka indicates:

> . . . self-government for a national minority seems to entail guaranteed representation on *intergovernmental* bodies, which negotiate, interpret, and modify the division of powers, but reduced representation on *federal* bodies which legislate in areas of purely federal jurisdiction from which they are exempted.[26]

After discussing the systematic discrimination and the self-government justifications for group-based representation, Kymlicka identifies what he considers the most serious problems afflicting this form of representation. Perhaps the most intractable of these problems is the question of which groups should be represented. Kymlicka suggests that the same criteria that was used for justifying group representation could be employed to identify which groups should be entitled to such representation, namely, self-government rights and systematic discrimination or disadvantage. Groups with claims to self-government, he says, are more easily identifiable than groups who have been subjected to systematic disadvantages. There are many ways in which groups can be disadvantaged, he notes, and it is not clear whether we can rank in a nonarbitrary way the different forms of disadvantage or discrimination to which different groups have been, and continue to be, subjected. Kymlicka recognizes that the problem of identifying which disadvantaged groups merit special forms of representation is formidable, and thus far unresolved.

Even if we could identify in a nonarbitrary way which disadvantaged groups merit group representation, we must still determine how many seats a group should have in the relevant governing bodies. Kymlicka distinguishes two common approaches to this issue, namely, proportional and threshold representation. According to the proportional representation approach, a group is adequately represented in a governing body only when the number of representatives from that group reflects the proportion of group members in the general population. The threshold approach maintains that demographic accuracy it is not necessary, and that it is enough that members of the relevant group hold a sufficient number of seats to ensure effective expression of their needs and interests. Kymlicka maintains that determining whether proportional or threshold representation is more appropriate in a particular case may depend on the nature of the relevant political institutions and on the broader political context in which they function. That is, if a legislative body employs a consensual process—such as a consociational or supermajority approach—for arriving at political decisions, a threshold number of group representatives may be sufficient, while a system based on simple majority voting rules may require proportional representation. In some cases, effective representation may require an even greater number of representatives than indicated by proportional representation, as in situations in which the number of minority group members is so small that they can be simply ignored or excluded, or in political contexts in which cultural groups are so polarized that there is little possibility of compromise or mutual understanding.

The final problem with group-based representation that Kymlicka discusses is that of political accountability. This issue concerns the mechanisms by which we can ensure that group representatives actually serve the interests of the group they purportedly represent. Here again Kymlicka identifies two ways of addressing the problem. According to the approach taken by the Maori in New Zealand, a separate electoral list is drawn so that only the Maori can elect certain legislators. Since these legislators are elected by the Maori only, they are wholly accountable to them. In this approach, it is accountability and not the cultural characteristics of the candidate that is crucial, because it is entirely possible (though improbable) for a non-Maori to be elected to one of these seats. The Maori model is used primarily for cultural minorities that are numerically small or territorially dispersed.

According to the second model, the focus is on the characteristics of the candidates. In this model, the accountability problem is resolved when candidates are elected that reflect the characteristics—such as ethnic, religious, or linguistic background—of the cultural group. Candidates in this model are not elected just by the members of the relevant group, but by the electorate as a whole. This approach assumes that because the elected officials share certain characteristics, experiences, and perspectives with the underrepresented group, they will faithfully advocate for their needs and interests. However, as Kymlicka points out, since these officials are chosen by the general electorate, it is not clear in what sense they would be accountable solely or even primarily to the ethnocultural group they purportedly represent. In fact, there is reason to think that they would not want to alienate the general voting population that elected them, including members of the dominant groups, by advocating too strongly for the concerns of their ethnocultural group. Kymlicka is skeptical that this second form of representation adequately resolves the accountability problem, and he leans in favor of the Maori model, even while recognizing that according to this approach it may be possible for cultural groups to end up not being represented by one of their own members. Kymlicka concludes his discussion by noting that even though no model of group-based representation has successfully resolved the three problems he identifies, these forms of representation do not violate principles of justice or of liberal democracy, and that they are worthy of careful consideration.

Evaluating Kymlicka's Theory of Self-Determination

Before evaluating the adequacy of Kymlicka's account of cultural and political self-determination for ethnocultural groups, it is important to appreciate the significance of his achievement. By making a plausible case for group-differentiated rights and group-based representation that is grounded on liberal ideals, he provides a much needed corrective to traditional theories of liberal democracy that neglect the impact of ethnocultural diversity. A theory of justice for liberal democracies cannot possibly be adequate or complete without an account of how ethnocultural groups affect the conceptualization of such fundamental issues as the nature of political rights. Since ethnocultural conflict is one of the most significant sources of tension and instability in multicultural democracies, the failure to take cultural diversity into account is not merely a theoretical shortcoming, it also reflects an inability to come to terms with one of the most significant problems facing democratic societies.

In order to understand the overall structure of Kymlicka's scheme, it would be instructive to briefly contrast his position with Tamir's. In contrast to Tamir, Kymlicka does not sharply divide political and cultural self-determination. His conception of group-differentiated rights includes both cultural and political rights, and his emphasis on group-based representation is partly motivated by the realization that cultural rights alone are unlikely to ensure that ethnocultural groups can control either their cultural or political destinies. Thus, he recognizes the complex dynamics involved in the ongoing intercultural negotiation of differences in needs and interests, and the continued vulnerability of cultural minorities to the decisions of the majority.

Moreover, Kymlicka's position is much more comprehensive and fully developed than Tamir's. He recognizes the diverse goals and varying historical circumstances of different ethnocultural groups, and distinguishes clearly between the kinds of culture-based rights merited by different groups. Earlier we observed that Tamir's account, while useful for understanding the goals of national minorities, was not helpful for understanding the case of accommodationist ethnic groups, that is, cultural groups who want to integrate and function within the socioeconomic and political institutions of the majority society while retaining aspects of their cultural traditions. Kymlicka recognizes the important distinction between national minorities and ethnic groups, and gives due recognition to their different conceptions of self-determination by introducing the notions of polyethnic and self-government rights. Polyethnic rights address the needs of accommodationist groups, who unlike national minorities do not want to create a distinct public sphere for the institutionalization of their societal culture. To address the needs of national minorities, Kymlicka introduces the concept of self-government rights. These rights typically promote the self-determination of national minorities by devolving power to the regions where they are concentrated or, in the case of territorially dispersed groups, by developing political mechanisms that allow them to duly influence the formation of policies that affect them.

For Kymlicka, cultural self-determination goes hand in hand with political self-determination. He recognizes that the political and cultural components of self-determination are mutually reinforcing and that self-determination for ethnocultural groups should not be confined or reduced to a single sociocultural or political dimension. He also resists reductionist attempts to understand the needs and goals of ethnocultural groups by using classificatory standards that gloss over important differences between them. In these respects, Kymlicka's position conforms in important ways with the conception of ethnocultural self-determination that I described at the beginning of this chapter. As we will recall, I stipulated three conditions that an adequate conception of self-determination for ethnocultural groups should observe. First, I proposed that self-determination should be understood as an integrated principle linking cultural, political, and economic forms of empowerment. Second, I maintained that self-determination should take into account the diverse goals of the different ethnocultural groups seeking control over their destinies. Third, I suggested that the agents who exercise self-determination should include not only individuals and sovereign states, but also the substate groups and communities who are forming, in an increasingly globalized environment, multiple and overlapping intra- and international associations with other groups, communities, and states.

Kymlicka's theory of group-differentiated rights fully accords with the second stipulation. He clearly recognizes the relevant distinctions between national minorities and accommodationist groups, and makes the appropriate adjustments in his theory of minority rights. Moreover, to the extent that he realizes that cultural and political self-determination are interconnected and mutually supportive, he also partly observes the first stipulation. I say partly because he does not deal systematically with the third form of empowerment, namely, economic empowerment. Likewise, concerning the third stipulation for self-determination, Kymlicka does not provide an analysis of how ethnocultural groups can achieve self-empowerment at the level of intrastate and international associations. He does not take sufficiently into account recent global economic and political developments that undermine the capacity of ethnocultural groups, and political and cultural communities in general, to control their domestic economic and political affairs.

Kymlicka's distinction between national minorities and ethnic groups, while very useful for making ethnocultural group distinctions that have been neglected by most political philosophers, is not sufficiently precise to capture important distinctions between ethnocultual groups that are relevant for their self-determination. As we shall see in the next two chapters, the classificatory system that I have proposed, consisting of three major categories comprising five kinds of ethnocultural groups, is more adequate for understanding the meaning and justification of self-determination for these groups.

In short, even though Kymlicka's theory of minority rights goes a long way towards satisfying the proposed stipulations for a comprehensive theory of self-determination for ethnocultural groups, it nevertheless falls short in the ways indicated. In the section that follows I develop my critique of Kymlicka by elaborating on the reasons why it is important for an adequate theory of ethnocultural self-determination to take systematic account of economic factors. I will argue that in many cases the absence of economic empowerment can seriously hinder the exercise of cultural and political self-determination, and that material inequalities undermine the cultural and political autonomy of ethnocultural groups in distinctive ways. I will conclude the chapter by commenting briefly on the reasons why it is important to consider systematically the effects of globalization on ethnocultural group self-determination. I will also identify the issues that need to be considered and resolved in order for a theory of ethnocultural group rights to satisfy this third stipulation concerning self-determination.

The Importance of Economic Empowerment for Cultural and Political Self-Determination

Even though scholars who specialize in normative issues concerning ethnocultural groups would no doubt acknowledge that economic factors are an important concern of just multicultural liberal democracies, they have not provided a systematic analysis of such factors. Authors such as Charles Taylor, Yael Tamir, and Will Kymlicka, for example, have not tried to examine systematically the impact of material factors on the cultural and political self-determination of cultural minorities. Though it is difficult to fathom the precise reasons for their neglect of economic considerations, the assumption underlying their position seems to be that, while of general importance, economic issues do not raise special problems for the theorist concerned with understanding the self-determination of ethnocultural groups in liberal democracies. That is, the assumption appears to be that ethnocultural diversity does not give rise to any distinctive economic issues that do not arise for the theorist concerned with the general problems of economic justice in liberal democracies. Thus, according to this line of reasoning, questions of economic justice, while of general importance, are not properly the concern of the philosopher trying to develop a theory of minority rights for multicultural liberal democracies.

I believe that the assumption underlying this way of thinking is mistaken, and that neglecting the impact of material factors on ethnocultural self-determination represents a serious shortcoming in the theories of those authors seeking to ground minority rights within the normative framework of liberalism. I would contend that neither cultural nor political self-determination for ethnocultural groups can be understood or achieved without considering how economic factors affect these forms of empowerment, and that a theory of minority rights in liberal democracies must therefore take systematic account of these factors.

Economic Inequalities and the Loss of Cultural Autonomy

Significant material inequalities between cultural groups in a multicultural society can undermine the capacity of disadvantaged groups to make autonomous choices in the cultural sphere. Autonomous choice-making regarding culture involves making individual and collective decisions that affect one's life and the fate of one's cultural group. Such decisions may concern the preservation and intergenerational transmission of cultural traditions, the proud acceptance of one's cultural self-identity, and the desired degree of assimilation into the majority culture. Because cultural membership has a "high social profile," these decisions can be greatly affected by socioeconomic status and the corresponding public perceptions of one's cultural group. When membership in one's cultural group is associated with lower economic and social standing, and when the option of cultural assimilation is available, individuals will generally be more reluctant (other things being equal) to retain their cultural identity.[27] Members of disadvantaged cultural groups may feel ashamed of embracing their culture, and may justifiably believe that being perceived as a member of an "inferior" group will place them in a position of socioeconomic disadvantage relative to the members of the dominant culture. In these situations, retention of one's culture may come at a price that is too high for some individuals to pay.

A case in point concerns Mexican-Americans living in U.S.-Mexico border areas. Many of these Chicanos are keenly aware of the negative stereotypes and images associated with being Mexican. They know that Mexicans have traditionally been characterized as, among other things,

lazy, immoral, dumb, untrustworthy, envious, uncouth, poor, and vio-
lent. In comparison to the Anglo society, Mexicans have traditionally
been perceived as an "inferior race." Standards of beauty, of moral recti-
tude, and of social taste and grace are based on Anglo characteristics, and
thus to be Mexican is by implication to fall short of these standards. Some
Mexican-Americans therefore make great efforts to deny their cultural
heritage and embrace Anglo culture. They refuse to teach their children
Spanish, despite the great advantages of knowing Spanish in an area that
is heavily populated by people of Mexican descent, and they anglicize
the pronunciation of their names in an effort to appear less Mexican and
more Anglo-Saxon.

Even though many of the negative stereotypes of Mexican-Americans
are no doubt due to ethnocentric prejudice, they are greatly reinforced by
class differences. A low degree of assimilation into the dominant Anglo
culture is generally associated with low economic status. For instance,
many of the recent immigrants from Mexico, particularly those that are
undocumented and live in the U.S. illegally, tend to be poorer and less assimilated than Chicanos who have lived longer in the U.S. Persons of
Mexican descent who speak little or no English, who adopt traditional
Mexican values, and whose aesthetic tastes (in music, for example) are
more Mexican are thus seen as belonging to a lower economic and social
class. Since functioning successfully in the economic and social institutions of U.S. society requires knowledge of English and the cultural
norms of the mainstream society, greater assimilation is seen as the route
to upward economic mobility. Moreover, those Mexican-Americans that
are poor are seen as being in that condition partly because they have
been unwilling or unable to successfully assimilate into Anglo culture.

Given the high social visibility of cultural group membership, the perceived connection between being Mexican and being lower class can undermine the self-respect of Chicanos. When one's cultural distinctiveness
carries heavy negative associations, unflattering and self-defeating attitudes can be internalized in one's cultural psyche. Perhaps an example
from my own experience will clarify this point. I recall my older brother
half-jokingly saying, "I wish that someone would point out in what ways
I am Mexican, so that I would rip them from myself." We would all laugh
at his sarcastic remark, but at some level we knew that it had the ring of
truth, insofar as some Chicanos felt this way. Our sense of cultural self-
deprecation was no doubt reinforced by the fact that we were migrant
farm-workers, living in labor camps, doing stoop labor, occupying the
bottom of the socioeconomic totem pole.

The effects of connecting cultural identity to lower class status can also
be seen at the familial level. Because of the association between level
of assimilation and economic status, the concern of some Mexican-
American parents that their children not be "too Mexican" is to an extent

understandable. Since it is the members of the dominant Anglo culture who hold most positions of authority involving economic decisions, for many Chicano parents successful socioeconomic achievement can come about only by wholehearted acceptance of the Anglo culture. Whether it is actually true or not that it is economically advantageous to fully assimilate into the Anglo-American culture, the connection between lower class status and Mexican identity and the desire to maximize economic opportunities for their children leads some Mexican-American parents to restrict the intergenerational transmission of their Mexican heritage.

In short, lack of economic self-reliance for Mexican-American communities exerts pressures on the members of those communities to assimilate, and thus undermines their cultural autonomy by introducing extraneous considerations that affect cultural decisions concerning their self-identity and preservation of cultural traditions. If Mexican-Americans were on equal economic footing with Anglos, they would enjoy greater autonomy in the cultural sphere. Chicanos would be able to retain and transmit their cultural self-identity and traditions without feeling that they are compromising their opportunities, and those of their children, for economic advancement. They would also be able to make decisions concerning cultural assimilation based on their own conceptions of what is valuable to accept of the mainstream Anglo culture, rather than on what is needed to survive economically in a different, and sometimes antagonistic, cultural environment. At a more general level, the phenomenon of "disglossia" in which the dominant language in a society is associated with business transactions and high class status while the language used by impoverished ethnocultural groups is associated with informal usage and low socioeconomic status (and is therefore to be avoided), reinforces the point I am making here regarding the connection between economic empowerment and cultural autonomy.

There are other ways in which economic disempowerment hinders the capacity of ethnocultural groups to exercise cultural autonomy. An important condition for the formation of cultural group identity involves the collective capacity of a group to conceive or imagine itself as a united cultural community, that is, as a community sharing a history and cultural practices, values, and aspirations.[28] Since most contemporary ethnocultural groups are too large and dispersed for their members to be personally familiar with one another, they have to rely on cultural images, narratives, aesthetic works, and other allusive devices to imagine themselves as members of a particular ethnocultural group. In advanced technological societies, and increasingly in developing countries as well, media technologies are the primary vehicles for creating and disseminating cultural images. It is through commercially produced films, television programs, books, magazines, tapes, compact disks, and other cultural products that conceptions of cultural group membership are formed and conveyed. However, the mastery and employment of these media technologies require, respectively, a relatively high degree of technical expertise and capital financing. Unlike traditional forms of cultural expression—such as storytelling, painting, folk songs, and traditional dance forms—sophisticated media technologies are infrequently used by impoverished cultural communities to depict their own visions of reality and of themselves.

Given the economic and technical prerequisites for employing modern media technologies, it is very important for ethnocultural groups to have the financial means and the educational and social resources to create and propagate those cultural images through which they can define and sustain themselves as a distinct ethnocultural group. And yet economically disadvantaged ethnocultural groups, particularly national minorities and impoverished communities in developing countries, often do not have the financial resources to create and disseminate their collective self-images. Technological and economic limitations function as impediments to their cultural agency. In many developing countries, for example, local television stations do not have the economic resources to produce their own programming and have to rely on foreign shows to fill air time. Often this means that domestic artists, screenwriters, directors, and technical assistants do not get the opportunity to develop their talents and convey their artistic visions of their own culture.

Economic Empowerment and Political Self-Determination

Economic disempowerment not only hinders the cultural agency of ethnocultural groups, it also significantly restricts their capacity for political self-determination. In Chapter 3, our discussion of epistemological egalitarianism revealed the many ways in which effective political participation can be impaired by economic inequalities. As we observed in that discussion, political empowerment for ethnocultural groups in part requires equal access to information and information technologies, equal educational opportunities to develop the critical thinking abilities for analyzing and evaluating that information, and equal access to the social and material means necessary for the intracultural and intercultural exchange of that information. Significant economic inequalities make the satisfaction of these conditions extremely difficult. Economic resources often determine accessibility to information and information technologies, as well as the educational training needed to employ knowledge effectively to defend one's needs and interests in political contexts. In what follows I will elaborate on the connection between material empowerment and political self-determination, and thus strengthen my contention that we need to conceptualize self-determination in an integrated, expansive fashion.

As we obtain a deeper understanding of political self-determination, we will realize that besides diminishing access to the epistemic resources needed for effective political defense of interests, there are other ways in which economic inequalities hinder political empowerment. Even assuming that cultural minorities enjoy special representation rights that ensure equitable political representation in legislative bodies, participatory inequalities brought about by economic disadvantage can still hinder their political empowerment. This is particularly true in the case of accommodationist groups who do not enjoy self-government rights but have to defend their interests by competing with cultural majorities within the framework of a common political community.

Construed broadly, political participation includes three principal dimensions: resources for political participation and influence, motivational factors, and social networks which promote political activity.[29] As we shall see, economic factors play a role in each of these dimensions affecting political engagement. But before examining how economic factors impact political participation and influence, it is worthwhile to understand why participatory inequalities are normatively significant for liberal democracy. A basic tenet of liberal democracies is that, because each citizen is worthy of equal dignity and respect, the needs and interests of all members of the polity should be taken into account in policy formulation and implementation. Universal suffrage and other democratic rights, such as the rights to form political parties and run for political office, are intended to ensure that all citizens can advocate equitably for their interests. Since government responsiveness to citizens' needs generally depends on political participation, however, when citizens are unable to participate and therefore influence the political process, they are incapable of adequately protecting their interests.

Generally speaking, the inability to participate entails inequality in the relative attention and concern given to one's interests, and to this extent is a violation of the democratic ideal that the needs and interests of all citizens should receive equal consideration. Participatory inequalities are particularly problematic for liberal democracies when the factors responsible for the inability to participate are, on the one hand, systematically interconnected and mutually reinforcing and, on the other, are not the result of volitional decisions on the part of the relevant political actors. For instance, when the inability to participate is brought about by a lack of resources resulting from structural social conditions—such as pervasive ethnocultural discrimination—rather than autonomously made decisions, participatory inequalities violate the normative tenet of political equality of all citizens.

And just as important from our perspective, imposed participatory inequalities have the practical consequence of impeding political self-determination because of the reduced impact that ethnocultural groups will have on the political process. Are the economic inequalities that beset some ethnocultural minorities responsible for imposed participatory inequalities in the three principal areas of democratic participation mentioned above, namely, resources for participation, motivational factors, and social networks of recruitment for political activity? And are these economic inequalities likely to hinder ethnocultural political participation and influence, and therefore political self-determination, even in the presence of the special representation rights for cultural minorities discussed by Kymlicka? I believe these questions must be answered in the affirmative for the following reasons.

Starting with the first question, one of the most intuitively obvious limitations to political participation concerns the absence of resources. Lack of money, for example, clearly limits one's capacity to make political contributions. Even when one is not indigent, one's influence on the political process can be less than those of individuals of greater financial means. In countries in which there are no limits to what can be spent on political campaigns, or where there are ways of circumventing limits to financial contributions, money emerges as a very significant factor influencing the political process. Those with greater financial resources can have greater influence on politicians and policy formation by financially supporting those parties and politicians that reflect their interests.

Moreover, there are less direct, more subtle, ways in which political influence can be exerted through the use of financial resources. By funding think tanks and institutes that promote specific ideological agendas, for example, individuals and organizations with great economic resources can influence public opinion and set the terms for political debate on particular issues. Through the financial support of scholars who write books and articles on important political issues, wealthy individuals and organizations can promote political objectives in which they have a proprietary interest. Members of the legislative and judicial branches of government can be influenced by economic elite through conferences and workshops, funded by the latter, in which these government officials are exposed to philosophies and doctrines which reflect the viewpoints and interests of the wealthy.

By contrast, individuals with few economic resources are limited in the financial contributions they can make to political parties and campaigns. They do not have the access to politicians and party officials that wealthy contributors have, and their concerns are less likely to be heard and heeded. And when they do participate politically, their involvement can have less impact than that of financially powerful individuals; for example, a call or letter from the CEO of a major corporation is likely to have more influence than one from a poor, unknown person. Indigent individuals are also limited in the financial contributions they can make to public interest organizations which advocate in favor of ethnocultural political causes. In recent years in the U.S., for example, ethnocultural interest organizations, following the general trend of public interest organizations, have come to depend more and more on the financial contributions of individuals who support their causes. Organizations like the Mexican-American Legal Defense Fund (MALDEF), the United Farmworkers (UFW), and the National Association for the Advancement of Colored People (NAACP) are relying less on grassroots involvement and more on the financial contributions of supporters they contact through computerized mailing lists. That is, involvement in ethnocultural organizations now depends less on direct political engagement by individuals and more on the financial contributions they can make. This shift of emphasis increases the importance of economic resources for participation in political interest organizations.

Civic skills are also important resources for political participation. Skills such as the ability to organize or lead a meeting, to write and speak effectively, or to coordinate a business presentation, prepare individuals to engage effectively in political activity. Civic skills developed in a nonpolitical environment like the workplace or university can be usefully employed in political organizing. People who have developed civic skills will have more confidence in their efficacy as agents of social change and will be more effective in performing political organizational tasks than those who have never had the opportunity to develop such skills. Moreover, civic skills are often developed in environments that are positively correlated with greater income. High-income jobs in which employees supervise other workers, carry out complex organizational tasks, or engage in conceptually challenging projects are more likely to develop capacities which are useful for effective political participation. There are, for example, large discrepancies between the opportunities for developing civic skills available to a high-school dropout working in a fast-food restaurant and an individual with an advanced degree working as a division manager in a large business.

Besides participatory resources such as money and civic skills, motivational factors and recruitment opportunities are also important for political participation. A high level of educational attainment, for example, is more conducive to greater knowledge and interest in politics than a low level of education. People who are more educated will generally have greater access to sources of information and will be more aware of political developments than the less educated. In addition, social networks can function as sources for recruitment for political participation. In the workplace, in civic associations, and at church, people can receive requests for political participation, and they are more likely to engage in political activity as a result of such requests.

It is worthwhile to note that acquiring the resources for political participation is cumulative, and that education plays a special role in this process of resource accumulation. As Verba, Schlozman, and Brady indicate in *Voice and Equality*, their landmark work on political participation:

> Circumstances of initial privilege have consequences for educational attainment which, in turn, has consequences for the acquisition of nearly every other participatory factor: income earned on the job; skills acquired at work, in organizations, and to a lesser extent, in church; psychological engagement with politics; exposure to requests for activity.[30]

Thus, individuals who come from a background in which their family had a high income and a high level of education are themselves more likely to become highly educated and reap the benefits that derive from more education, including acquiring greater means for political participation and influence.

However, the impact of economic inequalities on motivational factors and recruitment opportunities is less than on resources for participation and influence such as money and civic skills. In countries such as Japan and Austria, where institutional affiliations (to parties and other political organizations) play a significant role in political participation, the influence of economic inequalities on political activity is to an extent offset by the opportunities and dispositions for participation provided by these affiliations.[31] And in the U.S., association with religious institutions can play a significant role in providing poor individuals with motivations and requests for political activity that, respectively, they would not otherwise develop or be exposed to. This is particularly true for blacks, since Protestant churches have traditionally been important sources of political mobilization in black communities. Nevertheless, despite the mitigating effect of these institutional affiliations, economic inequalities remain a very significant, if not the single most important, factor determining political influence and participation.

It is also crucial to note that the most economically disadvantaged members of ethnocultural groups are likely to be doubly disadvantaged with regards to political influence and participation, because economic factors will be coupled with the ethnicity-related factors that are responsible for the underrepresention of ethnocultural groups in general. That is, the political influence of the poorest and least educated of ethnocultural groups' members will be diminished not merely by the politically marginalizing factors that afflict ethnocultural minorities (such as lack of familiarity with the modes of discourse and normative assumptions and values of the majority), but also by the effects of economic disadvantage. Moreover, as socioeconomic gaps within minority groups widen, the political interests of privileged and underprivileged minority group members are likely to widen as well. The greater political voice of minority elites becomes problematic to the extent that it does not reflect the needs and interests of the most disadvantaged members of their ethnocultural group (who may have distinctive concerns that need to be addressed) but coincides more closely with the preferences of the more privileged members of the majority society. Thus, ethnocultural groups who are already disadvantaged in terms of political influence and participation due to their lower socioeconomic status will be further disadvantaged when those who presumably speak for them do not really represent their needs and interests. This is an important dilemma, because political self-determination should apply to all members of ethnocultural groups, and not just to the most gifted or elite group members. We should note that this problem is likely to persist despite the use of special representation rights for ethnocultural minorities that ensure their equitable representation, because this dilemma is exacerbated by socioeconomic differences among minority group members themselves.

Thus far I have argued that economic inequalities provide the members of privileged groups with inordinate advantages in influencing the political process, and that such inequalities violate the democratic ideal that the needs and interests of all should be equally taken into account in political decision making. To the extent that ethnocultural groups are economically underprivileged, as they are in many democratic societies, they will be at a disadvantage relative to cultural majorities with regard to political influence and participation. However, I have not proposed any remedies to the problem of material disparities, and more generally, to the problem of economic self-determination. In Chapters 8 and 9, I will argue that in order to address this problem we need to challenge conventional conceptions of property rights. As we shall see, property rights as conventionally understood represent a fundamental inconsistency at the heart of liberal democracy, because they undermine in significant ways the individual autonomy which is granted pride of place in this form of democracy. In these chapters I will also consider how systematic and pervasive discrimination and oppression of ethnocultural groups has deprived them of economic empowerment, and what measures are appropriate in redressing their lack of material self-determination.

This section on economic inequalities and political self-determination can be summarized by noting several salient points. First, in addition to the negative effects of economic inequalities on epistemological parity that we discussed in the third chapter, we have seen that economic resources can be used to inequitably influence the political process in a variety of ways. Second, economic inequalities often play a significant role in creating participatory inequalities which involve the development of civic skills as well as opportunities and motivations for political activity.

Third, we observed that there are special problems concerning socioeconomically underprivileged ethnocultural group members, because they are doubly disadvantaged with regard to political influence and participation. In short, the powerful influence of economic factors on the political process and on political participation calls our attention to the fact that the formal mechanism of rights, even when tailored to ensure the equitable representation of ethnocultural minorities, is not sufficient for bringing about political self-determination for these groups. This is particularly true for accommodationist groups and communal contenders, who must defend their needs and interests *vis-a-vis* those of cultural majorities within the context of common political institutions. Even national minorities who enjoy rights of self-government, however, must contend with the impact of economic inequalities when these place them in disadvantageous positions (involving epistemological inequities, for example) in their political negotiations with the majority society.

Ethnocultural Self-Determination in a Globalized Environment

In this final section I address briefly the third component of self-determination I mentioned at the beginning of this chapter, namely, the impact of globalization on the empowerment of ethnocultural groups and the states in which they live. In an increasingly globalized world in which states and communities of different kinds are forming numerous connections and interdependencies, it is unrealistic to conceive of ethnocultural groups and states as economically, culturally, and politically isolated units. At the beginning of the twenty-first century, self-determination for states and substate collectivities can no longer be understood in traditional state-centered terms. That is, self-determination for states is not merely a matter of exercising sovereignty and, for substate collectivities, not merely a matter of obtaining political, social, and cultural rights guaranteed by the state. Ubiquitous global economic and social forces are in many cases undermining the capacity of states and ethnocultural communities to determine the course of their own futures. At the economic level, for example, globalization has meant the internationalization of labor forces, the opening of domestic markets to foreign investment capital, and the increased influence of economic institutions, such as transnational corporations, international banks, supranational lobbies, and the World Bank and the International Monetary Fund (IMF). The convergence of these developments has made it more difficult for countries to make decisions to protect the interests of their citizens and practice self-determination. Consider the impact of the internationalization of labor forces. As capital becomes more mobile due to changes in international investment regulations and technological advances in telecommunications and transportation, transnational corporations can more readily relocate their manufacturing operations and subcontract with businesses in other parts of the world where labor costs are lower. Workers in different countries find themselves competing with one another to provide the most favorable conditions for foreign investment, which often means lower wages, fewer worker benefits, and less auspicious working conditions. States and substate communities that adopt labor standards beneficial for workers have to contend with the likelihood that investment capital will be redirected to countries with lower or nonexistent labor standards.

For many multicultural democracies in the developing world, integration into the global economy has resulted in the imposition of "economic discipline" by the IMF and the World Bank in the form of conditions of structural adjustment which, among other things, restrict what these countries can spend on education, social and health benefits, and staple food subsidies. Many Third World countries must accept these conditions of fiscal austerity in order to receive the loans they need to repay debts incurred by previous borrowing from these same financial institutions.[32] The capacity of many developing countries to control their economic affairs has been severely compromised by these developments.[33] And when a country cannot decide for itself how many of its material resources it can utilize for educational or public health purposes, for example, it has lost an important dimension of democratic self-governance. As former World Bank officer Herman Daly has pointed out, the inability to determine fiscal priorities weakens national and subnational communities and eliminates the single most important way in which societies can carry out policies for the common good.[34]

Globalization has also undermined cultural self-determination for countries and ethnocultural communities throughout the world. Cultural products such as movies, compact disks, television programs, music videos, magazines, books, and children's toys are the means by which cultures throughout the world are being commodified and homogenized by media conglomerates. Many of these cultural products are targeted at the young, who are the most susceptible to foreign cultural influences because they are in the process of consolidating their personal and social identities. Technological innovations and the concentration of corporate power have created an unprecedented degree of centralized control of the creation and dissemination of cultural products.

Even though cultures are not static and undergo constant change, the negative influences of commercial culture on traditional cultures are particularly intrusive and pervasive. Commercial culture commodifies cultural expression and undermines traditional cultures through an ideological orientation that validates a person's existence on the basis of consumption and acquisition and not on the quality of their relationships to other human beings. While traditional cultures enable people to cope with universal human experiences and dilemmas such as facing death, growing old, relating to the transcendent, and providing narrative unity to one's life, commercial culture gives rise to truncated and vulnerable forms of personhood. Traditional cultures make possible comprehensive and sustainable human connections to family and community because they are maintained and conveyed in communal contexts, but commercial culture is individualistic and detached from situated communities. Moreover, intergenerational continuity, one of the basic functions of traditional cultures, is severed by commercial culture. The stories, wisdom, and skills preserved and transmitted by older people in traditional cultures are replaced by ever-changing, youth-oriented cultural fads and symbols. In brief, the communally fragmenting impact of commercial culture can diminish the capacity of ethnocultural communities to maintain the shared practices and understanding necessary for social cohesion, and thus to use their cultural resources for self-determination.

The goal of achieving comprehensive self-determination in an increasingly globalized world is one of the most important dilemmas facing states and ethnocultural communities. There are a number of complex issues that need to be addressed in meeting this challenge, including the development of economic self-reliance, cultural agency, and ecologically sustainable communities. The complexity and scope of these problems are such that I will not be able to address them in a comprehensive manner in this book. I will, however, provide the foundations for economic self-determination for ethnocultural minorities, as well as for members of cultural majorities, with the doctrine of property rights that I present in Chapters 8 and 9.

Regarding cultural self-determination, it is clear that global cultural homogenization introduces issues not usually examined in discussions of cultural rights. Often overlooked in discussions of cultural rights is the corrosive and surreptitious impact of commercial culture and the ethos of the competitive market on the solidarity and stability of ethnocultural communities, even though such impact can be as great, if not greater, than that exerted by states in their efforts to assimilate cultural minorities into the majority culture.[35] I will argue in the last chapter that ecological consciousness, besides having salutary effects on social solidarity in multicultural societies, can function as a much needed corrective to the influences of a culture of consumption.

In the next two chapters, I discuss the meaning of self-determination for the different categories of ethnocultural groups I have identified, namely, accommodationist, autonomist, and secessionist groups. My discussion will reflect the integrated nature of the different components of self-determination I have discussed.

Notes

1. S. James Anaya, *Indigenous Peoples in International Law* (New York: Oxford University Press, 1996), p. 75, footnote 2.

2. Ibid., p. 78–80.

3. Yael Tamir, *Liberal Nationalism* (Princeton: Princeton University Press, 1993).

4. Ibid., p. 72.

5. Ibid., p. 72.

6. For a discussion of some ethnocultural groups who have basically followed accommodationist approaches, see Ted Robert Gurr, *Minorities at Risk: A Global View of Ethnopolitical Conflicts* (Washington, DC: United States Institute of Peace Press, 1993), chapter 6.

7. Lani Guinier, *The Tyranny of the Majority* (New York: The Free Press, 1994), chapter 5. It is difficult to understand the reasons behind the double standard implicit in the Supreme Court's decision. Even though we cannot assume that all of the members of an ethnocultural group living in a certain area will necessarily share the same needs, interests, and values, neither can we make this assumption concerning, say, tobacco farmers. And surely there are some districts in which Blacks and Latinos will share a sufficient number of social, political, and economic concerns to justify considering them as communities of interest. It cannot simply be assumed that grouping the members of a cultural minority into the same congressional district will always be illegitimate and a case of "political apartheid." The Supreme Court's decision in effect deprives some ethnic minorities of the protection of fair representation that groups of white citizens enjoy.

Moreover, even though in order to declare a particular case of ethnic-based redistricting as unfair it is necessary to show that it would unjustly deprive some group of adequate representation, the Court failed to provide such evidence. The Court did not establish that white residents or any other group in the district would be denied fair representation by the ethnic-based redistricting. In fact, the district in question is one of the most integrated in North Carolina. Given the arbitrary exclusion of ethnic minorities from the community-of-interest standard and the absence of evidence to establish the unfairness of the congressional district in question, it is difficult to avoid the conclusion that the Supreme Court's decision was based not on sound legal reasoning but on prevailing ethnocentric attitudes against cultural minorities that consider socioeconomic or political policies intended to benefit such minorities as unfair to the white majority. These Supreme Court decisions can be seen as part of a broad social backlash in the U.S. against programs and policies, such as affirmative action, that try to rectify past discrimination by providing cultural minorities with special considerations in social, economic, and political institutions and organizations.

8. Will Kymlicka, *Multicultural Citizenship: A Liberal Theory of Minority Rights* (Oxford: Oxford University Press, 1995).

9. In the following exposition of group-differentiated rights, I rely on chapters 2 and 6 of Kymlicka, *Multicultural Citizenship*.

10. Ibid., p. 76.

11. Ibid., p. 81.

12. Ibid., p. 83.

13. I may fail in my goal of being a medical doctor or a self-supporting artist, for example, but my membership in a cultural community is relatively more secure and less prone to annulment.

14. Ibid., p. 89.

15. Ibid., p. 90.

16. As evidence of this, he points to the decline in the preservation of native language and cultural practices among second and third generation immigrants. Even though it is not impossible for a cultural group to retain its culture in the absence of state institutional support (note the capacity of certain American Jewish groups to preserve their culture), Kymlicka is surely right to claim that it is much more difficult for a culture to survive without institutional embodiment.

17. Kymlicka assumes that the groups in this category left their country of origin voluntarily under noncoercive conditions. However, we can recognize that in some cases some of these groups may have been motivated or even compelled to leave due to economic, political, or environmental exigencies.

18. Kymlicka, *Multicultural Citizenship*, pp. 31 and 114.

19. Ibid., p. 120.

20. Ibid., p. 122.

21. Questions arise here concerning how we determine that the freedoms denied to majority group members are of less importance than the sacrifices to which minority groups would be subjected by the denial of group-differentiated rights. Kymlicka would most likely maintain that restricting individuals from recreational activities in tribal homelands or fishing in tribal controlled waters, for example, are of less moral consequence than denying indigenous peoples the right to control their traditional territories. Of course, the situation is complicated if the restrictions in liberty of the majority group members living in the minority controlled territory are of such a substantial nature that they compromise fundamental interests. In these cases the notion of cultural minority rights may have to be invoked to protect the fundamental interests of these majority group members. In these more difficult cases we would have to take into account how basic the interests are that are being compromised for either minority or majority group members and the relevant historical agreements and developments (concerning territorial control, for example) that have an impact on the issues at hand.

22. Ibid., p. 132.

23. Ibid., p. 150.

24. Ibid., p. 137.

25. Ibid., p. 141.

26. Ibid., p. 143.

27. Pressures to assimilate are particularly strong for cultural group members living in societies that are receptive to, or that expect, their assimilation into the mainstream society.

28. For an account of the factors involved in the construction of cultural group identity, see Benedict Anderson, *Imagined Communities: Reflections on the Origin and Spread of Nationalism* (London: Verso, 1983).

29. For one of the most extensive and excellent studies of the most important factors influencing political participation in the U.S., see Sidney Verba, Kay Lehman Schlozman, and Henry E. Brady, *Voice and Equality: Civic Voluntarism in American Politics* (Cambridge, MA.: Harvard University Press, 1995). Even though this study is based on the U.S., economic factors are undoubtedly of primary importance in understanding political influence and participation in most democratic countries. As economic inequalities widen in more countries around the world, the impact of money on political processes is likely to increase.

30. Ibid., p. 514.

31. For an account of the ways, and extent, to which political organizations offset the effects of socioeconomic status, see Sidney Verba, Norman H. Nie, and Jae-on Kim, *Participation and Political Equality: A Seven Nation Comparison* (Cambridge: Cambridge, U.K.: University Press, 1978), chapters 6 and 7.

32. The story of how so many developing countries ended up burdened by a mountain of debt is complex and fascinating. What seems clear is that Western bankers and officials at the IMF and World Bank adopted a policy of pushing loans on many of these countries at favorable interest rates, which later were dramatically increased, for projects of economic development many of which were not successful. For an account of these developments, see Paul Valleley, *Bad Samaritans: First World Ethics and Third World Debt* (Maryknoll, NY: Orbis Books, 1990).

33. Sub-Sahara African countries provide some of the clearest examples of this loss of sovereignty. They have such staggering debts that the World Bank and the IMF are now making many of their economic decisions for them.

34. Ralph Nader and Lori Wallach quote Herman Daly in "GATT, NAFTA, and the Subversion of the Democratic Process," in *The Case Against the Global Economy and for a Turn Toward the Local*, eds. Jerry Mander and Edward Goldsmith (San Francisco: Sierra Club Books, 1997): pp. 71–77.

35. The influences of commercial culture are surreptitious and more effective than efforts by the state to repress cultural traditions because the latter are usually transparent and vigorously resisted by ethnocultural groups, while the former appeal to easily exploited prurient interests and a penchant for the novel and technologically alluring. There are whole industries (such as advertising) full of highly skilled people using their intelligence and sophisticated technologies to devise ever more clever and effective ways of transforming peoples' conceptions of themselves and their needs.

6

Self-Determination for
Accommodationist Groups

My primary objectives in this chapter and the next are to apply the integrated conception of self-determination I have articulated to accommodationist, autonomist, and secessionist groups. Applying this comprehensive conception is a complex matter because, as we have observed, self-determination has different meaning for each of these groups, and the normative justification of their claims for empowerment will be correspondingly different. However, our task will be facilitated by the fact that we have already initiated our discussion of the justification of cultural and self-government rights for some of these ethnocultural groups. In our examintion of Kymlicka's theory of self-determination, we discussed a plausible rationale for cultural rights and we observed that self-government rights and systematic discrimination can justify special forms of group representation.

But Kymlicka does not systematically discuss secessionist groups or the normative criteria that justify dividing existing states into two or more sovereign political entities. Understanding such criteria is crucial for a general theory of ethnocultural self-determination. Examining normative criteria for secession is also important because, after a long period of international stability regarding state boundaries, in the last decade approximately twenty-five new states have been formed and many other groups are currently engaged in secessionist struggles.[1] Further, Kymlicka's theory of self-determination is not sufficiently fine-grained to distinguish between indigenous groups and non-indigenous national minorities. As we shall see in what follows, there are important cultural, political, and economic differences between these groups and these differences will be relevant for developing adequate theories of self-determination for them. In addition, Kymlicka's account of ethnocultural group self-determination is state-centered, in the sense that it does not take into account the effects of globalization on ethnocultural political, economic, and cultural empowerment. In understanding self-determination in a globalized environment, the state should no longer be the sole focus of analysis. Especially when considering autonomist and secessionist groups, inter- and intra-state interconnections and associations complicate the empirical and normative considerations relevant for understanding self-determination. In short, there are very important issues yet to be examined concerning ethnocultural empowerment. I begin my analyses of self-determination for the three ethnocultural group categories by focusing on empowerment for accommodationist groups.

The Meaning of Self-Determination
for Accommodationist Groups

We have already seen that accommodationist groups differ from autonomist and secessionist groups in significant ways. Accommodationist groups do not want to create a separate and autonomous public and political sphere in which to exercise self-governance, but seek to retain aspects of their cultural traditions while achieving socioeconomic progress and political empowerment within the institutions and organizations of the majority society. In addition to attaining formal civil, political, and cultural rights, it is of primary importance for accommodationist groups to attain three objectives: equitable political representation[2], socioeconomic progress, and the removal of discriminatory social barriers. In a word, they need to attain full and equal status as members of the larger social and political community. Formal civil, political, and cultural rights constitute the foundation of equal citizenship for accommodationist groups, but these rights by no means exhaust the goals that are necessary for them to achieve true empowerment. Substantial political, social, and economic inequalities can afflict accommodationist groups in democratic societies despite formal recognition of civil and political rights. In order to understand self-determination for these groups, we must therefore examine the additional factors that are necessary for them to achieve full and equal status as members of the polity.

In Chapters 2 and 3 I argued that deliberative democracy has significant and distinctive advantages for multicultural societies comprised of accommodationist ethnocultural groups. We examined some of the ways in which political equality can be enhanced for these groups so that they can articulate and defend their needs and interests in the forums of public deliberation characteristic of deliberative democracy. We identified economic resources and level of formal education as factors of particular importance for political participation and equality in such democracies, and observed that the skills and capacities useful for political engagement are best developed in autonomy-enhancing occupations requiring a relatively high level of formal education. Since socioeconomic status is determined to a large extent by level of education, two of the objectives important for accommodationist self-determination, namely effective political functioning and socioeconomic upward mobility, are linked to economic resources and education.

Access to education, however, is not dependent merely on individual economic resources; it is also the result of the human resource policies of the society in question. The structure of the state's educational institutions, federal grant money to support the educational expenses of indigent students, funding policies for primary and secondary schools, and regional availability of higher education, for example, are typically the result of the state's educational policies. Accommodationist ethnocultural minorities, in order to have equitable access to good education, must be able to sufficiently influence the political process to affect educational policies. Thus, education, which is important for socioeconomic progress and political empowerment, is itself made more accessible by achieving these very goals. Likewise, economic resources, which contribute to effective political functioning and make good education accessible, are themselves attained by the latter factors. It thus appears that there is no simple linear path for disadvantaged accommodationist minorities to take to achieve empowerment. There is no single starting point on the road to self-determination; rather, there are multiple areas in which accommodationist groups must simultaneously make progress in order to control their own destinies. Progress on any of the fronts we have identified—economic, political, educational, and cultural—would contribute to self-determination.

Given the complexity of achieving accommodationist self-determination, the various relevant factors to achieve this goal will be discussed in separate chapters. The crucial issue of socioeconomic empowerment for accommodationist minorities, and for ethnocultural groups in general, is discussed in Chapters 8 and 9. Since we already examined epistemological inequalities and cultural rights in previous chapters, my focus here will be on the forms of political representation that are conducive to accommodationist empowerment. Before proceeding with this task, however, we should briefly discuss the third goal of accommodationist self-determination, namely, the elimination of discriminatory social barriers. It is important to understand what is involved in ethnocultural discrimination and, in keeping with our integrated conception of self-determination, how it relates to the other kinds of disadvantage we have identified.

Roughly, invidious ethnocultural discrimination could be defined as the practice in which members of ethnocultural groups are treated unjustly on the basis of perceived or self-ascribed cultural group membership. That is, discriminatory behavior is directed not only against those individuals who identify themselves as members of certain ethnocultural groups, but also against those who are perceived by others as being members of such groups; thus the self-ascriptive aspects of ethnocultural group membership are not necessarily relevant. But more important, discriminatory practices are generally based on ethnocultural prejudice and involve not merely negative attitudes towards the members of minority groups, but are accompanied by the power to inflict harm on these individuals or place them in positions of absolute or comparative disadvantage. This most important aspect of ethnocultural discrimination, namely, the economic, political, or sociocultural power to inflict harm on cultural group members, points to the fact that discrimination is often an institutionally supported phenomenon. It is when prejudicial attitudes are accompanied by institutionally backed power that ethnocultural discrimination has its most negative and pervasive consequences. If a prejudiced individual is my supervisor at work, a politician who represents my district, a judge who is presiding over my court case, a police officer who stops my car because of a routine traffic violation, or a civil service worker who can make decisions that affect me and my family, the prejudiced beliefs and attitudes of this individual can have significant, and on some occasions devastating, consequences for my economic, political, social, and emotional well-being.

Concern is also warranted in a second case, namely, when an individual (or group) with prejudiced attitudes is predisposed to harm me, even if his actions violate formally guaranteed protections and privileges, and the majority society is unwilling to defend me or punish him appropriately. This can occur in societies in which ethnocultural minorities have the same formal rights and opportunities as members of the majority or dominant society, but where there is a tacit understanding that violations of such rights and opportunities will not be punished, or are punished using more lenient standards. In this second case the harmful consequences of discrimination arise not because the individual inflicting harm is institutionally empowered to make decisions that affect my well-being, but because he can violate my rights and opportunities without fear of sufficient societal retribution.

A third case involves discriminatory mechanisms such as measurement instruments, admission standards for educational and training institutions, and criteria for hiring and promotion. Examples of these discriminatory mechanisms include standardized examinations that are culturally biased and promotion criteria for university faculty that do not take into account the differential circumstances of minority professors.[3] The discriminatory procedures here are more subtle, and there may be no malicious intent in the individuals designing these instruments and criteria, who may believe that they are being fair and neutral. Nevertheless, due to lack of knowledge of ethnocultural minorities and the circumstances they face, these institutionalized means for determining opportunities and meting out rewards may subject the members of ethnocultural groups to very real disadvantages and injustices. These more subtle discriminatory mechanisms could be minimized if more cultural minorities were in positions of decision-making authority regarding the formulation of the means by which individuals are offered opportunities and rewards. The expertise of minority psychologists, office managers, judges, university faculty, and social service workers, for example, would contribute to more informed decisions in the design and implementation of measurement instruments and employment criteria.

In all these cases it is the lack of minority political power or socioeconomic equality that makes the negative consequences of ethnocultural discrimination possible: in the first case because as a member of a disempowered minority group I am socially situated in a variety of contexts in which individuals with ethnocultural prejudice can make institutionally sanctioned decisions which affect my well-being; in the second case because I am vulnerable to harm by prejudiced persons or groups who are aware that they enjoy the protection of double standards of enforcement concerning violations of formally guaranteed rights and opportunities; and in the third case because formal measurement mechanisms and criteria for employment and promotion are formulated without the input and expertise of minority professionals. The harmful consequences of ethnocultural discrimination demonstrates the importance for ethnocultural minorities to achieve equitable representation across the wide spectrum of political, social, legal, and economic positions of power, authority, and expertise in a society. The greater the inequities between minority and majority groups with regard to such positions, the greater the likelihood that ethnocultural prejudices or lack of knowledge concerning minorities will, respectively, move beyond being merely negative psychological attitudes or epistemic deficiencies and create tangible inimical consequences for minority group members.

In emphasizing the function that inequalities in institutionalized power, authority, and technical expertise play in rendering ethnocultural discrimination harmful, I do not mean to underestimate the importance of the psychological dimensions of prejudice. Much discriminatory behavior results from the negative psychological attitudes that individuals have towards the members of ethnocultural groups. As I indicated in the third chapter, at least partial transformation of these attitudes could be achieved through multicultural education and the expansion of forums of public deliberation. My point here is to show that invidious discrimination is not simply a matter of subjective feelings or beliefs of particular individuals. Understanding discrimination as a purely subjective phenomenon manifested by persons in random or isolated situations obscures the systematic and institutional components of discrimination, and conceals the role that political and economic power play in reinforcing systems of discrimination which place the members of ethnocultural minorities in positions of pervasive disadvantage. Moreover, emphasizing the institutional, power-based components of discrimination helps us avoid the mistake of believing that the fact that ethnocultural minorities can also have prejudiced attitudes towards the members of dominant groups equalizes the situation as far as discrimination is concerned. That is, we will resist the temptation to think that since prejudice works both ways, ethnocultural groups have no reason to complain of special injuries caused by discriminatory attitudes.

Focusing on the systematic, institutionalized aspects of discrimination is also crucial for understanding the historical role that structures of discrimination have played in maintaining social orders that further the interests of groups in power. The major historical developments responsible for the pervasive disadvantages afflicting ethnocultural groups around the world include conquest, nation-building, and the labor needs of post-industrial societies.[4] Invasive settlement and conquest by Europeans subjugated many indigenous peoples throughout North and South America. Indigenous peoples suffered massacres, enslavement, and systematic destruction of their cultural traditions at the hands of Europeans. Settler societies have also used ethnocultural groups as slaves in plantation economies as well as in less oppressive roles, such as servants in colonial bureaucracies and as sources of cheap and exploitable labor for service economies. Aymara Indians in Bolivia, Nahualt-speaking Indians in Mexico, African-Americans in the U.S., Turkish immigrants in Germany, Maghrebins in France, and Palestinians in Israel are examples of ethnocultural groups who have been, and continue to be, subjugated in a variety of ways by systematic structures of discrimination and oppression. In many cases dominant groups created these structures to efficiently organize social relations to maintain their positions of political and socioeconomic power over these accommodationist, autonomist, or secessionist ethnocultural groups.

It is therefore not surprising that members of the dominant society would not want to relinquish the political, social, and economic privileges and advantages they have over these ethnocultural groups. Indeed, an interesting and important insight concerning accommodationist empowerment is that, since accommodationist minorities live within the same political and social community as majority groups, they will most likely compete directly with majority group members for desirable and scarce employment opportunities and positions of authority. In contrast to autonomist groups who typically seek empowerment through the creation of their own separate political and social institutions, accommodationist groups are therefore more likely to encounter resistance and backlash reactions from members of dominant groups who see their positions of advantage and power eroding as the result of efforts by accommodationist groups to achieve self-determination.[5] For these reasons, in some cases (such as where deep antagonisms or racial differences between accommodationist and majority groups exist) it may actually be easier for the majority society to grant self-determination to autonomist groups than to accept the changes necessary for accommodationist groups to achieve full equality within a common social and political community.[6]

It is also worthwhile to note that the problems that we have identified with ethnocultural discrimination can only be partially remedied through legal or other procedural mechanisms designed to ensure that equality of rights and opportunities is respected. In the first place, as we have already pointed out, there is the problem of enforcing existing formal rights and opportunities of ethnocultural groups. There are numerous examples of democratic countries in which rights for cultural minorities exist only on paper, and where there are significant failures of enforcement of existing protections and guarantees.[7] In the second place, guaranteed rights and opportunities for ethnocultural groups can be circumvented in a variety of ways, for example, code words can be used to identify the race or ethnicity of job applicants where laws prohibit explicit mention of such characteristics, or legal criteria for what constitutes probable cause can be interpreted differently when police officers deal with suspects belonging to certain racial or ethnic groups. In short, without socioeconomic empowerment or equality of representation in positions of political, legal, and professional authority, it is highly unlikely that ethnocultural groups can attain full and equal status as members of the multicultural polity.

From these observations on the effects of ethnocultural discrimination we can see that attaining the third objective that we identified at the beginning of this section as being of primary importance for accommodationist groups, namely, the removal of social barriers involving discrimination, principally depends on empowering these groups politically, legally, and socioeconomically *vis-a-vis* the majority society.[8] In other words, the removal of the negative consequences of invidious ethnocultural discrimination (though not necessarily of ethnocultural prejudice itself) is largely a matter of achieving the two other objectives, viz., upward socioeconomic mobility and equitable political (including legal) representation, that we identified for accommodationist groups. As indicated before, I will deal with issues of socioeconomic empowerment in Chapters 8 and 9. Addressing inequities in political and legal power, on the other hand, is primarily a matter of ensuring equitable political representation in the society's political and legal institutions. It is to this issue that I now turn.

Political Empowerment for Accommodationist Groups

I have identified equitable political representation as a fundamental feature of accommodationist self-determination because these groups strive to coexist with the majority society in a common social and political community. The normative justification for equitable political representation for accommodationist groups is therefore fairly straightforward, namely, that in a democratic society the needs and interests of all individuals should be equally taken into account. The core principle of the equality of the needs and interests of all members of a democratic polity is in turn based on the fundamental principle of the equal worth and dignity of all human beings. Because no person or group has an *a priori* or intrinsic superior moral status over any other person or group, in a democratic society there should be a basic belief in the equal consideration of everyone's needs and interests.

The fundamental equal moral worth and dignity of every member of the polity, however, does not in itself entail the need for proportional or equitable political representation for ethnocultural groups. Why is it necessary for cultural minorities to have their own representatives in order for their needs and interests to be protected and taken into account? Why must political representatives "mirror" the relevant ethnocultural groups in terms of ethnic or racial characteristics before the principle of equal consideration of needs and interests can be satisfied? Why should we assume that ethnocultural minorities cannot be adequately represented by politicians from the majority society?

In responding to these questions, it is important to differentiate between a strong and a weak formulation of the mirror representation thesis. In its strong version, the thesis states that only members of ethnocultural groups can truly understand, and have the necessary commitment to defend, the needs and interests of these groups, and therefore are the only ones who can adequately represent them. In its weak formulation, the thesis states that it is more likely, other things being equal, that ethnocultural minorities will be effectively represented by individuals who exemplify their cultural, racial, and social characteristics and who have familiarity with the experience of being an ethnocultural minority in the society in question.

It seems to me that the strong version of the mirror thesis is clearly implausible, given that it is certainly possible that persons who are not members of an ethnocultural group can be effective political advocates and representatives of that group's needs and interests. In cases in which the members of an ethnocultural group have been deprived of the opportunity to receive an education and develop the capabilities for political participation, and where there are individuals who have long experience working with such groups and have a genuine commitment to their cause, it may be in the best (short-term) interest of the group for these individuals to function as their political representatives. Of course, it should be a long-term goal for ethnocultural group members to acquire the resources, capacities, and opportunities that will enable them to speak for themselves and defend their own needs and interests. However, holding the latter view is certainly compatible with recognizing that on some occasions the most effective political representatives available need not mirror the characteristics or have the experiences of the ethnocultural groups they represent.

While the strong version of the mirror representation thesis seems implausible, this cannot be said of the weak version. According to the weak formulation of the thesis, it is reasonable to suppose that, other things being equal, a minority representative will for the most part do a better job than a non-minority of representing the needs and interests of the ethnocultural group of which she is a member. The rationale for the weak thesis is that familiarity with the experiences of being a member of the ethnocultural group in the society in question provides an individual with knowledge and affective insights important for understanding the problems and aspirations of that group. The facility to communicate with ethnocultural group members, the understanding of shared cultural assumptions, the first-hand experience of being a member of that minority group, the sense of social responsibility to fellow cultural group members, and the capacity to identify with and understand the basis of cultural group identity, for instance, are all factors that are likely to enhance the capacity of minority representatives to be particularly effective political spokespeople for their own ethnocultural group. To the extent that minority political representatives mirror relevant group characteristics and capacities, it is surely reasonable to suppose that possessing the latter increases their capacity to politically represent the ethnocultural group in an effective manner.

The "all things being equal" proviso in the weak version of the mirror representation thesis is important, because it is meant to neutralize factors that may affect in obvious ways the effectiveness and adequacy of political representatives. An uninformed, corrupt minority candidate would in all likelihood be less capable of adequately representing the ethnocultural group to which she belongs than an upright non-minority candidate with knowledge of the relevant political issues and a strong commitment to the group. It is probably impossible to specify with a high degree of precision the extent to which mirroring the characteristics and experiences of ethnocultural group members overrides particular differences in political skill and effectiveness. For practical purposes, however, it is not necessary to do this; it suffices to recognize that it is generally desirable for ethnocultural political representatives to mirror

minority group members regarding not simply ethnic or racial characteristics, but also the experiences and knowledge generally associated with
membership in that group. Unless we are willing to argue that ethnocultural minorities are essentially incapable of acquiring the political capabilities necessary for effective political representation, or that they are
more inherently predisposed to corruption than non-minority politicians,
we should recognize that, other things being equal, the experience of being an ethnocultural minority in a society in which that minority group
has been traditionally marginalized and discriminated against, will provide them with insights and experiences relevant for effective political
representation of their group's needs and interests.

Further, as Melissa Williams and others have argued, representative-
constituent political trust tends to be higher when marginalized groups
are represented by one of their own members than when they are represented by a member of the dominant group.[9] This trust, which facilitates
communication between representatives and their constituents, makes it
easier for citizens to approach their representatives, and thereby promotes the political dialogue which is central for political accountability.
When members of ethnocultural minorities who have traditionally been
marginalized from the political process believe and feel that their concerns will be heard, understood, and heeded, they will be more willing to
communicate them to their representatives. Moreover, in addition to the
fact that there is empirical evidence indicating that representatives who
are members of marginalized groups are in fact more likely to uphold positions that support the interests of these groups[10], minority constituents
are well aware of the fact that the issues with which they are concerned
will most likely affect their representatives if they are also members of
their group. This latter realization will in turn reinforce the belief of constituents that their minority representative will advocate in good faith for
their interests. In brief, the trust which ethnocultural minorities are more
inclined to have for minority representatives is not merely a subjective
feeling without a factual basis, but is grounded on reasonable assumptions concerning the factors that affect the interests and well-being of
their representatives.

An additional reason for maintaining that it is desirable for ethnocultural groups to be politically represented by one of their own members is
that given the "high social profile" of ethnocultural group membership
in many multicultural societies, the self-identity and self-respect of minorities will be positively affected by political representation by their
own members. It is important for ethnocultural minorities to feel that
they are an accepted and legitimate part of the political community. If
ethnocultural minorities are constantly excluded from political representation, they will think and feel that their concerns and preferences are not
taken seriously by the majority. The public recognition of their presence

and participation in the political process has a salutary effect on the general civic culture of a multicultural society.

If it is desirable, for all of these reasons, for ethnocultural groups to elect minority representatives to political office, what conditions must be met by electoral systems that are adequate for accommodationist self-determination? Perhaps the most important of these conditions is that appropriate electoral systems must be capable of taking into account the fact that the identities of some accommodationist ethnocultural groups are less likely to be entrenched and enduring than those of autonomist groups. More precisely, systems of political representation should be capable of allowing for the hybrid ethnocultural identities of some accommodationist minorities and the dynamic, voluntaristic character of accommodationist group boundaries.

The hybridity of ethnocultural identity refers to the capacity of individuals to simultaneously see themselves as members of diverse cultural groups, or as members of an ethnocultural group and of the larger social and political community. Accommodationist group boundaries are dynamic to the extent that they allow for the emergence of new group affiliations, the decline or disappearance of traditional groups, and the coalescing of group identities. The third characteristic of this conception of ethnocultural group identity, which Kymlicka calls the "cosmopolitan" view, is that group affiliation should be a voluntary individual decision rather than a collectively predetermined fact.[11] According to this view, it is the individual, and not the society or the ethnocultural group, who decides, or should decide, cultural group membership. Thus, an American child of a Puerto Rican father and an Asian-American mother, for instance, might identify herself, and should be given the option to identify herself, as Puerto Rican or Asian-American, as neither, or as both. The cosmopolitan view is thus at once descriptive and prescriptive, that is, it claims to accurately describe what is going on in some liberal multicultural societies containing accommodationist groups while also maintaining that it should be accepted because it conforms with the respect for individual choice and autonomy which is a central feature of liberal democracies.

As Kymlicka has argued, there are good reasons for advocating the cosmopolitan perspective of accommodationist group identity.[12] By focusing on civic identity as a basis for common citizenship, this approach has worked remarkably well in incorporating new ethnocultural immigrant groups into mainstream society in many contemporary democracies. In the U.S., it has certainly been successful in enabling Western European immigrants to become full-fledged social and political members of the polity, and it also promises to work well for more recent Latin American, Arab, and Asian immigrants. In the U.S. and Canada, rates of intermarriage among accommodationist groups, and among these groups and members of the majority society, have been rising in recent years. In Canada, mixed race groups are increasing, while in the U.S. intermarriage between whites and Latinos and Asian-Americans has been greatly increasing in recent years.[13]

However, rates of intermarriage in the U.S. between African-Americans and whites, though increasing, are much lower than those between other accommodationist groups and the majority society. The case of African-Americans raises an important point, namely, that not all accommodationist groups fit easily into the cosmopolitan model. It may be much more difficult to implement the cosmopolitan model in certain situations where racial, ethnological, or religious differences exist between accommodationist and majority cultural groups. The general social and cultural character of a society can also play a crucial role in whether these differences will be relevant. Americans are more reluctant than the British, for example, to fully integrate with blacks in common social organizations, close relationships, and intermarriage.[14] And in countries such as Germany, where conceptions of ethnological heritage are important for determining German citizenship, ethnic immigrants are not easily integrated into the social, economic, and political institutions and organizations of the society. The cosmopolitan model of accommodationist identity is much less likely to be implementable in these societies.

Given that in some situations accommodationist group boundaries are open-ended and dynamic while in others they are relatively closed and enduring, what are the implications of these observations for electoral systems which are adequate for accommodationist political empowerment? On the one hand, a consequence entailed by these observations is that systems of representation that treat accommodationist groups as monolithic, involuntary, and permanent are not suitable for accommodationist political self-determination. In order to conform with the cosmopolitan character of accommodationist group boundaries, electoral systems must allow for the members of the polity to freely affiliate according to their political interests and self-ascribed cultural membership. But on the other hand, allowance must also be made by fair systems of representation for those accommodationist groups whose identity may be perceived by the dominant society, and perhaps by themselves as well, as being relatively deep-rooted and enduring. At first sight these might seem to be contradictory requirements, in that no electoral system could comply with both of these conditions. But as we shall see below, it is possible to consistently accommodate these adequacy conditions. To see how this could be done, it would be useful to begin by distinguishing between different forms of proportional representation. Because some of these electoral systems allow individuals to determine for themselves their group identity and affiliation, they seem like promising systems for accommodationist political self-determination.

Generally, systems of proportional representation could be classified as being of two types, rigid proportional representation (RPR) and flexible proportional representation (FPR). In the former type of system ethnocultural groups are guaranteed a predetermined number of seats in governing bodies or institutions of political authority in proportion to their percentage of the population. Such seats or positions can be filled only by the members of pre-selected ethnocultural groups. Systems of rigid proportional representation are more suitable for multicultural democracies comprised of autonomist groups or where power-sharing arrangements are agreed upon by different ethnocultural groups. In these societies— such as Belgium and Malaysia where ethnocultural group divisions are more deep-rooted and enduring—systems of rigid proportional representation recognize and reinforce the distinctness of the separate social and political communities which the different groups inhabit.

Electoral systems of flexible proportional representation, on the other hand, are designed to accommodate the fluidity and open-ended nature of cultural group (as well as other) affiliations and coalitions. These systems do not pre-identify certain ethnocultural groups as needing special forms of political representation, but facilitate the representation of minorities while allowing individuals to define for themselves their principal interests and group affiliations. These systems are still categorized as involving proportional representation, however, because they are structured in such a way that they facilitate the election of political representatives in proportion to the support they received in elections. As we shall see in what follows, systems of flexible proportional representation do not have the drawbacks of assuming that the boundaries of ethnocultural group identity are permanent, that the interests of all members of an ethnocultural minority coincide, or that only ethnocultural minority candidates can advocate in favor of their groups' needs and interests.

But perhaps most important, these flexible electoral systems do not depend on a prior identification of the ethnocultural groups which merit proportional representation. Identifying such groups in a normatively nonarbitrary manner is difficult to do. As we noted in the last chapter, the two most plausible ways of identifying such groups is on the basis of self-government rights and systematic discrimination. Since we are considering accommodationist groups, the self-government criterion, which applies to autonomist groups, is not relevant here, and this leaves us with the systematic discrimination criterion only. Even though this standard can be readily applied to certain ethnocultural groups, such as African-Americans and Chicanos in the southwestern parts of the U.S., it is much more difficult to determine whether it applies to other accommodationist groups whose historical or present circumstances of institutionalized, pervasive, and systematic discrimination may not be as clearly established. Claims of systematic discrimination are particularly difficult to

evaluate in multicultural societies with a large number of accommodationist groups, some of whom may have experienced pervasive discrimination in the past but no longer endure such discrimination and some of
whom are recent immigrants without a history of subjugation but who
suffer significant discrimination at the present. Given that neither self-
government rights nor systematic discrimination provide an adequate
basis for employing rigid proportional representation in multicultural
democracies with accommodationist groups, let us examine electoral systems of flexible proportional representation.

Prominent examples of systems of flexible proportional representation
are the party-list system, the single-transferable vote (STV) system, and
cumulative voting.[15] In the party-list system, political parties nominate a
list of candidates for the contested seats in multimember districts, and
voters cast their ballots for a whole party list. The seats that parties receive are determined by their share of the vote. If a party wins 30 percent
of the vote in a ten-seat district, for example, it receives three seats. Thus,
it is not necessary for a party to obtain a majority or plurality of votes to
win some seats. In the STV system, candidates are elected in multimember districts, with parties nominating candidates for the contested seats.
Candidates are listed individually in the ballots, and voters get to rank
the candidates in order of their preference, so that a voter's first choice
gets a 1, his second choice a 2, and so on. Voters are not confined to voting for candidates in only one party, but can vote for candidates from different parties. In order to determine which candidates get elected, a
threshold or quota is set to determine the number of first-place votes a
candidate needs to get elected. Usually the threshold number of first-
place votes is calculated by adding one vote to the total number of ballots
cast divided by the number of contested seats plus one. For example, in
an election in which 100,000 votes were cast in a race where nine seats
were contested, the threshold number would be

$$100,000/9+1 + 1 = 10,001.$$

This number represents the smallest number of first-place votes that are
required to ensure that a candidate gets elected.

Once a candidate attains the required number of threshold votes, any
surplus ballots (i.e., votes that exceed the threshold) that she received are
transferred over to the next preferred candidates on her ballots. That is,
the number two candidates on the surplus ballots get those votes, which
in turn count towards their attaining the required threshold number of
votes. Once the surplus ballots are redistributed in this manner, the votes
are counted again to determine if any of the other candidates has reached
the threshold number. If no candidate has reached it, the votes of the candidate with the fewest first place votes are redistributed to the second-

choice candidates on their ballots and the votes are counted again to see who has reached the required number of votes to be elected. The process continues in this manner until all of the contested positions are filled. Most of the votes cast in an election using the STV system count towards the election of some candidate and practically all voters get to elect one of the candidates they most strongly prefer.

In cumulative voting, the votes that electors get to cast is equal to the number of seats that are being contested, except that, unlike more conventional electoral systems, electors can concentrate their votes in any way they please. Thus, citizens can cast all of their votes for one candidate, rather than having to distribute them among the candidates running for each contested seat. For instance, in an election in which there are seven contested seats, electors can cast four of their votes for one candidate and three for another, or can cast all of their votes for one candidate only. In cumulative voting, voters can express the intensity of their support for particular candidates by the number of votes they cast in their favor.

The party-list, STV, and cumulative voting systems provide greater opportunities for minorities to elect candidates of their choice. These electoral systems stand in stark contrast to the winner-take-all single-member plurality (SMP) systems in which a plurality of votes is need in order to elect a candidate. In SMP systems, candidates run in single-member districts and the candidate with the most votes wins the election. In these winner-take-all systems, a sizable portion of the electorate may end up without a representative to advocate for their views on the issues. Unless there is universal agreement among the citizenry regarding policy matters, which is rarely the case, the person elected will defend a position which reflects the needs and interests of those individuals who voted for her. And it will not do to argue here that the people who voted for a losing candidate in a given district will have their interests represented by another candidate from another district who holds views similar to their own, so that the political system will take their preferences into account after all. This argument mistakenly assumes that candidates representing the views of the people who voted for the losing candidate will in fact be elected in another district. But there is no guarantee that this will happen, and the citizens who voted for the losing candidate could very well be left without someone to represent their point of view. The dilemma of voters who end up without actual representation is particularly problematic in multicultural societies in which there are deep differences in the preferences and concerns of the citizenry.

Another serious problem with the SMP system is that it can give rise to *manufactured majorities*. This occurs when three or more parties nominate candidates in single-member districts and some candidates win without receiving a majority of the votes. As a result, a party may receive more than half of the seats in a legislative body even though it received less than 50 percent of the vote. For example, suppose that the candidate nominated by party A receives 38 percent of the vote and that the candidates of party B and party C received, respectively, 32 and 30 percent. If a similar distribution of votes is replicated in a sufficient number of districts, party A would receive more than 50 percent of the seats in the legislature even though significantly more than half of the electorate voted against this party. As Douglas Amy has indicated, this type of scenario is not unusual in SMP systems, but can be quite common.

> In a study of elections in six plurality and majority countries from 1945 to 1980, Arend Lijphart found that 45 percent of those elections resulted in manufactured majorities, while in Great Britain the figure was an impressive 91 percent. A good example was the 1987 British elections for Parliament. The Conservative party won 42.3 percent of the vote, the Labour party won 30.8 percent, and the Alliance of Social Democrats and Liberals 22.8 percent. The peculiar workings of the plurality system, however, resulted in the Conservative party receiving 58 percent of the seats in Parliament. The large majority of seats garnered by Thatcher's party gave the illusion of a strong public mandate for the prime minister and her conservative ideology ... but the opposite was in fact the case. The clear majority of British voters (53.6%) supported parties considerably to the left of the Conservative party—either liberal or socialist. But these parties were allocated substantially fewer seats than they deserved, particularly the Social Democrats and Liberals, who received 22.8 percent of the vote but were given only 3.4 percent of the seats. ... This electoral travesty was repeated in the 1992 British elections that saw the Conservative party—with John Major at the helm—gain yet another majority in Parliament, this time with only 41.9 percent of the vote.[16]

Another case of such democratic travesties occurred in the 1980 U.S. senate race in New York in which Republican Alphonse D'Amato won with 45 percent of the vote, while his opponents Democrat Liz Holtzman received 44 percent and Liberal party candidate Jacob Javits received 11 percent. Polls showed that D'Amato would have been defeated by Holtzman in a head-to-head race.[17] Due to the SMP system, even though a majority of the New York electorate preferred a senator with ideological orientations different than those of D'Amato, they ended up with him as their senator. It is important to note that this would not have happened had the STV system been used, because many of Javits's votes would have been redistributed to Holtzman, who would have obtained a majority of the votes and won the election. By taking into account the second strongest candidate preferences of Javits's ballots, a more democratic and just outcome to the senate race would have been obtained, one that more accurately reflected the will of the citizenry.

As we can see from these examples, in the SMP system a sizable number of voters can have their votes nullified or "wasted" because they will not count for the election of a candidate of their choice. SMP electoral systems do not exemplify very well the idea that all or practically all votes cast by the electorate should count towards some candidate's election. By contrast, in party-list, STV, and cumulative voting systems most or all votes count towards the election of some candidate or other, and in this sense they are more democratic and fair. These systems of flexible proportional representation allow the representation of minority interests to a much greater extent because in these systems it is not necessary to obtain a majority or a plurality of votes to get a candidate elected.

Since in SMP systems many voters are left without actual political representation, these electoral systems violate the democratic principle that voters are politically empowered only if their vote counts toward the election of a candidate who represents their needs and interests. Only in a conceptually perverse sense can it be said that a politician, even though she defends policies which are opposed to those you advocate, is *your* representative. Of course, in no democracy is the implementation of one's position on policy issues guaranteed. However, if a society is to call itself a democratic republic, it is surely imperative that the position of most of the voting citizenry on policy issues should be at least represented in the governing bodies which make collectively binding decisions. If those decisions are to be democratically legitimate and if citizens are morally bound to obey them, then they should have their point of view represented in the appropriate legislative bodies. If an electoral system thwarts the opportunity of a sizable portion of the citizenry to elect representatives who will voice their positions on policy issues, and if there are alternative systems available that do a much better job of fair democratic representation, then the members of the polity have a right to demand that the state employ the latter electoral systems. Available flexible systems of proportional representation are more democratically fair because in these systems the election of candidates more accurately reflects the proportion of voter support they had in the election.[18]

Do party-list, STV, and cumulative voting systems satisfy the conditions we identified above for accommodationist political empowerment? As we observed above, adequate systems of accommodationist political representation must simultaneously allow for groups that fit the cosmopolitan model of group identity and groups whose identity is seen as more exclusive and enduring. To see that these electoral systems satisfy these conditions, consider that they allow the members of accommodationist ethnocultural groups to determine their own primary political interests and cultural affiliations. Unlike systems of rigid proportional representation, these three systems respect the open-ended and dynamic nature of accommodationist group boundaries. At the same time, however, these electoral systems permit the self-organization of those accommodationist groups, such as African-Americans, whose group boundaries are treated by the majority society, and perhaps by themselves as well, as being more enduring and entrenched than that of other accommodationist groups. Such groups would be able to employ their more deeply entrenched group identity for political mobilization. Regarding accommodationist groups which do not fit easily into the cosmopolitan model, there would be no need to pre-identify them and grant them special representation status, as is sometimes done through race-conscious districting. And even though these systems have the desirable feature that they greatly facilitate the election of minority representatives that are accountable to minority voters, they do not rule out the possibility that minorities may decide under exceptional circumstances to elect non-minority representatives. As we observed earlier, the strong version of the mirror thesis is implausible, and in certain situations it may be the wisest choice for ethnocultural groups to elect non-minority candidates to represent them.

Party-list, STV, and cumulative voting would also encourage minority participation and cross-group coalition building among minority groups. Since with these electoral systems ethnocultural groups would not need a plurality or majority of votes to win seats, they would be encouraged to participate in political institutions in which they were formerly marginalized. In fact, there is empirical evidence that shows that when these systems are implemented, traditionally marginalized ethnocultural groups are able to elect their own representatives.[19] Moreover, in these systems ethnocultural groups would not have to defer to majority interests to elect representatives responsive to their needs. Minority political autonomy would be enhanced by the realization that since they have a realistic chance of electing their own representatives, they do not need to tailor their interests so that they conform to majority preferences. To the extent that different minority groups have similar interests in such areas as civil rights, affirmative action, social service programs, and criminal justice policies, they could more successfully implement cross-group coalitions which would increase their effectiveness in affecting policy-making. Such coalitions would also have the salutary effect of compelling majority legislators to consult and compromise with minority representatives to achieve the required support to pass legislation.

Finally, the party-list, STV, and cumulative voting systems have the advantage of being more adequate than SMP systems for representing not merely the interests of ethnocultural minorities, but the interests of the citizenry in general. Parties representing the interests of women, environmentalists, libertarians, and workers, for example, would have a greater opportunity to elect candidates of their choice. Flexible systems of proportional representation are also desirable because they promote the representation of minority interests while respecting the principle that each vote should have equal political value. That is, they restrain the potential domination of policy making by the majority without relying on mechanisms which grant minority votes disproportionate electoral weight.

The point made above regarding the greater political autonomy that accommodationist groups would attain with flexible systems of proportional representation raises the question of whether these systems would undermine political cooperation by fragmenting the polity. Wouldn't the polarization resulting from the enhanced capacity of minority parties to elect their own representatives ultimately work against minority interests? And would minorities, even if they were able to obtain proportional representation with these electoral systems, really fare better in competitive, polarized governing bodies given that they could still be outvoted? Here the question arises regarding the kind of discursive ethos of governing bodies that is most appropriate for accommodationist group empowerment. It is reasonable to suggest that in order for the needs and interests of everyone to be taken into account, public deliberation should involve not merely the citizenry, but legislative bodies as well.

That is, if the ideals of mutual understanding and cooperation are important for a multicultural society, the principles of deliberative democracy should be applied to the legislative process itself. This entails legislative decision making guided by the ideals of deliberative democracy, such as a concern for the common good, a commitment to consider the needs and interests of all members of the polity, a willingness to evaluate one's background assumptions and subject one's positions to critical scrutiny, and a commitment to find reasons that, as far as possible, are mutually acceptable. To the extent that these principles are the basis of legislative decision making, the dialogical relationship between legislators, including those from ethnocultural minorities and the dominant groups, would be guided not by an ethos of unyielding competitiveness, but by the goals of mutual recognition, understanding, and compromise. When legislative decision making is guided by such a dialogical ethos, minority representatives have a crucial role to play in legislative bodies attaining a greater comprehension of the common good, that is, attaining an understanding that includes the perspectives of all members of the polity.

In decision-making bodies that adopt the dialogical principles of deliberative democracy, the limited number of ethnocultural legislators would not seriously hinder the capacity of these legislators to implement policies that take the interests of their constituents into account. Since the goal of public deliberation is not to impose the interests of the majority on the rest of the polity, but to reach deliberative outcomes which grant equal consideration to the concerns of all citizens, the fact that ethnocultural legislators are in the minority would not represent as great a disadvantage as it would in a competitive framework of legislative decision making. Nevertheless, proposals in democratic governing bodies must still be subjected to a vote, and minority legislators can still be outvoted on proposals that would protect the interests of ethnocultural minorities. Are there institutional mechanisms that could lessen the position of relative disadvantage of minority representatives while promoting the ideals of deliberative democracy in the legislative decision-making process?

Melissa Williams has suggested that adopting supermajority requirements for the passage of legislation would strengthen the ethos of deliberative democracy in legislative bodies and diminish the impact of the numerical disadvantage faced by minority legislators in passing legislation.[20] Supermajority requirements would compel majority legislators to seek a greater degree of agreement concerning legislation and to court the vote of minority representatives. Since supermajority rules require more than a simple majority to pass legislation, in would be in the interest of majority legislators to seek the support of minority representatives, and it would induce all legislators to engage in deliberative procedures aimed at producing a greater level of agreement on policy issues. Supermajority requirements would provide an incentive for members of governing bodies to engage in deliberative procedures involving mutual recognition and the presentation of reasons for legislative proposals that take the interests of all into account. As Williams points out, it is too idealistic to believe that legislators will readily adopt the demanding requirements of deliberative democracy, and therefore it is important to adopt institutional measures that encourage the adoption of the principles of reasoned public deliberation. Williams also indicates, however, that there is a disadvantage to supermajority requirements, namely, that they could lead to legislative gridlock. Such legislative paralysis would not be in the interests of minorities, since it could likely entrench the status quo. For this reason, she recommends that supermajority rules be used in a careful and limited manner, for example, that they be restricted to crucial legislation such as budget and appropriations bills. Since budget decisions have to be made in order for the government to continue to function, legislators would have to negotiate with one another to reach such decisions. This would enhance the importance of minority representatives as potential allies in passing budget and appropriations bills, and this would in turn provide incentives for majority representatives to take the interests of minority legislators and their constituents into account.

In this section we have examined the importance of adopting electoral systems of proportional representation for achieving accommodationist political self-determination. In addition, we have observed that it is important to extend the principles of deliberative democracy to legislative decision making. Regarding the adoption of systems of proportional representation, it is worthwhile to note that most democracies already have some form of proportional representation in place, with the notable exception of the U.S., Canada, and Britain. The situation of political empowerment of ethnocultural minorities is particularly critical in the U.S., given the recent Supreme Court decisions declaring race-conscious congressional districting, one of the few mechanisms providing ethnocultural minorities in the U.S. with a measure of political equality, as unconstitutional. Another factor worsening the situation of U.S. minorities is the extremely high incarceration rate of African-Americans and Latinos. Regarding African-Americans, they are five times more likely to be arrested for drug offenses than white men, even though the prevalence of illegal drug use is about the same in both groups. About half of the inmates in the U.S. are black, and approximately twenty-five percent of black males are likely to go to prison during their lifetime.[21] If present trends continue, by 2020 about one third of all black males will be ineligible to vote. These facts represent a serious obstacle for black political empowerment, because they undermine the political capacity of black communities to control their own destinies. These developments make it imperative that measures such as proportional representation and deliberative democracy be adopted in the U.S. to provide ethnocultural minorities with a greater degree of political self-determination and that existing statutes concerning disfranchisement for certain felony convictions be scrutinized in public deliberation.

Finally, it bears repeating that in attaining political empowerment the goal of accommodationist groups is not to fragment the larger political community, but to achieve full and equal citizenship, and thereby greater integration in the common political union they share with the majority society. Ethnic resentments, suspicions, hatred, and segregation fester when ethnocultural groups are denied the opportunity to equitably influence the political process. It is when groups are marginalized and their political influence excluded or diluted that the most dangerous kinds of separatist identity politics emerge. A culturally pluralistic democracy with accommodationist groups that is truly willing to integrate them into its political, economic, and social institutions will fare much better concerning intercultural relations than one that refuses to recognize the reality of ethnocultural political disempowerment arising from structurally unjust systems of democratic representation.

Notes

1. Allen Buchanan, "Democracy and Secession," in *National Self-Determination and Secession*, ed. Margaret Moore (New York: Oxford University Press, 1998), pp. 14–15.

2. As we shall see in what follows, political representation will be construed broadly here to include representation in positions of legal authority, such as the positions of judges, police officers, parole officers, and so forth.

3. When I was on a tenure-track position in a research oriented university, I recall talking to my department chair concerning the additional obligations I had as a minority faculty. I told him how minority students would often come to my office seeking advice, sponsorship of their campus organization, participation and input into an upcoming cultural event, and so forth. I also indicated how often I was contacted by organizations and individuals in the university and in the community asking for my participation in a variety of organizations and events. Though I did not always agree to participate, far too often I found myself unable to deny them (particularly the students) my help and expertise. I knew only too well that the scarcity of minority faculty made it imperative for me not to refuse their requests. Moreover, I felt (as I still do) a responsibility to them and to those who came before me who helped me when I was going through the educational system. My department chair, a decent man sympathetic to minority issues, was totally oblivious to these special circumstances that I faced as a minority faculty, and admitted that the university criteria for promotion and tenure did not recognize them or take them sufficiently, if at all, into account. Though some skeptics may dismiss these insights as anecdotal accounts, they are very real to a great many minority faculty in this country, as well as in others.

4. For an account of how dominant groups have systematically used and oppressed ethnocultural groups, see Ted Robert Gurr, *Minorities at Risk: A Global View of Ethnopolitical Conflicts* (Washington, DC: United States Institute of Peace Press, 1993).

5. For a fuller discussion of this point, see Gurr, *Minorities at Risk*, chapter 6.

6. In some cases, additional considerations may complicate the granting of autonomist objectives. In the Middle East, for example, security concerns and the fact that the same territories have deep religious and cultural significance for Jews and Palestinians makes autonomist claims very difficult to resolve.

7. For an account of the discriminatory and oppressive practices inflicted on ethnocultural minorities around the world, see Gurr, *Minorities at Risk* and Hurst Hannum, *Autonomy, Sovereignty, and Self-Determination: The Accommodation of Conflicting Rights*, revised edition (Philadelphia: University of Pennsylvania Press, 1996).

8. Such forms of empowerment are particularly important for accommodationist groups who, because they are committed to living in a unitary social and political community with the majority society, will find themselves in direct competition with majority group members for positions of authority and power.

9. On this point, see Melissa S. Williams, *Voice, Trust, and Memory: Marginalized Groups and the Failings of Liberal Representation* (Princeton: Princeton University Press, 1998) chapter 5, and Jane Mansbridge, "In Defense of 'Descriptive' Representation," paper presented at the annual meeting of the American Political Science Association, San Francisco, 29 August–1 September 1996.

10. Williams, *Voice, Trust, and Memory*, p. 107.

11. Will Kymlicka, "American Multiculturalism in the International Arena," *Dissent*, (Fall 1998): pp. 73–79.

12. Ibid., p. 74.

13. Ibid., p. 74.

14. Leonard Steinhorn and Barbara Diggs-Brown, *By the Color of Our Skin: The Illusion of Integration and the Reality of Race* (New York: Dutton, 1999), p. 23.

15. Strictly speaking, cumulative voting is a system of semi-proportional representation. This is because it is possible in this system for the representation of a party or group not to reflect its voting strength. If too many candidates are nominated by a party, for example, proportional representation will not necessarily result. For discussions of cumulative voting, see Douglas J. Amy, *Real Choices/New Voices* (New York: Columbia University Press, 1993), pp. 186–87 and p. 232. See also *United States Electoral Systems: Their Impact on Women and Minorities*, eds. Wilma Rule and Joseph F. Zimmerman (New York: Greenwood Press, 1992), p. 183–196 and p. 214.

True systems of proportional representation all share the following three characteristics: (i) they are applied in multimember districts, (ii) it is not necessary for candidates to obtain a majority or plurality of votes to get elected, and (iii) they allocate seats in proportion to voting results. For a fuller discussion of these systems see Amy, *Real Choices/New Voices*.

16. Ibid., p. 34.

17. Ibid., p. 35.

18. The viability of flexible systems of proportional representation is amply demonstrated by the fact that the vast majority of liberal democratic governments use these electoral systems. For a response to arguments showing the problems with proportional representation, see Amy, *Real Choices/New Voices*, chapter 8, and Williams, *Voice, Trust, and Memory*, chapter 7.

19. For instance, see Richard L. Engstrom, Delbert A. Taebel, and Richard L. Cole, "Cumulative Voting as a Remedy for Minority Vote Dilution: The Case of Alamogordo, New Mexico," *Journal of Law and Politics* 5(3) (1989): 469–97; Richard L. Cole, Delbert A. Taebel, and Richard L. Engstrom, "Cumulative Voting in a Municipal Election: A note on Voter Reaction and Electoral Consequences," *Western Political Quarterly* 43 (1) (1990): 191–199; and Richard L. Engstrom and Charles J. Barilleaux, "Native-Americans and Cumulative Voting," *Social Science Quarterly* 72 (2) (1991): 388–93. These references are cited in Williams, *Voice, Trust, and Memory*, p. 217. For further evidence establishing the effectiveness of proportional representation in electing ethnocultural minorities, see also Leon Weaver and Judith Baum, "Proportional Representation on New York City Community School Boards," in *United States Electoral Systems*, Rule and Zimmerman, pp.197–205.

20. Williams, *Voice, Trust, and Memory*, pp. 226–27 and p. 235.

21. See, Eric Schlosser, "The Prison Industrial Complex," *Atlantic Monthly*, Vol. 282, no. 6 (December, 1998): 51–77, p. 54.

7

Self-Determination for Autonomist and Secessionist Groups

Because autonomist and secessionist claims to self-determination are both essentially based on appeals to self-governance, their normative justifiability is best examined together. The political arrangements that would satisfy these appeals for self-governance can range from limited local or regional jurisdiction over political and cultural functions to independent statehood. The core rationale underlying autonomist and secessionist claims is that they constitute a distinctive people or nation with a right to autonomously determine their sociocultural, political, and economic affairs. To attain an adequate understanding of autonomist and secessionist self-determination, the single most important error we must avoid is the imposition of a model of ethnocultural relations that is inappropriate for these groups. Unless we recognize the important differences between the three categories of ethnocultural groups I have identified, we cannot attain a proper understanding of either the normative or empirical issues involved. Because some writers on multiculturalism fail to draw the appropriate distinctions between these groups, they repeatedly make serious mistakes in their conceptualization of the empirical and moral issues confronting these groups and the societies in which they live.[1]

Our analysis of accommodationist political self-determination focused on equality within the majority society's political institutions. Given the normatively well-grounded status of political equality, our emphasis was not on the normative justification of the latter but on identifying the appropriate resources and institutional mechanisms to ensure equitable political representation for accommodationist groups. Due to the disputed nature of rights to self-governance, when we consider autonomist and secessionist political self-determination our focus will shift to normative considerations, even though the institutional means for achieving self-determination for these groups will also be considered. A number of different factors will emerge as normatively relevant when discussing autonomist and secessionist self-determination, including, *inter alia*, issues of more deeply entrenched group identity, historical claims of coerced or unjust incorporation into the state, cultural survival and, most important, claims invoking a *sui generis* right to self-governance.

Writers who have examined the normative justification of the right to self-governance usually refer to it as the right to self-determination. To avoid confusion in the discussion that follows, it is important to keep in mind this terminological distinction: while I have used, and will continue to use, the notion of self-determination to refer to the varied and complex issues related to the political, cultural, and economic empowerment of the three categories of ethnocultural groups I have identified, most other writers use the concept of self-determination in a more narrow sense, namely, to refer to claims by national minorities to form their own autonomous political community. In this more restricted sense, self-determination denotes the disputed right of nations or peoples to control their own destinies through rights of self-governance, which are usually understood as involving either secession or partial autonomy. I will use the term "self-governance" to refer to the two latter forms of political empowerment, and will continue to use "self-determination" to refer to my more inclusive conception of ethnocultural empowerment. It is also important to note that when discussing the moral rationale for autonomist and secessionist claims, some of the arguments will apply primarily to indigenous, ethnonationalists, and secessionist groups, and less so to communal contenders. I will specify when normative or empirical considerations apply to all of the groups in the autonomist and secessionist categories (by using these terms without qualification) or to indigenous, ethnonationalist, and secessionist groups only.

Two advantages of using the notion of self-determination in the way I do are that, on the one hand, it makes it easier to avoid the mistaken view that accommodationist minorities (since they don't clamor for "self-determination" in the way autonomist and secessionist groups do) already have the requisite rights and resources for self-determination and, on the other, it helps us to appreciate the complexity of self-determination and the interconnections between its various components. In what follows I will draw upon the different aspects of self-determination I have articulated to evaluate autonomist and secessionist claims. As we shall see, our previous discussion of such themes as the function and justification of political communities and the various dimensions of ethnocultural empowerment will help us arrive at a more adequate assessment of the moral justifiability of their claims.

My discussion of the meaning and justifiability of self-determination for autonomist and secessionist groups is divided into four parts. I begin by discussing several general objections against ethnocultural group claims for self-governance, continue by articulating a general normative justification for autonomist and secessionist claims, and then examine some objections that are directed specifically against secession. I conclude the chapter by discussing the factors, other than political self-governance, that are necessary for autonomist and secessionist groups to achieve self-determination in the expansive and integrated sense described in Chapter 5.

The Moral Justification of Self-Governance

Self-governance could be understood as a process in which a group of individuals establish and maintain their own autonomous political community. This political community could either be situated within a larger political body, such as a confederated state, or it could consist of a sovereign and independent state. At first sight, the right of a collectivity to form a political union, at least in countries that recognize principles of democratic governance, may seem to be morally unproblematic. After all, the right of association is recognized by democratic polities as a fundamental civil right, and the effort to form an autonomous political body could be seen as a case of associational freedom. However, the formation of an autonomous political community cannot be seen merely as an exercise in liberty of association because, as pointed out in Chapter 4, the formation of such political communities usually involves territorial control, including powers to appropriate natural resources and determine immigration policies, that affect the members of other political societies. Unlike cases of associational freedom, in which typically the welfare of others is not significantly affected, the formation of a political society changes the physical and moral universe in which other individuals and political communities function. Given the moral consequences of the formation and maintenance of political bodies, reliance on associational freedom is by itself not sufficient to justify self-governance claims. In addition, to understand the claims of autonomist and secessionist groups for self-governance merely as appeals to exercise freedom of association fails to capture an essential feature of their demands, namely, that they are a people with the right to control their own political affairs. Indeed, the debate on the justifiability of autonomist and secessionist claims has centered primarily on whether nations or peoples have the right to self-governance.

As noted earlier, one of the forms that autonomous governance can take is regional autonomy within a larger, sovereign political body. Though such forms of self-governance do not involve divorce from the existing state, they entail a significant bifurcation of the existing political community. The depth of the political bifurcation depends on the kind and degree of autonomy involved. Institutional arrangements for ethno-cultural group autonomy can include federalism, regionalism, administrative decentralization, various forms of local government, and the use of offices for community development.[2] These various arrangements give rise to different degrees of autonomy and provide control of political and cultural institutions that is at least partly independent of the central government. Secession, on the other hand, involves complete alienation from the existing political community and the subsequent creation of a sovereign state or irredentist integration with another political community. As might be expected, secessionist struggles are generally more contentious than claims for autonomous governance, and additional normative and pragmatic obstacles have to be overcome before secessions can be justified and successfully implemented.

General Arguments against Self-Governance

A number of general arguments could be raised against claims for self-governance. First, it could be argued that autonomist and secessionist demands undermine certain key factors important for the functioning of democratic societies.[3] According to this argument, the cultivation of civic virtues important for democratic polities requires a stable political community. In particular, for the members of a democratic society to make a commitment to develop civic virtues, they need to believe that they and their progeny will be subject to the collective decisions made by that political community. Unless citizens have a reasonable expectation that their political community will be stable enough that they and their children will actually get to live by the collective decisions made by the members of the polity, they will have little incentive to take the time and effort required to deliberate in a conscientious manner regarding the alternatives before them. Why would individuals stay informed about political issues, learn the skills of civic dialogue and compromise, and strive to understand the needs and interests of their fellow citizens, for example, without a reasonable assurance that their political community will be sufficiently enduring to implement their decisions? A political community that lives under the threat of being fragmented by groups that demand their own separate and autonomous political institutions is not a stable civic environment in which the virtues of democratic citizenship can be developed.

Moreover, the threat of political fragmentation not only frustrates reasonable expectations that the political community will live by the decisions arrived at, it also undermines the conviction among the citizenry that they constitute a common political body. Without the belief that they are a united political community with a shared political future, it will be difficult for members of the polity to compromise and moderate their demands for the sake of the common good. The social solidarity necessary for the effective functioning of a political union will be lacking when some sectors of the citizenry refuse to make a definite and reliable commitment to the general welfare of their political society and to their fellow citizens. In short, demands or threats to fragment the political society through autonomous governance or secession engender a political milieu fraught with resentment and suspicion between cultural groups.

Another argument that could be raised against demands for self-governance is that they unjustly deprive the majority group in the existing political community of their right to preserve the cultural and political character of the society they have established. If a political community was founded on specific cultural traditions, the founding group has a right to require that all of the members of that political body respect and grant their allegiance to those cultural traditions. In making these demands the members of the majority cultural group are simply exercising their right to determine the character of their own political community, that is, they are preserving their culturally distinctive way of life. If self-governance in a cultural community of their choosing is a fundamental right of collectivities, then the majority society, as much as any other group, should be able to determine the course of its own future by preserving the character of the political community it has created. All groups within the political union should seek empowerment within the institutional framework of the political society of which they are already a part, and not try to destroy this union by demanding their own separate and autonomous political institutions or communities.

These arguments, if effective, would seriously undermine secessionist claims, and they would also have considerable force against autonomist demands, since autonomous governance involves a partial fragmentation of the existing political community. The soundness of these arguments, however, is questionable. The argument concerning the need for the citizenry to be assured that their political community will maintain its unitary character neglects the reasons that ethnocultural groups use to challenge the political boundaries of existing states. While it is important for a democratic polity to support the cultivation of civic virtues and mutual political commitments by maintaining its institutional integrity and territorial boundaries, it is not the case that these goals always morally outweigh all other considerations. In some culturally pluralistic democracies, there may be compelling reasons why some sectors of the citizenry may not have a vested interest in remaining part of the political community. As we observed in our discussion of political inequalities in Chapter 2, in some multicultural societies the differences in worldview between cultural groups may be so great that it is highly improbable that mutual understanding can be reached. In such situations, ethnocultural minorities are likely to be constantly on the losing end of democratic deliberations. When this occurs, ethnocultural minorities will suffer serious political inequalities and lose the capacity to effectively influence political decision making. It is reasonable to question whether maintaining the existing political union should morally outweigh democratic equality and empowerment. There is no prima facie reason to believe that preserving the status quo should take normative precedence over the fundamental right of the members of ethnocultural minorities to determine in a democratic manner the course of their own lives.

Against the argument that autonomist and secessionist claims undermine the capacity of the members of the majority cultural group to preserve the character of their political community, we could respond that appeals for self-governance do not at all pose this threat to the majority society. If ethnocultural groups were provided with the opportunity to create and maintain their own separate political and cultural institutions, the members of the majority society could still preserve their cultural and political traditions within their own political community by, for example, retaining control of the language for conducting state transactions, preserving the structure of their political institutions, determining the educational content required in schools, and deciding on state symbols and official holidays. Granting ethnocultural minorities the right to self-governance, whether in the form of autonomous governance or secession, would provide them with a right that the majority already enjoys, namely, the right to determine their own political and cultural destinies by creating an interconnected system of political, cultural, and economic institutions that expresses and sustains their way of life. While granting autonomous governance or independence to an ethnocultural group would obviously change the character of the existing political community, the majority society would not be deprived of its right to maintain, in Walzer's terms, a self-governing cultural community of character and memory. Of course, there may be other considerations, particularly in the case of secession, that could override autonomist and secessionist claims, but the appeal by the majority to live in a political community that reflects its cultural traditions is not by itself a decisive or even persuasive reason for rejecting self-governance claims.

Those intent on preserving intact the existing political community, however, may be dissatisfied with the reasons I have given. They may argue that the crucial issue is not whether the members of the majority society retain the right to determine the nature of their political community, but whether they can preserve the state in its existing form, with its territorial boundaries intact. After all, this is their land, the land they have cultivated and defended with their sweat and blood, and which they are now trying to prevent from being torn asunder. Living in this land should be done on their terms and in a way that respects their cultural traditions and way of life. Any group living within the territorial boundaries of their country should take whatever steps are necessary for them to adapt to living in their political community.

Two Rationales for Self-Governance

In responding to the latter argument, the most important, and I believe decisive, rejoinders can be given by ethnocultural groups seeking self-governance. The first of these responses, which applies primarily to indigenous, ethnonationalist, and secessionist groups, is that they never voluntarily joined the political community from which they want to partly or completely separate; rather, they were coercively incorporated into this political community through conquest, forced annexation, invasive settlement, or territorial transfer or partitioning between imperial powers. By emphasizing the historical fact of coerced incorporation, these ethnocultural groups would challenge a fundamental assumption made by members of the dominant society, namely, that they and the minority group form a common political community. In this way, these ethnocultural groups would change the issue from one in which they appear to unjustifiably renege on a commitment to live in a unitary political community to one in which they have been unjustly deprived of their fundamental right of self-governance. Indigenous, ethnonationalist, and secessionist groups would maintain that, far from failing to live up to a prior commitment, they never made such a commitment in the first place, and have for many years been denied of their right to democratically determine the course of their own lives. Their claims thus involve a re-appropriation of a long denied fundamental right, one which the majority society already enjoys and takes for granted, for certainly the members of the majority society believe they constitute a distinct nation or people with rights to maintain a political community with territorial borders over which they have exclusive control. The majority society cannot consistently deny these ethnocultural groups a right that it already possesses and that it recognizes as fundamental to the well-being of its members.

The argument could be raised here that the group that was coercively incorporated into the existing political community consisted of different individuals than those who presently comprise the ethnocultural communities, and that therefore the harm was strictly speaking not done to the latter persons but to individuals who no longer exist. Thus, the present members of these minority communities cannot demand that a right of which they were deprived now be recognized, because this right was not denied to them in the first place.

In answering this argument, it is important to realize that typically the identity of the ethnocultural groups who make these self-governance claims is grounded on the idea that they are a culturally distinct people with ancestral connections to formerly self-governing communities who were forcibly incorporated into the existing state. Their sense of political alienation, which is all too often reinforced by a *de facto* marginalization from equitable participation in the political life of the majority society, stems partly from the fact that they lost their status as a distinct self-governing political community. For the members of indigenous, ethnonationalist, and secessionist groups, historical facts concerning forced incorporation and loss of territorial control of their homelands have moral relevance because they see themselves as the existing members of the communities that were deprived of their autonomy, that is, they have intergenerational and cultural connections with the former members of those communities. If we are to make any sense at all of the identity of political and cultural communities through time—as we certainly must in order to recognize the territorial collective rights and the sovereignty claims of the present members of established states—then we must acknowledge the meaningfulness of the transtemporal membership of distinct individuals in political and cultural communities. Further, to admit that it is meaningful to say that different individuals can belong to the *same* community at distinct and non-overlapping times is to recognize that the members of ethnocultural groups can make legitimate claims regarding past injustices committed against *their* community. Thus, assuming that there are no compelling normative considerations that override the rectification of past harms, it is legitimate for these groups to demand the restoration of the autonomy and territorial control of which their community was deprived. How morally compelling their appeals are will of course depend on the historical accuracy of their claims regarding lost autonomy, but the fact that the members of the ethnocultural groups presently making self-governance claims were not the actual individuals whose collective autonomy was violated does not present a problem for the legitimacy of their claims.[4]

The second way in which indigenous, ethnonationalist, and secessionist groups can defend their self-governance claims is by arguing that by living in the same political community with the majority society, they do not have sufficient or adequate control of the decisions they make in the cultural, political, and economic dimensions of their lives. These groups often maintain that by being forced to live with the majority society, which they regard as an alien or even hostile cultural group, their autonomy is significantly impaired or denied altogether. The impairment or denial of autonomy can take various forms, including systematic discrimination and oppression, prohibition of the preservation of culture, political marginalization resulting from radical cultural incommensurability and, in the most extreme cases, endangerment of physical security. The crux of this defense of self-governance is not the restoration of lost autonomy, but the appeal to a *sui generis* right to self-governance and the corresponding limitations in cultural, political, and economic autonomy that result from being denied the right to live in a political community in which they can sustain their common way of life.

Even though the autonomy-denying injustices inflicted on indigenous, ethnonationalist, and secessionist groups are in themselves serious harms, these groups take these injustices as prima facie reasons for altering or dissolving their political union with the majority society. That is, they see the harms they have suffered as evidence that they cannot exercise political, cultural, and economic autonomy as long as they remain part of the political union from which they want to separate. For these ethnocultural groups, it would not do merely to rectify these injustices if the existing political arrangements remain the same. In other words, the normative relevance of this second rationale lies not so much in the injustices these groups have experienced, as in the fact that these injustices are the result of their being denied self-governance. If the point at issue were merely state-inflicted harms, the state could wholly undermine their claims to self-governance by rectifying these harms and developing institutional mechanisms to prevent their reoccurrence.

To be sure, state-inflicted harms often do play a role in an ethnocultural group's articulation of its claim to self-governance, but this role is essentially a supportive one, that is, these injustices serve to establish the marginalized, second-class status of the members of the ethnocultural minority in the political community. The *de facto* status of the group members as second-class citizens lends credibility to their claim that they are not perceived by the dominant society as political equals or full members of the political community. This insight also supports their contention that the best way to ensure that these injustices will not occur in the future is by granting the group powers of self-governance. In brief, if we understand autonomist and secessionist claims simply as appeals to be treated justly by the dominant society, we will fail to see an essential feature of their claims, namely, that they do not form, and do not want to form, a common unitary political community with the majority society. For these groups the only proper way to rectify these harms is by attaining partial autonomy or secession.

Communal contenders would also rely on the second rationale to justify self-governance. That is, they would maintain that they have a right to determine their own affairs because they are a distinctive people or nation with the *sui generis* right to self-determination. In contrast to states in which indigenous, ethnonationalist, and secessionist groups live, however, in democracies with power-sharing or consociational arrangements among communal contenders there is already a general understanding that the society consists of distinct groups deeply divided by ethnicity, religion, language, race, or national origin. Whereas in countries in which the former groups live it is a more common occurrence for the majority society to contest the status of indigenous, ethnonationalist, and secessionist minorities as distinct peoples or nations—and even try to forcibly assimilate them into the majority culture—in consociational democracies the major problem is finding fair institutional arrangements that will allow autonomous governance and the stable sharing of political power among communal contenders. Even when just autonomous governance and power-sharing arrangements are found, in some of these democracies there can be an ongoing problem of insuring that the most powerful group does not use its political or economic advantages to undermine the distribution of power or the well-being of the other ethnocultural groups.

Communal contenders are also not likely to emphasize coerced incorporation into the state as a justification for self-governance. But for communal contenders, the absence of a history of coerced incorporation or of systematic discrimination does not diminish the moral justifiability of their claim to be a distinct ethnocultural group with the right to partly determine its own affairs. Their appeal to a *sui generis* fundamental right to self-governance is conceptually independent of other group claims to regain status as autonomous cultural-political communities.

To be sure, consociational political arrangements sometimes come at a cost. Devising institutional structures that guarantee different ethnocultural groups political representation will entrench group divisions and formalize the fragmentation of the political community. On the other hand, when cultural identities are deep-rooted, long-standing, and likely to persist, it seems preferable to develop democratic structures in which the ethnocultural groups constituting the society are guaranteed democratic representation, rather than pretend that the body politic is a unitary political community in which the representatives of the dominant groups genuinely protect the needs and interests of other groups. It is important to remember that while some consociational arrangements have failed (Lebanon), others have been stable and democratically fair (Belgium and Switzerland). A multicultural society with communal contenders needs to reinforce democratic institutions and civil life, and minimize such factors as ethnocultural discrimination, intercultural economic differences, and intolerant religious fundamentalism. Consociational arrangements work best in settings in which the influence of these elements has been arrested. As long as such elements are pervasive, any democratic structure in a pluralistic society is likely to be subverted.

Thus, there are two rationales to which an ethnocultural group can appeal in justifying its claims for self-governance. One involves the re-appropriation of lost political autonomy and of control of territory that was formerly under its jurisdiction. The other involves the claim that it cannot properly determine the course of its own political, cultural, and economic future without powers of self-governance. The moral force of the first rationale depends on the justness of retrieving something that was unjustly appropriated, while that of the second rests on the notion that, at least under certain circumstances, an ethnocultural group can claim a right to form its own political and cultural community. As we have observed, the second rationale, though often couched in terms of injustices committed by the state, is normatively underpinned by a *sui generis* appeal to collective autonomy and by the contention that the only appropriate remedy for these injustices is the granting of self-governance. We should also note that the second rationale can be employed even though an ethnocultural group may have never had its own independent political community. Examples of groups who might rely primarily on the first rationale are the Palestinians and the Tamils of Sri Lanka, while the Kurds could be considered as an example of a group who would rely on the latter. In many cases ethnocultural groups try to strengthen their case for self-governance by appealing to both of these rationales, whenever the historical evidence warrants such appeals.

Even though in practice these rationales can be treated as distinct, they are theoretically connected in the sense that the first rationale is less basic than and dependent on the second; in other words, the moral justifiability of the former depends on the justifiability of the latter. Presumably the claim of a people or nation to regain their autonomy and territory is morally compelling because, as a people or nation, they had the basic right to govern themselves in the first place. Unless we assume that the ethnocultural group had a legitimate prior right to form and maintain their own political community, it is unclear why their present claim to regain the autonomy and territory of which they were deprived would have any moral weight. It is thus questionable whether it can be consistently maintained, as writers such as Allan Buchanan have done[5], that ethnocultural groups do not have a positive right to self-governance, but that they have the right to regain the autonomy and territorial control they formerly possessed. This is not to deny that there may be normative and practical considerations that may constrain the form of autonomy a group should now obtain (particularly if secession is involved), but it is questionable whether we can categorically deny a positive or *sui generis* right to self-governance while acknowledging the justifiability of reparatory or remedial claims to the same right.[6]

It is worthwhile to note the basic *sui generis* right to self-governance of autonomist and secessionist groups is ultimately the same as the justification which grounds the right of the members of established states to preserve their own political community. Since the underlying justification for the formation and maintenance of political communities, namely the promotion of human flourishing, is basically the same for established and aspiring political bodies, it is illegitimate to demand that fundamentally different normative conditions be met before autonomist and secessionist groups can exercise self-governance. I emphasize this point because in the literature on self-determination a double standard is often assumed concerning the justification of emerging political communities. Some writers introduce a host of criteria that ethnocultural groups must meet (such as a set of necessary and sufficient conditions that guarantee that they are a distinct people or nation) before self-governance rights can be granted even though such criteria could not be met by most established states. Again, as I have noted repeatedly, there may be normative and practical considerations which in particular cases override self-governance claims, but in general we should not treat the justification of established and emerging political communities as essentially distinct moral cases.

Buchanan's Theory of Secession. It would be instructive to evaluate my justification of self-governance, particularly secession, by examining Allan Buchanan's theory of secession, which is perhaps the most fully developed normative theory on the subject. This will help clarify certain aspects of my position as well as identify some shortcomings of his theory.

Buchanan has proposed a theory of secession according to which secession is justified if it is a response to serious injustices, is the only feasible way to prevent the genocide of an ethnocultural group, results from a mutual agreement between the established state and the seceding political community, or involves the exercise of a pre-existing constitutional right.[7] He also requires that certain supplementary conditions be met, such as the negotiation of a bilateral agreement regarding payment of the national debt, partitioning of federal properties, and the demarcation of borders. In addition, credible guarantees need to be provided by the seceding political community regarding the protection of the basic rights of the minorities that will live in the new state. In short, according to Buchanan, secession is justified if it is a remedial response to substantial injustices, prevents gross harms, or results from bilateral agreement.

I believe that Buchanan is correct to require the above-mentioned supplementary conditions for a justifiable secession, and he is also on solid ground in maintaining that a secession can be justified if it results from a mutual agreement or the exercise of a constitutional right. Further, because the genocide of a people is one of the most morally repugnant actions a state can perpetrate, he is correct to maintain that genocidal policies override whatever claims the state has to the territory inhabited by the persecuted group. However, the rationale for secession based on serious injustices requires more careful consideration.

In examining what is involved in the remedial rationale for secession, it is crucial to be clear about precisely what constitutes a serious injustice. According to Buchanan, among the most important of injustices is the coerced annexation by a state of a political community and its territory. He believes that secession is justified as a reparatory measure to regain unjustly appropriated territory. Other serious injustices include infringe-ments of rights such as those of democratic governance, equality of economic opportunity, physical security, and liberty. To count as reasons for secession, these violations must be systematic and widespread. Thus, if a society systematically deprives ethnocultural minorities of their voting rights, if it instigates or allows pogroms against them, or if it implements policies which redistribute economic benefits and resources in a discriminatory and morally arbitrary manner, the ethnocultural group is justified in making secessionist claims as a means of rectifying these injustices. These examples of human rights are generally recognized as protecting fundamental interests, so it is incontrovertible to regard their violation as constituting serious harms. But conspicuously absent from the list of injustices deemed serious enough to warrant secession are violations of rights to cultural survival.

Buchanan contends that the justification of secession based on cultural survival has limited force.[8] He argues that the right to maintain one's culture cannot be reasonably construed as the right of a group to preserve its culture in perpetuity. In the contemporary world, Buchanan points out, there are some cultures that do not have a good chance of surviving, and it would be unreasonable for the members of these cultures to demand whatever resources are necessary for them to preserve their culture. Even though he recognizes the centrality of cultural membership for meaningful choice-making and for communal relationships that preserve self-identity, he argues that it would be detrimental, in at least some cases, to provide ethnocultural groups with the resources for what is essentially a doomed project. He contends that it is morally problematic to help them try to perpetuate an endangered culture when there are viable cultures available that they and their children would be able to enjoy if they only stopped their futile efforts of cultural preservation.[9] In other words, by helping them maintain an unviable culture, we are preventing them from recognizing the futility of their project and therefore from adopting a sustainable culture in which they and their children could enjoy the benefits of cultural membership. He qualifies these remarks by admitting that changing cultural membership may be very difficult or impossible for the members of some groups, but he emphasizes the unreasonable character of rights to the preservation of cultures that are not viable in the contemporary world.

One of the conditions that Buchanan requires before cultural survival can be used to justify secession is that neither the established state nor any other political community makes claims to the seceding territory.[10] He imposes this condition because he believes that violations of the right to cultural survival are insufficiently serious to override the state's claim to its territory. This is a very stringent condition for the normative legitimacy of a rationale for secession, because in the vast majority of cases the established state will claim as its own all of the territory under its control.

If neither the state nor any other political community had any claims to the contested territory, it is highly unlikely that the difficult issue of secession would even arise. By imposing this condition, Buchanan in effect makes it practically impossible for ethnocultural groups to employ cultural survival as a basis for defending their claim to secede.

Finally, Buchanan contends that if cultural preservation is of concern to ethnocultural groups, there are political arrangements short of secession that could protect their culture. By granting these minorities rights that preserve their language, that provide their children with public education on their cultural traditions, and that recognize public holidays commemorating culturally significant historical events, for example, a political community could protect the preservation of minority cultures. Thus, Buchanan argues, the goal of cultural preservation, even if we grant it central importance, does not in itself entail secession. Certain state guarantees, institutional structures, and devolutions of power can accomplish the goals that secession is intended to achieve.

Buchanan maintains that another common way of justifying secession, namely, by appealing to a pure or *sui generis* right to self-governance, also fails.[11] He critiques this purported right, when it is understood as entailing a plebiscitary right to secede, by arguing that it is morally unjustifiable because it is fraught with ambiguities and has detrimental consequences. The claim that every group that comprises a "people" has a right to its own sovereign state, he maintains, is questionable because it is difficult to clarify the meaning of "peoples." The characteristics which are usually invoked to explain the distinctiveness of a people or nation, such as a common language and a shared culture, are problematic. Buchanan argues that what counts as a distinct language is hard to determine given the different existing dialects which often exist of what is purportedly the same language. And because most cultural groups have had infusions from diverse cultural traditions, and their members have assimilated to various degrees into other cultures, it is difficult to make sense of the notion of cultural distinctiveness.

A *sui generis* right to self-determination, Buchanan contends, is also problematic because its implementation is not possible.[12] He notes that there are so many different cultural groups in the world that they could not all exercise the right to form a state. The earth's surface is too limited to allow the formation of sufficient autonomous political bodies for each of these groups. What's more, some of these ethnocultural groups are dispersed across different territories and are intermixed with other groups in complex patterns. The attempt to create culturally homogeneous states would inevitably involve morally objectionable policies of exclusion, forced assimilation, or extermination. Finally, recognizing an express right to self-determination would be "a recipe for limitless political fragmentation." In short, the practical and moral costs of acknowledging and implementing self-governance, when this right involves a right to secede, are practically and morally prohibitive.

Even though Buchanan maintains that there is no pure or *sui generis* right to self-governance, he believes that self-governance is instrumentally valuable.[13] He maintains that autonomous governance is valuable to the extent that it achieves other objectives, such as the protection of a group's physical survival or the freedom of its members, but that in itself it is not intrinsically valuable. Having discredited self-governance as a *sui generis* right, Buchanan argues that secessionist claims can be justified on the basis of the injustices that secession would prevent or rectify. Thus, the pure right to self-governance, as an independent rationale for secession, is dropped from consideration in favor of a remedial justification based on the injustices committed or threatened by the state against the secessionist group.

In summary, Buchanan contends that neither cultural survival nor self-governance are in themselves acceptable rationales for secession. The former falls short because it has very limited applicability, while the latter turns out not to be a right after all. But how compelling are Buchanan's arguments against cultural survival and self-governance as rationales for secession? I begin by examining his claims that cultural survival has extremely limited moral relevance as a justification for secession.

Concerning his contention that the cultural survival argument is indefensible because it is unrealistic for ethnocultural groups to demand whatever means are necessary for preserving their culture in perpetuity, we should note that this is an inaccurate account of what most cultural minorities seek. Ethnocultural groups want the rights to and control of resources needed to determine for themselves which aspects of their culture will change and which will be retained. Most of these groups want autonomy in the cultural sphere—the same autonomy that the majority society takes for granted. These groups are not so naïve as to believe that they can completely isolate themselves from the outside world so that their culture can remain intact forever. On the contrary, they are well aware of the external influences and the internal forces which inevitably transform cultures, but they want to have greater control of the conditions and terms under which cultural change occurs. Many indigenous groups, for example, welcome modern conveniences and technologies which facilitate their daily activities and empower them socially and economically, as long as they have control of how these resources are introduced and employed. What they do not want, however, is to be the passive objects of cultural, technological, and economic influences which undermine the continuity and integrity of their cultural traditions. For most ethnocultural groups, cultural survival signifies possessing the legal entitlements, resources, and political influence necessary to maintain control of their cultural traditions and the extent, content, and rapidity of cultural change.

Moreover, Buchanan's claim regarding the likely demise of at least some minority cultures has limited applicability and reveals his misunderstanding of the conditions that threaten minority cultures. The key term that needs to be clarified here is the world "likely." If national and international distributions of political and economic power remain the same, Buchanan is correct to point out that a significant number of minority cultures are not likely to survive. But when ethnocultural groups claim that they have a right to preserve their culture, their point is to transform the present configurations of political and economic power which deprive them of the wherewithal to control their own destinies in the cultural sphere. While it may be true of a very small number of cultures that they are unlikely to survive in the contemporary world in anything resembling their present form—small tribal groups in the Brazilian rain forest come to mind—this is not the case for most ethnocultural minorities. For the vast majority of ethnocultural groups, whether their culture will change and survive in a form that is acceptable to them will depend to a great extent on whether they attain the rights and resources necessary to make autonomous decisions regarding the preservation and transmission of their culture. Thus, Buchanan is incorrect to assume that the effort of cultural minorities to preserve their culture is a doomed project because the demise of their culture is inevitable.

In refusing to consider cultural survival as a factor of sufficient normative importance to justify secession, Buchanan fails to grant due consideration to the purpose and justification of political communities. As I argued in Chapter 4, the promotion of human flourishing is the central function of political bodies and is a crucial factor in their legitimation. If cultural membership is vital to human flourishing, we have a straightforward reason to regard the failure of the state to provide the rights and control of resources necessary to retain one's culture as a serious injustice. Moreover, to the extent that the state fails to perform its central function, it undermines its own legitimacy, including its claim to sovereign control of its territory.

Buchanan argues that the right of a state to its territory is so strong that it should take moral precedence over the right of cultural survival, so that violations of the latter cannot be used to nullify the former. But how did the state acquire the right to its territory in the first place? I will discuss this question in more detail in Chapter 8, for now it will suffice to note that in the vast majority of cases existing states acquired their territories through conquest, invasive settlement, partitioning between colonial powers, and other morally illegitimate means. Partly for this reason, the territorial rights of states are conditional rights, that is, they are rights whose legitimacy depends, among other things, on their fulfilling the fundamental needs and interests of *all* of their citizens. If a political community undermines in a serious way the capacity of some of its members to flourish, it violates a fundamental pre-condition of its own legitimacy. Thus, if a state denies the members of an ethnocultural group the rights and control of resources necessary for them to preserve their culture, and if the state refuses to countenance more limited forms of autonomy than secession, that group can employ cultural survival as an independent rationale to secede, provided that it meets the supplementary conditions discussed earlier, such as providing credible assurances that the rights of any minorities in the seceding territories will be protected.

We should note that Buchanan is correct to maintain that in some cases certain forms of autonomy short of secession may suffice for the preservation of a culture. If the state is willing to grant these forms of self-governance, the ethnocultural group's claim to secession based on cultural survival loses its moral force, unless the group can show that these more limited forms of autonomy are not adequate to protect its culture. Finally, the possibility that another group or political community may have a claim to the disputed territory should certainly be considered, particularly if they were unjustly displaced from that territory and its repossession remains vital to their well-being. However, this scenario will be relatively rare, given that many secessionist groups typically support their claims by pointing to their long-standing, and most recent, occupation of the disputed territory.[14] In summary, we can see that Buchanan's position that cultural survival can almost never serve as a legitimate basis for secession is not well justified.

I now turn to Buchanan's arguments against employing a *sui generis* right to self-governance—understood as entailing a right to form a sovereign government—as a rationale for secession. As we will recall, one of his arguments against this rationale was the alleged impossibility of identifying in a nonarbitrary way which groups constitute a people. Buchanan maintains that since the criteria for identifying peoples or nations is unclear, we cannot determine to which groups the principle of self-governance applies. Evidently what Buchanan requires are necessary and sufficient conditions to pre-determine which groups are entitled to their own sovereign state. Underpinning his argument is the assumption that unless we can identify the rightful bearers of a right, we cannot grant that right moral legitimacy.

A simple solution would be to say that all identifiable cultural groups merit their own sovereign state. The problem with this solution, Buchanan points out, is that the number of identifiable cultural groups far exceeds the number of autonomous states that could viably exist. Without clear criteria for identifying non-arbitrarily the groups to which the principle applies, the principle is bound to be implemented in a morally capricious and unjustifiable way. Buchanan concludes from these considerations that a *sui generis* right to self-governance can never be used as a rationale to justify secession from a just democratic state, even when the supplementary conditions he specifies for secession are satisfied.

The argument that identity criteria cannot be provided for the groups entitled to self-governance is probably the most common objection made against this rationale for secession. Despite its appeal and familiarity, this argument is unconvincing. First, it is problematic to the extent that it assumes that providing necessary and sufficient characteristics is essential for adequately defining a category. As recent research in cognitive science and psychology has shown, often we cannot provide, and we do not need to provide, necessary and sufficient conditions for many meaningful and useful categories.[15] The human mind often forms and employs categories on the basis of "prototypes," which are exemplar representatives of categories that permit categorial membership in which members have different degrees of similarity to the prototype. Even though in theoretical contexts we should certainly strive for clarity in identity criteria, the absence of necessary and sufficient conditions for a category does not automatically render it illegitimate in either informal or formal contexts. The relevant question is not whether completely precise identity criteria can be provided for the members of a theoretical category, but whether the criteria of identity are sufficiently precise to allow the category to serve the theoretical purposes for which it is intended.

When the issue is framed in this manner, it is reasonable to maintain that it is not particularly problematic to identify which groups comprise peoples who can appeal to a right to self-governance, including secession. Such groups are often territorially concentrated, identify themselves as members of a culturally distinctive group, share a common history and cultural tradition, were incorporated into the state in a nonvoluntary manner and, most important, maintain that self-governance is essential for their individual and collective flourishing. Again, these criteria are not intended as unambiguous necessary and sufficient conditions, and they do not rule out borderline cases, but in general they are adequate for identifying those groups who have a prima facie case for appealing to rights of self-governance, including in some cases secession. Their appeals to autonomous governance or secession can be overridden (particularly in the case of secession) by normative or pragmatic considerations, but these are the groups whose claims to self-governance should be granted a serious hearing.

In the criteria listed above, I noted the special importance of self-governance for achieving individual and collective flourishing. This condition is crucial because it is the primary moral basis for justifying self-governance. In the account I have given here, human flourishing is a fundamental function of self-governing political communities and a central factor in their justification. The ethnocultural groups that can rightfully claim the right to self-governance to alter existing political arrangements are those for whom regional governance or secession is an essential condition of their flourishing as human beings. These are the groups for whom the existing institutional distributions of political power are inadequate for accomplishing the goals of self-actualization and empowerment in the cultural, economic, and political spheres.

In democratic societies, it is the members of ethnocultural groups who should decide for themselves if self-governance is a necessary condition for their self-realization and flourishing, as well as what form self-governance should take. In order for ethnocultural groups to be able to do this, multicultural democracies must respect the civil and democratic rights that will allow groups to self-organize on the basis of shared interests and a self-ascribed common ethnocultural identity. This process of self-identification is best accomplished in a political environment in which the members of all groups have the opportunities, resources, capacities, and sources of motivation for meaningful political participation. As discussed in Chapters 2 and 3, an important goal of just multicultural democracies is to insure that everyone in the society has the wherewithal for effective participation in public deliberation. Under these conditions, ethnocultural groups will have the wherewithal to mobilize politically and to collectively chart the course of their own future. In a broadly egalitarian political milieu that prizes public deliberation, it will also be more difficult for certain developments—such as efforts by elites to manipulate nationalistic sentiments for their own political gain—to skew the process by which groups mobilize to attain genuine political empowerment.

The processes that generate and validate a group's conviction that self-governance is necessary for their well-being are deeply influenced by such factors as the political culture of the existing state, the response to previous efforts by the ethnocultural group to attain various degrees of autonomy, the degree of animosity between the group and the majority society, the perceptions by the minority of the political and economic costs, or advantages, of autonomy or secession, and so forth. The factors that determine what an ethnocultural group considers necessary for its flourishing are often context-dependent, so it is difficult to identify which groups will make claims to autonomous governance or secession merely by looking at objective internal characteristics of ethnocultural groups, such as the degree of cultural homogeneity they exhibit.

However, merely because a group considers that secession is necessary to determine the course of its future, it does not mean that its claims should go unchallenged or that these claims cannot be outweighed by moral and practical considerations. In justifying secessionist claims, groups must show that forming their own sovereign state, and not merely attaining more limited forms of autonomy, is necessary for their individual and collective flourishing. In establishing their position, ethnocultural groups may provide evidence that the state has bargained in bad faith and has reneged on its commitments in the past, that it is unwilling to dismantle systems of pervasive discrimination or unjust distribution of resources, or that it is unwilling to implement electoral systems that provide equitable political representation. But even if this could be established, normative factors, such as the unwillingness of the seceding group to politically accommodate the minorities in the new state, or practical considerations, such as the economic or military nonviability of the seceding political community, may still outweigh moral justifications for secession.

Emphasizing the moral and practical factors that may override claims to secession undercuts Buchanan's argument that granting moral legitimacy to a right to self-governance is a license for endless political fragmentation. Condoning unrestricted secession follows only if we grant a right to self-governance without qualification; that is, if we do not place appropriate constraints on it. What's more, at the practical level, some ethnocultural groups will not desire self-governance in the first place because they will be satisfied with attaining accommodationist objectives. And even for those groups who do desire self-governance, some more limited form of autonomy may respond to their needs. In fact, there is evidence to show that in regions with secessionist movements, many people would settle for some form of autonomous governance short of secession.[16] There is no evidence to suggest that a large number of ethnocultural groups would seek secession at all costs if a heavily conditioned right to secession was recognized. Of the approximately 5,000 identifiable ethnocultural groups in the world, the number who have even contemplated secession is extremely small.[17] In brief, those who recognize a suitably restricted right to self-governance are not vulnerable to the charge of defending a position that is morally untenable or has devastating practical consequences.

This brings us to an important point that can be made against Buchanan's position. By admitting that a right to self-governance, including secession, is significantly restricted in its application, we do not thereby deny that such a right exists. That is, just because the right to self-governance is significantly constrained by a number of conditions does not mean that it is not a *sui generis* right, that is, a right which, in certain circumstances, an ethnocultural group can legitimately employ as an independent justification for autonomous governance or secession. Buchanan is correct to maintain that a pure, express right to self-governance, understood as involving a unilateral, plebiscitary right to secede, is not normatively defensible, but advocates of a *sui generis*, independent right of autonomous governance or secession need not adopt such a extreme view. There is nothing inconsistent in upholding the moral legitimacy of a constrained right.[18]

Neither does it follow, as Buchanan contends, that self-governance does not have intrinsic value, but merely instrumental value. Placing conditions on the exercise of a right does not entail that what the right is intended to protect does not have intrinsic value. Self-governance can be intrinsically valuable even if the bearers of this right must meet certain conditions before they can exercise it, that is, if self-governance can be overridden by other moral considerations.[19] It is a mistake for defenders of liberal democracy to hold that autonomous governance has only instrumental value. As I argued in Chapter 4, autonomy in liberal democracies has a dual role. On the one hand, liberalism maintains that autonomy is instrumentally valuable because it is the best and most reliable means through which individuals and collectivities can achieve human flourishing. But on the other hand, autonomy is intrinsically valuable because it is the institutional expression of the liberal conviction that human beings are moral agents capable of self-direction. It is intrinsically valuable for individuals to govern their lives according to their own conceptions of the good. In the liberal perspective, we support and respect individual and collective autonomy not merely because of its beneficial consequences, but also because it is an intrinsic good. Even when individuals and collectivities make what we would regard as poor decisions, as long as they do not violate individual or collective rights we acknowledge the legitimacy of those decisions and their right to make them, and this attitude indicates our respect for the intrinsic value of autonomy.

Furthermore, regarding individual and collective autonomy as having merely instrumental value opens the door to paternalistic and even authoritarian forms of governance. If the only reason why self-governance is morally justified is because of its beneficial consequences, on what principled basis can we reject non-democratic forms of governance that might achieve greater economic progress and social stability than democracy? Considering this possibility is not merely an intellectual exercise, since recent discussions of the viability of democracies in developing countries have raised the possibility that in a global economy authoritarian forms of governance may be more suitable for these countries. Some authors have argued that in order to achieve economic progress, developing countries need, *inter alia*, a disciplined labor force, social and political stability, and a government with sufficient authority to create an attractive environment for international capital. These social characteristics, they argue, are best achieved by authoritarian, non-democratic regimes, because in democratic societies certain sectors of the populace, such as labor unions, environmental organizations, and indigenous groups, are more likely to raise issues and make demands that create an unfavorable environment for economic growth and foreign capital. Given the possibility of subverting democracy by, ironically, appealing to the common good, it is important for advocates of liberal democracy to defend autonomous governance as intrinsically valuable, and not merely as a means to socially beneficial ends. Buchanan fails to give due consideration to this important dimension of the value of autonomy in democratic societies.[20]

The reasons why Buchanan maintains that self-governance has no intrinsic value and is not a *sui generis* right are not difficult to fathom. He wants to foreclose the possibility that self-governance could ever be used as an independent justification for secession. In admitting that self-governance is intrinsically valuable, we countenance the possibility that an ethnocultural group could use self-governance by itself as a rationale for secession. It is not clear, however, that this should be a serious concern. A unilateral plebiscitary right to secede is in any case not normatively justifiable given the significant conditions—such as a mutually agreeable pact concerning the fair distribution of federal properties and repayment of the national debt, and credible indications establishing that the rights of minorities within the seceding territory will be protected—that must be satisfied before secession is justified. An additional justifiable condition that could be imposed on groups desiring secession is a supermajority requirement. Since it is reasonable to suppose that a fairly high level of social solidarity and civic mutuality will be important for the effective functioning of the new sovereign political community, it could justifiably be required that more than a majority of its members be in favor of secession. Moreover, an ethnocultural group appealing to the right to self-governance must show why the particular form of self-governance it seeks is necessary for accomplishing its goals of individual and collective flourishing. If they seek secession, this would entail establishing why secession, and not some other form of more limited autonomy, is indeed necessary. In short, if a substantial number of hurdles are placed on the road to secession, a *sui generis* right to self-governance can be recognized without legitimizing or inviting the endless and pointless fragmentation Buchanan is so concerned about.

Evaluating Self-Governance Claims

Several factors should be kept in mind in determining the strength of particular appeals for self-governance. Claims regarding secession and territorial control that are based on the rationale of recovering unjustly appropriated territory weaken with the passage of time. As succeeding generations of new occupants are born in a particular political community and develop a sense of place for the land in which they were born and raised, the strength of the claim of the ethnocultural group that was last displaced from the disputed territory diminishes. This position may appear to be unjust because it neglects the normative entitlement that the displaced group has to the territory it previously occupied. However, two considerations strongly mitigate and even override the apparent injustice involved as a group gradually loses its claim to self-governance in its former territory.

First, it is doubtful whether there is any adequate criterion besides length and stability of occupancy for granting a political community collective rights to a territory. If we are to recognize the right of communal self-determination at all, we have to grant political communities the concomitant right of territorial control, and it is very difficult to determine how the latter can be concretely specified other than through length and stability of occupancy. If a political community is to be able to control its own destiny, it must have some control over its territorial boundaries. But which territory is to be recognized as belonging to which political community? Unless we opt for the wholly unrealistic alternative of dividing the earth's surface and allotting portions to each political community using criteria which everyone, or at least the majority of the world's people, would agree with, we have to recognize that the territory that a political community is most entitled to is the one to which its members already have a deep attachment, the territory that forms an intrinsic part of national consciousness, the one that the political community has fought for and defended for many generations. And it is precisely through length and stability of occupancy that a political community develops these attachments and historical connections to a particular territory.

Second, the group whose claim to a given territory weakens with the passage of time is in the same position as the group that they displaced when they acquired dominance over that territory. Since practically all of the world's political communities live in territories that were formerly occupied by other groups, the latest displaced group—which claims that a great injustice is being perpetrated if we maintain that its claim to its former territory weakens over time—itself acquired rights to that territory through length and stability of occupancy. The latest displaced group thus has no absolute moral status concerning ownership of the disputed territory, it is merely the latest in a long list of displaced groups.

However, an important consideration that supports reparative claims for lost territorial control and autonomy is whether the group in question has managed to successfully integrate into another political community. If the group continues to have refugee status and if its members are treated as pariahs in a foreign land, then their claims to their former homelands remain strong, despite the fact that a long time may have passed since they were formerly autonomous. On the other hand, if the group has been accepted as a legitimate part of another political community, if its members have attained full citizenship and a reasonable degree of social and economic well-being in the society of which they are now a part, and if its members have accepted their status as members of the new political community, then the moral strength of their claims to regain their former territory and autonomy significantly diminishes.

An interesting normative case is that of indigenous groups who were unjustly displaced from large territories. According to the position I have defended here, these groups do not have a legitimate moral claim to the recovery of all of their former territory if it is not necessary for their flourishing within a self-governing political community and if members of the majority society need parts of those territories for their subsistence.[21] This is so even if there is clear and compelling historical evidence that they were unjustly displaced from their homelands. Given the needs of the present occupants of those territories and their reliance on these territories for their well-being, indigenous groups may not justly claim the recovery of all of the land they previously occupied. The members of indigenous groups have no greater claim to parts of nature to satisfy their needs than members of the majority society. As long as indigenous peoples have control of sufficient land to preserve their culture and achieve individual and collective flourishing, they should not lay claim to additional territories from which it would be very difficult or impossible to displace members of the majority society, for the latter also have a right to the resources necessary for the promotion of their collective flourishing.

Self-Determination in the Contemporary World

I end this chapter with a brief discussion of what self-determination, in the expansive and integrated sense described in Chapter 5, means for indigenous peoples, ethnonationalists, communal contenders, and states in a global context.[22] I have maintained that the promotion of the flourishing of its members is the central function of a political union and a crucial factor in its justification. The flourishing of the members of a political community, I have also argued, is best understood and achieved in terms of the self-determination of their community. In turn, the self-determination of a political community involves the capacity of its members to decide their affairs in the political, social, cultural, and economic spheres. In the contemporary world, however, the capacity of states and substate political bodies to make decisions that promote the well-being of their citizens has been significantly compromised by such factors as economic interdependence, cultural homogenization, and regional and global associations that influence political decision making. Self-determination can no longer be understood solely in state-centered terms. That is, whether an ethnocultural group can determine the course of its collective future now depends as much on its capacity to employ its economic, cultural, and political resources to form the local, regional, and global associations that would best promote the well-being of its members as on the rights, concessions, and devolutions of power that it might obtain from the state. It does an ethnocultural group little good, for example, to obtain local control of the state's civil service administration if the state is heavily burdened by external debt which prevents it from providing its citizens with much needed educational, medical, and technical resources. Likewise, the capacity for economic self-determination of an ethnocultural group who has attained concessions from the state to control the development of regional natural resources can be severely undermined by the numerous exit options available to the owners of capital in that region and by the need to defer to the interests of foreign capital.

As we observed at the end of Chapter 5, in the present globalized environment more and more decisions that affect the lives of people all over the world are being made by transnational corporations, international economic organizations, and supranational bodies and associations. Often, the people most affected by these decisions have no role in making them. To attain true self-determination, ethnocultural groups have to bring under democratic control the regional and global processes and the institutional structures that limit the efficacy of political communities to determine their own affairs. What is needed is a democratic framework that, on the one hand, provides self-governing ethnocultural groups with local and regional autonomy and, on the other, enables these groups to subject the regional and global forces affecting their lives to democratic standards of representation, public accountability, legitimacy, and reasoned public deliberation. As we shall see in what follows, there are important connections between these two components of such a democratic framework. I now examine each of these components in turn.

The Content of Self-Determination

Assuming that an ethnocultural group merits rights to self-determination, what are the specific areas over which it needs to have control? Hurst Hannum has provided a useful account of the areas over which self-governing ethnocultural minorities need to have regulatory authority.[23] He identifies five areas which are of particular importance for self-governance: language, education, government civil service and security forces employment, control of land and natural resources, and representative local government structures.

Since language is one of the most important ways in which culture is preserved and transmitted, ethnocultural groups should be at liberty to use their language without fear of discrimination, and they should have the freedom to preserve and transmit their native language. Self-governing ethnocultural minorities need to manage the institutional mechanisms through which their language is learned and transmitted, as well as determine the ways it is used in the public sphere. Control of the former primarily entails deciding the language used in the schools, and in the latter it involves the capacity to make decisions concerning the language used in such areas as the judicial system, civil services, electoral procedures, and the news media.

Language policies can be a source of great disagreement and conflict, particularly in states where there is only one major linguistic minority. Such states are likely to be less tolerant of the linguistic minority than states that are multilingual. In the latter, the existence of several linguistic groups is more likely, relatively speaking, to create an atmosphere of mutual tolerance than a bilingual state, where the dominant group will tend to see the minority as a threat to its cultural homogeneity and dominance.[24] In bilingual states it is important for the linguistic minority to acquire sufficient proficiency in the majority language so that its members can function effectively in the greater society, since in the contemporary world there will likely be a fairly high level of interaction between the majority and minority groups, even in societies in which the latter exercise rights of regional self-governance. On the other hand, the state should realize the importance of language retention for the minority group, and should recognize that in many cases in which states have tried to officially suppress minority languages, such policies have had the opposite effect of reinforcing ethnic identity. Moreover, the existence of states in which the right to use one's language is officially recognized, such as Belgium, Switzerland, and Finland, shows that a state's recognition of the linguistic diversity of its citizens need not lead to social fragmentation or disintegration.

Another area important for self-governance is education. In addition to language, education is a primary vehicle for the transmission and preservation of cultural traditions.[25] It is well known that education functions as a primary means of socialization and acculturation into the social values and behavioral patterns of the dominant society. For this reason, most states will be very reluctant to transfer complete control of the educational process to ethnocultural minorities.[26] Nevertheless, ethnocultural groups have to insist that the curriculum of the public schools educate their children in their cultural values, traditions, and history. For ethnocultural minorities, education is an essential form of empowerment. In addition to transmitting their cultural traditions, a culturally relevant education should provide their children with the historical perspective necessary for them to understand the struggles which their predecessors have endured for the sake of maintaining their cultural identity and traditions. The point of such an educational approach is not to resuscitate age-old conflicts and animosities, but to provide new generations of vulnerable minorities with the information and understanding necessary to safeguard their needs and interests in a society in which their predecessors have had to struggle to achieve the dignity and respect taken for granted by other members of the society. A culturally relevant curriculum should also emphasize the progress (or lack of progress) made by the ethnocultural group in achieving full citizenship, as well as the contributions they have made to the development of the state. It is especially important for groups whose cultural differences with the majority society are particularly pronounced, such as indigenous groups, to have considerable influence over the educational process, particularly with regard to curriculum content, pedagogical methodologies, and teaching personnel.

Other areas in which self-governing ethnocultural groups need to have regulative authority are in government civil service employment, provision of social services, and participation in security forces.[27] Deliberate exclusion of ethnocultural minorities in the administration of government services and in governmental decision making can be a primary reason behind the social and economic marginalization of minorities. When regionally concentrated minorities see that governmental administrative functions are carried out by members of the dominant group, their belief that they are perceived as second-class citizens will be reinforced. It is reasonable to maintain that the administration of government services should be conducted by individuals who understand the local populace, because they are generally in a better position to know their particular needs as well as their values and points of view.

Of particular importance is equitable representation of ethnocultural minorities in police and security forces. Because the latter have powers to detain and arrest individuals, are officially commissioned to carry weapons, and are the enforcers of the states' laws and regulations, it is important that they be seen by local populations as "impartial arbiters of the law" and not as illegitimate occupation forces.[28] But it is very difficult for them to be seen in this way if they are comprised primarily or overwhelmingly of members of the dominant group. For this reason, equitable group representation in security forces is crucial for the acceptance of these forces by local communities. In situations in which the police and/or the army are comprised largely of members of dominant groups—as is the case in Northern Ireland, Sri Lanka, Fiji, Spain, Malaysia, and many African countries—the absence of a neutral and credible police force makes it far more difficult for mutually agreeable resolutions to problems of intercultural conflict and self-governance to be reached and implemented.[29]

Control over land and natural resources is also important for self-governing, particularly for indigenous and ethnonationalist groups.[30] An ethnocultural group's influence in policies of immigration into the territories under its jurisdiction is crucial for its sense of autonomy. Such authority can in effect function as a symbolic surrogate for sovereignty and can diminish the prevalence of calls for secession within the group. In the case of indigenous groups, territorial control may be necessary for maintaining their culture. By retaining exclusive hunting and fishing rights in certain regions of their native lands, for example, they can preserve their cultural practices and protect the material base for their forms of life. Since many indigenous groups also have a deep spiritual connection to their homelands, territorial control can safeguard the integrity of sacred sites, burial grounds, and natural bodies of spiritual and historical significance. However, indigenous groups are not the only groups with profound connections to territories. Many other ethnocultural groups have deep religious and historical attachments to their traditional homelands. The notion of regaining control of the "motherland" figures prominently in many ethnocultural movements for self-governance. In addition, control of territory can also serve the function of providing protection for persecuted ethnocultural groups. Because violation of a political community's territory is widely condemned by the international community, territorial control can serve as a form of protection not otherwise afforded to persecuted ethnocultural groups.

Having authority over the use and development of natural resources can safeguard the economic and cultural interests of ethnocultural groups. But obtaining control of such resources is difficult for these groups because of the strongly held conviction by most states that subsoil resources, as well as fisheries, forests, and other natural resources, are part of the patrimony of the state that should be used at the discretion of the state's central authorities.[31] In these areas strong conflicts of interest are likely to arise, particularly in a globalized economy in which states are often willing to exploit their natural resources to generate foreign currency or attract capital investments from private enterprises. What is important to ethnocultural groups in many cases is not so much exclusive ownership of their natural resources as much as effective participation in the decision-making processes involving economic development. Minority groups, especially indigenous peoples, are often concerned about the impact that indiscriminate economic development and exploitation of natural resources will have on their way of life. The negative consequences of such development can include displacement of indigenous communities from their traditional lands, rapid and uncontrolled intrusions into their communities of foreign cultural and technological influences, and deterioration or destruction of the ecosystems which form the material base for their way of life. Indigenous peoples are also particularly vulnerable to resource exploitation because the discovery of new natural resources is more likely to occur in yet undeveloped areas of the state, where indigenous people often live. What's more, their lack of political organization and formal education makes it difficult for them to effectively defend their interests.[32] For these reasons, it is imperative that ethnocultural groups include, as an essential component of self-government, the right to play a central role in economic decision making and in the implementation of economic development policies.

Adequate political frameworks for self-governing ethnocultural groups should also include representative local governmental structures.[33] The primary function of these governmental structures should be to exercise control over local matters within the basic political parameters set by the state. Meaningful autonomy would include a locally elected legislative body with the authority to formulate legislation that is immune from nullification by the central government as long as the legislative body does not exceed its powers as defined by constitutional or other foundational documents.[34] Also included in effective autonomous governance is a chief executive, elected by the local populace, who has the authority to administer and enforce local and state laws. Even though this chief executive could be accountable to both local and state authorities, ideally chains of command should be clearly articulated to prevent possible conflicts in accountability.[35] The latter clarification is particularly desirable in regions where political communities have a strong sense of their independence from the central state authorities. Also important is the establishment of an independent local judiciary with the authority to interpret laws that apply to local populations. The resolution of conflicts between the local government and the state concerning such matters as judicial interpretations or jurisdictional authority would ordinarily be decided by the state's highest court or, ideally by a joint body specifically created for dispute settlement. Finally, areas of joint concern could be dealt with through institutional mechanisms in which power is shared between the local and central government. Such areas may include the regulation of ports, highways, bridges, communication facilities, and other general infrastructures as well as administrative functions that serve both the regional and central communities.

Particularly in the case of indigenous groups, it is very important that representative local governmental structures recognize already existing traditional organizations and leadership. In devolving power to indigenous regions, some central governments may want to coopt local governments by instituting new political organizations which are under the control of the central government. In Bolivia, for example, the state government developed Territorial Base Organizations to oversee local political functions. The latter organizations, however, were sometimes linked to the country's political party in power and overlooked traditional indigenous organizations. The purpose of this maneuver by the central government was to undermine the devolution of autonomy to indigenous communities. This case serves to remind us of the tactics that can be used by central governments to undermine self-determination for ethnocultural groups even when they have formally granted these groups autonomous governance.

In order to obtain self-governance, communal contenders, like indigenous peoples and ethnonationalists, would need to have regulative authority in the areas just described, even though control over land and natural resources would not be as critical to their autonomy as it would be to indigenous groups. But there is another requirement that is of critical importance for communal contenders to acquire self-determination, namely, commensurate political representation and influence in the central governing institutions of the state. This latter requirement is essential because the power-sharing democracies in which they live are ruled by governing coalitions of ethnocultural groups. Arend Lijphart has studied extensively the subject of power-sharing or consociational arrangements in deeply divided pluralistic democracies. He defines consociational democracies in terms of the primary principles of grand coalition and segmental autonomy and the secondary principles of proportionality and the minority veto.[36]

Lijphart describes a grand coalition as an executive body in which all of the leaders of the recognized ethnocultural groups in the society participate. In parliamentary systems this executive body would take the form of a grand coalition cabinet, while in a presidential system it could consist of the presidency and other high offices distributed among representatives from the different ethnocultural groups. In either form, the power-sharing character of these arrangements could be strengthened by distributing the membership of important state committees and advisory councils among representatives from the different groups. The other major component of consociational democracy, segmental autonomy, is to be understood in terms of the devolution of decision-making power to the ethnocultural communities making up the society. Segmental autonomy has a complementary function relative to the grand coalition component—while the latter governmental institution represents a commitment to the idea that issues of common concern should be jointly decided by the different groups, the former is the institutional mechanism by which issues of regional or local interest are to be decided by the different ethnocultural communities. Segmental autonomy can take a territorially-based form, when ethnocultural groups are regionally concentrated, or a non-territorial form when they are geographically dispersed.

The principle of proportionality refers to the commitment by the society to achieve proportional influence or representation of the different ethnocultural groups in positions of political power, civil service assignments, and the allocation of public funds. The most important of these areas, proportionality of political representation, could be achieved by the electoral systems of rigid or flexible proportional representation that were discussed in the last chapter. In culturally pluralistic societies where ethnocultural identities are deeply entrenched and the major groups are clearly identifiable, it may be appropriate to employ rigid proportional representation. But in societies in which ethnocultural group identities are contested, unclear, or overlapping, it would be more appropriate to employ systems of flexible proportional representation in which members of the polity would determine for themselves their cultural or political affiliations. Flexible electoral systems of proportional representation also have the advantages of avoiding the permanent entrenchment of ethnocultural identities and divisions, the involuntary ethnocultural group classification that some individuals may find objectionable, and the difficult problem of deciding in a fair and objective manner the ethnocultural groups that merit representation in governing institutions. In a system of open and fair political competition, flexible systems of proportional representation would allow individuals, even those from smaller groups or parties, to obtain representation. This is particularly true if the threshold for representation is set at a relatively low level, that is, if a political party needs to obtain only a small percentage of the votes in an election in order to obtain seats in governing institutions.

The fourth main principle of consociational democracies is the minority veto. This institutional mechanism, which allows any of the ethnocultural groups participating in the power-sharing arrangements to veto political decisions, is intended to protect a group's vital interests in case they are outvoted or overruled. It can be used in a general way to apply to any governmental policy or in a more restricted sense to apply only to policies that directly affect an ethnocultural group's vital interests. Given its potential for deadlocking governmental decisions, unless the democracy in question has a strong political ethos of solidarity and compromise, it might be wise to employ the minority veto in the latter sense only.

Cosmopolitan Democracy

Even if an ethnocultural group obtained the appropriate concessions from the state to exercise self-governance, it would still face the constraints imposed by globalization. Given the complex ways in which globalization affects the self-determination of ethnocultural groups—as well as political communities in general—here I will do no more than provide some broad guidelines for the kind of political framework appropriate for self-determination in the contemporary global environment. As noted earlier, an appropriate political framework that provides ethnocultural groups with genuine self-determination is one that enables them to employ the economic, cultural, and political resources at their disposal to deal with the processes and institutional structures that affect their political community. Cosmopolitan democracy seems particularly suitable for this task since it recognizes both the important role that culture plays in the formation and maintenance of political communities and the urgent need to develop democratic institutions to subject regional and global processes to democratic accountability. This emerging form of democratic governance attempts to find a middle ground between a world government and a Westphalian, state-centered international order.

There is an institutional as well as a moral rationale for cosmopolitan democracy. These rationales require that we reconceptualize and extend the scope of traditional democratic categories. At the institutional level, the adequacy of conventional democratic structures to deal with the problems that confront state and substate communities must be questioned in light of interstate connections and dependencies. As David Held has stated:

> National boundaries have traditionally demarcated the basis on which individuals are included and excluded from participation in decisions affecting their lives; but if many socioeconomic processes, and the outcomes of decisions about them, stretch beyond national frontiers, then the implications of this are serious, not only for the categories of consent and legitimacy, but for all the key ideas of democracy. At issue is the nature of a constituency, the role of representation, and the proper form and scope of political participation. As fundamental processes of government escape the categories of the nation-state, the traditional national resolutions of the key questions of democratic theory and practice are open to doubt.
>
> Against this background, the nature and prospects of the democratic polity need re-examination. The idea of a democratic order can no longer be simply defended as an idea suitable to a particular closed political community or nation-state. We are compelled to recognize that we live in a complex interconnected world where the extensity, intensity and impact of issues (economic, political or environmental) raise questions about where those issues are most appropriately addressed. . . . If the most powerful geopolitical interests are not to settle many pressing matters simply in terms of their objectives and by virtue of their power, then new institutions and mechanisms of accountability need to be established.[37]

Even though the advocates of cosmopolitan democracy sometimes disagree regarding the precise nature of the institutions of a transnational democratic order, they agree that the members of all political communities should have rights of democratic representation in international political institutions and should play a role in making the regional and global-level decisions that affect them. Defenders of cosmopolitan democracy are also in general accordance with the need to develop publicly funded forums of democratic deliberation in which the views and interests of all political communities can be discussed and represented. Regional bodies such as the European Union are sometimes cited as examples of mediating institutions that could represent the needs of state and substate political communities in larger global forums.

Some advocates of cosmopolitan democracy have suggested that the development of the institutional structures appropriate for cosmopolitan democracy could begin with reforms of existing international organizations, particularly the United Nations.[38] Rather than trying to create from scratch institutions based on the ideals of cosmopolitan democracy, they maintain that it would be more realistic to make the necessary transformations to organizations like the United Nations. Reforms that would make the United Nations more democratic and egalitarian could include restructuring the Security Council to provide developing countries with a greater voice in its decision-making processes, organizing an international constitutional convention to establish a United Nations second chamber, and creating a stable, accountable, and effective transnational military force. Other measures might include providing an official voice to domestic and transnational civil society associations in the decision-making processes of the United Nations and the establishment of a new Human Rights Court with compulsory submission by all countries to its jurisdiction.[39]

The moral rationale underpinning cosmopolitan democracy is the fundamental equality of all human beings and the recognition of their intrinsic dignity and moral agency. This acknowledgement of equal moral worth is institutionally expressed through systems of democracy that enable them to govern their own lives. It is significant to note that cosmopolitan democracy does not contravene but rather upholds the normative justification for self-governing political communities. This is because if the right to communal self-determination is ultimately grounded in the conviction that such form of governance is the most suitable means for ensuring the well-being and flourishing of the members of a political community, then cosmopolitan democracy, to the extent that it empowers a political union to attain true self-determination, can be seen as contributing to the fulfillment of that political union's primary goals and functions. In other words, despite appearances to the contrary, the members of state and substate political communities will actually be more empowered by cosmopolitan democracy, because the latter will enable them to achieve greater control of the transnational forces that affect them. The capacity of cosmopolitan democracy to further the goals and functions of political communities shows the moral complementarity of this form of democracy with the foundational rationale for the existing system of sovereign political communities.

However, in order to access the greater control that cosmopolitan democracy can provide over regional and global processes and institutions, countries will have to alter traditional Westphalian conceptions of the state as a political body with near absolute, centralized, sovereign powers. Needless to say, this is an important hurdle in the implementation of even moderate conceptions of cosmopolitan democracy. Any viable form of cosmopolitan democracy will have to develop institutional structures that demarcate clearly the areas and the ways in which the authority of the state will be superseded by transnational democratic bodies, so that there is a clear understanding by all parties concerned regarding the nature and limits of transnational democracy.

Writers concerned with providing a moral rationale for cosmopolitan democracy often turn to Kant for guidance. In the essay, "Toward Perpetual Peace: A Philosophical Sketch,"[40] Kant conceived of a peaceful global order emerging from the worldwide expansion of institutions based on the rule of law. Kant believed that commercial interests and the heavy cost of continuously preparing for war would lead states to form a peaceful federation of sovereign states based on legal institutions and committed to repudiating violence as a means of resolving their differences. This federation would observe a cosmopolitan law, applying above the level of sovereign states, that would recognize the rights of world citizens, while the independent states comprising the global federation would grant their citizens basic human rights. Kant maintained that strict publicity would be among the most important factors necessary for global peace. Educated and critical world citizens would maintain, within their societies, a cosmopolitan public sphere in which domestic governments would be held accountable for violations of human rights before global public opinion. Kant's federation of sovereign states would not be a powerful centralized world government; rather, it would consist of independent republics founded on the rule of law and principles of self-governance. Only such governments, Kant believed, would be able to respect each other's democratic sovereignty and successfully employ peaceful means of influence rather than coercion to ensure international security. Kant's decentralized cosmopolitan vision would allow for a noncoercive transnational public sphere while respecting the sovereignty of states.

Despite the initial usefulness of Kant's views for identifying a normative rationale for cosmopolitan democracy, there are significant limitations to his perspective. First, certain contemporary social, political, and economic developments hinder the attainment of a peaceful, sustainable, and just global order. While the avoidance of interstate conflict of course remains of primary importance, the major threats to the stability of political communities now include internal ethnocultural conflict, the grinding poverty of developing countries, and extreme interstate economic inequalities that translate into unfair political advantages for the most economically powerful countries. While global commerce has increased the incentives for peace, it has also exacerbated, entrenched, and institutionalized serious economic inequalities between states that make it practically impossible for the most impoverished nations to develop the civil societies necessary for democratic self-governance and, more generally, to provide their citizens with the resources necessary for human flourishing. Kant's perspective, with its emphasis on peace and security based on the rule of law, is too limited to deal adequately with these dilemmas of the contemporary world. Second, Kant's vision of a peaceful global order grants almost unqualified recognition to state sovereignty. But certain global problems, such as environmental degradation and violations of human rights, demand that in at least some cases the sovereignty of states be overridden. Kant does not articulate an adequate normative basis for overriding state sovereignty. A much stronger moral basis than that provided by Kant is needed for justifying the institutional mechanisms of cosmopolitan democracy that resolve problems which transcend state sovereignty, such as the problems of global economic injustice and environmental sustainability. I will return to the issue of providing an adequate moral basis for cosmopolitan democracy that is not subject to the limitations of Kant's approach in my discussion of the collective property rights of states.

The moral rationale for cosmopolitan democracy aside, at a practical level the possibility exists that internationally influential countries and powerful interest groups in some of these countries will resist cosmopolitan democracy because they will see it as diminishing the inordinate power they presently wield in global affairs. Member states of the United Nations security council, transnational corporations, leaders of international economic organizations, and other economic and political powerbrokers would likely be threatened by any form of cosmopolitan democracy that might diminish their global influence and power. States that possess inordinate power in international affairs and organizations like the United Nations might resist calls for reforms that would make global decision making more democratic and egalitarian. Similarly, multinational corporations and managers of transnational investment capital would probably view with suspicion institutions of cosmopolitan democracy that could enforce regulations in such areas as the exploitation of natural resources, the use of an international minimum wage, the recognition of a global right to unionize, the establishment of environmental regulations, and restrictions on the use of child labor. On the other hand, impoverished developing countries who have the most to gain from acquiring a voice in global political and economic developments have less influence in international affairs and are less politically organized and funded than their wealthier, more powerful counterparts. In other words, powerful countries and interest groups who could promote cosmopolitan democracy the most might have little incentive to do so, while developing countries, who would have greater incentive to implement such a system of democratic governance, have relatively fewer resources to do so. The realization of cosmopolitan democracy would also likely encounter resistance from states that are strongly nationalistic (particularly states that are profoundly influenced by religious fundamentalism), who might be reluctant to relinquish internal authority in a variety of areas to a form of governance inspired by Western political traditions.

Despite the existence of these countervailing factors against cosmopolitan democracy, including the predictable general reluctance of states to accept limitations to their sovereignty, there are a number of factors that enhance the prospects for cosmopolitan democracy. First, as already noted, state and substate political communities are recognizing that their capacity to make sovereign decisions in the economic and political spheres has already been significantly compromised by global developments, and that it would be in their best interest to bring the influence of these developments under systematic democratic control and accountability. Second, there is an emerging global consensus, whose importance should not be underestimated, on a number of values and interests, such as human rights, the rule of law, democratic participation, and ecological sustainability.[41] Third, technological developments in communication and transportation make it more feasible than ever for the appropriate infrastructures to be developed that would make transnational democracy possible. Fourth, there are certain issues, such as environmental dilemmas and problems of overpopulation, that by their very nature can be adequately addressed only by globally coordinated institutions and forums. Environmental and population issues are particularly relevant here because they are not likely to resolve themselves, will get worse if left unaddressed, and are at a more critical point than at any time in human history. Finally, the great increase in recent years of domestic and international civil society organizations (CSOs), testifies to the emergence of a transnational civil society that can play a crucial role in the realization of cosmopolitan democracy.

The development of a transnational civil society is particularly important for making cosmopolitan democracy a reality. As Janna Thompson has pointed out, a cosmopolitan democratic order, like any stable and well-functioning political community, needs a sense of solidarity and identity among its constituent members. She maintains that the political will to implement the principles of cosmopolitan democracy will not come about merely by espousing universalistic principles of human justice and equality or designing cosmopolitian democratic institutions. Rather, attention must be paid to the creation of a political culture appropriate for transnational democracy. Advocates of cosmopolitan democracy such as Thompson, Daniele Archibugi, and David Held maintain that civil society has a crucial role to play in the development of the sense of global political community important for cosmopolitan democracy.[42]

These advocates of cosmopolitanism have suggested that a sense of global citizenship could be forged by transnationally interconnected systems of CSOs which are rooted in particular political communities but which also engender among their members a consciousness of the various ways in which citizen interests, responsibilities, and identities are linked across national boundaries. Over the last several decades the number of such associations—which deal with such issues as economic development, civil liberties, women's issues, democratic development, indigenous rights, and environmental pollution—has greatly increased. These domestic and international CSOs are building a transnational public sphere by exchanging information, influencing government decision making, building social awareness, and developing a sense of solidarity and common purpose across national boundaries. The legitimacy of these CSOs is also increasingly recognized by domestic governments and international organizations such as the United Nations, who rely on them to acquire information on grassroots activities and concerns and to receive input about the problems faced by local communities. Even though it would be easy to overstate the importance of these CSOs, many of which remain focused primarily on domestic developments, they do represent a significant movement in the direction of an emerging transnational civil society on which cosmopolitan democracy can rely for its own development.

It is not difficult to see how ethnocultural groups would benefit from cosmopolitan democracy. By obtaining a voice in the political, economic, and social decisions that affect them, ethnocultural groups would obtain a greater degree of self-determination. Since these groups do not constitute sovereign states, at present they do not have the status in international forums and organizations that states do, and cosmopolitan democracy can provide a political and structural framework within which they can be recognized as distinct and legitimate political communities. Second, by forming transnational coalitions with ethnocultural groups in other countries, they would gain leverage for influencing domestic policies to protect their needs and interests. By employing transnational CSOs to bring their plight to international forums and organizations, they could rally international support in their favor and pressure their government to respond favorably to their demands. This is particularly important for indigenous groups, who often have few material resources and organizational means to protect their interests.

But ethnocultural groups would not only benefit from cosmopolitan democracy, they can also play a notable role in its realization through the development of a transnational public sphere. Indigenous groups in different countries in Latin America, for example, have developed Pan-Indian associations for the purpose of addressing cultural, political, and economic issues confronting indigenous communities. They have developed support networks and associations that build a commitment to shared values and a sense of identity and loyalty that transcends state boundaries. In South America, for example, numerous indigenous peoples have joined transnational indigenous organizations which have effectively influenced governments to respond to their positions on domestic issues.

Other ethnocultural groups are engaged in developing substate political communities which do not fit the Westphalian model of the nation-state. As Michael Keating has shown in his detailed study of Catalonia, Scotland, and Quebec, some territorially concentrated ethnocultural groups are devising new ways of coping with globalization. The groups in these regions rely on a strong sense of ethnic and historical territorial identity to articulate strategies of nation building at the substate level. Keating clarifies key orientations of these three regions and rejects commonly made assumptions regarding these forms of ethnic nationalism.

> So minority nationalism is not mere ethnic particularism, as so many observers continue to insist. National identity has become an organizing principle for the society as a whole, even if not everyone is a committed nationalist. . . . These are becoming global societies, the reference points for political debate and social integration, rather than mere fragments of wider societies. . . .
>
> National identity promotes a public domain within which policy can be debated and issues decided, where issues of culture, economy, and social justice can be brought together. This is underpinned by common identity and shared values. . . . Language policies in Quebec and Catalonia are a mechanism for maintaining social cohesion, not against the international market but within it. All three societies have traditions of contractualism, or pact-forming, favouring accommodation and compromise across class, ethnic and national boundaries.
>
> This national identity cross-cuts other forms of political and social alignment, notably that of class. Trade unions, working class organizations and the political left are increasingly committed to the new nationalism, though to varying degrees in the three cases.[43]

Keating emphasizes that in these three ethnic regions, self-determination is a matter of balancing and structuring the new international dependencies and creating new forms of self-reliance. Scotland, Catalonia, and Quebec, among other ethnocultural regions, want to adapt to globalization in the contemporary world on their own terms. This adaptation is primarily based on a national identity that is not a mere reversal to the past, but which provides the social cohesion to attain self-determination in a world of overlapping identities and weakening loyalties to the state. Even though retention of ethnic identity remains important (as evidenced, for example, in language policies and efforts to assimilate new-comers), national identity is plural and not singular or exclusivist. An open and democratic civil society is vital to the dynamic character of these regions and is crucial to their capacity to adapt effectively to the global changes that are affecting them. Keating indicates that in all three societies, there is an awareness that the nationalist project cannot succeed unless it is rooted in a democratic and open civil society.

Even though the observations regarding these ethnocultural regions cannot, of course, always be generalized to all territorially concentrated ethnic groups, these societies provide examples of the ways in which some ethnocultural minorities are developing new forms of political community that, given their orientation to accommodate transnational connections and dependencies while retaining social solidarity through reliance on their own historical identities, are more receptive to the forms of democratic governance characteristic of cosmopolitan democracy.

To be sure, the goal of making cosmopolitan democracy a reality will be difficult to achieve. As we observed earlier, there are powerful inter-ests that would be threatened by the implementation of an egalitarian and inclusive system of transnational democracy. Those who benefit from international agreements regulating trade and economic organiza-tions granting development capital, such as the World Trade Organiza-tion (WTO) and the International Monetary Fund (IMF), respectively, would be reluctant to accept modifications to these international organi-zations based on the input of grassroots communities. Organizations such as the WTO and the IMF, which are at present elitist and democrati-cally unaccountable, represent the institutionalized global entrenchment of the neo-liberal economic paradigm which favors the free market over democratic regulation of economic development and investment. These powerful international organizations, and the individuals who influence the formation and implementation of their policies, pose a formidable hurdle to be surpassed before any effective form of cosmopolitan democ-racy can be implemented.

However, if the ultimate purpose of cosmopolitan democracy is to cre-ate a more just and egalitarian democratic global order, the most serious obstacle to the achievement of this objective may very well lie elsewhere, namely, in conventional systems of restricted property rights. As long as existing systems of property rights, including intellectual property, re-main in place, it is likely that the inequalities that afflict domestic democ-racies will be replicated at the global level in a system of cosmopolitan democracy. Differences in economic and political power within and be-tween countries are so egregious that only a fundamental reconceptual-ization and implementation of property rights at the domestic and inter-national levels provides a realistic hope for developing a truly just and egalitarian global order. Universal rights to natural property, by transferring greater economic control to communities, could effectively constrain the power of transnational corporations and international capital. Ownership of land and natural resources by the members of local communities would democratize and decentralize economic decision making, and lead to greater economic self-reliance for these communities. In the next two chapters I address what I consider to be the greatest flaw in constitutional liberal democracies, namely, their unconditional and uncritical acceptance of conventional conceptions of restricted rights to material and intellectual property. The discussion of property rights will complete my account of self-determination for ethnocultural groups.

Notes

1. For example, see David Hollinger *Postethnic America: Beyond Multiculturalism* (New York: Basic Books, 1995). Hollinger, by failing to make the distinction between accommodationist and autonomist ethnocultural minorities, seeks to apply a model of intercultural relations to the latter groups that appropriately applies only to the former. For a criticism of Hollinger's approach, see Will Kymlicka, "American Multiculturalism in the International Arena," *Dissent* (Fall 1998): 73–79.

2. For an account of the various forms of autonomous governance that have been used in different countries, see Claire Palley, "The Role of Law in Relation to Minority Groups," in *The Future of Cultural Minorities,* eds. Antony E. Alcock, Brian K. Taylor, and John M. Welton (London: Macmillan Press, LTD, 1979).

3. A version of this argument has been presented by Albert O. Hirschman, *Exit, Voice, and Loyalty* (Cambridge, MA.: Harvard University Press, 1970) and discussed by Allan Buchanan in *Secession: The Morality of Political Divorce From Fort Sumter to Lithuania and Quebec* (Boulder, CO: Westview Press, 1991).

4. Another tempting but ineffective way in which we could try to show that a state's unjust origin does not undermine its legitimacy is by arguing that a state could rehabilitate itself by adopting and implementing just democratic ideals and institutions. David Copp has argued that the fact that most states originated through morally devious means does not necessarily imply that they are normatively illegitimate, since they could, by subsequently treating their citizens justly and satisfying their needs, in effect become legitimate states. This approach would not work here because the claim by autonomist ethnocultural groups is that the state, by denying them self-governance, is *perpetuating* a historical injustice. Approaches like those of Copp that depend on moral rehabilitation are plausible only in cases in which the present members of the relevant political community come to regard the political society where they live as one which through its just actions and policies enables them to flourish as human beings. But this, of course, is precisely what is denied by autonomist groups when they advocate for self-governance. See David Copp, "The Idea of a Legitimate State," *Philosophy and Public Affairs* 28, no. 1, (1999): 1–45. Even though Copp's argument cannot be used to show the unjustifiability of autonomist claims, efforts by states to genuinely incorporate an ethnocultural group into the mainstream society by treating its members as full and equal citizens sometimes do affect a group's concep-

tion of what political arrangements are needed for their well-being. Groups who were forcibly incorporated into the state may come to adopt an accommodationist perspective as a result of such efforts by the state. This, however, is the exception rather than the rule, and rehabilitative efforts by the state are in any case only one factor in this change in orientation by an ethnocultural group.

5. See, for example, Allan Buchanan, "Democracy and Secession," in *National Self-Determination and Secession*, ed. Margaret Moore (New York: Oxford University Press, 1998). Below we will discuss in detail Buchanan's views on secession.

6. In order to see the latter point more clearly, it would be useful to recall our discussion in Chapter 4, where I argued that the most important factor that justifies the formation and preservation of autonomous political communities is the promotion of human flourishing. Self-governance is a means for attaining this goal and can be justified to the extent that it actually promotes or achieves it. By providing a proper political and cultural context for maintaining their self-identity and way of life, for example, these institutions contribute essential elements for living a satisfying existence. By providing secure cultural and social frameworks for the development of the capacities and potentialities of its members, the institutional structures of a political community promote their self-actualization and flourishing as human beings. Likewise, by securing control and use of natural resources for economic self-reliance or providing safety and protection from prosecution or oppressive treatment from other cultural groups, a political community furthers the interests and well-being of its members. In short, aspiring political communities, no less than established states, are morally justified by reference to the role they play in furthering human self-actualization.

Focusing on human flourishing as a justification for self-governing political communities calls our attention to an important connection between such communities and the context within which they currently exist, namely, globalization. Clarifying this connection buttresses the normative case for self-governance. The globalization of the economic, political, and cultural dimensions of life are increasingly undermining the capacity of states to discharge their traditional functions of providing for the needs and protecting the interests of their citizens. The members of political communities all over the world are deeply affected by economic and political decisions they have no role in making. Ethnocultural groups are realizing that decentralized, regional control of their natural, economic, and cultural resources is important for regaining control of their lives in a globalized environment. I will return to this issue below, when I discuss the content of the expansive, integrated conception of self-determination I advocate for political communities. The point I wish to make now is that if the proper function of a political community is to further the flourishing of its members, autonomist and secessionist claims are strengthened to the extent that it can be shown that existing political communities fail to perform this function while institutional arrangements for self-governance offer better opportunities for accomplishing this goal.

7. Allen Buchanan articulates his theory in (among other sources) the following publications: *Secession: the Morality of Political Divorce*, "The Morality of Secession" in *The Rights of Minority Cultures*, ed. Will Kymlicka (New York: Oxford University Press, 1995), and "Democracy and Secession," in *National Self-Determination*, ed. Moore (New York: Oxford University Press, 1998).

8. Buchanan, "The Morality of Secession," *The Rights of Minority Cultures*, p. 355–364.

9. Ibid., p. 357–364.

10. Ibid., p. 363–364.

11. Ibid., p. 351–354.

12. Ibid., p. 351–352.

13. Ibid., p. 353.

14. The possibility that another group, that was also unjustly displaced from the disputed territory, may make claims to it raises complicated moral questions. A complete theory of secession would provide an account of how competing moral considerations should be weighed in these cases. For example, should the most recently displaced group have a greater moral priority to the territory than a group that held the territory a long time ago but who for other reasons, such as protection from prosecution, has a greater need of that territory? I will not attempt to answer such questions here, since limitations of space and time restrict the extent to which these questions can be addressed.

15. For a review of some of this research, see George Lakoff, *Women, Fire, and Dangerous Things: What Categories Reveal About the Mind* (Chicago: University of Chicago Press, 1987). It is also well known that Wittgenstein questioned the need to provide necessary and sufficient conditions in understanding categories. Lakoff shows how recent research substantiates Wittgenstein's position.

16. John McGarry, "Orphans of Secession," in *National Self-Determination*, ed. Moore (New York: Oxford University Press, 1998), pp. 225–26.

17. On this point, see Hurst Hannum, *Autonomy, Sovereignty, and Self-Determination: The Accommodation of Conflicting Rights*, revised edition (Philadelphia: University of Pennsylvania Press, 1996) and Ted Gurr, *Minorities at Risk: A Global View of Ethnopolitical Conflicts* (Washington, D.C.: United States Institute of Peace Press, 1993).

18. In general, it is not the case that merely because certain conditions must be satisfied before a right can be applied that it is therefore not a right. This is true of many rights, such as voting rights and inheritance rights.

19. It is not a morally incoherent position, for example, to consider non-human sentient creatures as having intrinsic value, even while maintaining that protecting their interests can be overridden in situations in which human lives would be lost by engaging in this practice.

20. It is worthwhile to note that by claiming that self-governance is not a *sui generis* right, i.e., is not a right at all, Buchanan's position is threatened by incoherence. This is because he acknowledges that a group that was unjustly displaced from its territory has a right to secede and form a sovereign political community in the territory it formerly occupied. But it is not at all clear whether we can make sense of remedial claims of ethnocultural groups to regain lost territorial control and autonomy unless we assume that they had a legitimate moral right to self-governance in the first place.

21. For an analysis of the complex issues involved in rectifying historical injustices against indigenous groups, see Jeremy Waldron, "Superseding Historic Injustice," *Ethics* 103, no.1 (October 1992): 4–28.

22. The observations in the next section (on regional self-determination) will not apply to accommodationist groups. Since accommodationist groups share the

basic social, political, and economic institutions with the majority society, only the observations in the last section of the chapter (the cosmopolitan democracy section which discusses the self-determination of states in a global context) will apply to them. Regarding secessionist groups, the comments concerning regional self-determination are relevant to them as long as they remain a part of the state from which they want to secede. Of course, if and when they become independent states, the comments on cosmopolitan democracy will then be applicable to them.

23. Hannum, *Autonomy, Sovereignty, and Self-Determination*, pp. 454–477.

24. Ibid., p. 459.

25. Ibid., p. 460.

26. Ibid., p. 461.

27. Ibid., p. 461–463.

28. Ibid., p. 463.

29. Ibid., p. 461–463.

30. Ibid., p. 463–466.

31. Ibid., p. 465.

32. Ibid., p. 463–466.

33. Ibid., p. 466.

34. Ibid., p. 467.

35. Ibid., p. 467.

36. See, for example, Arend Lijphart, *Democracy in Plural Societies: A Comparative Exploration* (New Haven: Yale University Press, 1977) and "Self-Determination versus Pre-Determination of Ethnic Minorities in Power-Sharing Systems," in *The Rights of Minority Cultures*, ed. Kymlicka. In the account of consociational democracies that follows I rely primarily on the second of these works.

37. David Held, "Democracy and Globalization," in *Re-imagining Political Community: Studies in Cosmopolitan Democracy*, eds. Daniele Archibugi, David Held, and Martin Kohler (Stanford: Stanford University Press, 1998), pp. 22–23.

38. For a discussion of the role of institutions such as the United Nations in promoting cosmopolitan democracy, see Richard Falk, "The United Nations and Cosmopolitan Democracy: Bad Dream, Utopian Fantasy, Political Project," and David Held, "Democracy and Globalization," in *Re-imagining Political Community*, Archibugi, Held, and Köhler.

39. Ibid., p. 25.

40. Immanuel Kant, *Perpetual Peace and other Essays*, trans. by Ted Humphrey (Indianapolis: Hackett Publ. Co., 1983), pp. 107–143.

41. Martin Köhler, "From the National to the Cosmopolitan Public Sphere," in *Re-imagining Political Community*, Archibugi, Held, and Köhler, p. 231.

42. See, for example, *Cosmopolitan Democracy: An Agenda for a New World Order*, eds. Daniele Archibugi and David Held (Cambridge, U.K.: Polity Press, 1995), David Held, *Democracy and the Global Order* (Stanford, CA: Stanford University Press, 1995), and Janna Thompson, "Community Identity and World Citizenship," in *Re-imagining Political Community*, Archibugi, Held, and Köhler, pp. 179–197.

43. Michael Keating, *Nations Against the State: The New Politics of Nationalism in Quebec, Catalonia and Scotland* (New York: St. Martin's Press, Inc., 1996), pp. 218–219.

8

Property Rights in Multicultural Liberal Democracies

Because my examination of property rights is significantly more extensive than that provided for other rights, it is important to be clear about the reasons for this more extensive treatment. First, conventional theories of property rights do not address the specific issues concerning property ownership that arise in multicultural societies. One of the most important of these issues concerns the claims to collective property ownership made by indigenous groups. The evaluation of such claims involves considerations not usually discussed in traditional theories of property rights, such as questions concerning cultural survival and group ownership of tribal territories. Second, discrimination and oppression of ethnocultural groups have created group-based economic injustices different in nature from economic injustices against random individuals. Such group-based historical injustices, and the impact they have on the current socioeconomic status of disfranchised ethnocultural groups, cannot be adequately understood by traditional, individual-centered, economic justice approaches that assume a culturally homogeneous polity. Of particular importance in examining these group-based economic injustices is the issue of rectifying inequalities in ownership of mediated property. Third, the practice of biopiracy, in which transnational corporations appropriate and patent plant varieties and ethnobotanical knowledge of indigenous communities without compensating them, raises important issues not generally considered in theories of intellectual property. The fact that these plant varieties and ethnobotanical knowledge are possessed by ethnocultural groups within the context of community, and not market, economies raises questions concerning the special form that intellectual property rights for these communities should take or, conversely, whether it is even desirable to grant them intellectual property rights in the first place.

Fourth, cultural group differences in property ownership facilitate the discrimination and marginalization of vulnerable ethnocultural groups and undermine intercultural understanding. Forms of oppression and discrimination made possible by economic inequalities represent one of the most serious problems facing multicultural democracies. Wealth provides, *inter alia*, differential access to political power, private sector positions involving authority and influence, media centers of information dissemination and attitude formation, and educational resources which make possible the effective political defense of needs and interests. Material deprivation, on the other hand, besides depriving disfranchised groups of these advantages, can reinforce negative forms of social behavior and engender self-defeating attitudes and dispositions. Such behaviors and attitudes in turn reinforce negative cultural stereotypes which make the mutual respect and understanding necessary for fruitful intercultural civic engagement more difficult to attain.

Fifth, as we observed in our discussion of self-determination, economic inequalities between cultural groups undermine the capacity of disfranchised groups to make autonomous choices in the cultural sphere. Poverty and material inequalities can negatively affect the self-respect of many cultural group members and compromise their ability to critically reflect upon and make autonomous choices concerning assimilation and preservation of cultural traditions. For instance, the fact that inferior socioeconomic status may be associated with membership in a particular ethnocultural group can undermine the capacity of the members of that group to identify and appreciate the merits of their cultural traditions.

In addition to these specific ways in which ethnocultural diversity requires that we reconsider the role of property rights in multicultural democracies, at a more general level there is another important reason for providing an extensive treatment of property rights, namely, that there are serious theoretical problems with the justification of property rights as conventionally understood. In articulating the foundations for multicultural liberal democracies, it is essential to attain a correct understanding of property rights, not only because they are the single most important factor determining the material structure of these societies, but also because we cannot adequately assess the impact of cultural diversity on such rights unless we have an appropriate understanding of their nature and justification. Without such an understanding, the particular property rights dilemmas that arise in multicultural democracies cannot be resolved.

In keeping with this line of reasoning, I begin this chapter by examining the philosophical justification of ownership rights to land and natural resources, and then analyze the justification of collective property rights for indigenous groups.[1] In the next chapter I first analyze general ownership claims to property mediated by human labor and to intellectual property, and then examine dilemmas concerning these forms of property that arise from injustices committed against ethnocultural groups.

Property rights are enforced by legal authority and state sanctions. The moral and legal force of property rights as conventionally understood is great indeed, because they restrict individuals from the unauthorized use of property even if its use is necessary to satisfy their basic survival needs. In certain situations, restricting a person's access to another's property may endanger her life and the life of those for whom she is morally responsible. It is in the nature of rights to place limitations on people's behavior, but it is rather unusual for a right to restrict access to something which may be crucial for survival. My rights to life and liberty, for example, restrict the ways you may act towards me, but typically they do not limit the actions you need to take to insure your own survival. Since property rights often apply to objects that are limited and scarce, such as land and natural resources, the limitations imposed by ownership claims are all the more significant. Property rights do not merely place limitations on individuals in a society, they structure in fundamental ways the conditions under which they relate to one another. In multicultural societies, ethnocultural group differences in property ownership underpin intercultural socioeconomic inequalities that contribute to discriminatory and exploitative practices.[2] It is important to recognize from the outset the wide-ranging implications of conventional property rights, because their legitimacy is often taken for granted. It is only our pervasive and deeply rooted cultural conditioning that makes conventional ownership claims appear unassailable and sacred.[3]

Before proceeding with our analysis of property rights, several terminological distinctions are in order. The term "property" denotes land and natural resources, while the term "mediated property" refers to capital goods (including supporting physical and technological infrastructures) and manufactured commodities. To emphasize the distinction between property and mediated property I will sometimes refer to the former as "natural property." "Intellectual property" refers to intangible entities such as copyrights, patents, and trade secrets. "Private property right" denotes a set of claims to property that includes some or all of the following: the right of use, control, management, income, sale, lease, alienability, and bequeathal.[4] "Weak private property right" refers to a set of ownership claims that includes only some of the rights in this cluster, while "strong private property right" refers to a claim to property that includes all of the rights just mentioned. "Intellectual property right" is a set of ownership claims to intellectual objects that includes some or all of the following: the right of use, reproduction, income, public display, dissemination, bequeathal, and protection from misappropriation. "Strong intellectual property right" denotes a set of ownership claims that includes all of the latter, while "weak intellectual property right" includes only some of the rights in this set.

Most of the arguments for private property ownership try to justify it not as a universal or general right, but as a restricted right, that is, as a right that individuals may acquire through certain means or actions but do not have as a matter of course. Even though it is commonly assumed by those who defend nonuniversal property rights that everyone is at liberty to acquire ownership rights to property, they do not believe that people are automatically entitled to property ownership.[5] In this discussion, the notion of the right to property will refer to the actual possession of ownership rights over property and not merely to the capacity or possibility of obtaining such rights. Since the focus of most philosophical discussions is on defending property rights as restricted or nonuniversal rights, in what follows I concentrate on the justification of schemes of nonuniversal property ownership; that is, on schemes of property ownership in which some individuals own property and others do not. Later in this chapter I examine arguments in favor of property ownership as a general or universal right.

Locke and Original Appropriations of Property

One of the most influential defenses of property rights is provided by John Locke in his *Second Treatise on Government*.[6] Establishing the legitimacy of private property ownership and inequitable property holdings was one of Locke's concerns as a social and political philosopher. He maintained that in the state of nature—a state prior to the establishment of civil societies—the earth belonged to all in common, because everyone has a right to use land and natural resources to satisfy those needs, such as food and water, required for self-preservation. From this initial condition of common ownership of land and natural resources, how could private appropriations of property be justified?[7]

Locke's answer was that individuals could legitimately acquire exclusive and permanent rights to parts of nature, without obtaining the consent of others, by mixing their labor with nature. For instance, by picking apples from a tree growing in the wild or by clearing and tilling a tract of land, individuals could lay claim to the products of their labor, since these products resulted from combining something that is indisputably theirs, namely their labor, with nature. But Locke stipulated that in order for these property claims to be legitimate it was necessary to respect two provisos, namely, to leave "enough and as good in common for others"[8] and to take from nature only what one could use before it spoils. Thus one should not pick more apples than one could eat or cultivate more land than one could use[9] because this would, respectively, lead to spoilage and waste and diminish the capacity of others to satisfy their own needs. The fundamental purpose of these two provisos is to safe-guard the right of everyone to use land and natural resources to satisfy sustenance needs. If these provisos are honored, it is not necessary to ob-tain the consent of others in making original appropriations of property because such appropriations do not violate their right to use property as a means of self-preservation.

According to Locke, in a situation in which abundant unappropriated useful land exists, the two provisos are readily satisfied by original non-wasteful property appropriations, since such acquisitions do not involve excessive appropriations of property or deprive others of the capacity to make their own acquisitions. Further, Locke maintains that in a situation of land scarcity in which no useful land would be left to appropriate, original nonwasteful appropriations would still be legitimate as long as the right to use property as a means of self-preservation was protected by guaranteeing that nonproprietors have access to appropriated land to satisfy their sustenance needs. In effect this means granting those with-out property the right to earn their living by laboring on the private property of others. Thus, according to Locke, private property acquisi-tions are justified, even in a context of land scarcity, as long as: (i) original appropriations resulted from mixing one's labor with nature and (ii) ei-ther these appropriations conformed with the two provisos, or the non-wastefulness proviso was satisfied and nonproprietors are not deprived of the right to earn their subsistence.

Despite an initial plausibility of Locke's account, it is not difficult to see the problems with his justification of private property. First, if this ac-count is understood as an attempt to legitimize existing private property claims, we can point out that most of the private property claims in the world cannot be traced to original appropriations obtained by laboring or to voluntary transactions between individuals. Existing holdings of land and natural resources in most parts of the world came about through conquest, intrusive settlement, coerced annexation, broken treaties, fraud and deception, and outright assault and murder.[10] The set-tlement of North and South America by Europeans, for instance, did not for the most part proceed through peaceful and voluntary exchanges of tracts of land for precious metals or money, but through conquest. In Peru, for example, after land was forcefully appropriated by Europeans, indigenous people were forced into slavery to extract silver and gold that was subsequently shipped to Europe. The gold and silver expropriated from the Americas more than tripled the value of the reserves of the Eu-ropean colonial countries and was an important factor in their emergence as world powers.[11]

Besides the fact that Locke's account has dubious validity for justifying existing property rights, it is problematic in a more philosophically basic way. It is not clear how mixing labor with nature justifies original private appropriations of property in the first place. If I cultivate a tract of land and plant corn, for instance, it may be reasonable for me to claim the resulting crop of corn, since it resulted directly from my added labor, but why am I entitled to permanent ownership of that tract of land? What justifies me in claiming not only the added value created by my labor, namely the crop, but also the raw materials which enabled it to grow and which belong to all in common? Why am I entitled to the subsoil, minerals, and other materials that were untouched by my labor?[12] In his discussion of this issue, Locke greatly exaggerated the value created by human labor *vis-a-vis* the contributions of nature. He states that human labor creates 99 percent of the value of land, implying that uncultivated land is largely worthless. His strategy is obvious: if 99 percent of the value of a tract of land is created by something that I contribute to it, namely my labor, then it is reasonable that I can claim that land as my own. In asserting an ownership claim to property I am merely appropriating something that has been thoroughly transformed and permeated by my labor, and that prior to my labor had little worth.

This, of course, is a false picture of the contribution of human labor to the value of land. Even land that is uncultivated can have great value, as is the case with terrain that can be used for grazing animals, for military purposes, or as a source of valuable resources such as water or minerals. Further, when I plant a crop, nature does most of the work in nurturing and helping the crop grow. While the farmer may work the fields for parts of the day or season, the complex biological processes that maintain the fertility of the soil and enable the crop to grow are continuous. Nature provides raw materials which are of great value independently of the added value that human labor may provide. But most important, even if it could be established that cultivating a tract of land so thoroughly mixes my labor with that land that my labor could never be extricated from it—in itself a questionable claim[13]—it would not follow that I am entitled to ownership of those parts of the land, such as the subsoil and subterranean minerals, that were untouched by, and therefore unmixed with, my labor.

Furthermore, the provisos that Locke introduces to safeguard the equal rights that everyone has in the initial situation of common ownership are not satisfactory because they do not comprehensively protect all of the fundamental interests that people have in property. Using property as a means of self-preservation does not exhaust all of the advantages of property ownership. The autonomous satisfaction of sustenance needs, the connection to a life-place, and the development of positive human qualities promoted by property ownership, for example, are benefits of proprietorship that Locke's provisos do not protect. The inadequacy of Locke's provisos emerges with particular clarity in the situation of land scarcity. Locke maintains that even here restricted private property ownership and inequitable accumulations of property are legitimate as long as the right of self-preservation of nonproprietors is safeguarded. But why must we assume that this is the only right that needs to be protected? Nonproprietors may be placed in a position of serious disadvantage by being dependent on wage-labor for their subsistence. Even if a right to work is guaranteed, it is a very minimal right that protects only accessibility to property to earn the bare necessities for life. Such a minimal right is compatible with living in poverty and being in a constant state of dependence on property owners for one's survival. It is reasonable to maintain that being in such a state of dependence represents a serious infringement of agency and autonomy, which are paradigmatic examples of rights that should be protected. If it is plausible to maintain, as I will argue more fully in one of the following sections, that property rights are of fundamental importance for the exercise of agency and autonomy, then Locke's account is inadequate without an explanation of why such prima facie candidates as agency and autonomy should not be included among the rights that need to be protected in the area of property ownership.

Locke's position cannot be saved even if we use the alternative interpretation advocated by Tully and Sreenivasan.[14] According to these authors, the proper way to understand Locke's principal argument concerning property appropriations is not in terms of mixing labor with nature, but rather in terms of the natural ownership rights that creators have over the objects they create. Taking the creative activity of God as a standard, this "workmanship model" maintains that it is self-evident and undeniable that if something is created *ex nihilo* by a free, intelligent agent, what is thus created belongs to that creative being. Of course, people laboring in nature do not create objects *ex nihilo* but instead transform pre-existing materials; that is, the case of God involves creation, while that of people involves making. But this difference can be disregarded, according to the workmanship model, if human agents are entitled to use the materials from which making begins. And, the argument continues, this entitlement can be obtained by satisfying Locke's two provisos. Assuming that the provisos are satisfied, the activity of making is sufficiently similar to the process of creating—since both involve bringing objects into existence by the intentional acts of free, intelligent beings—that we should grant the right of ownership of those objects to their makers.

But even if we grant that making is sufficiently like creating *ex nihilo* to justify ownership rights over the objects brought into existence by working on pre-existing materials, the workmanship doctrine faces an insurmountable objection, namely, that private property rights involve ownership claims over entities that were not made by human labor. As we observed above, when people cultivate land they bring into existence objects of value, such as crops, that would not exist were it not for their labor. But from this it does not follow that they are entitled to those parts of the land that they did not make, such as the subsoil, its fertile nutrients, underground aquifers, and minerals in the land. At most they are entitled to the things they made by using commonly owned materials, not to these materials themselves or to materials they never engaged with their labor. Note that it cannot be argued here that by satisfying the two provisos, legitimate ownership can be obtained of those raw materials, namely land and natural resources, that the laboring person did not create. The function of the provisos (assuming their adequacy, which we have found reason to question) is to ensure that others do not lose out by original, unilateral property appropriations; they do not on their own justify appropriations.

Finally, it is worth noting that there are certain unsubstantiated cultural assumptions, if not biases, in Locke's account of private property acquisition. It is not entirely clear why land cultivation, but not other forms of subsistence, provides a moral basis for property acquisition. Unlike an individual who cultivated land, an individual or group who used hunting and fishing as forms of subsistence would supposedly not merit ownership rights to the territory they used for these purposes. Perhaps Locke might argue that while the latter merely took what they needed from nature, the farmer improved the land through cultivation. But "improved the land" in what sense? Surely it does not matter to nature whether land is cultivated or not, and the clearing and tilling of land is more likely to disrupt natural ecosystems than hunting and fishing. Presumably, the value of the farmer's contribution is that it increases the stock of available food and materials vital for sustaining human life.[15] The value of this contribution is therefore contingent on the existence of people who need these food and materials to live. But if the cultural groups who depended on hunting and fishing satisfied the sustenance needs of all of their members and lived in an environmentally sustainable way, why should we hold it against them that in their society there were no people in need of the food and materials that could be produced through land cultivation? Why should leading a materially simpler life within bioregional limits count against one's claims to property?[16] It seems that if questions like these are to be answered in a way that supports Locke's position, some culturally loaded assumptions will have to be made concerning the moral superiority of more technologically complex forms of life, of the instrumental use of nature, and of certain forms of consumption-oriented initiative.

Recognizing the numerous problems with Locke's position, three strategies could be taken to justify private property rights: the consequentialist strategy, the strategy based on desert, and the agency and autonomy strategy. Even though some of these justificatory strategies are inspired or based on some of Locke's arguments, they can be considered

Property Rights in Multicultural Liberal Democracies

as independent arguments for private property rights. And this is just as well, because we do not want to confine ourselves to Lockean arguments in searching for a justification for restricted or nonuniversal private property ownership. We should note from the outset that these arguments, though sometimes apparently couched in terms that apply only to natural property, often also include mediated property.

The Consequentialist Strategy

According to the first strategy, defended by Robert Nozick, original individual appropriations of property, and correlative strong ownership rights over that property, are justified because they have beneficial consequences, such as improved material prosperity, that on balance do not worsen the position of those unable to make original appropriations. Nozick's point of departure is different from Locke's state of nature in which land and natural resources were owned by all in common. Nozick starts with the more neutral assumption that land and natural resources were initially owned by no one, thus dispensing with the need to justify common ownership by appealing to a more fundamental right of self-preservation. Despite his different starting point, however, an analogous problem arises for Nozick concerning the legitimacy of original appropriations made without the consent of others. Even though land and natural resources originally belonged to no one, everyone was equally free to use them. But the institution of private property changes the moral universe in which everyone acts, because it restricts the access they previously enjoyed to land and natural resources. Thus, Nozick must also address the issue of justifying original appropriations in the absence of general consent.

Nozick resolves the consent problem by first pointing out that Locke's provisos regarding leaving enough for others and not wasting resources were motivated by the moral concern that the situation of others not be made worse by the appropriation of property. Nozick then argues that Locke's provisos are not the only ways of insuring that the situation of others is not worsened. He maintains that the material and social advantages of allowing private property—and by implication mediated property—balance or outweigh the disadvantages that nonproprietors suffer by not being able to make original appropriations. Since these advantages entail that no one's position is worse off than it was before property acquisitions, their consent can be dispensed with.

Is the situation of persons who are unable to appropriate (there being no more accessible and useful unowned property) worsened by a system allowing appropriation and permanent property? Here enter the various familiar social considerations favoring private property: it increases the social product by putting means of production in the hands of those who can use them most efficiently (profitably); experimentation is encouraged because with separate persons controlling resources, there is no one person or small group whom someone with a new idea must convince to try it out; private property enables people to decide on the pattern and types of risks they wish to bear, leading to specialized types of risk bearing; private property protects future persons by leading some to hold back resources from current consumption for future markets; it provides alternate sources of employment for unpopular persons who don't have to convince any one person or small group to hire them, and so on.[17]

According to Nozick, nonproprietors are better off in a system which permits private appropriations than they would be if no one was allowed to own private property. Nonproprietors have no reason to complain of the unfairness of original appropriations since their position does not deteriorate by systems that allow them. Accordingly, the Lockean moral concern underlying the provisos can be satisfied even if there is no new property to appropriate. Nozick also indicates that the purpose of calling attention to these advantages is not to establish a utilitarian justification of private property, but to show that because the spirit of the provisos can be satisfied, original appropriations can be morally justified from a neo-Lockean perspective after all.[18]

There are several difficulties with Nozick's position. We should first of all notice that Nozick's argument that nonproprietors would be worse off in a system in which no one owned private property does not establish the unique preferability of systems of nonuniversal strong private property ownership. Since he uses the no-ownership situation as the base line of comparison, any property ownership scheme that provides more than or as many material advantages as a system of no-ownership is equally justified by Nozick's argument. Thus, since practically everyone would be worse off in a system of no-ownership than they would be in systems of worker owned cooperatives or systems of universal private property ownership, for example, the latter property schemes are also preferable to the no-ownership system. Nozick might respond that nonproprietors would be better off in systems of nonuniversal strong private property ownership than they would be in any alternative system of property ownership, but it is highly unlikely that he can successfully make this case.

Consider a predominantly agrarian society in which a small percentage of the population owns most of the land and productive resources. In such a system, nonproprietors would surely be at a great disadvantage. They would be forced to sell their labor to landowners and rent land from the property owners to have a place to live. In countries like Brazil and Guatemala, the great disparities in wealth and power between the wealthy elite and the poor working classes can be largely attributed to the ownership of land and natural resources by the elite. And even in technologically complex nonagrarian societies where individuals have a wide range of options for earning a living, nonproprietors would still be at a significant disadvantage. If they wanted to start a business, for example, they would have to rent or buy land from proprietors, not to mention that in order to have a place to live they would also have to pay rent or buy property from property owners. It is certainly reasonable to suppose that in these two scenarios the situation of nonproprietors would improve if they owned property. In some of the sections that follow I will elaborate more fully on the advantages of property ownership. For now the important point to note is that since Nozick fails to establish that the nonproprietor's situation would be better in systems of nonuniversal strong private property ownership than in other alternatives to the no-ownership scheme, his justification for the unique preferability of nonuniversal strong private property rights is unconvincing.[19]

Another problem with Nozick's position is that even if schemes of nonuniversal private property ownership lead to general material prosperity and other social benefits, there is an unfair asymmetry in the advantages enjoyed by owners and nonproprietors. Proprietors benefit twice—once by the general well-being that private property produces and then again by owning private property—while nonproprietors benefit only once. Further, it is not clear why the mere fact that proprietors improve the general material and social well-being of a society by itself justifies providing them with such a significant advantage as strong private property rights. Nozick does not answer such questions as: How many social and material benefits have to be produced to outweigh the disadvantages to nonproprietors? How would such benefits have to be distributed to justify the fact that only some own property? Does the fact that some people may be deprived of basic needs in such schemes of nonuniversal ownership nullify the justification of such schemes? Nozick's failure to answer these questions weakens his case considerably for nonuniversal strong private property ownership.

Finally, Nozick, like Locke, does not recognize that there are other important advantages of owning private property, such as developing at least partial material self-reliance and a connection to a life-place, that nonproprietors will be deprived of by not owning property. Nozick construes the notion of being well-off in purely economic terms. He does not consider that there may be additional benefits to property ownership that have little to do with material wealth and more to do with human qualities and dispositions that are constitutive of developed personhood. In addition, as we shall see below, for some indigenous groups maintaining ownership and control of their land can have great religious and cultural significance, and their very survival as distinct cultural groups may depend on ownership of their homeland. In a multicultural society it would be grossly misleading to understand the significance of property to these ethnocultural groups solely in material terms.

Despite appearances to the contrary, Nozick did not intend his arguments concerning the Lockean provisos to be purely utilitarian justifications of private property; rather, he was concerned with salvaging the fairness or moral legitimacy of original appropriations along Lockean lines. Nevertheless, utilitarian considerations are often cited to defend private property rights. For this reason, we will consider utilitarian justifications of private property independently of Lockean considerations. The more strictly utilitarian arguments that follow—which apply to the ownership of private property and mediated property—are intended to show the beneficial consequences of nonuniversal schemes of private property ownership. I will charitably construe these arguments as intending to legitimize weak nonuniversal private property rights, with the understanding that if they cannot justify such rights neither can they justify strong nonuniversal private property rights.

The most common utilitarian reason adduced for the private ownership of property and mediated property is that they maximize economic productivity and efficiency. Defenders of this view make the correlative assumption that social and political institutions that support free markets are needed for private property to have these beneficial consequences. If we do not create and maintain the institutional mechanisms needed for free enterprise, so the argument goes, the advantages of private property cannot be realized. Thus, this argument is best construed as purporting to show that nonuniversal schemes of private property ownership accompanied by free markets are conducive to economic productivity and efficiency. Here private property is defended in an indirect way, by maintaining that it is an essential component of an economic system that has desirable consequences.

We can critique this argument by questioning whether economic productivity and efficiency should have normative priority over values like egalitarianism, ecological sustainability, social justice, or community cohesion. It may well turn out, after an examination of the relative importance of different social values, that economic productivity and efficiency should override all others, but we cannot simply assume that this is the case. Granting normative priority to economic productivity and efficiency would not be a problem if the systems of nonuniversal ownership championed by the proponents of this argument also supported values such as ecological sustainability or social justice, but such systems do not necessarily uphold values like these. Take ecological sustainability as an example. The conceptions of productivity and efficiency that underpin contemporary systems of nonuniversal ownership externalize ecological costs; that is, they do not take into account the depletion of natural resources or the degradation of ecosystems brought about by its "productive" and "efficient" economic methods.

Failure to internalize ecological costs creates a faulty understanding of productivity and efficiency. By clearing its rain forests and turning them into grazing lands for cattle or by using petrochemical herbicides and pesticides to increase crop yields, for instance, a country can greatly increase its economic productivity and efficiency in the short run. Yet it is highly questionable whether these economic methods are truly productive and efficient since they degrade the natural resource base from which all nourishment and life derives. Deforestation contributes to global warming, destroys numerous plant and animal species, and increases desertification, while the heavy use of petrochemicals in agriculture kills microorganisms in the soil that maintain its fertility and contributes to topsoil erosion due to a decreased capacity of the soil to absorb water. How productive and efficient can an economic system be if it systematically destroys the biological viability of the earth on which we and future generations must depend for our sustenance and well-being?

Utilitarian arguments based on productivity and efficiency also fare poorly with regard to the ideals of egalitarianism and social justice. As I observed earlier in my discussion of Nozick, ownership schemes in which only some individuals own private property place nonproprietors in positions of economic and social disadvantage. Nonuniversal ownership schemes create asymmetries in power that are conducive to abuse and oppression. The potential for such abuse and oppression is not a mere theoretical possibility but an ever present real danger, as the history of such systems amply demonstrates.[20] In any case, it is not at all clear why utilitarian considerations should override principles of justice and equality. From a moral standpoint, it is untenable to maintain that gains in economic productivity and efficiency will necessarily supersede the rights of every human being to be treated equally and justly. In short, the utilitarian argument based on the desirability of present systems of nonuniversal ownership that promote economic productivity and efficiency fails to establish the legitimacy of restricted or nonuniversal private property rights, because it does not establish the moral primacy of productivity and efficiency over all other social values.

Another utilitarian argument often cited in defense of private property is that it is necessary for democracy.[21] This argument is similar to the one just considered, though it is more plausible to the extent that it is easier to argue for the primacy of democracy as a social desideratum. Here again the defense of private property is indirect, because properly speaking it is capitalist systems coupled with private property ownership (including ownership of mediated property), and not private property by itself, that are necessary for democracy. The idea is that capitalist systems, and the correlative right of private property, place significant political and legal restrictions on what a government can and cannot do, and that capitalism creates a political climate which promotes civil liberties and the rule of law, the open exchange of information, and democratic self-determination. According to this view, private property and free markets go hand in hand with democratic self-governance. Capitalism lays the necessary groundwork for democratic rule, and any government that does not respect an individual's right to own private property and to transact freely with the fruits of her labor will also deprive that individual of the right to democratic governance.

Some of the claims on which this argument is based are plausible, particularly the desirability of democratic self-rule and the contention that free markets impose certain constraints on government regulation of economic and social activity.[22] The argument falters, however, to the extent that it insists that democratic governments can exist only where systems of *nonuniversal* private property ownership are in place. Indeed, there is a covert shift in the argument from the general claim that private property ownership is necessary for democracy to the more specific contention that systems of nonuniversal or restricted private property ownership are necessary for democracy. But even if we grant the argument's contention that private property and free markets are necessary to create a civil environment appropriate for democracy, why do we have to suppose that such a civil milieu can exist only where schemes of nonuniversal private property ownership exist? For example, why couldn't a market system of universal property ownership in which all workers own private property and are either self-employed or collectively own the business cooperatives where they work support democracy?[23] In such a system of universal ownership, private property would not be under state ownership or control and market competition would exist for goods and services. The market mechanisms that constrain government regulation would be in place and workers would have greater control over their economic lives. Actually, it is plausible to suppose that in such schemes there would be a higher degree of democratic empowerment and participation than in schemes of nonuniversal private property ownership.

Systems of nonuniversal private property ownership, to the extent that they underpin significant class differences, also undermine equitable democratic empowerment.[24] Among the greatest causes of political disempowerment and alienation in democratic societies are differences in educational resources and social advantages that are caused primarily by economic inequalities.[25] When these inequalities reflect differences among cultural groups, they will tend to exacerbate intercultural tensions and conflicts. A society that enables its citizens to achieve economic self-reliance through universal property ownership (either private or communal) is more likely to foster equitable and fair democratic participation for all members of the polity. Vast concentrations of wealth create problems for democratic societies. In schemes of nonuniversal property ownership the democratic process is distorted by the disproportionate political influence of elites with great concentrations of private capital.[26] More equitable distributions of property ownership would likely undercut these distorting and unjust political influences in democratic societies. Far from being necessary for democracy, existing schemes of nonuniversal private property ownership tend to undermine political equality in democratic societies.

The Strategy Based on Desert

The second strategy for justifying restricted private property rights centers on the notion of desert. The basic idea behind this strategy is that expending effort and time in improving land merits compensation, and that private property rights to cultivated land is the commensurate and morally appropriate recompense for one's labor. Our analysis of this strategy actually encompasses two different arguments, both based on desert. The first argument deals with original appropriations of property while the second circumvents questions of original ownership and focuses on the private property rights of present owners. I will consider each of these arguments in turn.

Imagine an individual who has invested a great deal of effort and time in cultivating unclaimed land and improving its value and productivity, and in the process has provided goods and benefits to others. Through her own initiative, and under no moral obligation to do so, she has labored to add value to an unclaimed tract of land with the specific aim of owning it. It is clear that this individual deserves some benefit for the efforts that have increased the value of uncultivated land. However, this benefit has to fulfill several conditions to be morally appropriate: first, the benefit must be proportionate, that is, it must be commensurate to the value produced by the labor expended; second, the individual's interests in performing the labor must be taken into account in determining an appropriate benefit (particularly if the agent performed the labor with the intention of acquiring property); third, granting the benefit must not violate the rights of others; and fourth, other people besides the appropriator must have benefited by the labor performed.[27]

Various problems beset this justification of restricted private property rights. Consider the proportionality requirement. It is very difficult to maintain that the only, or the most fitting, reward for cultivating land is the granting of private property rights. Envision a situation in which an individual cultivates a tract of land for a year and obtains an ownership claim to it. In the second and third years she hires someone to continue cultivating it in the same manner and pays him wages as a recompense. From the perspective of desert, the wage-laborer is equally or more deserving of ownership rights than the proprietor, for he has expended twice as much effort as the owner.[28] It will not do to argue that the second individual has already been appropriately compensated by wages, since he could claim that if ownership rights were a fitting reward for the owner, he also deserves the same ownership rights as compensation. And neither can we convincingly maintain that the temporal priority of the first individual's labor is of decisive moral relevance. If what entitles someone to private property ownership is time and effort expended in improving property, why did that apply at the earlier time but not later? Of course, it will not do to respond that the property was already owned at the time the second individual expended effort cultivating it, because it is precisely the legitimacy of the original appropriation that is in question here. Finally, we cannot successfully argue that the second individual lacks the independent initiative of the first, if he was forced into wage labor because there was no more new land for him to improve and appropriate through his labor.[29]

It is also questionable whether the third condition dealing with the non-violation of others' rights is satisfied. One could argue that granting private property rights to a tract of land violates the original common right that everyone had to that land. Even though a particular tract of land may not be claimed by any particular individual, that does not mean that the members of the community or society do not have a collective claim to it. Since originally no one had a privileged claim to exclusive ownership of common resources, when someone unilaterally (i.e., without the consent of others) appropriates a tract of land held in common, there is an infringement of the rights of others, because they no longer have the same access to it as before. Unless the members of a community or society agree that an individual who cultivates land in a certain way merits private property rights to it, that individual cannot claim that land as her own. Here the argument from desert breaks down, since it is based on the assumption that desert by itself is sufficient for justifying unilateral private property nonuniversal ownership rights. One could try to ameliorate the moral seriousness of the infringement on others' rights by arguing that their situation is not really worsened by schemes allowing original private appropriations in which some will not own private property, but we have already seen the inadequacy of this response.

The other argument based on desert eschews attempts to justify original private appropriations of property and concentrates instead on defending existing private property claims. According to this argument, many present owners of private property have invested a great deal of time, effort, and money in acquiring and improving their property and, regardless of the possible illegitimacy of the original appropriation of the property they now own, the efforts they have taken to acquire it merit ownership rights. Even if we cannot provide a sound justification for original private appropriations of property, the argument continues, we should recognize that most present owners acquired their property legitimately under the terms set by existing social and legal frameworks. We cannot ignore the fact that numerous existing owners have invested their money and efforts in acquiring their property with the clear expectation that they would have legitimate ownership claims to it. The refusal to recognize the legitimacy of their ownership claims violates a reasonable social expectation they had in acquiring their property. We have a collective moral responsibility to honor the contractual agreements that we as a society have made with proprietors.

In responding to this argument we should note that when something is obtained illegitimately, formalizing rules and procedures for acquiring and transferring it does not mean that we can obtain legitimate rights to it. Imagine a tribe that illegitimately obtained some property from another tribe and then instituted a set of acquisition and transference rules for that property. No one could justifiably claim that a member of the pilfering tribe deserved ownership rights to that property by expending labor or money to acquire and improve it. A member of the pilfering tribe could not acquire legitimate ownership rights even if she paid a "reasonable" price for the property and adhered faithfully to the collectively determined acquisition rules and procedures set up by her tribe. Even if she improved the stolen property through her labor and added to its value, this would still not justify ownership rights to it because the property was illegitimately appropriated in the first place. Finally, the fact that a long time may have elapsed since the property was stolen would not change the basic fact that the present ownership claim of the member of the pilfering tribe is illegitimate. While not all past injustices create a moral imperative for rectification—either because it is impossible to determine what form the rectification should take or because present circumstances override the moral obligation for rectification[30]—nonuniversal private appropriations of property are different because, as we have seen, they sustain *present* socioeconomic inequalities and injustices, and hinder the development of autonomy of nonproprietors. And, as we shall see below, there are workable procedures through which the injustice of exclusive appropriations of property and the concomitant nonuniversal schemes of property ownership can be rectified.

These arguments, however, must be qualified in the following way. Because present proprietors may have arranged their lives on the basis of the reasonable expectation that they have legitimate ownership claims to their property, compensation for expropriation is in some cases morally justified. The kind and degree of compensation is to be determined by such factors as the number of nonproprietors in the political community, the amount of private property the proprietors hold, the available resources of the society in question, the amount of property necessary to provide a base level of material autonomy, the advantages the proprietors may have unjustly achieved by inequalities in property ownership, and historical considerations regarding unjust modes of property appropriation. Though a more precise examination of the relative importance of these factors will not be provided here, these are among the most important considerations to be taken into account in determining the need and extent of compensation.

The issue of whether property can ever be privately appropriated in the first place thus remains of central importance for the legitimacy of present private property ownership claims, even if such claims are part of an institutionalized social and legal framework. If we fail to provide a sound justification for original unilateral nonuniversal appropriations, we cannot claim that present private property claims are legitimate. Again, this does not mean that present owners do not merit moral consideration or compensation for their labor and investments; the point is that the arguments from desert do not establish that granting individuals private property rights within a scheme of nonuniversal ownership is the only or most fitting compensation for their efforts.[31]

The Agency and Autonomy Strategy

The third strategy for defending property rights is based on the claim that private property (again in the extended sense that includes mediated property) is necessary for exercising agency and achieving autonomy. With the possible exception of arguments from utility, this defense of property rights is the one most commonly used by contemporary advocates of private property.[32] This strategy maintains that human beings are choice-making agents who have the fundamental right to choose and implement their own values, projects, and conceptions of the good life. According to this view, to exercise agency and achieve autonomy at least two things are required: first, one must be allowed to acquire control over the material objects (property in particular) needed for one's basic sustenance needs and life projects, and second, socioeconomic institutions must be maintained that enable one to act freely regarding the control and disposition of these objects; that is, market institutions must be sustained that allow and support free transactions of one's property.[33] If these two necessary conditions are satisfied, individuals will have the minimal resources and autonomy needed to pursue their own vision of the good life. In addition to making possible the self-reliant satisfaction of sustenance needs, private property rights will provide the stability and security of expectation necessary for long-term planning, while the economic framework of the free market will provide the freedom necessary for autonomous self-determination.

The advocates of this strategy believe that the cardinal virtue of private property and free markets is that they make possible the autonomy of the individual. As John Gray states: "The free market enables the individual to act upon his own goals and values, his objectives and his plan of life, without subordination to any other individual or subjection to any collective decision procedure."[34] Private property and free markets, by providing a sphere of action characterized by the absence of interference from others, makes it possible for the individual to attain the self-determination and independence that are essential for autonomy. In addition, the individual's innate capacity for agency is best realized in a context of autonomy characterized by economic self-reliance and independence from the decisions of others.

This strategy also upholds the corollary principle, which is sometimes not explicitly stated, that the exercise of agency and autonomy requires the control of one's body and labor. An autonomous individual must be able to determine how to use her labor to satisfy basic needs and carry out her life projects. The management of one's labor includes the freedom to enter into voluntary transactions concerning the use of one's labor and body and the right to retain the rewards of one's efforts. Forced labor or control of a person's labor by a centralized state agency, for example, would undermine agency and autonomy in significant ways. Any community or society that respects agency and autonomy must abide by this principle of individual control over one's body and labor.

Of all of the strategies we have examined for justifying private property rights, the arguments based on agency and autonomy are the most plausible. However, we must sharpen our analysis of this strategy to determine its most tenable formulation, because as it stands several aspects of this approach are inadequately articulated. The most important qualification is that, to the extent that it is justifiable, this strategy establishes that private property rights are universal and not restricted rights; that is, it shows that everyone has a right to private property. If private property ownership is necessary for the self-reliant satisfaction of basic needs and the exercise of the fundamental capacities of agency and autonomy, then it is essential for everyone to own private property. For this reason, this strategy does not *per se* support schemes of nonuniversal private property ownership in which some do not own private property. In order to defend private property ownership as a restricted right one has to provide rational and morally adequate criteria for granting legitimacy to schemes of nonuniversal private property ownership and, as we have seen, the arguments that try to justify nonuniversal unilateral acquisitions of property fail.[35]

In addition, this strategy in itself establishes only that people are entitled to sufficient private property to fulfill basic needs and to exercise a level of agency and autonomy compatible with a similar degree of agency and autonomy for others, it does not justify private property holdings in excess of what is needed to fulfill basic needs and exercise this level of agency and autonomy. The latter point is crucial, because this strategy is often used to legitimize existing systems of property ownership in which some have large property holdings while others have no property or insufficient property to fulfill agency and autonomy needs. Thus, far from justifying present schemes of property ownership, the agency and autonomy strategy actually undermines the legitimacy of these schemes. Particularly in cases in which large property holdings make it impossible to satisfy everyone's needs for useful and accessible land, this strategy can be used to justify land redistribution.[36]

But the strength of the agency and autonomy argument as a justification of private property ownership should not be overstated. As we will see below, the case of certain indigenous groups shows that individual ownership of private property is not universally necessary for the exercise of agency and autonomy. For some of these groups, collective ownership of property concurs more appropriately with their conceptions of human flourishing. Thus, rather than making the universalistic statement that private property is necessary for agency and autonomy, it would be more accurate to say that the institution of private property is needed to promote agency and autonomy in market-based, technologically complex societies with individualistic cultural orientations.

Concerning the misgivings that some individuals concerned with social justice might have about defending capitalism and private property, I should point out that it is not the market system and private property *per se* that are problematic but rather schemes of nonuniversal private property ownership. The fact that not everyone has ownership rights to land and natural resources, and the technologies needed to usefully employ them, is at the root of economic and sociopolitical inequalities.[37] Market systems need not be coupled with inegalitarian schemes of nonuniversal ownership. As indicated below, there are feasible systems of universal property ownership that incorporate market principles. Market systems involving private property ownership are particularly appropriate for technologically complex societies because of the indispensable epistemological functions of the market in providing information about supply and demand and in coordinating the complex division of labor required in these societies. Even in a perfectly altruistic technologically complex society, markets would still be necessary for providing this information and performing these coordinating functions. However, for traditional small-scale agrarian communities with a high degree of communal cohesion, as well as for intentional communities built on egalitarian values, various schemes of collective ownership might be more appropriate. Indeed, the most sustainable and egalitarian schemes of property distribution in human history have been decentralized systems of communal property ownership in which meeting the basic needs of all of the members of the community was a social priority.

It is extremely ironic that systems of nonuniversal private property ownership praised for their promotion of agency and autonomy actually impose significant limitations on the agency and autonomy of a large number of people. To see this we need only ask the question: Whose agency and autonomy is enhanced by these systems of property distribution? Surely these systems do not enhance the agency and autonomy of those members of society who must depend on wage-labor to survive and who are in positions of economic dependence *vis-a-vis* the owners of private property.[38] Market systems of nonuniversal ownership maximize the agency and autonomy of the owners of private property at the expense of those without private property. A central mistake of those who defend these systems is the failure to realize that agency and autonomy can be thwarted not only by interference by a central state or collective body but also by systems of nonuniversal private property ownership that lead to grossly inequitable positions of economic power.

Even though there is no straightforward necessary correlation between wealth and ownership of land and natural resources, the nonuniversality of property rights makes possible the concentrated accumulation of vast amounts of private capital at the national and international level. Restricting rights to natural property, and the technological means for its efficient use,[39] undermines economic self-reliance for the majority, and is an important aspect of class inequalities.[40] In the U.S., the richest 1 percent of the population at present own about 40 percent of the wealth. Apart from stocks owned by pension funds, the wealthiest 10 percent of Americans own 83.1 percent of stock market wealth.[41] In third world countries such as Guatemala the concentrations of wealth are even greater. Approximately two percent of Guatemalans own 75 percent of the land and resources.[42] Even in relatively egalitarian countries such as Sweden the concentrations of wealth are substantial. In 1992, the richest 2 percent of Swedish households owned 23 percent of the country's wealth and 62 percent of the value of the shares on their country's stock exchange.[43]

Technological advances in transportation, telecommunications, and information processing have made possible unprecedented levels of international economic coordination among global elites. At present, about half of the world's largest 100 economies are not countries but transnational corporations. In a world increasingly dominated by market systems of nonuniversal ownership, global concentrations of wealth have increased greatly in the last thirty years. In 1950 the average income of the 20 percent of people living in the world's richest countries was about thirty times that of the 20 percent living in the poorest countries, but by 1989 this difference in wealth had increased to sixty times.[44] These figures are based on national averages and represent inequalities between countries; when the global distribution of wealth is measured in terms of individual incomes rather than national averages, the average income of the world's richest 20 percent is *150 times* greater than that of the poorest 20 percent. The poorest 20 percent of people in the world receive 1.4 percent of total world income.[45] Even though the cost of living in technologically advanced societies is greater than in developing countries, these figures still represent enormous standard-of-living differences between developed and Third World countries. These inequitable accumulations of wealth are made possible by systems of restricted private property rights that are morally and rationally illegitimate, and that unjustly confer great advantages to the few at the expense of the majority, while undermining the autonomy of billions of people.

Since material factors affect so many aspects of peoples' lives, when individuals lose control of their economic lives their capacity to choose and pursue their vision of the good life is greatly diminished. As far as agency and autonomy are concerned, systems of nonuniversal ownership are socially unsound because they do not promote general economic self-determination. For many hundreds of millions of people in Brazil, Uruguay, India, Pakistan, Thailand, Mexico, Peru, Kenya, Guatemala, Chile, Haiti, Panama, Colombia, Ecuador, Egypt, Honduras, Zaire, Indonesia, Ethiopia, Turkey, Cameroon, and the Philippines (among many others), systems of nonuniversal ownership have been a resounding failure. Approximately 1.3 billion people in the world—the overwhelming majority of whom live in systems of nonuniversal ownership—exist in conditions of abject poverty in which they face starvation or severe malnutrition and lack other necessities of life such as clean water and adequate shelter.

In order to be judged as adequate, an economic system of property distribution must be able to provide at least the basic necessities of life.[46] By this criterion of adequacy—and surely this is a rational and fair standard by which to judge economic systems—the vast majority of systems of nonuniversal ownership are categorical failures. A tempting but inadequate response here is to argue that the reason these countries have failed to thrive economically is due not to nonuniversal property ownership but to the endemic political corruption of their elites. What this argument fails to acknowledge, however, is that the political power of these elites to undermine economic reforms, fair democratic procedures, and equitable distributions of wealth is due to the economic power they possess by virtue of their rights of ownership of a major share of the land and natural resources of their countries. It is the existence of nonuniversal private property schemes that make the existence of such elites possible in the first place.[47]

Another common argument is that existing systems of nonuniversal ownership, while not ideal, nevertheless make possible a higher degree of agency and autonomy than systems of centralized state ownership, and that the demise of socialist systems at the end of the 20th century bears this out. However, the relevant standard of comparison should not be centralized systems of property ownership, but schemes of universal property ownership in which everyone either owns private property or has the right to participate in the decision-making processes that determine how property and natural resources are to be used. Contrary to the claim that there are no feasible alternatives to market systems of nonuniversal ownership, a number of countries have vibrant sectors of worker-owned cooperatives. In the United Kingdom the number of cooperatives increased from less than twenty in 1975 to approximately 1,600 in 1989. Italy has about 1,200 cooperatives that employ some half a million people, while France has about 1,200 cooperatives with around 40,000 workers. The failure rate of cooperatives is between 6 and 11 percent per year, which is the same or better than other types of small businesses.[48] In these cooperatives, workers achieve a higher degree of agency and autonomy than in most systems of nonuniversal ownership. Even though these examples do not conclusively show that a whole economy based on worker-owned businesses would be viable, they do establish that we cannot automatically assume that all alternatives to schemes of nonuniversal ownership are in principle unfeasible.

The Incoherence Objection

But the defenders of nonuniversal private property ownership have one last card up their sleeves.[49] They will argue that my position on property rights is not viable because it is not sustainable. My rationale for granting universal property rights was based on their indispensability for exercising agency and autonomy, but the exercise of these capacities involves deciding for ourselves how to use what we own, what risks to take regarding our property, to whom we will bequeath what we have, and what economic partnerships and alliances we will make. Over time, these decisions will invariably lead to some individuals acquiring a disproportionate share of property and wealth, while others will lose most or all of their property. Those that are economically successful will typically bequeath their wealth to their descendants, further exacerbating inequalities. The only way to prevent these inequities is to severely restrict what individuals can do with their property, that is, to delimit the very agency and autonomy that property rights were supposed to make possible. Thus my position is incoherent because the only way to sustain universality of property ownership is to restrict the economic freedom, and therefore the agency and autonomy, of individuals. We would do much better to opt for schemes of nonuniversal private property ownership because in these schemes individuals have the economic freedom that makes agency and autonomy a reality.

To answer this argument, we should begin by noting that even though in a system of universal property ownership certain restrictions on property transactions, such as denial of unrestricted powers of bequeathal, would have to be implemented to maintain general property ownership, these restrictions need not be so onerous and pervasive that they thwart agency and autonomy. As we noted at the beginning of this chapter, property rights actually involve a bundle of distinguishable rights over property. Denying the power to sell or transfer those portions of one's property necessary for self-reliance would not interfere with other property rights, such as rights of property exchange, property lease, or qualified income rights.[50] Since my argument for universal property ownership was not based on the goal of achieving a completely egalitarian society, but on providing everyone with the wherewithal for a base level of economic security and autonomy, many economic transactions would be permissible.[51] The specific form that property rights would take in a particular society would be determined in the forums of public deliberation in which collective decisions should be made in a multicultural society. Cultural groups with long traditions of economic autonomy and self-sufficiency might endorse stronger private property rights than cultural groups with communal orientations. In any case, the right to participate in economic arrangements of a given kind is not an all or nothing affair, but can be delimited in several ways. In practice there are always restrictions on economic transactions and contracts; the difference is that in a just multicultural society restrictions would be designed to protect the basic property rights of all and to provide incentives for egalitarian socioeconomic conditions and practices, such as the development of technologies that promote economic self-reliance and retention of property ownership for all.

Property Rights and the Territorial Powers of States

Some important clarifications need to be made concerning the legitimacy of the territorial claims of states. I have argued that existing systems of private property rights are illegitimate because no morally defensible basis for the nonuniversal unilateral acquisitions of property by individuals can be found. Implicit in my position, however, is the idea that states have a legitimate claim to their territories, because as I maintained in Chapter 4, communal self-determination is not possible without the right to control membership and residence in a political community. But since most, if not all, existing states acquired their territories through conquest, invasive settlement, broken treaties, and other morally improper means, their territorial ownership claims should also be considered illegitimate.

Moreover, even if an existing state acquired its territory peacefully, it still did not do so through the common agreement of all the world's inhabitants, who have an equal claim to the territories in question. In short, if we subjected state territorial claims to the same adequacy criteria we have used to determine the moral legitimacy of individual property ownership claims, the territorial claims of states would surely fail. The only consistent position, it would seem, is to declare existing property claims of both individuals and states as equally unjustified.

There are normative and pragmatic reasons why I do not advocate the latter position. First, without the right to exercise territorial control a political society could not implement the right of self-determination. Unless a political body can control immigration or set standards for civic membership, for example, it cannot effectively maintain its character as a distinctive political and cultural community. For instance, imagine an indigenous political community that lives in a beautiful, undeveloped territory. A number of wealthy individuals in a neighboring community find the indigenous peoples' territory ideally suited for vacations and recreational activities. They move en masse into the indigenous land and in a few short years radically change the ecological balance of that bioregion through extensive commercial development and the building of private homes, thereby destroying the material base of the indigenous group. If a sufficient number of the outsiders move in, they could even constitute a majority in the area, and outvote proposals by the indigenous group to maintain the ecological integrity of their territory. In short, without the capacity to regulate immigration and set conditions for political membership in their community, the indigenous group would be unable to sustain the cultural, material, and political character of its community.

Similarly, without the right to determine how its natural and financial resources are to be used, a political society cannot set policies concerning the use of its economic resources. Think of a political community whose members make the collective decision to set aside part of their gross domestic product to take care of the medical and social needs of the elderly, young children, and other members of the polity unable to provide for themselves. Many people living in other political communities who have made less of a collective investment in their most vulnerable citizens and have consumed their surplus revenues decide, when they are elderly, to move to the first political community, knowing that they will enjoy the generous social benefits provided there. This process would soon make it impossible for the first political community to fulfill its promise to its necessitous citizens due to the uncontrolled influx of immigrants.

Furthermore, there are strong pragmatic reasons for granting conditional recognition to the territorial claims of states. At this point in human history, it is simply not feasible to countenance a global redistribution of natural property guided by the ideal that all land and natural resources belong to all of humanity in common, however fair this ideal may be in theory. Should there come a time in collective human evolution when this ideal could be implemented, I would certainly be in favor of it. For the foreseeable future, however, we must live with distinct political communities. But while global redistribution of natural property is an unrealistic possibility, land distribution policies are by no means unprecedented in the history of states. Even though revolutionary change would be needed to implement such policies in most countries, the breakup of the former Soviet Union and the abolition of apartheid in South Africa have shown that revolutionary changes on a grand scale are possible with relatively small degrees of violence, particularly if the ideals motivating the changes are sufficiently compelling, such as appeals to autonomy and fundamental human rights. I would maintain that the proposal I am outlining is the most feasible one that respects the universal, fundamental right to property under existing political circumstances.

There are significant advantages to recognizing states and their territorial boundaries.[52] Many states already have in place the institutions and legal structures essential for safeguarding and implementing other basic human rights, such as civil and democratic rights. Even though in many countries these rights are only formally recognized and not always observed, there is growing consensus in many countries that a legitimate government should respect the most fundamental civil and political rights. The existing legal and political structures of states could be modified to incorporate property ownership as a fundamental human right. In the absence of global institutions with sufficient authority to effectively mediate the process of specifying and implementing property rights, states provide the most viable political centers for the discursive and legal processes through which the basic human right to property ownership could become a reality. While it is theoretically possible to envision global institutions that are so powerful that they could implement and safeguard universal property ownership, it is very questionable whether the creation of such institutions would be a more feasible, or desirable, project than implementing general property rights within the context of states. State-centered implementation of property rights would also allow for the cultural variability in the interpretation of these rights that is necessary for their acceptance and sustainability.

It is important to note that in recognizing state territorial boundaries, we are in effect granting an essential constitutive condition for the existence of states, since without territorial boundaries states as presently conceived cannot exist. This significant concession of territorial legitimacy is contingent on several requirements. The most important of these is that states must guarantee rights of property ownership to all of their citizens. Since the rationale for recognizing national territorial boundaries is based on the role states can play in facilitating and safeguarding universal property ownership, they must live up to this responsibility. Thus, when a state denies universal property rights to its citizens, it violates not only a fundamental human right but also an essential pre-condition for its own legitimate existence. The members of a polity are therefore justified in dissolving or overthrowing the state if it fails to fulfill this basic stipulation underpinning its moral legitimacy. In refusing to grant universal property rights, a state declares itself to be not only unjust, but also *illegitimate*.

Another requirement for the legitimate recognition of state territorial boundaries is that states deal justly with territorial challenges from ethnocultural groups. Without this requirement, our proposal for state recognition would rule out by fiat the claims for rectification made by ethnocultural minorities who were displaced or forcibly incorporated by existing states. As we observed in our discussion of the doctrine of self-determination, these territorial challenges cannot be rejected offhand. In more specific terms, the stipulation that states deal fairly with the territorial claims of ethnocultural minorities entails that these countries should respect the territorial principles of self-determination for the particular group in question. Thus, in some cases a morally acceptable response may involve providing the legal and institutional mechanisms to enable a forcibly incorporated ethnocultural group to obtain political control over its traditional homeland within the state.

Some might object that the decision to grant legitimacy to present territorial boundaries of states for the sake of facilitating the realization of universal property ownership leaves the members of certain states at a distinct disadvantage. The citizens of those countries with a shortage of fertile land and with poor natural resources will fare badly under this strategy in comparison to the citizens of countries that enjoy rich natural property. In answering this objection, it would not help to argue that since it was a historical accident that the citizens of resource-impoverished countries were born in their native country, no compensatory measures are morally obligatory on those who had nothing to do with bringing about their present predicament. The citizens of resource-poor countries could correctly respond that if everyone has an equal initial ownership claim to the earth's natural property and if they are willing to accept a disadvantaged position in carrying out a pragmatically necessary measure (namely, recognizing state territorial legitimacy) that benefits everyone, then compensatory measures are required from those who arbitrarily, or unjustifiably, fared better in the distribution of the natural property to which all have an equal claim.

The disadvantaged citizens from resource-poor countries thus appear to have a legitimate objection after all. This objection brings us to the third stipulation that must be placed on the recognition of state territorial legitimacy, viz., that countries with rich natural resources have a responsibility to help those countries with poor natural property. The idea here is that those countries whose natural property is insufficient to enable them to achieve a basic level of material well-being should be aided by countries with richer land and natural resources.

Even though this stipulation would significantly mitigate the disadvantages to some individuals wrought by the strategy of recognizing existing state territorial boundaries, this requirement is the most difficult one to satisfy because of several complicating factors. Mere possession of rich natural resources does not mean that a country enjoys a high level of material well-being, because oftentimes a country's level of technological and economic development determines the effectiveness of its use of land and natural resources. Resource-rich but impoverished countries such as Guatemala and Honduras that do not have a high level of industrial and technological development cannot offer significant aid to resource-poor countries, so we cannot advocate a uniform and straightforward policy of resource shifting from resource-rich to resource-poor countries. Another complicating consideration is that states must surely take some responsibility for their success or failure in developing their natural resource bases and distributing justly the goods produced from these resource bases. Since political corruption, nepotism, and disrespect for social justice, among other factors, play important roles in the level of effectiveness in using natural resources and in improving the material well-being of the populace of a country, any policy of international resource redistribution which entirely disregards the meritorious or censurable collective efforts of states to use their natural resources efficiently and fairly seems to be prima facie unfair.

Despite these complications, the stipulation of resource-redistribution still has some force. The first complicating factor, involving the problem of identifying resource-rich with prosperous countries, can be ameliorated by simply discharging those resource-rich but technologically underdeveloped countries from the responsibility of assisting resource-poor countries, or at least adjusting, based on their level of technological development, the degree of aid they should provide. The significance of the second complication, concerning the collective moral responsibility of states, must be strongly qualified by recognizing that the development of the political, economic, and social institutions of many underdeveloped countries has been greatly hindered by colonialism and is currently hampered by unjust global economic structures (such as systems of intellectual property rights and credit provision for economic development) that benefit the technological, highly industrialized nations. Even the development of effective and just democratic structures has been negatively affected by colonial domination, to the extent that trust in public institutions, a large middle class, and high levels of literacy—which are essential for establishing sound democratic structures—were less likely to develop in countries oppressed by colonial powers. Furthermore, we should acknowledge that the technological advances of many industrialized countries were assisted by such developments as colonial exploitation, which included the enslavement of Third World populations and the massive extraction of valuable natural resources from overseas and internal colonies. Thus, the lack of technological achievement, the inefficiency in natural resource use and development, and even the absence of just and effective political institutions, are not merely manifestations of deficiencies in the collective will of underdeveloped countries, but in part reflect the influences of colonial domination and, perhaps more important, the continuing economic structural disadvantages that burden underdeveloped countries.

Moreover, since the most impoverished citizens of indigent or resource-poor, technologically developing countries are often politically disempowered or disadvantaged, they have not had the opportunity to make democratic decisions concerning the development of their material bases and the most fair form of economic exchange and distribution. Given their lack of political empowerment, it is hardly fair to charge them with neglecting to effectively employ their natural property. These considerations mitigate the charge that their present condition of poverty and lack of development is entirely their own fault.

For these reasons, it is still reasonable to maintain that technologically advanced, resource-rich countries have a moral obligation to provide aid to resource-poor developing countries and, perhaps less strongly, to countries that have rich natural resources but have been hindered from developing them properly. The primary form of assistance should be technological aid to enable these countries to make optimal use of their available land and natural resources. Due to the impact of advanced technologies on resource use and development, such technical aid would be more important than an outright transference of natural resources. Given the fact that resource-poor countries often bear some responsibility in succeeding or failing to develop their natural property, while technologically advanced countries often bear some responsibility for their own level of material prosperity, *complete* equalization of resources (even if such a goal could be feasibly accomplished) is not a moral obligation created by the inequality of natural property among states. Finally, the resource-redistribution stipulation should involve not merely pro-active measures to help developing countries, but should also include the modification of existing international systems of capital investment, use of foreign labor, intellectual property rights, and so forth, so that they are more just to developing countries. Unjust systems of economic development and exchange often exploit the vulnerable position of developing countries, to the advantage of the rich, highly technological nations, and make it very difficult for these indigent countries to work their way out of their state of underdevelopment.

We can summarize this section by stating that there are compelling reasons for granting *conditional* legitimacy to the territorial claims of states. This concession of legitimacy is based on the important role that states can play in implementing universal property rights, and is contingent on their compliance with the following stipulations: (i) the guaranteeing of property rights to all of their citizens, where this can take the form of universal rights to private property or rights to participate in democratic decision-making concerning the use and development of natural property, (ii) settling in a just manner the territorial claims of ethnocultural groups and, where appropriate, (iii) providing aid to indigent, technologically underdeveloped, resource-poor countries, and in some cases, providing aid to indigent underdeveloped countries even when they are not resource-poor. There are many complex issues that I have not discussed concerning these stipulations and, more generally, the recognition of state territorial boundaries. My modest purpose in this section has been to provide a sketch of the arguments that should be used to justify such recognition, and the conditions that should be placed on states before their particular claim to territorial sovereignty can be respected.

In the last chapter, I indicated that my position on the collective property rights of states would provide the rudiments for an adequate moral rationale for certain theoretical components of cosmopolitan democracy. I argued that Kant's position on cosmopolitan democracy suffers from two deficiencies. First, it does not address the significant problems of material inequalities between states and global economic injustice and second, it does not provide a normative justification for overriding state sovereignty.

Regarding the issue of inequitable access to natural resources, my position is that there are significant obligations that resource-rich states have to resource-poor states. Because natural property—that is, the earth's land and natural resources—belongs to all in common, if it belongs to anyone at all, the world's inhabitants have an equal claim to the totality of natural property. This claim, however, is superseded, *albeit* not completely, by the territorial sovereignty of states and substate political communities which must be observed in order for the members of these collectivities to exercise self-determination. But because the territorial powers of existing political bodies were not acquired through the common consent of the world's people, but unilaterally or through force, coercion, or other morally illegitimate means, these territorial powers cannot have morally unconditional status. Rather, as we have seen, they have the status of qualified rights, which are contingent upon political communities fulfilling the conditions stated above.

Consider now the second problem with Kant's approach, namely, the practically unqualified recognition given to state sovereignty. To be sure, Kant proposes a right of universal hospitality, according to which an alien, if she behaves peaceably, should not be treated as an enemy but allowed to associate with the members of other political communities. Even though this right is, according to Kant, binding on all political bodies, it is clearly not broad enough to include all of the ways in which state sovereignty must be overridden in an adequate system of cosmopolitan democracy. In contrast to Kant, my view is that sovereignty is a conditional right. To the extent that territorial powers, that is, the powers to appropriate natural property and control borders, are essential to the existence of states and substate political communities in their present form, the very legitimacy of these political collectivities depends on the willingness of the global community to recognize their territorial powers. These observations raise the question of whether there are other conditions that should be imposed, other than those already identified, on the recognition of territorial sovereignty.

Though I will not develop this argument here, it is reasonable to maintain, on the basis of moral reciprocity, that political communities should refrain from systematically undermining the capacity of other political communities to flourish. Since territorial powers are essential for the self-determination and flourishing of political bodies, the recognition of these powers should be morally reciprocated by a commitment on the part of political societies not to interfere with what the employment of territorial powers is intended to accomplish. One of the most important ways in which the self-determination and flourishing of political communities is hindered at present is through the maintenance of unjust systems of economic production and exchange, credit provision, and debt repayment. It is pertinent not only to question the inherent justness of these systems, but also to inquire into whether their existence itself violates minimal expectations of moral reciprocity that arise from the recognition of sovereign territorial powers. Indeed, I would maintain that it is reasonable to believe that a fundamental restructuring of present international economic relations and institutions is morally obligatory. In addition, to the extent that a political community sustains such unjust systems or fails to satisfy the stipulations on sovereignty we have identified, it also undermines its right to exercise sovereign control over its territory, including the use of coercive mechanisms to control illegal immigration.

Indigenous Groups and Collective Property Rights

A pertinent observation on the agency and autonomy strategy that I have used to justify property rights is that it is unclear about the conditions under which agency and autonomy can be exercised. Even though in many societies *individual* ownership of property is considered essential for self-determination, it is by no means obvious that the only way in which people can exercise agency and autonomy is by owning private property. Here enter considerations of the kind and degree of control of material objects required to exercise agency and autonomy. Individualistic cultures will want to maximize individual agency and autonomy and will see their attainment as contingent on the possession of individual property rights. In a multicultural society, however, we should not assume that all ethnocultural groups will want to adopt a framework of individual property rights. In some cultural traditions autonomy of the individual, understood as self-sufficiency and freedom from communal dependencies and commitments, is not seen as necessary or even desirable for human flourishing.

Indigenous cultures provide the clearest example of the communal view of human development. Members of indigenous cultural groups have strenuously resisted agrarian policies that involve the breaking up of communal lands and the granting of private land titles because these practices run counter to their cultural values and undermine their cultural survival.[53] For many indigenous groups, human flourishing is best nurtured in communal contexts of interconnection and interdependence, and private property is undesirable because it promotes social detachment and economic independence among individuals. Typically, in these communities the level of social cohesion and value convergence is sufficiently high that individuals do not feel encumbered by social interdependencies and do not believe their agency and autonomy is compromised by their communal way of life. The independence and self-reliance provided by private property in individualistic cultures is replaced by the communal security made possible by collective property rights. Indigenous groups also oppose granting private property to their members because it makes possible the selling of part or all of their tribal lands. They recognize that the partitioning of tribal lands by granting individual land titles and their purchase by wealthy members of the majority society (and more recently by foreign capitalists) is one of the principal ways in which indigenous groups have lost their ancestral territories after the colonial period.

Agency and autonomy are still relevant for justifying the property rights to which the members of these ethnocultural groups are entitled, but these ideals need to be seen in communal rather than individual terms. That is, it is the agency and autonomy of the group which is of critical importance for many indigenous peoples, and correspondingly, it is the collective claim to property of the cultural group that is relevant and not the ownership claims of their members to individual parcels of land. This fact is substantiated by the ubiquitous emphasis placed by indigenous peoples on territorial autonomy in their struggles to survive as distinctive cultural groups. They point out that only through collective property ownership can they ensure the sustainable preservation of their material and cultural forms of life.

Even though the emphasis in these cultural traditions is on collective property rights, within the indigenous communities individuals have the right to participate in the use of communal property to satisfy their basic needs and to carry out their life projects within the parameters set by the needs of the other members of the community. Thus members of indigenous communities have property rights in the sense that they have tacitly understood access to the use of communal land and to participation in the decisions concerning how land and natural resources are to be used. The case of indigenous groups thus demonstrates that there are a variety of ways in which property can be used to satisfy the adequacy criterion of providing for basic needs as well as supporting agency and autonomy.

In determining the property rights that indigenous groups should have in a multicultural society, it is important to remember their unique and essential relationship to the land. Collective territorial rights are essential for both material and spiritual reasons. The modes of production through which they sustain themselves often involve hunting and fishing or farming on ancestral lands. These forms of material subsistence possess intrinsic cultural significance and are deeply interwoven into their cultural worldview. On the spiritual side, the territories they inhabit often contain sacred sites and ancient burial grounds, which are also of central importance for preserving their cultural traditions. As stated in a study by a United Nations commission on indigenous peoples,

> all indigenous communities have, and uphold, a complete code of rules of various kinds which are applicable to the tenure and conservation of land as an important factor in the production process, the foundation of family life and the territorial basis for the existence of their people as such. The whole range of emotional, cultural, spiritual and religious considerations is present where the relationship with the land is concerned . . . The land forms part of their existence.
>
> Between man and the land there was a relationship of a profoundly spiritual and even religious nature. They spoke of Mother Earth and its worship. For all those reasons it was in no way possible to regard it as a mere possession or still less as a commodity . . .
>
> The only rights that were available, and could be granted, to them by tradition and legal custom were usufruct and priority of use of the ancestral plot, with the consequent obligation to make use of it in the manner required by ecology and custom and not to leave it unused indefinitely.
>
> The expropriation, erosion, pillage, improper use and abuse of, and the damage inflicted on, indigenous land are tantamount to destroying the cultural and spiritual legacy of indigenous populations. Forcing them to hand

over such land is tantamount to allowing them to be exterminated. In a word, it is ethnocide.[54]

Thus, the self-identity of indigenous peoples is inextricably grounded in their cultural traditions and the very meaningfulness of their values and life-options depend on their cultural practices, which in turn are indissociably connected to their homeland.

One of the central tenets of liberal democracy is that individuals have the right to pursue their own conception of the good life. Since the exercise of cultural practices may be, and often is, essential to one's attainment of a satisfying existence, such practices can be straightforwardly legitimized on the basis of this tenet.[55] Freedom of religion, for example, is a paradigmatic case of a cultural practice grounded on the right to the pursuit of one's vision of the good. Once we recognize that the freedom to exercise cultural practices is protected by one of the core principles of liberal democracy, collective property rights for indigenous peoples can in turn be justified on the basis of their necessary role in safeguarding these practices. But why is it necessary to suppose that the liberty of indigenous groups to engage in their cultural traditions can be protected only by granting them collective property rights? Why not grant them private property rights and let them decide for themselves how to use the property under their control?

The historical and contemporary experiences of indigenous peoples provide ample evidence for the fact that the preservation of their way of life is highly vulnerable to the machinations of domestic and foreign interests.[56] Since the start of the colonial period in the middle of the sixteenth century, indigenous groups all over the world have suffered pervasive and profound oppression at the hands of settler societies and foreign colonial powers. Such oppression has taken many forms, the most serious of which have included extermination, enslavement, territorial displacement, exploitation of natural resources, and loss of sovereignty. Indigenous groups have experienced serious injustices even in liberal democratic countries with constitutionally protected civil rights. These rights, despite their centrality in such democratic systems, have not been sufficient to protect them from pervasive and systematic discrimination and oppression. In the U.S., for example, indigenous groups have suffered—among other abuses—broken treaties, pogroms, unjust court decisions, and exploitation of natural resources in their homelands. This centuries-long legacy of oppression has been a constant threat not only to the preservation of their way of life, but also to the maintenance of their land and natural resources. Constitutionally protected collective property rights, by institutionalizing group territorial ownership within a secure political framework, safeguard their natural property and ways of life better than private property rights.

The special institutional protections provided by the group right of collective property ownership also makes the members of indigenous groups less susceptible to the effects of competitive market societies. Due to lack of access to education and resources for human development, members of indigenous groups have not acquired the specific skills and knowledge needed to protect their interests in the economic and legal institutions of majority societies. The decision-making procedures that indigenous communities have to employ before arriving at resolutions concerning collective property are generally longer, more deliberative, and more inclusive than individual decision-making procedures involving private property. These decision-making procedures in effect function as an institutional and cultural defense against deception and fraud by domestic and foreign interests. Exacerbating the potential for the transgression of indigenous interests are recent developments—such as increases in population, diminishing natural resources, and the global expansion of neoliberal, consumption-oriented economic systems—that have increased the likelihood of exploitation of the natural resources in indigenous territories. In brief, given the historical record of discrimination and oppression against indigenous peoples, and their lack of equitable resources to protect their interests, it is reasonable to maintain that the liberty to practice their cultural traditions is best safeguarded by collective property rights that grant them the necessary autonomous control over the material resources needed for the enjoyment and preservation of their culture.

Even though granting collective property rights to indigenous groups would most likely impose limitations on the general population, such as fishing restrictions on tribal lands, the negative consequences for these ethnocultural groups of denying them such rights would be much greater, since it would involve their cultural destruction as a people. But are rights to collective property unlimited? Are there factors which constrain these rights? To answer these questions, it is necessary to recall the considerations which motivated our recognition of the legitimacy of property rights in the first place, namely, the exercise of agency and autonomy. These considerations can be used to articulate the limits of collective property rights for indigenous peoples.

Since the justification for property rights was based on their role in securing the agency and autonomy of all members of a multicultural society, collective rights to property should not violate this general rationale. That is, collective property rights cannot place such severe burdens on the majority population that their agency and autonomy is seriously hindered. The bearers of collective territorial rights cannot, for example, categorically deny material resources to the majority society which it needs for its survival. Since indigenous groups are still members of the state and obtain rights based on that membership, they bear certain responsibilities to the non-indigenous members of the society. Articulating precise guidelines for determining what these responsibilities are is very difficult and perhaps not possible, given the large number of ways in which the needs and interests of indigenous groups and majority societies can come into conflict and the different types of autonomous governance that can be practiced by indigenous groups. However, in the public deliberations in which these issues are to be resolved, several general considerations should be kept in mind.

First, even though indigenous groups are part of the state, the nature of their political relationship to the latter will generally be different than that of the other members of the society. Since indigenous peoples, before the arrival of the settler societies, lived in autonomous communities with their own sociopolitical and economic institutions, and since most of them were incorporated into the state under coercive conditions, the majority society should respect their status as distinct, self-governing political entities located within the territorial boundaries of the state.[57] The majority society should not expect to have the same kind of ready access to indigenous natural resources as it has to resources in other areas within its territorial boundaries. Second, the majority society should not simply take for granted the legitimacy of its existing modes of economic production and consumption, and justify its access to indigenous resources on this basis. Issues of ecological sustainability and wasteful consumption, for instance, should be put on the table in the deliberative process. It may well turn out that the majority society employs methods of economic production and consumption that are environmentally harmful and unsustainable, and that the resources it considers essential to its material well-being would not be necessary if it adopted more reasonable levels of consumption. Indeed, one of the greatest serendipitous effects of granting indigenous peoples collective property rights is that it may force technologically advanced majority societies throughout the world to examine critically their economic policies and philosophies, many of which are based on overconsumption.

Still, there may be situations in which indigenous groups will have to concede that resources within their territories are in fact essential for the majority society's survival or reasonable level of well-being. The possible negative impact on the indigenous communities of granting the majority society the needed resources will have to be weighed against the urgency with which those resources are needed. In granting access and use of indigenous resources, participation of the indigenous groups in the development and implementation of the policies guiding the extraction and use of those resources is imperative. The primary purpose of such participation would be to minimize the possible negative effects of resource extraction on the cultural integrity and material base of the indigenous communities.

The position we have reached concerning rights to property in a multicultural society can be summarized as follows. Since it is untenable to construe property rights as restricted rights and since the use of property is necessary to satisfy sustenance needs and exercise agency and autonomy, every member of a multicultural society is entitled to natural property that is accessible and sufficiently useful to achieve these ends.[58] Given the cultural diversity of conceptions of agency and autonomy and differences in the availability of natural property, the precise nature of the property rights to which individuals are entitled may vary in different societies, but in all cases individuals should have ownership rights to private property and/or the right to participate in decision-making processes for determining how land and natural resources are to be used.[59] All individuals will also have the correlative right of the control of their body and labor. This involves lack of coercion regarding one's body and labor and the right to transact freely regarding one's body and labor. In addition, a multicultural society should recognize the collective rights to natural property of indigenous groups who have maintained a high degree of social cohesiveness, a material and spiritual connection to their traditional land, and most importantly, whose survival as a distinct cultural group depends on maintaining territorial autonomy over their homeland.

Notes

1. I will not attempt to provide a comprehensive analysis of property rights; rather, my goal will be to sketch a rationale for such rights and reveal the failure of the major traditional justifications of rights to nonuniversal or restricted private property ownership.

2. Economic inequalities set the groundwork for a wide variety of exploitative practices between ethnocultural groups, including discriminatory employment practices, unfair contractual agreements between labor and the owners of capital, and greater access to, and abuse of, political power. Of course, these practices also take place in societies that are culturally homogeneous, but in multicultural societies they have the added disadvantage of exacerbating intercultural conflicts and resentments.

3. Communal land ownership, rather than private property ownership, has been the norm throughout much of human history. For a discussion of community economies and their conception of ownership, see Stephen Gudeman, "Sketches, Qualms, and Other Thoughts on Intellectual Property Rights," in *Valuing Local Knowledge*, eds. Stephen B. Brush and Doreen Stabinsky (Washington, D.C.: Island Press), pp. 104–108.

4. Thus, the right to private property ownership need not be seen as a single, univocal right, but can be understood as a set of distinguishable rights. In what follows, we shall see that different rights in this set can be justified by different arguments.

5. It is interesting to contrast restricted property rights with other basic rights. While one need not satisfy some qualifying criterion to be entitled to the right to liberty or life, for example, this is not the case with restricted property rights. This asymmetry between restricted property rights and other rights should alert us to the peculiar (and as we shall see questionable) nature of restricted property rights.

6. John Locke, *Two Treatises of Government*, Critical Edition, Peter Laslett, ed. (Cambridge, U.K.: Cambridge University Press, 1960).

7. Lockean scholars disagree on whether Locke's arguments justify strong private property rights or rights of use and possession only. This dispute does not matter for our purpose here, which is to determine whether original private appropriations of property can be justified in the first place. If it turns out, as I will argue, that they cannot be legitimized, then it is a moot point whether strong or weak property rights are justified by Locke's arguments.

8. Locke, *Two Treatises of Government*, sect. 27.

9. Cultivating more land than I can use is to be understood primarily as growing more food than I need to feed myself and my family. However, Locke maintained that the legitimate acquisition of large tracts of land was made possible by the introduction of money (and valuable jewels or minerals like gold) which enabled individuals, through voluntary exchanges of these items for the land of others, to obtain more land than they needed for sustenance needs.

10. The argument here applies to the legitimacy of appropriations of property by individuals. Later in this chapter I will consider the question of whether it is legitimate for states to collectively appropriate land and natural resources.

11. Jorge M. Valadez, "Pre-Columbian and Modern Philosophical Perspectives in Latin America," in *From Africa to Zen: An Invitation to World Philosophy*, eds. Robert C. Solomon and Kathleen M. Higgins (Lanham, MD: Rowman and Littlefield, 1993), p.104.

12. There are other questions regarding the notion of "mixing my labor with nature" that would be very difficult for Locke to answer: What degree of contact do I need to make with nature so that I can claim that I have mixed by labor with it? (Would watering a tree once make it mine?); What kind of contact establishes ownership, and why? (Could hunting or fishing serve as a basis for ownership, and if not, why not?); How do we adjudicate conflicting claims to ownership when different people have used land for different purposes at different times?

13. In the vast majority of cases, after a few years land that remains untouched by human labor will revert to its original condition. Thus, unless one continuously cultivates the land, it is unclear what becomes of the original labor that was the basis for my laying claim to that land.

14. See James Tully, *A Discourse on Property: John Locke and His Adversaries* (Cambridge, U.K.: Cambridge University Press, 1980) and Gopal Sreenivasan, *The Limits of Lockean Rights in Property* (New York: Oxford University Press, 1995), pp. 59–92.

15. Note that in the absence of constraints on how these food and materials are to be used, the moral laudability of the production of the latter is in question. After all, the farmer could hoard the food and materials, use them to extract unjust concessions from people in need (particularly if they have no property of their own to satisfy their needs), and so on.

16. We should note here that in the absence of clear criteria for what counts as mixing one's labor with nature (which Locke does not provide), it would be question-begging to say that land cultivation counts as mixing one's labor with nature but hunting and fishing do not.

17. Robert Nozick, "Distributive Justice," in *Readings in Social and Political Philosophy*, ed. Robert M. Stewart (New York: Oxford University Press, 1986), pp. 223–224.

18. I classify Nozick's argument under the consequentialist category, despite his disclaimer that it is not a utilitarian argument, because its plausibility depends on the beneficial consequences resulting from private appropriations of property.

19. Even if we modify the private property rights that Nozick defends from nonuniversal strong to nonuniversal weak private property rights, his general justificatory strategy still fails. Unless he shows that the situation of nonproprietors would be worse in all systems of property ownership in comparison to systems of nonuniversal weak private property rights, he has not established a justification for the latter.

20. For a discussion of the development of capitalist nonuniversal systems of property ownership and the effects they have had on many peoples around the world, see Paul Vallely, *Bad Samaritans: First World Ethics and Third World Debt* (Maryknoll, NY: Orbis Books, 1990) and Eric R. Wolfe, *Europe and the People Without History* (Berkeley: University of California Press, 1982).

People all over the world suffer from oppression as a result of the present systems of nonuniversal private property ownership. Needless to say, people can also be oppressed by systems of property ownership in which the state owns and manages the use of property.

21. See, for example, Milton Friedman, *Capitalism and Freedom* (Chicago: University of Chicago Press, 1962) and R. Selucky, *Marxism, Socialism, and Freedom: Towards a General Democratic Theory of Labour-Managed Systems* (London: Macmillan Publishing Co., 1979).

Strictly speaking, it is liberal democracy, and not democratic systems in general, that the advocates of this argument have in mind when they contend that free markets and private property are necessary for democracy. Democracy can take many forms, but liberal democracy, with its emphasis on civil and political rights, the rule of law, and state neutrality concerning the good, is generally considered the most desirable form of democracy. The objections that I present here against the private property-democracy argument apply to the most compelling form of this argument, namely, the one that assumes that liberal democracy is the relevant democratic form under consideration.

22. This statement has to be qualified by pointing out that market systems are clearly not sufficient for democracy. As countries like Singapore illustrate, a society can have a market system and yet be authoritarian. Also, rather than making the blanket statement that capitalism supports civil liberties and democratic rights across the board, it would perhaps be more accurate to say that market systems support only certain kinds of liberties and rights.

23. Later I will argue that certain market schemes of universal property ownership, characterized by worker ownership and self-management of cooperative

enterprises, are economically feasible and more conducive to general democratic empowerment and political participation than existing market systems.

24. The plausibility of this claim increases when we consider the impact of universal ownership of land and natural resources on mediated property. As we shall see in the next chapter, universalizing private property rights places important constraints on mediated property, which in turn further equalizes socioeconomic status and political empowerment among cultural groups.

25. In one of the most extensive analyses of the socioeconomic and civic factors that affect political and community participation, Sidney Verba, Kay Lehman Scholzman, and Henry E. Brady in *Voice and Equality* (Cambridge, MA: Harvard University Press, 1995) argue that such participation is rooted in the structures of inequality in American society, including differences in socioeconomic status (particularly level of educational attainment).

26. For an excellent examination of the ways in which concentrations of wealth distort the democratic process in the U. S., see Kevin Phillips, *Arrogant Capital: Washington, Wall Street, and the Frustration of American Politics* (Boston: Little, Brown, and Co., 1994).

27. I am basing these conditions on Lawrence C. Becker's discussion of desert in *Property Rights* (London: Routledge and Kegan Paul, 1977), pp. 49–56.

28. With minor alterations, this example is taken from David Miller, "Justice and Property," *Ratio*, 22 (1980), p. 7.

29. Ibid., pp. 7–8.

30. Evidence of electoral fraud in a state election 150 years ago is a case of the former (because we cannot identify who to compensate or how to compensate them), while discrimination against German-Americans during World War I is a case of the latter (because as a group they are highly assimilated into the mainstream society and do not presently suffer from systematic and pervasive discrimination). Jeremy Waldron, in a well-known essay, argues that the moral obligation to rectify historical injustices can be superseded by present circumstances. The obligation to return indigenous lands to the existing descendants of wronged groups, for example, can be superseded by the need of present non-indigenous inhabitants to use those lands for their subsistence. See Jeremy Waldron, "Superseding Historic Injustice," *Ethics* 103, no. 1 (October 1992):4–28. Waldron's arguments do not undermine my position here, because my case against unilateral, nonuniversal original appropriations partly rests on their role in sustaining present inequalities and injustices. If anything, present circumstances strengthen rather than weaken the need for rectification. Moreover, as Waldron points out, even when a property appropriation occurred under just conditions (at a time when no one was deprived of property), changing circumstances, such as changing needs and increases in population, can make private ownership of the justly acquired property unjust at the present time. Thus, strictly speaking, it is not necessary for defending my position to assume that all property acquisitions occurred under unjust conditions (though no doubt most of them did). It is also worthwhile to note that my position is not strictly egalitarian, and that it is compatible with granting some proprietors more than a threshold level of property as recompense for past efforts, as long as everyone has the threshold level of property to satisfy a base level of agency and auton-

omy (to be determined through an egalitarian process of public deliberation) and the additional property is not used to obtain unjust advantages over threshold proprietors.

31. The recompense which present proprietors of inordinately large land holdings are due would be determined by several considerations. Among these are the mode of acquisition of the property in question, the procedure by which it was improved, and the benefits already obtained from ownership. Did the individual acquire the property through unfair political advantage, fraud, coercion, or bequeathal? Or was the property entirely paid for by the individual? Was the property improved through wage-labor? Or did the individual improve the property through her own labor? Has the individual already enjoyed many benefits and advantages over nonowners as the result of owning that property? Or has the individual recently acquired that property and not enjoyed any of the benefits of ownership? The way in which we answer these, and other, questions will determine the degree of moral consideration that the present proprietor is due. For instance, an individual who paid a fair price to obtain her property, improved it through personal toil, and has not used ownership of that property to obtain social or political advantages over nonowners deserves greater moral consideration than a proprietor who obtained a large tract of land at an unfair price through political privilege, hired wage-laborers to improve it, and has enjoyed for a long time the economic and social advantages of ownership. These questions concerning the moral consideration which present property owners deserve raise complex and important issues which are beyond the scope of the present discussion. Here the relevant point is that arguments based on desert do not convincingly establish that we must grant nonuniversal private property rights as a reward for efforts expended in investing in and/or improving property.

32. See, for example, John Gray, *The Moral Foundations of Market Institutions* (London: IEA, 1992), F. Hayek, *The Fatal Conceit* (London: Routledge and Kegan Paul, 1990), and L.E. Lomansky, *Persons, Rights, and the Moral Community* (Oxford: Oxford University Press, 1987).

33. Actually, the requirements for achieving autonomy under this strategy are more complex, involving not only free contractual transactions of private property but also of mediated property and capital. I will consider these other factors in the next chapter, where I discuss ownership rights to mediated property. As we shall see, ownership claims to mediated property differ from those that can be made regarding property. In any case, the major points I will make in the present discussion will not be affected by the simplifying assumption of considering only property and not mediated property or capital.

34. Gray, *The Moral Foundations*, p. 19. Needless to say, in this statement he is assuming the existence of private property.

35. Jeremy Waldron, in one of the most detailed and outstanding analyses of private property available, reaches conclusions regarding property ownership which are similar to mine. Even though he takes a Hegelian "self-development" approach to the justification of universal property rights, his rationale for these rights is similar to my own. See Jeremy Waldron, *The Right to Private Property* (Oxford: Clarendon Press, 1988).

36. If possible, the implementation of universal property ownership should proceed with a minimum of redistribution of existing holdings, particularly if these are small or medium-sized holdings (the relative size of an average property holding being determined partly by the total available useful and accessible land and the number of nonproprietors or owners with insufficient property holdings). Redistribution is justified only to the extent that it is necessary to satisfy universal agency and autonomy needs and the other constraints placed on the equitable access to natural resources, such as clean water, important minerals, and energy resources, which by nature are unevenly distributed.

The ecological impact of developing large tracts of land to satisfy the universal need for land should also be taken into account in determining the number and size of property holdings to be expropriated and redistributed. In sum, all of these considerations will make it very likely that large private property holdings will not exist in a just multicultural democracy.

37. In the next chapter we will see how also universalizing ownership rights to *certain* forms of mediated property will promote general economic self-reliance and greatly ameliorate class differences.

38. Again, the situation is more complex, in the sense that it is ownership of mediated property and capital that is primarily responsible for economic inequalities in many countries. Nevertheless, for many individuals, the purchase of property and a dwelling is their major initial investment, which in turn facilitates individual and transgenerational capital accumulation. Dwellings are forms of mediated property, and in what follows I will argue that the resources and technologies needed for certain forms of mediated property should also be universalized. This move would prevent morally intolerable situations like those found in the U.S., in which about one million homeless people coexist with millions of wealthy individuals in the same political community.

39. In the next chapter, where I discuss mediated property, I will argue that we should also universalize rights to those forms of mediated property (technological means) that will enable people to employ the natural property to which they are entitled in a way conducive to economic self-reliance.

40. The connection between nonuniversal property rights and inequalities in economic power will become clearer in the next chapter, when I examine mediated property. As we shall see, universalizing rights to ownership of land and natural resources places important constraints on the ownership of mediated property. Even though these constraints will not be so strong as to generally entail universal or social ownership of mediated property, they will significantly diminish the likelihood of large accumulations of private capital among a small percentage of the population.

41. David C. Korten, *When Corporations Rule the World* (Hartford, CT: Kumarian Press and San Francisco, CA: Berrett-Koehler Publ., 1995), 106–109.

42. *Guatemala Health Rights Support Project* (Washington, DC: Guatemala Health Rights Support Project, 1987).

43. Korten, *When Corporations Rule,* p. 95.

44. Korten, *When Corporations Rule,* pp. 107–108.

45. Korten, *When Corporations Rule,* p. 107–108.

46. Here I am of course assuming the availability of sufficient productive resources to satisfy these needs.

47. In some Latin American countries, for example, wealthy elites exert a grossly disproportionate influence on political elections through financial campaign contributions, bribes, and intimidation of progressive candidates and reformers. In some cases they hire private security agents to kill or bully political candidates and social activists.

48. Julian Le Grand and Saul Estrin, eds. *Market Socialism* (Oxford: Clarendon Press, 1989), pp. 166–167. We should note that many of these cooperatives do well despite economic environments that are either hostile or nonconducive to the success of cooperative enterprises. In his essay in this volume, Saul Estrin addresses the economic weaknesses of cooperative enterprises and makes realistic suggestions for resolving them.

49. Robert Nozick essentially makes the argument that follows in *Anarchy, State, and Utopia* (Oxford: Basil Blackwell, 1974), Pt. III. In a different vein, Proudhon argues against the coherence and stability of universal systems of private property because he thinks such systems will necessitate the constant redistribution of property holdings due to increases in population and differential needs. Such redistributions, according to Proudhon, will negate the control over property that property rights are supposed to provide. (In contrast to Nozick, however, Proudhon is not defending restricted property rights, but seeks to do away with private property altogether.) In response to Proudhon's argument, Jeremy Waldron points out that he overstates the need for redistribution of property by overestimating the shifts in population and the different needs that would have to be accommodated by such changes. Waldron correctly maintains that in a society which controls immigration and has a fairly stable level of population, there is reason to believe that there would be sufficient stability in property rights to justify short and long-term economic planning. I would add that universal property rights would actually contribute to the control of population, as people acquire the capacities and dispositions (such as the disposition for responsible, long-term planning and the capacity for self-determination) that would be promoted by property ownership. See Waldron, *The Right to Private Property*.

50. In my discussion of mediated property in the next chapter, I will argue in favor of a market economy with certain constraints on property rights.

51. Included in the permitted transactions could be the disposition of property beyond the base limit necessary for a basic level of sustenance and material autonomy.

52. The remarks that follow concerning the advantages of recognizing states apply primarily to liberal democracies, and not to illiberal states, since the former are better institutionally and ideologically equipped to implement basic rights. However, both liberal democracies and illiberal states need to guarantee their members universal property rights in order for their territorial boundaries to be considered legitimate.

53. See, for example, Nina Pacari, "Taking on the Neoliberal Agenda," *NACLA: Report on the Americas*, Vol. XXIX No. 5 (March/April 1996): 23–29.

54. United Nations, *Study of the Problem of Discrimination Against Indigenous Populations*, UN Doc. E/CN.4/Sub. 2/1986/7 and Adds. 1-4 (1986), no. 4, pp. 28–29. Cited in Hurst Hannum, *Autonomy, Sovereignty, and Self-Determination: The Accommodation of Conflicting Rights*, revised edition (Philadelphia: University of Pennsylvania Press, 1996), p. 92.

55. Note that the claim here is not that individuals have a right to the indefinite preservation of their culture. This stronger claim does not immediately follow from liberal principles of autonomy and pursuit of happiness.

56. For an account of past and present injustices in the U.S. against indigenous populations that have threatened their physical and cultural existence, see *The State of Native America: Genocide, Colonization, and Resistance*, ed. Annette Jamies (Boston: South End Press, 1992). For a corresponding account of oppression against indigenous people around the world, see *State of the Peoples: A Global Human Rights Report on Societies in Danger*, ed. Marc S. Miller (Boston: Beacon Press, 1993).

57. For a defense of the special political status of indigenous groups in liberal democracies, see Will Kymlicka, *Multicultural Citizenship: A Liberal Defense of Cultural Rights* (Oxford: Oxford University Press, 1995).

58. The amount of private property to which an individual is entitled will depend on such factors as total availability of useful and accessible land, the number of people for whom he or she must provide, and the productivity and value of the land available.

59. Everyone's agency and autonomy would be additionally safeguarded by the fact that in a multicultural society they would have the "right of exit," i.e., the right to leave their cultural group.

9

Rights to Mediated and Intellectual Property

In this chapter, I begin by examining rights to mediated property, the appropriate constraints on such rights, and the compensatory measures merited by certain ethnocultural groups regarding the acquisition and development of mediated property. I then examine rights to intellectual property and pay particular attention to the issue of whether intellectual property rights should be granted to indigenous communities to protect their ethnobotanical knowledge and plant varieties. My general approach will be similar to the one I adopted in the last chapter, where I dealt with natural property. There my first concern was to clarify the nature and justification of ownership rights to natural property, and then to examine the impact of ethnocultural diversity on such rights. Similarly, here I examine ownership rights to mediated and intellectual property before examining certain key issues raised by ethnocultural groups for the understanding of these rights in multicultural democracies.

The Justification of Rights to Mediated Property

When we consider rights to ownership of property mediated by human labor, such as capital goods and manufactured commodities, it is not plausible to make the claims to universal ownership we have made regarding land and natural resources. While the latter are found in nature and are not the product of anyone's labor, mediated property (particularly in technological societies) usually embodies a high degree of transformation of the raw materials found in the natural world.[1] The degree of conceptual and physical labor exerted by specific individuals to manufacture commodities and to design and construct the tools, machines, and other technological implements necessary to manufacture them is sufficiently great that straightforward claims to universal ownership are clearly inappropriate. Ownership claims to the various forms of mediated property should be based, at least in part, on the labor, risks, and investments made by the particular individuals or groups responsible for their creation. Similar considerations apply to intellectual property, such as patents and copyrights, which also require conceptual and physical labor for their creation. Given the intangible character of intellectual property, however, special factors will constrain ownership claims to these forms of property.

Assuming that an individual possesses legitimate private property rights to her share of land and natural resources in a society that respects universal property ownership and the other property rights we have discussed, what is the nature and justification of her rights to mediated property? People will labor, individually and in groups, to transform and refine the natural property in their legitimate possession to create goods for their own use and the use of others. They will also want to make short and long-term economic transactions with other individuals and groups for the purpose of expanding their access to material goods and services. In technologically complex societies these transactions cover a gamut of choices that include monetary, employment, and partnership agreements, while the goods transacted will involve varying degrees of physical and conceptual labor. Since the primary rationale for granting property rights was the exercise of agency and autonomy, and agreements involving mediated property certainly seem to promote the latter, there is an initial prima facie case for granting individuals the freedom to enter into voluntary, mediated property transactions.

Complex societies need a mechanism with which to coordinate the numerous and varied needs and desires of individuals with the production of the goods and services that satisfy them, that is, a mechanism is needed to regulate supply and demand. Here again the initial presumption is in favor of a market system of free exchange in which the price mechanism signals relative demand for goods and services. Markets provide indispensable information concerning, *inter alia*, the variety and intensity of existing needs and desires, needed specializations in the division of labor, and the cost of goods, services, and resources. In complex industrialized societies, no other mechanism as efficiently provides this information as markets.[2] This is not to say, of course, that existing market systems always provide accurate information in these areas. National and international corporate monopolies, for instance, can manipulate prices, affect availability of resources, create artificial needs and desires through advertising, and externalize ecological costs. Such machinations distort the legitimate epistemological and regulating functions of markets. For instance, in externalizing ecological costs—as when the price of gasoline does not include the medical expenses incurred in treating respiratory illnesses caused by air pollution—false information is provided to consumers regarding the true costs of using environmentally harmful products.[3] Despite the shortcomings of present market systems, however, properly structured markets are still the best mechanisms for fulfilling the epistemological and labor-coordinating functions needed by efficient and viable economic systems in industrial, technological societies.[4]

Since we have considered ownership of one's body and labor as a kind of property right, individuals should also have the right to transact freely regarding the use of their bodies and labor, thus giving rise to labor markets. Agency and autonomy are clearly enhanced when individuals can make their own decisions regarding how to employ their knowledge, skills, and labor power. In addition to markets in goods, services, and labor, individuals will also have an interest in establishing the legal and economic institutions, such as contract law and capital markets, to support a market system of economic production and exchange. Within the context of this economic and social framework, individuals will be entitled to own those forms of mediated property that they have made through their labor (or in collaboration with others) and those that they have acquired through voluntary transactions.

In providing a rationale for ownership claims to mediated property, the workmanship model, the agency and autonomy strategy, and consequentialist arguments could all be put to good use. Recall that the workmanship argument, as a justification for nonuniversal private property rights, faltered when it extended ownership claims to entities that the individual did not make through her labor, such as the subsoil, subterranean minerals, and underground aquifers. In the case of mediated property, however, the ownership claims under consideration are confined to entities made from materials that the individual (or group she is voluntarily cooperating with) legitimately owns. Unlike the Lockean case in which one was trying to unilaterally appropriate a part of something that belonged to all in common, here there is no question that the individual (or group) is laboring on something to which she already has a legitimate ownership claim. Now the full force of the insight that one is entitled to what is brought into existence through one's physical and conceptual labor can be brought to bear on the justification of rights to mediated property.

We could also appeal to agency and autonomy in justifying rights to mediated property. In carrying out life projects one needs to have short and long-term control of objects that is not dependent on the collective decisions or restrictions of others. If one had to convince a collective body of the desirability or plausibility of one's life projects and of the corresponding need for the objects required for their implementation, agency and autonomy would be severely hindered. Further, individuals will not be content to confine their projects to those that use objects as they are found in nature. People will seek, typically in cooperation with others, to transform and refine those objects in a wide variety of ways and to enter into economic transactions to attain the materials needed for their technical transformation. In some cases, specialized knowledge will be needed to carry out the desired technical refinements of raw materials. This entails providing individuals and groups with the freedom to make the necessary educational and training agreements with other individuals and organizations to achieve these ends. By allowing people and groups to enter into such agreements, a wide variety of autonomy-enhancing specialized services will be made possible. In brief, the exercise of agency and autonomy depends to a significant extent on the capacity to acquire, refine, and expand our technological knowledge of mediated property.

Consequentialist arguments of social utility further strengthen the case for rights to mediated property. In most societies individuals are not indifferent to economic opportunities and/or to their financial well-being. Having the right to retain profit from what one creates and sells, either singly or in cooperation with others, provides incentives for innovation, productivity, risk-taking, and economic alliances that coordinate talents and maximize creative potential. The creative synergy that results from ownership rights to mediated property gives rise to a diversity of products and services that benefit society as a whole. Advances in manufacturing, medicine, transportation, information technologies, and many other areas improve social as well as economic well-being not only for the providers of these goods and services, but also for their recipients.

General Constraints on Rights to Mediated Property

These arguments in favor of rights to mediated property, however, must be qualified in several ways. These qualifications will in turn indicate how these rights should be constrained. The workmanship or labor argument, based on the intuition that one has a right to own what one creates or makes, would appear to establish the rights of use, control, management, and alienability. But in itself this argument does not establish the prerogative to full income rights—in the sense of obtaining market value for the commodities and capital goods one constructs—for the simple reason that market value is not something the individual makes. As Hettinger has argued, the market value of a product is contingent on many factors that the individual is not responsible for, such as demand and availability of that product. Hettinger states:

> Market value is a socially created phenomena, depending on the activity (or nonactivity) of other producers, the monetary demand of purchasers, and the kinds of property rights, contracts, and markets the state has established

and enforced. The market value of the same fruits of labor will differ greatly with variations in these social factors.

Consider the market value of a new drug formula. This depends on the length and the extent of the patent monopoly the state grants and enforces, on the level of affluence of those who need the drug, and on the availability and price of substitutes. The laborer did not create these. The intuitive appeal behind the labor argument—"I made it, hence it is mine"—loses its force when it is used to try to justify owning something others are responsible for (namely, the market value). The claim that a laborer, in virtue of her labor, has a "natural right" to this socially created phenomenon is problematic at best.[5]

The claim that market value is not something for which the maker of capital goods or commodities can take credit is buttressed by recognition of the cooperative social labor that creates and maintains the numerous institutions and infrastructures that make possible the efficient functioning of market systems. This background labor includes the maintenance of judicial systems, penal institutions, regulatory agencies, physical infrastructures like roads and bridges, consumer and environmental protection agencies, public sanitation, and even normative practices like the cultivation of social capital. Consider social capital, which is perhaps the least understood of the factors contributing to the effective functioning of market systems. Included in social capital are all of those attitudes, practices, and values in the personal and civic spheres (such as personal responsibility, social trust, and belief in democratic institutions) that are conducive to social solidarity and law-abiding, prosocial behavior. Given the importance of social trust and adherence to the rule of law, for example, for the successful operation of market systems, it is highly unlikely that such systems could do without social capital. Similarly, the functioning of markets is likely to be seriously hindered without mediating institutions such as the criminal justice system and the judiciary, which not only enforce laws but also ensure due process in case one is accused of a crime. And yet it is society and not the market system that plays the essential role in supporting such non-market institutions and the foundational environments for social capital that make possible the efficient operation of systems of free enterprise.

The upshot of these observations is that since market value is not created by the makers of commodities and capital goods, and since the market system itself depends on extensive non-market social labor for its efficient functioning, society has the right to delimit income rights to mediated property. Typically, these restrictions on income rights will take the form of tax laws to gather revenue to support the physical infrastructures and social institutions (including those that cultivate social capital) that are necessary for market systems of economic production and exchange.[6] And even though the limitation of income rights at first glance also appears to limit agency and autonomy, it is a necessary measure to ensure the exercise of these capacities. Without judicial institutions to protect due process or penal institutions to enforce compliance of contracts, for example, individuals could not confidently enter into the economic agreements necessary to accomplish their life-goals.

The agency and autonomy argument in support of private ownership rights to mediated property needs to be qualified in the following way. If rights to mediated property are justified because they make possible more extensive forms of agency and autonomy, then their nature must reflect this fact. That is, the legal articulation and social impact of these rights must actually enhance the agency and autonomy of the members of society. This entails that schemes of mediated property that systematically undermine autonomy and economic self-reliance by allowing, for example, monopolies and great concentrations of wealth, will be unacceptable.

Likewise, when considering social utility arguments for rights to mediated property we should be ever vigilant that the social and legal institutions governing these rights actually promote beneficial social consequences. Just because ownership rights to mediated property *can* lead to socially desirable consequences does not mean they actually will. The most socially beneficial and useful products, services, and innovations are not necessarily the most profitable, and in a laissez-faire market system it is profit and not altruism that will guide research and innovation. Advocates of the free market extol the social utility of markets with great zeal, but turn a blind eye from existing market systems that give rise to socially detrimental consequences, such as widespread poverty and environmental degradation. As with the agency and autonomy strategy, if we take seriously the social utility argument we need to make sure that the social and legal institutions that govern rights to mediated property actually contribute to socially desirable ends.[7]

Constraints on the Ownership of
the Primary Forms of Mediated Property

In addition to these qualifications, there are considerations of a more basic nature that constrain in important ways the private ownership of certain kinds of mediated property, namely, the primary means of production.[8] These forms of mediated property—such as capital goods and technologies for energy production, habitat construction, food production, medical care, water purification, and modes of transportation—are primary in the sense that they are essential for satisfying basic needs and constitute the foundation of economic self-determination. Because of their centrality for maintaining life itself and making possible the exercise of material self-reliance, everyone has a fundamental interest in having access to these forms of mediated property. But how does this fundamental general interest affect the ownership and development of the primary forms of mediated property? And how does the universal right to ownership of natural property, which includes the raw materials from which the primary forms of mediated property are constructed, affect the ownership of the primary forms of mediated property?

In answering these questions, we should start by remembering that since natural property is not the product of anyone's labor and no justifiable basis for the unilateral, nonuniversal appropriation of natural property can be found, everyone has an equal ownership claim to natural property and, correlatively, to essential natural property, that is, those portions of natural property—arable land, potable water, and valuable natural resources—that are essential for constructing the primary forms of mediated property. In addition, given that the primary forms of mediated property are necessary for satisfying sustenance needs and exercising agency and autonomy, everyone has a fundamental interest in owning essential natural property.[9] The equal ownership claim and basic general interest in essential natural property in turn entail that it should be distributed in a way that respects everyone's equal ownership claim and everyone's fundamental interest in it. Essential natural property, however, is not parceled out by nature in a way that facilitates its fair distribution. Clearly, it would not do to simply divide all of the available land into equal-sized parcels and distribute one parcel to each individual in the society, because different people would end up with land that differed greatly with regard to its usefulness and concentration of valuable natural resources.

Moreover, since nature does not provide essential natural property in ready-made, refined form, it has to be accessed and transformed through socially coordinated labor into technologically usable forms. Minerals have to be extracted and smelted, materials for constructing buildings have to be culled and reshaped, energy sources have to be harnessed, and arable land has to be cleared and cultivated. The need to technologically refine essential natural property before it can be usefully employed means that everyone also has a fundamental interest in the development of primary forms of mediated property that are autonomy-enhancing and procurable. There is little point in having an ownership claim to essential natural property if one does not have the technological means to use it, or if those technological means exist but are inaccessible.[10] In short, not merely the distribution of essential natural property, but also the development of the technological means for accessing, using, and transforming it must be consistent with the original rationale for general property ownership, namely, the nondependent satisfaction of basic needs and the exercise of agency and autonomy.

Thus, a democratic society that recognizes ownership of natural property as a basic human right has to address two distinct but closely related issues: (i) the fair distribution of essential natural property, that is, water, arable land and the natural resources needed to construct the primary forms of mediated property, and (ii) the development of autonomy-enhancing primary forms of mediated property. The first issue emerges from the legitimate universal claims to ownership of natural property and the basic general interest in obtaining the means for material self-determination, while the second arises from the need to technologically refine essential natural property and from the important role played by technologies in attaining material self-reliance. In resolving these issues, it might be suggested that while collective decision making certainly appears necessary to ensure the fair distribution of essential natural property and to protect everyone's fundamental interest in it, the market is better suited to achieve the most efficient and productive development of the primary forms of mediated property. The inclination here is to adopt a bifurcated approach that resolves the first issue through democratic means, but employs free market mechanisms to develop the primary forms of mediated property. After all, there are important advantages in efficiency, innovation, productivity, and fiscal discipline to be gained by the market-guided development of technology, particularly in advanced technological societies.

This inclination, however, must be resisted because even though the distributive and developmental aspects of essential natural property are conceptually distinct, in practice it is not possible to separate them. In order to resolve the issue of fair distribution of essential natural property it is necessary to decide upon a certain path of technical development, because the eventual value of any portion of natural property allotted to individuals will depend to an important extent on the ways it can be developed technologically. With few exceptions, such as highly fertile land and fresh water sources, a society cannot identify its essential natural property, much less distribute it equitably, independently of questions of technological access and development. There are many paths of technological development possible, not all of which are consistent with the universal interest in material autonomy and self-reliance. Even if we could somehow carry out a prior identification and fair distribution of essential natural property, and then let the market determine how the latter was developed, some individuals could very well be left with relatively unusable or worthless portions of "essential" natural property. Therefore, since the point of owning essential natural property is to promote material self-determination, the development of the primary forms of mediated property (including technological forms) cannot be left entirely to market forces, but must be guided by procedures involving democratic decision making.[11] Nevertheless, as we shall see below, our considerations do not entirely rule out the possiblity of employing market mechanisms, within circumscribed economic contexts, to further the development of autonomy-enhancing primary forms of mediated property.

Markets and the Ownership of Essential Natural Property and the Primary Forms of Mediated Property

In predominantly agrarian societies, such as Guatemala and the Philippines, the democratic processes involving the just distribution and appropriate technological development of essential natural property could focus on private and collective arable land distribution, state-subsidized infrastructural and technical support, and provision of credit and capital to support agriculturally based material self-reliance for a significant percentage of the population. In technologically advanced societies, however, it will generally not be feasible, barring a massive simplification of technological development, to achieve economic self-determination through physical distribution of arable land and provision of the technological and financial resources needed for its cultivation. Income flows are seldom derived from agricultural production in technologically complex economies. Alternative means for achieving material self-determination have to be found that, on the one hand, are consistent with the universal equal ownership claims to essential natural property and that, on the other, conform to the existing levels of technological and economic development of the societies in question.[12]

Differences between agrarian and nonagrarian societies also emerge regarding the development of autonomy-enhancing primary forms of mediated property. In agrarian societies the machinery and technologies that need to be developed to promote economic self-determination will be more apparent than in advanced technological societies, where it will be far from clear how material autonomy and self-reliance can be achieved given extensive national and international economic specialization and interdependence. In complex economies, most capital goods and technologies function not so much to provide for basic needs, but to coordinate and maintain highly differentiated market systems of global production and exchange. Material autonomy and self-reliance acquire a very different meaning in societies in which the capacity to function effectively in a variety of technological niches is more important for economic self-determination than the ability to grow one's own food or build one's own shelter.

Assuming that technological societies want to continue to operate within a complex globalized economic system (though there are compelling reasons to resist globalization in its present form and work to embed decentralized economies within local and regional communities[13]), are there economic models available that take into account the con-

straints on the ownership of mediated property which we have discussed? In recent years a number of theorists have developed economic
systems that combine market mechanisms with such collective goals as
public ownership of the means of production, general social distribution
of profit income from firms, and worker-managed and owned business
enterprises. It is useful to look at these systems to get an idea of the available economic frameworks that are consistent with the mediated property rights structures I have elucidated and defended thus far. As we
shall see, it is possible to establish economic systems, even in technologically complex societies, that take advantage of market mechanisms while
adequately resolving the dilemmas of fair distribution of essential natural property and the development of autonomy-enhancing primary
forms of mediated property.

The separation of ownership and management in the modern corporation makes possible the construction of economic frameworks that combine markets and democratic control of a society's productive resources.
Firms in these economic frameworks are not publicly owned in the narrow sense of being under direct and exclusive state control, but operate
under boards of directors representing either workers or institutions—
such as banks, mutual funds, or pension funds—which hold stock in the
firms or are responsible for the financing of the respective firms.[14] The
idea is to avoid the well-known problems of centralized state ownership
by creating institutional buffers between centralized political control and
the management of firms. Within this tradition, John Roemer has developed an economic system characterized by public ownership of business
enterprises, equalized distribution among the populace of profit income
from capital, freedom for individuals to select their own investment port-
folios, management of firms by individuals accountable to local, regional,
and national level agencies, and a stock market to induce firm managers
to maximize profits for shareholders.[15] Financing of firms could be done
by a Japanese-style *keiretsu* system.[16] In this economic model, every adult
member of the society receives an equal number of nontransferable certificates from the state that can be used only to purchase shares of mutual
funds, which in turn can purchase shares of firms. Prices of mutual funds
and corporate shares would be stated in certificates, and would change
according to supply and demand for shares. Mismanagement of a firm
would lead to a decrease in the value of the firm's shares in the stock
market, and thus discipline its managers to rectify deficiencies in performance. Small privately owned firms would be permitted to provide incentive for innovation and profit[17], and differential interest rates would
be used to encourage investment in autonomy-enhancing technologies
and other socially desirable technological forms. In short, in this system
market principles that ensure competition, fiscal accountability, creativity, and initiative would be maintained, while the society would exercise

democratic control over the means of production and share equally profit income.

In adapting this system to our purposes, we would restrict public ownership to essential natural property and to the enterprises involving the primary forms of mediated property. Profit income from these public enterprises would still be equally distributed among the members of society through the use of state-issued certificates, and their financing would follow the *keiretsu* system. Firm managers, who would be accountable to the public, would be induced to perform efficiently by the competitive participation of their firms in a stock market. Private ownership of small firms dealing with the primary forms of mediated property would be permitted to promote innovation and provide profit incentives. In other respects, the economic system would be basically like conventional market systems. How would this modified Roemerian economic framework fare in its capacity to protect the fundamental general interest in material self-determination? While it would not achieve the kind of extensive societal income equalization that market socialists like Roemer find desirable, it would resolve the dilemmas discussed earlier of the fair distribution of essential natural property and the development of autonomy-enhancing forms of mediated property. The first dilemma would be resolved by not having to physically distribute essential natural property at all, since it, and the economic enterprises through which it is developed, would be publicly owned. The second dilemma would be addressed by the use of democratically determined economic instruments (e.g., research grants and differential interest rates) to steer research and investment toward the development of kinds of mediated property and technological forms, such as solar energy technologies, that promote material self-determination for individuals and communities.

The autonomy-enhancing aspects of our adaptation of Roemer's model could be further strengthened by its incorporation of worker-owned and managed business enterprises. As Thomas Weisskopf has argued, Roemer's system fails to promote the development of community and democratic self-governance in the workplace because it does not provide for worker participation in enterprise management.[18] This additional modification of Roemer's system brings to light the notion that material self-determination, particularly in complex economies, involves dimensions of social agency, such as development of negotiation skills, a sense of efficacy, and a capacity for independent judgement. Workplace democracy can play an important role in the cultivation of these capacities and dispositions. These skills and dispositions are particularly important in multicultural societies such as the U.S., which contains groups in the accommodationist category, that is, cultural groups seeking a greater degree of incorporation into the main social and economic institutions of the mainstream society. Though these skills and capacities are important in any complex society, they are especially needed to maintain intercultural socioeconomic parity in this particular kind of multicultural society, since here there will be a greater degree of ongoing negotiation concerning cultural group economic needs and interests.

The dramatic world-wide failures of socialist economies at the end of the twentieth century revealed in a clear and compelling way the pitfalls of collectivized economies. An important advantage of the market social-ist resolution of the dilemmas of fair distribution of essential natural property and the development of autonomy-enhancing forms of medi-ated property is that it embeds the resolution of these dilemmas within an economic framework that recognizes and rectifies the deficiencies in centralized economic planning. Detailed analyses of these deficiencies have led to the construction of economic models that grant a significant role to market mechanisms and that appreciate the importance of factors such as innovation, economic incentives, the resource allocating func-tions of markets, and the need to separate political influence and eco-nomic accountability. To be credible, any economic model that advocates either partial or total public ownership of a society's productive re-sources must take these factors into account.

We should also note that the imperative to protect the universal equal ownership claim to essential natural property and the universal interest in autonomy-enhancing primary forms of mediated property cannot be overridden by economic criteria of efficiency and productivity. Thus, a market system of nonuniversal property ownership would not be morally preferable, even if it had greater *overall* productivity[19], to a less productive economic system that respected fundamental property own-ership rights.[20]

In this section I have merely drawn out the logical consequences of universal ownership of essential natural property and the basic general interest in autonomy-enhancing primary forms of mediated property. In defending my views I have not relied on normative appeals to concep-tions of distributive justice, such as equalization of social conditions and socioeconomic opportunity, though nothing in my position precludes the possibility of appealing to such notions to arrive at a more thoroughly egalitarian position. Given this possibility, the question naturally arises: Why not apply a full-scale market socialist model to all of the means of production, and in a single stroke establish the conditions for a more egalitarian society? Indeed, there appears to be a reason for making this move, namely, that everyone has an equal ownership claim to all natural property, and not just to the essential portions of it. If this is the case, and if all forms of mediated property depend on natural property for their creation, it seems natural to socialize the ownership and profit income from the total means of production, so that everyone shares equitably in the benefits derived from the use of all natural property.

To understand the reasons why I have not opted for a full-scale market socialist model, recall that in our discussion of the rationale for private property ownership we recognized that there was a prima facie case for granting people a wide range of economic freedoms to further the realization of their life-projects. These economic freedoms, we noted, could be institutionalized by granting private property rights, which would provide individuals with: (i) the control of the material objects necessary to carry out their life-projects, (ii) the liberty to enter into a wide range of contractual economic relationships, and (iii) the stability of expectation necessary for long-term planning. If an individual had to convince a collective body of the desirability of her life-projects and petition for the resources to carry them out, her agency and autonomy would be significantly constrained. In tightly knit, culturally homogeneous communities with a high consensus of values, needs, and desires—such as indigenous communities or Israeli kibbutzim—it may be possible to collectivize all of the productive resources of the society without a substantial loss of agency and autonomy. The high degree of value consensus in these communities would decrease the likelihood that collective decisions would thwart the projects and aspirations of their members. In complex, culturally pluralistic societies with a wide diversity of conceptions of the good life, however, it is far more probable that collectivized ownership and control of all forms of mediated property would hinder agency and autonomy.

In short, sustaining agency and autonomy in complex pluralistic societies supports an initial case for private property rights over natural and mediated property. But, as we have observed, these rights are constrained by the equal ownership claim to essential natural property and the fundamental general interest in autonomy-enhancing primary forms of mediated property, because of the role these play in satisfying basic needs and promoting material self-reliance.[21] These ownership claims and economic interests, however, do not by themselves justify complete collective ownership of all of the means of production. They only justify democratic control of those productive resources necessary to protect these claims and interests. Those who want to argue that collectivized ownership of the total means of production promotes agency and autonomy better than any other alternative must bear the burden of proof to show that state ownership would most likely accomplish these goals. Here the jury is still out on full-blown market socialism. Serious concerns remain regarding the capacity of full-scale market socialist models to overcome problems in attaining material self-determination and in achieving an adequate level of overall efficiency and productivity.[22]

As previously noted, the hybrid economic system I have proposed is compatible with systems of economic redistribution designed to achieve objectives, such as equality of educational opportunity, that would further promote material self-determination in technologically advanced societies. These additional steps will most likely be necessary, because the economic measures I have proposed, while contributing significantly to material self-determination, are not sufficient to achieve it. Any adequate conception of material self-determination in complex technological economies will have to include a fairly robust set of competencies and opportunities, and thus go beyond the base level requirements I have advocated. For instance, educational training that provides individuals with the wherewithal to function competitively in a technological economy will be of paramount importance. A more thorough discussion of the full requirements for material self-determination, and the role that mediated property plays in the material base of multicultural democratic societies, is beyond the scope of this work. My purpose here has only been to draw out the implications that follow from universal rights to property ownership and to show that there are economic systems in which these consequences could be consistently observed. As we have seen, these rights, and the economic claims and interests that follow from them, must be respected by any economic system adopted by a just multicultural liberal democracy. In summary, we could say that at the most general level the economic policies of a multicultural society should be guided by the commitment to develop and maintain the means of production, socioeconomic institutions, and technological forms by which people and communities can satisfy their material needs in a self-reliant manner which promotes general agency and autonomy while eliminating economic and political exploitation.

Exploited Cultural Groups and the Acquisition of Mediated Property

The fact that some cultural groups have experienced systematic and pervasive discrimination and oppression[23] at the hands of majority societies raises some interesting issues concerning the need to promote accessibility to the ownership of mediated property for these groups. We have already observed that some indigenous groups can claim special property rights to protect territorial and cultural autonomy. These property rights concerned land and natural resources; are there similar moral obligations the state has to promote ownership and development of mediated property for indigenous and other ethnocultural groups? Due to the extensive and long-term effects of the discrimination and oppression some of these groups have suffered, a strong case can be made for remedial efforts to revitalize the economic and social institutions that will permit them to acquire an equitable share—measured against the median level of economic well-being of the majority society—of the society's mediated property. The need for revitalization becomes more compelling when we recognize that some of these groups cannot enjoy collective or individual autonomy without a viable material base.

There are many ways in which the capacity of some ethnocultural groups for owning and developing mediated property has been hindered or eroded. Territorial displacement, enslavement, debt servitude, denial of infrastructural and technical support, unequal educational resources, unjust taxation schemes, exploitation of natural resources in communal lands, and discriminatory financial and social policies are some of the ways in which the ability of ethnocultural groups throughout the world to attain material well-being by acquiring and developing mediated property has been undermined. Maya Indians in Guatemala and in the southern Mexican state of Chiapas, for example, have experienced most of these forms of systematic and pervasive discrimination and oppression by their respective governments. In Guatemala, the Liberal Revolution of 1871 brought about a shift from subsistence to export agriculture in which many Indians lost their land through confiscation and fraud. Forced-labor laws furthered the Mayas' loss of economic self-determination.[24] This legacy of oppression and discrimination extends to the present. In the area of education, for every quetzal (about 20 cents) the central Guatemalan government currently spends for education in the predominantly Maya western highlands, it spends three quetzales on the education of the mostly *ladino* population of the eastern region.[25] Lack of educational resources has hindered the development of economic self-reliance of Maya communities in Guatemala and continues to do so.

In Mexico, because of long-standing discriminatory government policies, more than 50 percent of the residents of the heavily Indian-populated state of Chiapas do not have running water, and about half of all households do not have electricity, even though Chiapas, comprising only 3 percent of the country's population, provides 54 percent of Mexico's hydroelectric power and 17 percent of its oil and gas.[26] Despite the richness of its natural resources, Chiapas is the second poorest state in Mexico. Its indigenous communities, which include Tzotzil, Tzeltal, Chol, and Tojolabal Mayas, have suffered a long history of oppression. In 1856 and 1863, for example, the Mexican government passed the Liberal Reform laws which legalized the purchase by non-Indians of Indian communal lands.[27] The loss of their land drove the Indians into wage-labor, and eventually into forms of debt-servitude akin to slavery. Thus, the oppression experienced by the Maya in Guatemala and Mexico have centered, on the one hand, on loss of control of their lands and natural resources and, on the other, on denial of equitable access to resources for human development, such as education. As a result, the capacity of Maya communities to own and develop forms of mediated property central for material well-being, such as technologies for energy and food production, was seriously impaired. In turn, this material impoverishment exacerbated their social and political marginalization.

It is important to recognize that the forms of oppression and discrimination suffered by the Maya were causal factors of decisive importance in bringing about their current economic and political disempowerment, and that the state either sanctioned or knowingly tolerated these injustices. Since the present condition of disempowerment of these cultural communities would most likely not exist were it not for the actions of the state, the latter must take responsibility for remedial efforts to rectify these injustices.[28] Among the factors to be considered in determining the nature of the rectification are the scope and degree of oppression suffered, the extent of state culpability, the resources available to the larger society, and the level of mediated property ownership and development the oppressed group can realistically achieve by having the same access to resources and opportunities as the majority society. A host of complex issues arise that require much more extensive treatment than I can provide here. But three points in particular should be made. First, the rectificatory procedures for groups such as the Maya should be directed not merely at individual members of the group, but at the cultural community as a whole. Unlike affirmative action policies involving preferential treatment of individual members of the wronged ethnocultural groups who are competing for limited opportunity positions with majority group members, the goal should be to revitalize the groups' economic and social institutions so that they can achieve a reasonable level of collective material and sociocultural well-being. What justifies the focus on community mediated-property revitalization is the highly cohesive and interdependent character of the cultural and material bases of these indigenous communities.

Second, the long-term responsibility for revitalizing the groups' economic and social institutions is inversely proportional to the degree of autonomy of the ethnocultural group in question. That is, the greater the regional political and material autonomy of the minority group, the less responsibility the larger society has to continually maintain their economic well-being at a level comparable to that of the members of the majority society. Though initially there would be strong moral imperatives for the state to correct past wrongs, its continuing responsibilities would be limited by the degree to which the cultural group has autonomous control over its own land, resources, and sociopolitical institutions. Of course, this assumes that the state would not be exploiting the group in other ways, for example, through more subtle discriminatory policies, exploitation of the region's resources, or inequitable economic relationships. Third, unlike rights to territorial autonomy, rectificatory procedures would not have the status of permanent, group-based rights, but would be temporary measures that would no longer be in force once their intended goals were achieved.

The regional concentration and strong communal orientations of groups like the Maya make it relatively easy to identify, respectively, the cultural communities which need revitalization and the nature of the rectificatory policies. But what about accommodationist groups, who may have experienced similar systematic discrimination and oppression, but who do not desire autonomous self-determination but rather greater participation in the social and economic institutions of the majority society? Typically these groups, such as African-Americans and Latinos in the U.S., are much less regionally concentrated than groups like the Maya, and a relatively greater number of their members have achieved mid-range socioeconomic status. Nevertheless, communities comprised primarily of members of these cultural groups are still identifiable, and in general these communities are more economically impoverished and have a lower rate of ownership of mediated property than communities comprised of majority group members. To the extent that it can be established that the cultural groups in this category have suffered pervasive and profound systematic state-sponsored or tolerated discrimination and oppression that have been major factors in their present condition of material and social disempowerment, they also merit corrective measures to ameliorate their lack of ownership and development of mediated property.

A very strong case can be made to show that in the U.S., cultural groups such as African-Americans and Mexican-Americans have suffered pervasive and profound discrimination of the latter sort. The enslavement for 200 years of African-Americans was not only a great and abhorrent crime against their humanity, it also undermined in numerous ways their individual and collective development. Among other things, chattel slavery fractured the black family, impeded black ownership and development of mediated property, and severely hindered the acquisition by blacks of those skills and capacities necessary for vying successfully for capital-accumulating positions in the competitive American society. By denying them such fundamental capacities and opportunities as literacy and access to capital, for example, chattel slavery greatly undermined the individual and collective social, economic, and political empowerment of African-Americans.

While recognizing the great moral turpitude of slavery, some might argue that this system which legitimized the sale and marketing of human beings was abolished almost 150 years ago, and that one and a half centuries of formal equality is surely sufficient to eliminate, if not all, at least most of the negative consequences of slavery. Even though slavery is a shameful part of world and American history, the argument goes, it should not be used as a justification for granting special privileges or compensation to African-Americans, since they have enjoyed equal rights for a sufficiently long time to justify their being judged by the same standards as everyone else. In response to this view, we should note that even if the effects of slavery on African-Americans could have been eradicated in this time period—in itself a questionable assumption—very severe forms of discrimination and oppression of blacks continued well into the twentieth century. Indeed, as we shall see, African-Americans at present still suffer from significant kinds of discrimination and oppression.

For a few years after the Civil War, some efforts were made to provide political and social equality for the freed slaves. During the period of Reconstruction, formal measures were instituted—most notably the Fourteenth and Fifteenth constitutional Amendments and the Civil Rights Enforcement Act of 1870—to ensure that blacks would be able to exercise their civil and democratic rights in the same manner and to the same extent as the white majority. Considering the proximity of this time period to the era of slavery, remarkable progress was made for a brief time towards the political and social empowerment of blacks. African-American leaders were elected to local, state, and federal seats, and the number of black registered voters equaled or outnumbered white registered voters in a number of Southern states. Blacks were major participants in the constitutional conventions that took place in the Southern states during Reconstruction; they even constituted a majority of the convention delegates in the South Carolina constitutional convention and equaled the number of white delegates in Louisiana's convention. The Freedmen Bureau, a federal organization designed to address the needs of the former slaves, provided them with such goods and services as food rations, medical attention, educational training, and even small portions of abandoned and confiscated land.

This remarkable period of interracial democracy was short-lived, however, and within a few years there was a full scale retreat from equality. A series of Supreme Court decisions negated the civil rights protections for blacks provided by federal legislation and the Fourteenth and Fifteenth Amendments. In the famous Slaughter-house cases of 1873, the Supreme Court distinguished between state and federal citizenship, and argued that since most civil rights derived from state citizenship, they could not be protected under the Fourteenth Amendment, whose proper function, according to the court, was to protect the rights of federal citizenship. The Supreme Court refused to specify the nature of federal citizenship rights, arguing that because the case before it concerned state citizenship rights, it had no obligation to specify the rights guaranteed by federal citizenship. The Slaughterhouse decisions set the stage for later decisions involving the interpretation of rights under the Fourteenth Amendment.

In 1876 the Supreme Court declared unconstitutional those sections of the Civil Rights Enforcement Act of 1870 that prohibited one or more individuals from conspiring "to injure, oppress, threaten, or intimidate any citizen, with intent to prevent or hinder his free exercise and enjoyment of any right or privilege granted or secured to him by the constitution or laws of the United States."[29] On the basis of this Supreme Court ruling, charges brought under the Enforcement Act against two white individuals were rejected. These individuals had conspired to falsely imprison and kill two blacks and deprive them of their lives and liberty without due process of law. The rationale for the court decision was that the Civil Rights Enforcement Act went beyond the prohibitions against discrimination provided by the Fourteenth Amendment. The U.S. Congress subsequently repealed the whole Enforcement Act in 1894.

In 1876 the court also ruled that since the Fifteenth Amendment only prohibited discrimination in the right to vote on the basis of race, color, or previous condition of servitude, the sections of the Enforcement Act that went beyond such protections were unconstitutional, and therefore had to be repealed. The final nails in the coffin of protective legislation came when the Supreme Court decreed in the Civil Rights Cases of 1883 that the Fourteenth Amendment forbade states, not individuals, from discriminating without due process.[30] Through semantic hair-splitting, the court decided that blacks could not seek protection under the Fourteenth Amendment for the violation of their civil rights by individuals, businesses, private clubs, organizations, and so forth, because this amendment prohibited only *states* from discriminating against them.

Thus, congressional legislation that protected the rights articulated by the Fourteenth and Fifteenth Amendments was repealed within a few years of its passage. Since the purpose of this legislation, as well as the Fourteenth and Fifteenth Amendments themselves, had been primarily to protect the civil and political rights of blacks, its nullification ushered in an era of Jim Crow laws in the Southern states where the vast majority of blacks lived. Jim Crow laws legalized the forcible separation of blacks from whites in many areas, including public transportation, schools, inns, hospitals, funeral homes, and cemeteries. Interracial marriages and eating establishments were legally prohibited, white educators could not teach black children, and white nurses could not provide medical treatment to black men.[31] The state-sanctioned Jim Crow system not only profoundly punished, controlled, limited, and humiliated the African-American people, it also systematized very serious forms of discrimination and oppression that had long-term social and economic disempowering consequences for blacks. The Supreme Court decisions undermined the newly acquired political rights of blacks, while the Jim Crow system institutionalized their social, political, and economic inequality.

One of the most important ways in which such inequality was institutionalized was through an inequitable system of education. In 1915, for example, South Carolina spent $13.98 for every white student, and only $2.57 for every black student. As late as 1933, there were no four-year public high schools for blacks in most parts of the South. Education is of primary importance not only because it a major entryway to positions of higher socioeconomic status, but also because of its role in self-development. To deprive a people of an adequate education is to rob them of the capacity to control their own destinies through the development and exercise of their potential skills and talents. Furthermore, lack of adequate educational opportunities forced many African-Americans into the highly exploitative system of share-cropping. Under this system, planters provided black tenants such resources as land, tools, animals, and fertilizer, and in return retained from one-third to two-thirds of the crops.[32] Planters charged usurious rates for the implements they provided, and the inability of many blacks to read made it easy for planters to cheat them. The net result of these factors was that many share-croppers fell into debt servitude from which it was very difficult to extricate themselves. In addition, the state-tolerated, organized terror of such groups as the Ku Klux Klan and the Knights of the White Magnolia kept the share-cropping system in place by intimidating, torturing, and killing blacks who dared to protest.[33]

It is very important to note that many African-American adults living today are only two generations removed from the Jim Crow era; that is, their grandparents lived under the pervasive discrimination and oppression of the Jim Crow system. It is unreasonable to maintain that two generations is sufficient to eradicate the long-term detrimental consequences of such an unjust system. Further, when land and credit was provided to white settlers to promote the settlement of the West, blacks were unable to take advantage of this opportunity because they had just been emancipated and were without capital or the means to acquire it. After Emancipation, the promise to distribute land to African-Americans and to provide the credit to develop it never materialized. In short, African-Americans in the U.S. never had the same opportunities as whites to acquire and develop land, mediated property, and the capital accumulation that derives from possessing the latter.

There are remarkable similarities between the forms of discrimination and oppression imposed by the majority society on African-Americans during the Jim Crow era and those forced upon Mexican-Americans living in Texas in the early part of the twentieth century. While the discrimination and oppression suffered by the latter was not as extreme or pervasive as that suffered by blacks, the discriminatory and oppressive mechanisms were nevertheless profound and similarly structured. For instance, just as the systematic denial of educational opportunities drove many Southern blacks to the share-cropping system, similar Jim Crow policies in education compelled many Mexican-Americans into agricultural labor and, in some cases, debt servitude. Sometimes organized groups such as the Texas Rangers and local sheriff departments played a role in maintaining and promoting systems of discrimination and oppression similar to that played by the Ku Klux Klan and the Knights of the White Magnolia.[34]

Several factors make it difficult to identify the most appropriate policies for rectifying disadvantages in mediated property ownership and capital-accumulation for accommodationist groups. The complexity of these factors precludes the possibility of providing even general guidelines for rectificatory policies for these groups. Here I will confine myself to making several germane observations concerning appropriate compensatory measures. First, because accommodationist cultural groups are generally not as socially cohesive as autonomist groups (to which the Maya belong), individual-centered rectificatory policies[35] will not necessarily improve the situation of the most disadvantaged members of their communities. Thus, unless communal socioeconomic factors are taken into account, affirmative action policies involving competition between minority and majority group members will tend to disproportionately benefit those ethnocultural group members who have already overcome some of the disadvantages associated with membership in their ethnocultural group. Furthermore, members of accommodationist groups who achieve upward socioeconomic mobility are likely to leave impoverished minority communities, thus lessening the positive impact they could have on the ethnocultural group members who need the most help.

Second, in rectifying the effects of discrimination and oppression on mediated property acquisition, it is reasonable to concentrate on the most disadvantaged cultural group members, because they are the ones most affected by discriminatory and oppressive practices. Whether due to socioeconomic disadvantages, problematic family environments, or lesser natural abilities, some ethnocultural group members are more vulnerable to the negative effects of these practices. Since it is the damage done by discriminatory and oppressive practices which must be redressed, it makes sense to focus rectificatory efforts where these practices have produced the most harm, rather than where their effects have been negated by a combination of social factors and individual talents. In connection with this point, it is instructive to note that even though some ethnocultural groups—such as Jewish Americans and Italian-Americans—have experienced significant discrimination in this country, the moral imperative for the U.S. to rectify, on a group-wide basis, past injustices against them is not compelling unless these injustices are responsible for existing disadvantages afflicting these groups.[36] This is particularly true if the injustices were experienced not by living ethnocultural group members but by their predecessors. The example of these cultural groups reinforces the view that it is not past discriminatory and oppressive practices *per se* that create a moral imperative for rectification, but the causal link between such practices and existing disadvantages experienced by the relevant ethnocultural groups. To the extent that discrimination and oppression have diminished the capacity of existing ethnocultural group members to acquire mediated property and enjoy the corresponding benefits derived from a base of capital-accumulation,[37] they merit compensatory policies that at least roughly equalize their position *vis-a-vis* members of the majority society.

Third, mediated property rectificatory policies that are individual-centered tend to undermine the political and social solidarity of ethnocultural groups by creating class-based cleavages between group members. Policies of preferential treatment that have primarily benefited middle-class blacks and Latinos in the U.S., for example, have played a significant role in widening the gap between the wealthiest and poorest blacks and Latinos. In fact, the difference between the wealthiest and the poorest quintiles of African-Americans is greater than the difference between the richest and poorest white quintiles. These class differences, and the residential segregation and occupational stratification that accompany them, have polarized black and Latino communities internally and have made it more difficult for them to speak with a unified voice or achieve effective political mobilization. Class-based divisions within black and Latino communities have also made it more difficult for the best educated minority members with the most resources to genuinely understand, and empathize with, the needs and perspectives of the most disfranchised members of their own groups.

Though issues involving ownership of natural and mediated property are important for developing an adequate theory of property rights for multicultural democracies, to accomplish the latter task it is also crucial to understand the role of intellectual property. Understanding rights to intellectual property is increasingly important given the prominence of advanced technologies in the contemporary world.

Intellectual Property

While rights to natural and mediated property have long been recognized as an important part of a general theory of property rights, intellectual property rights do not have a well-established niche in property rights theory. However, several developments at the end of the twentieth century—such as greater reliance of businesses and governments on copyrightable information systems, technological innovations in bioengineering that make possible the patenting of life-forms, and the emergence of transnational corporations seeking greater control and protection of lucrative telecommunication technologies—account for the increased prominence of intellectual property rights in domestic and international law and international trade agreements. In addition to these general developments, increased recognition of the importance of ethnobotanical knowledge and plant hybrids developed by minority communities make it imperative that issues regarding intellectual property be addressed in delineating the general character of property rights in multicultural democracies.

Generally, intellectual property is divided into three categories: (i) copyrights, which involve entities like writings, photographs, and software systems, (ii) patents, which include inventions, manufacturing processes, and compositions of matter (like pharmaceuticals and plant hybrids), and (iii) trade secrets, which in addition to copyrights and patents can include such information as plant layouts and sales and marketing data.

Different intellectual property rights grant the bearer different kinds of privileges. Copyrights confer rights to reproduce, distribute, adapt, perform, and publicly display the protected subject matter, and expire 50 years after the author's death. Patents grant the exclusive rights to make use of, sell, and produce the relevant subject matter, and provide protection from independent discovery or creation; that is, others are prohibited from using, selling, or producing the patented product even if they should discover or create it on their own. Patents expire after twenty years. Trade secrets grant the rights of use, management, income, and protection from misappropriation. The latter is important given the prevalence of commercial espionage and the susceptibility of trade secrets being revealed by former employees of firms. Trade secrets have no term limits, and they do not exclude independent creation or discovery. Thus it is permissible for others to appropriate them, for example, through the reverse engineering of protected inventions. Patents, on the other hand, require disclosure of the subject matter protected, but offer the advantage of granting a complete monopoly of that subject matter for twenty years.

From a philosophical perspective, interesting problems arise in the area of intellectual property because of the intangible nature of its subject matter. Unlike concrete forms of property, intellectual property is nonexclusive: it can "be" at different places at once and can be entirely used by different people at the same time and, unlike some forms of tangible property, is not consumed or worn out when used. Thus, if a patent covers a certain type of computer, properly speaking it is the abstract, nontangible *design* of the computer that is protected, and not any particular computer which instantiates that design (laws against theft already provide protection for the concrete object). The nonexclusivity of intellectual property means that it is sharable in ways in which concrete property is not. Unlike tangible property, other individuals besides the author can use the intellectual property without hindering the author's use of it. Thus the crux of intellectual property rights lies not so much in granting the bearer of those rights access to and use of the relevant intellectual objects, but rather in restricting others in certain uses of these objects, like reproduction, dissemination, and most important in a market system, profit from sale.

Justifying Intellectual Property Rights

Arguments similar to those provided for tangible property can be used to legitimize rights to intellectual property. The workmanship argument certainly has at least initial appeal, because when I bring an intellectual object into (abstract) existence it is my cognitive, willful activity that is responsible for its coming into being. On the basis of the natural right that a creator has to the objects of his creation, I could claim that the object is mine. As a corollary to creator's rights, it could also be claimed that given their nonexclusivity, if ownership of intellectual objects is to be a meaningful notion it must include income rights and control of their reproduction, disclosure, and dissemination. The state should respect the author's right of ownership to her own ideas by formalizing these rights through the legal institution of intellectual property rights.

The agency and autonomy argument can also be adapted to justify intellectual property rights. Two versions of this argument can be distinguished. The first version focuses on the role played by intellectual objects in realizing one's life projects and achieving self-definition. According to this view, control of the products of one's intellectual activity is just as important as control of objects in the physical environment for exercising agency and achieving autonomy, because carrying out some of our life projects may depend on our capacity to: (i) choose a way of life in which we earn a living through the products of our intellectual activity (either by selling them directly or by contracting out our intellectual labor) and/or (ii) enter into partnerships with others for a wide variety of projects involving cooperative intellectual labor. The only way these objectives can be accomplished is by granting individuals control over the products of their intellectual activity. In other cases, such as those involving artistic creations, control of the public access or reproduction of the objects of intellectual activity may play a crucial role in self-identity. For some individuals, the products of aesthetic creativity, and control of the conditions of their public accessibility, may be intimately connected to their sense of who they are and are thus of central importance in the process of self-creation. In brief, denying individuals the right to control the use of their intellectual labor could seriously infringe upon their autonomy and agency.

The second version, proposed by Lynn Paine, applies primarily to trade secrets, and maintains that respect for the privacy and autonomy of the individual grounds the right to control the disclosure of one's ideas. According to Paine, respect for an individual's moral agency entails respect for the privacy of her thoughts and ideas. She contends that people have a prima facie right to keep their thoughts to themselves and, should they choose to disclose them, to decide to whom they should be disclosed. Public regulation of peoples' inner life is a unjustifiable violation of their personhood. She states:

> To require public disclosure of one's ideas and thoughts—whether about "personal" or other matters—would distort one's personality and, no doubt, alter the nature of one's thoughts. . . . This sort of thought control would be an invasion of privacy and personality of the most intrusive sort. If anything is private, one's undisclosed thoughts surely are.[38]

Paine's principal arguments are based not on control of intellectual objects used as means for self-determined ends, but rather on respect for the privacy and moral integrity of the individual. In effect, she tries to place the burden of proof on the state to justify its right to set the conditions under which individuals can disclose, share, or transfer control of their ideas.

Arguments based on social utility are the strongest and most commonly used arguments to justify intellectual property rights. According to this justificatory strategy, intellectual property rights provide incentives for individuals and organizations to invest time, money, and labor in research that promotes technical progress. If the individuals and organizations responsible for the development of novel ideas, techniques, and inventions did not receive special rights over their intellectual property, they would not have the incentive to spend the resources necessary to create them. By granting control of the sale, reproduction, dissemination, and use of intellectual property to those responsible for its creation, the state maximizes beneficial consequences for the whole society. Even though granting a monopoly or placing restrictions on the use of intellectual property may in the short run limit the free flow of information, in the long term technical progress and the availability of information is increased because eventually nearly everyone benefits from technological progress. Yesterday's technological wonders are today's pedestrian devices.

Evaluating the Rationale for Intellectual Property Rights

Despite the initial plausibility of the notion that an intellectual object belongs to he who creates it, the workmanship argument runs into a serious problem. Inventions, theories, manufacturing processes, and the like are rarely, if ever, entirely new creations which do not depend on the prior intellectual labor of others. The development of a new process for manufacturing jet engine parts, for example, relies on extensive prior research in chemistry, physics, mathematics, and engineering. Similarly, a new software program depends on earlier research in computer programs, innovations in hardware, and historical developments in mathematical logic involving abstract algorithmic systems. Even groundbreaking artistic creations—which might be regarded as quintessential embodiments of creativity—assume mastery of established techniques for using an artistic medium and an art tradition within which their novelty and revolutionary character make sense. Their dependence on the accomplishments of previous human intellectual labor means that intellectual objects do not arise as totally new creations from the inventor's mind; rather, they are social products fundamentally dependent on collective labor.[39] This is particularly true in technologically developed societies in which inventions exemplify a high level of technical complexity. Much of the structural complexity characterizing intellectual objects protected by intellectual property rights in such societies is attributable to a long history of research and innovation by others. Moreover, a great deal of the research on which such prior innovations depend was made possible by institutions—such as public libraries, government data collection agencies, and state institutions to support research and development—that were either partly or wholly supported by public funds. The dependence of intellectual objects on collective social labor severely undermines the claim that they are the sole product, and therefore the sole property, of the inventor.

The fact that intellectual objects presuppose prior collective social labor does not entail that inventors should not have any special rights to their intellectual creations, or that the state has the right to appropriate them. It does mean, however, that no unconditional claim to strong intellectual property rights can be made solely on the basis of the workmanship argument. Besides, other considerations reinforce the notion that society can legitimately place constraints on intellectual property. In most cases involving intellectual property, the controversy centers on the inventor's right to income from her intellectual creations, and not on her use or access to them.[40] That is, the question is not whether someone who makes ownership claims to intellectual objects has the right to employ them for her own purposes at her own discretion, but whether society should legally restrict others from using them without paying her due compensation. Since it is the right to derive income in market transactions that is involved here, the arguments given earlier regarding mediated property also apply. In other words, since the market institutions that make possible financial recompense from intellectual property are supported by a great deal of social cooperation and labor, society has the right to place constraints on income rights to intellectual property.[41]

The first version of the agency and autonomy argument has limited force for justifying copyright, patent, and trade secret laws. Recall that according to this version of the argument, intellectual property rights are needed to enable individuals, on the one hand, to earn a living by means of their intellectual creations and to undertake projects involving cooperative intellectual labor and, on the other, to secure autonomy in self-creation and self-definition. The claim that intellectual property rights are necessary for individuals to earn a living is greatly undermined by the fact that most copyrights and patents, and practically all trade secrets, are held by institutions, such as corporations and universities, and not individuals. It is rare for individuals to independently employ intellectual property as their primary means of survival. And even in those cases where an individual's livelihood depends on her intellectual labor, intellectual property rights are not necessary. As Hettinger and others have pointed out, other alternatives to intellectual property rights are possible, such as monetary rewards or state support for writers and inventors in exchange for the placement of their works in the public domain. It is also implausible to maintain that intellectual property rights are necessary for engaging in cooperative ventures involving intellectual labor, since other monetary and nonmonetary benefits could be used to encourage and compensate such ventures. To be sure, denying intellectual property rights in their present forms would nullify the monopoly rights that corporations and other institutions can have over intellectual property, but limiting income rights to intellectual property cannot be straightforwardly equated with denial of economic self-reliance or sovereignty in self-definition, because such income limitations do not deny these organizations access to and use of the relevant intellectual property.

The autonomy argument is most persuasive with regard to copyrights that protect artists from the unauthorized reproduction and public display of their works. Given the profound self-identification that artists can have with their creations, it is reasonable to maintain that they should have some control over the way in which their works are publicly disseminated and reproduced. To the extent that copyright laws protect this form of self-creative activity, they have a well-grounded justificatory basis. Even so, we should note that most copyrights are held by corporations, such as publishing houses, and not individuals. Thus, the self-creation argument is most plausible in a limited number of cases, and is unconvincing in the case of patents and trade secrets held by large corporations, because generally the function of the latter is not to protect the conditions for exercising sovereignty in self-definition.

Still, putting aside the issue of self-definition, limitations on the income rights of either individuals or institutions could be seen as autonomy-diminishing, and thus as undesirable. Even though few individuals make their living from selling their intellectual property, many people earn income from their investments in corporations whose profit depends to a significant extent on ownership of intellectual property. The autonomy of these investors is diminished by restrictions on income rights. This raises the fundamental question of whether intellectual property rights, at least in their present forms, *generally* promote or diminish autonomy. In an era of increasing globalization, this question must be posed within an international and not merely a national context. Since the exercise of agency and autonomy is a universal human right, the situation of people in developing countries must also be taken into account. The organizations that we should be most concerned about in examining this question are corporations, because of their enormous economic and sociopolitical power.

More than half of the 100 largest economies in the world are now corporations. The vast majority of the approximately 4 million patents in the world (which form the heart of intellectual property) are owned by transnational corporations from technologically advanced countries, while Third World countries, which contain about 75 percent of the world's population, own only 1 percent of world patents.[42] The monopoly rights granted by patents entail private gains by corporations at the expense of the people of developing countries. The enormous discrepancy in patent holdings exacerbates already great differences in economic power and technological capabilities between highly developed nations and the Third World, and as a result the latter are unable to draw technologically abreast, or compete on equitable terms with, the former. Given that developing countries often struggle to satisfy even the basic needs of their populace and that the fulfillment of these needs is basic for pursuing life projects, patents in effect help perpetuate material conditions that are autonomy-limiting for billions of people. Thus, a plausible case cannot be made for the general autonomy-enhancing function of existing intellectual property rights; on the contrary, it is more reasonable to maintain that they actually limit autonomy in fundamental ways for most people.

An additional problem for the claim that existing intellectual property rights promote autonomy is that in some cases they restrict the employment mobility and opportunities of individuals. Trade secret laws restrict the occupational mobility of engineers and scientists because firms are sometimes reluctant to hire them for fear of exposing themselves to lawsuits from firms concerned that their former employees may divulge secret technical or scientific information. Surely the autonomy of these skilled individuals is not furthered by restrictions in their capacity to exercise the technical training they have worked long and hard to acquire and in which they have invested considerable amounts of money.

The second version of the agency and autonomy argument, which is intended to apply to trade secrets and is based on respect for the privacy and autonomy of the individual, is also not convincing. Paine's suggestion that the denial of trade secret laws would mean state control of the initial disclosure of privately created intellectual products is questionable, because this kind of state coercion is simply not entailed by the denial of trade secret laws. In societies without such laws, governments do not force individuals to divulge the products of their intellectual activity. But her claim that respect for individual privacy implies granting individuals the right to control the dissemination of their ideas is more plausible. Part of our understanding of privacy (at least in most societies) includes recognition of a person's right to choose the conditions of dissemination of her thoughts, including sources of disclosure and confidentiality conditions. Ordinarily, when we disclose information of a deeply personal nature we consider carefully to whom we disclose it and the likelihood of its being held in confidence.

The plausibility of the privacy argument, however, vanishes when we consider that corporations are the primary holders of trade secrets and that the subject matter of trade secrets does not involve personal matters, but business information that enhances competitive advantages in the marketplace. The function of trade secret laws is not to protect individual privacy, but to support business (primarily corporate) interests in controlling the accessibility of certain kinds of information. Of course, one could respond here that there are important independent reasons, such as providing incentives for innovation and increasing the long-term availability of knowledge, for controlling such information, but the rationale then shifts from privacy concerns to social utility.

The latter point brings us to the most widely held rationale for intellectual property rights, namely, social utility. Hettinger's description of the argument serves as a reminder of this legitimizing strategy.

> Without the copyright, patent, and trade secret property protections, adequate incentives for the creation of a socially optimal output of intellectual products would not exist. If competitors could simply copy books, movies, and records, and take one another's inventions and business techniques, there would be no incentive to spend the vast amounts of time, energy, and money necessary to develop these products and techniques. It would be in each firm's self-interest to let others develop products, and then mimic the result. No one would engage in original development, and consequently no

new writings, inventions, or business techniques would be developed. To avoid this disastrous result, the argument claims, we must continue to grant intellectual property rights.[43]

In evaluating the social utilitarian basis for intellectual property rights, it is important to note from the outset the familiar difficulty of grounding rights solely on a utilitarian basis. The problem with this approach is that the factors on which the justificatory basis depends vary depending on empirical contingencies which may yield different utility outcomes in different situations. Unless we have reason to believe that these factors are intrinsic and immutable (an unwarranted assumption given the diversity of motivational factors and normative social ideals in different cultural contexts), it is unlikely that a universal human right can be grounded on such a consequentialist basis. It may therefore be more appropriate, when trying to justify intellectual property rights on a socially utilitarian basis, to understand these rights as social policy goals rather than basic human rights.

Having noted this qualification, what claims over intellectual property should a society recognize on the basis of social utility? The most important consideration here is whether existing intellectual property rights actually promote socially beneficial consequences. Evidence suggests that they may not. We have already noted the function of patents in maintaining technological and economic inequalities between developing countries, which contain most of the world's population, and technologically advanced countries. Patents also reinforce inequities at the national level by creating monopolies that stifle competition and make it very difficult for small companies to compete against corporate giants. The practice of buying up patents, for example, is frequently used by large corporations to suppress competition[44] and create profits from the innovations of others, while their capacity to fund research gives them an inordinate advantage over small firms in obtaining new patents.

Furthermore, research and innovation are often guided by profit and not social utility. For instance, in the area of energy consumption, enormous amounts of money are spent perfecting highly profitable but ecologically unsound fossil fuel technologies that degrade the environment while making communities subject to centralized technocratic control of their energy needs. One of the most extensive and profitable areas of technological innovation is military research, that fuels a weapons industry which destabilizes societies throughout the world. In addition, trade secrets, by protecting the disclosure of information of a firm's most profitable products, prevents firms from focusing on one another's most successful products and thus stifles competition.[45] And, as observed earlier, trade secrets can also restrict the inter-firm mobility of scientists and engineers, and thus slow the transmission and use of technical innovations.

These considerations do not establish that intellectual property rights do not provide profit incentives for research and innovation, since there is little doubt that they do. Rather, the point is that in significant ways, existing institutions of intellectual property fail to produce socially utilitarian consequences. The relevant question should thus be whether existing property statutes can be modified or replaced by alternative regulations which produce socially beneficial goals while promoting competitive efficiency. Our discussion suggests that certain changes in intellectual property rights—such as restrictions in trade secret laws that stifle competition, changes in patent laws to arrest the formation of national and international monopolies, and public support of ecologically sound technologies that once developed would be part of the public domain—would be helpful in promoting social utility and competitiveness. Government has an essential role to play in providing incentives and imposing restrictions when they clearly further the common good. In their present form intellectual property rights promote neither social justice nor competitive efficiency.

It seems unadvisable, however, to eliminate all forms of intellectual property rights and replace them with public subsidy. Decentralized decision making is an important component of scientific, artistic, and technological research and progress. In technologically sophisticated societies it is important that incentives be provided for individual creativity to flourish in a diversity of ways. It is questionable whether centralized bureaucracies are always the best mechanisms for identifying the ideas and inventions most worthy of development or determining the serendipitous ways in which inventions and technological innovations can be used. Centralized control of technological and scientific development is also susceptible to the familiar problems of political favoritism and limitation of vision. In addition, certain intellectual property rights—copyrights in particular—play a crucial role in protecting the integrity of artistic works.[46] Deciding which intellectual property rights to retain, and in what form, is a complex matter that can only be decided by taking into account the kind of considerations we have discussed here. What is clear, however, is that intellectual property rights in their present form need to be significantly modified to promote ideals of social justice and utility.

Local Knowledge, Intellectual Property Rights, and Indigenous Groups

Concerns over loss of cultural and biological diversity has brought to the forefront many interconnected issues concerning local knowledge, indigenous groups, biological stewardship, and intellectual property rights. For centuries indigenous groups[47] in many parts of the world have developed plant hybrids, studied the medicinal uses of numerous plants, and preserved and enriched the natural world. Some of the most widely used crop varieties and the active ingredients in many pharmaceuticals are based on biological resources originally developed by indigenous people. It is estimated that the annual value of pharmaceuticals sold worldwide that are derived from plants discovered by indigenous peoples is 43 billion dollars.[48] Botanists have yet to classify and study thousands of species of biologically active flora in territories inhabited by indigenous groups. Despite the great proven and potential usefulness of the biological resources that exist in the regions they inhabit, both indigenous people and their territories have been increasingly threatened in recent years. On the one hand, deforestation, industrial expansion, and environmental degradation have caused serious depletions in the biological diversity of these areas, and on the other, economic displacement, forceful appropriation of their natural resources, continuing discrimination, and exogenous military conflicts threaten the members of indigenous communities.

There is an emerging realization among conservationists, natural and social scientists, indigenous and nonindigenous political activists, and even corporate parties that the ecological viability of the earth's most biologically diverse regions is intertwined with the fate of indigenous peoples. This realization is prompted by several factors: the most abundant repositories of genetic information lie in territories inhabited by native groups, these groups possess invaluable knowledge for classifying and accessing plants useful to pharmacology and industry, and they are the best and most experienced stewards of biological diversity.[49] Continued protection and nurturing of these biologically rich regions can best be accomplished by the continued existence and viability of indigenous communities. This is because the ethnobotanical knowledge and patterns of behavior of indigenous groups are by nature collective and cooperative and can best be maintained within the context of living, thriving communities.

Granting intellectual property rights to protect the biological resources and knowledge of indigenous communities has been proposed as a mechanism by which these communities can receive compensation for their contributions to the development and maintenance of biological diversity. Intellectual property rights for these groups appears to be a wise choice because it would simultaneously accomplish three important goals: first, it would rectify the continuing injustice of not compensating indigenous communities for their historical role in promoting biological diversification; second, by providing monetary compensation, it would further the self-determination and survival of communities whose cultural and biotic knowledge are valuable parts of the common heritage of humankind; and third, it would provide an incentive for these communities to retain their ecological knowledge and continue nurturing biologically fertile areas. The institution of intellectual property rights, given its widespread acceptability by the international community, seems to be a feasible mechanism for resolving some of the central issues related to the preservation of biological and cultural diversity.

Enthusiasm for intellectual property rights, however, has been dampened by the practical and structural problems that stand in the way of their implementation. For instance, if part of the motivation for granting such rights is compensation for contributing to ethnobotanical knowledge and the preservation of biodiversity, the source of particular biological and epistemic resources must be identified. But biological resources and knowledge have traditionally been treated in indigenous communities as components of a common heritage usually involving the contributions of many generations of farmers from different regions. Often there is no clear way to determine who should be compensated for specific medicinal knowledge, plant hybrids, seeds, and landraces, and it surely appears morally arbitrary to reward only those individuals or communities who happened to be in possession of these biological and epistemic resources at the time compensation was meted out.

To circumvent the practical problems of identifying the source of biological knowledge and resources, it has been suggested that intellectual property rights or remuneration should be based not on compensation for past contributions, but on rewards for future conservation services.[50] The latter is a forward-looking approach that compensates indigenous and peasant farmers for their role in conserving valuable genetic resources. The advocates of this approach point out that these farmers could obtain a higher income or produce more food by abandoning traditional crop genetic resources and using available new technologies and crop varieties to produce higher yields. By remunerating them with intellectual property rights or contracts, these farmers would be compensated for the losses they incur by foregoing more lucrative methods of cultivation for the sake of preserving biological resources. This solution, however, faces problems of its own. Under present intellectual property laws, geneticists can breed new commercial plant-varieties—using existing local plant-varieties—without being required to compensate farmers who claim ownership of those local plant-varieties. Also, in many breeding programs genetic materials from many different sources are used, so that it is difficult or practically impossible to isolate the value contributed by a particular biological source.

But there are problems of a more basic or structural sort with providing indigenous communities with intellectual property rights. These rights would likely weaken or destroy precisely those cultural characteristics which make indigenous communities such effective innovators and stewards of biological diversity. By importing a mercantile reward system that is essentially at odds with the community economies that exist in indigenous communities, we would be undermining the cultural and economic structures that sustain these communities. To appreciate the potentially detrimental effects of intellectual property rights on indigenous communities, it is instructive to contrast market and community economies.

Community economies are located in a particular region, are mostly confined to a community of people who share a heritage, and are primarily structured to sustain a way of llfe. In these economies, which are characteristic of indigenous communities, people produce mostly for themselves and live by what they make. A central feature of community economies is the commons, which includes land and its resources, ancestors, animals, and the material and conceptual resources of the community. All members of the community work to sustain the commons, which they inherited from their ancestors and which they will bequeath to their progeny. The commons represents the focal point of unity of a community; ultimately it is that on which everyone depends for their subsistence. Participation in maintaining the commons is not merely a means to an end, but has intrinsic cultural significance. The practices of planting, harvesting, weaving, making pottery, fishing, and so forth are not done merely for their instrumental value, but also to reinforce values, patterns of living, and modes of relating to one another.

Community economies depend for their effective functioning on a high degree of sharing and interdependence among community members. The level of solidarity required in these economies is sustained by fostering the values of trust, reciprocity, and reliance on others. All members of the community, regardless of their productivity or contributions, are entitled to the satisfaction of basic needs. Finally, and most important for our purposes, in community economies intellectual innovations are the product and property of groups and not individuals. Innovations in biological resources and knowledge arise through cultural practices and numerous trials across generations. Like songs, dances, productive techniques, methods of cooking, myths, and medicines, they represent the patrimony of communities of individuals bonded by a common heritage.

By contrast, in market economies people produce mostly for others, receive wages for their labor, and are unrestricted by regional or national boundaries in their economic transactions. In these economies great emphasis is placed on competition, productivity, and efficiency in allocation of resources.[51] Relationships in the public sphere in market economies are generally impersonal and contractual, and market transactions are constrained and enforced by legal statutes. While in community economies well-being is understood comprehensively in terms of integration into the life of the community, in market economies it is conceived in terms of individual acquisition. Production in market economies is geared for profit and accumulation of capital which accrues to the individual and not to the community as a whole. Intellectual property in market economies is a means to an end, namely the acquisition of monopoly rights which result in profits. The role of intellectual property is markedly different in community economies, where it serves the function of sustaining and enriching a shared cultural tradition from which everyone can draw.[52]

We can now appreciate the extent to which intellectual property rights as conventionally understood are incompatible with the basic principles of community economies. Privatizing intellectual property in indigenous communities could undermine the traditional cooperation that has made possible the communal attainment of many ethnobotanical innovations and the preservation of biodiversity. As observed earlier, trust and solidarity are of crucial importance in maintaining the social networks of reciprocity and mutuality in which cultural knowledge is developed and biological resources are cultivated. When external mechanisms are introduced that provide incentives for individuals or groups to refrain from sharing knowledge and innovations, the free flow of information so important for progress in indigenous communities could be severely hindered or come to a halt. In addition, intellectual property rights by their very nature presuppose that intellectual objects can be decontextualized and abstracted from situated communities. Intellectual innovations are not recognized as valuable by highly technological societies unless they can be transposed and applied in very different sociocultural contexts, particularly those of First World countries. This decontextualization of cultural knowledge is likely to distort and demean indigenous conceptual resources. For instance, treating indigenous knowledge imbued with religious significance as having only instrumental value neglects its deeper cultural meaning. By validating it according to alien secular standards, it distorts our understanding of its significance for indigenous communities.

Indigenous groups often have internal knowledge partitions which specify which individuals in the community can have access to particular kinds of knowledge. In certain communities some knowledge should be known only by shamans, or women, or men. Internal knowledge partitions may be necessary for maintaining structures of meaning and divisions of labor within the community. There may also be external knowledge restrictions, that is, restrictions specifying what knowledge should not be accessible to outsiders. These restrictions can have the important functions of maintaining group membership and identity, as well as safeguarding burial sites, sacred sites, and locations used for religious ceremonies. Western researchers, through the publication of restricted knowledge or the filming of secret religious rites, have at times endangered the cultural bases of indigenous communities.[53] The issue of decontextualization serves to remind us of the need to protect different kinds of indigenous cultural knowledge, not just biological knowledge that is potentially useful to First World countries. Indigenous communities are unlikely to remain vibrant and thriving, and hence effective stewards of biological resources and ecologically important knowledge, if we do not respect the constraints they place on outsider accessibility to their cultural knowledge.

But even though the problems with granting indigenous groups intellectual property rights are significant, the status quo is just as, if not more, problematic. Biological diversity needs to be protected from industrial intrusions, environmental degradation, and corporate biopiracy; ethnobotanical knowledge should be preserved; and indigenous groups should be provided with incentives for continued stewardship. Though intellectual property rights can in a limited number of cases play a role in accomplishing these goals, a variety of culturally appropriate strategies can be employed, such as community approved prospecting contracts for biological resources, trust funds for farmers promoting *in situ* conservation, compensation in the form of training and access to ecologically sound technology, and rewards and recognition for communities or individuals who have developed new biological resources. A number of organizations have implemented or proposed principles to regulate the preservation and transfer of biological and epistemic resources. The United Nations Convention on Biological Diversity, drafted at the Earth Summit in Rio de Janeiro in 1992 and signed by more than 150 nations, identifies key conditions regulating the international transfer of biodiversity. Among the most important requirements of the Convention are the following: that user countries share equitably with provider nations the benefits derived from the utilization of biological resources, that access to biological diversity be provided only for ecologically sound uses, that the interests of local and indigenous communities be protected, that communities have the right to set conditions of access to biological resources, and that traditional forms of life relevant to the preservation of biological diversity be respected.[54]

Indigenous groups also have formed national and transnational organizations to develop and implement principles for the transfer of biological resources and ethnobotanical knowledge. These organizations include the Coordinating Body of Indigenous People's Organizations of the Amazon Basin, Organization Indigena of Surinam, Native Seeds/ SEARCH, the Continental Commission of Indigenous Nations, and the Amerindian Association of Guyana. One of their most prominent recommendations is the need for indigenous communities to play a major role in the development and implementation of conservation policies. This is a very important condition, because given the history of oppression and abuse that states have perpetrated on indigenous peoples, the latter have little reason to trust that states will negotiate in good faith on their behalf. This recommendation is also consistent with the general sociopolitical view that when considering policies that particularly affect certain groups, a just multicultural society should ensure that those groups are included in the formulation and implementation of these policies. The indigenous communities that live in the most biologically diverse areas have indispensable knowledge concerning what is required for the preservation of that biodiversity and their own cultural traditions.

Indigenous communities have also emphasized the necessity of cross-cultural communication and training to achieve understanding between user and steward groups. Differences in ideals, concerns, needs, conceptions of rationality, and methods of justification can undermine effective dialogue and mediation between these groups. Many indigenous communities, for instance, are interested in protecting not only ethnobotanical knowledge and biodiversity, but other forms of cultural knowledge as well. As noted earlier, they are concerned with protecting the internal and external epistemic restrictions that apply to religious ceremonies, burial sites, shamanistic knowledge, and other culturally sensitive areas. Recognizing the broader scope of indigenous concerns for protecting cultural knowledge will facilitate our understanding of the motivations behind restrictions they may place on outsider access to their cultural knowledge. Better cross-cultural communication will also help indigenous groups appreciate some of the concerns of user countries. In those cases in which indigenous groups engage in unfair and corrupt internal practices, for example, they will be better able to understand the efforts of user countries to promote sociopolitical guidelines that are fair to all concerned.

Probably the most important point emphasized by indigenous groups is the connection between, on the one hand, the protection of biological and epistemic resources and, on the other, the exercise of political, cultural, and economic self-determination. Only if they can control their own destinies can they be effective stewards of biological resources and protectors of their ways of life. As long as industrialized countries continue to infringe upon their capacity for self-determination through industrial, military, and political intrusions, indigenous groups are unlikely to preserve those forms of life that have created and sustained biological diversity. In this connection it is particularly important to address the environmental degradation caused by highly industrialized countries. Stewardship efforts by indigenous groups will come to naught if industrialized countries and transnational corporations continue their policies of unrestrained industrial expansion and overconsumption of global natural resources.

Notes

1. It might be argued that since most natural property in the world has been transformed through human labor, practically all property is actually mediated

property. This would undermine claims in favor of universal property rights, since there is little property which is in its natural state and, given my own arguments, it is legitimate to restrict ownership to mediated property. This argument fails because, even though it is true that most accessible natural property in the world has been transformed through human labor, this can hardly be used as a basis for restricting ownership rights to it. If proprietors restricted others from laboring on the property under their control, it would be unjustifiable for these proprietors to claim that it belongs to them because only they have labored on that property. If nonproprietors were denied the opportunity to stake ownership claims to property because they were prevented from laboring on it, this denial of opportunity would disqualify this basis of restricting ownership to natural property. What is more, in many situations the ones who actually labor on the land do not own it, and if it is transforming property through one's labor that entitles one to own it, then these wage workers would have as much, or more, of a claim to that property as the proprietor.

2. Even in advanced technological societies characterized by an optimally high degree of altruism and social solidarity, the epistemological and coordinating functions of the market would still be needed. This consideration shows that the fundamental need for markets in complex societies cannot be dispensed with by changes in prevailing social values and attitudes. This insight also shows that socialists concerned with social justice in capitalist systems should focus their attention on present property ownership relations in such systems and on the introduction of constraints based on communal and ecological soundness, and not on the rejection of market systems.

3. For a discussion of cost externalization, see Herman Daly and John Cobb, *For the Common Good* 2nd ed. (Boston: Beacon Press, 1994), p. 164.

4. The task of specifying the nature of a well-structured market system is beyond the scope of this book. However, I will return to this issue in a future volume, where I will develop a theory of the material basis of multicultural democracies.

Even though some writers may lament the individualistic values and competitive attitudes commonly engendered by market systems, as well as the other problems that usually accompany markets, this is the price we pay for technological complexity (though this would be ameliorated with properly structured markets). In materially simple community economies, extensive market systems are not necessary because it is relatively obvious what commodities are needed for subsistence, as are the divisions of labor needed for the economy to function in an efficient manner. And once again, these small decentralized communal property systems have generally been the most sustainable, egalitarian, and proven material systems.

5. Edwin C. Hettinger, "Justifying Intellectual Property," in *Intellectual Property: Moral, Legal, and International Dilemmas*, ed. Adam D. Moore (Lanham, MD: Rowman and Littlefield, 1997), p. 23.

6. Covering the cost of creating physical infrastructures and supporting social capital are not the only reasons for a society to legitimately restrict profit rights. It can also tax revenues for the purpose of protecting universal rights, including those rights, such as autonomy, that form the basis for granting property rights in the first place.

7. By offering tax incentives and lower interest rates to businesses that provide ecologically sound, communally self-reliant forms of energy production, for example, a society could promote socially desirable consequences such as ecological sustainability and material autonomy for all.

8. Included in the category of mediated property are technological forms such as information-processing, medical, and advanced scientific technologies.

9. The idea here is that by owning essential natural property, one has control of the raw materials necessary to create the forms of mediated property required to satisfy sustenance needs.

10. From these observations we can see that there is a relationship of mutual dependence between essential natural property and the primary forms of mediated property. On the one hand, the simplest forms of mediated property, such as plows and hoes, and the most sophisticated technological forms, such as silicon chips and lasers, depend on essential natural property for their construction. On the other hand, essential natural property, such as iron ore and coal, are inaccessible and unusable without the proper technologies which are part of the primary forms of mediated property. This relation of mutual dependence reinforces the view that it is not possible to separate the procurement and development of essential natural property and the primary forms of mediated property.

11. The market cannot be relied upon to give rise to primary forms of mediated property that promote economic self-reliance because, in a market system, profit will determine where research funds are channeled and what gets produced. For instance, even though solar technologies would promote greater individual and community self-reliance in energy production than petroleum-based technologies, it is the latter which have been developed to a far greater degree.

12. Here I am proceeding on the assumption that most societies (particularly the most technologically complex societies) will want to retain their present level of technological development. By no means, however, do I want to rule out the possibility that some societies, or some groups within these societies, may decide that technological simplification is a desirable goal, and accordingly will find alternative ways of employing essential natural property so that its use is consistent with the goals of a materially simpler lifestyle.

13. Here I will not consider the views that argue for decentralization and the creation of community and regional economies, even though I consider these perspectives of great importance in reflecting on the future economic development of ecologically sound, politically autonomous multicultural societies. I will consider these issues in a future work; my purpose now is to show that economic alternatives exist that conform to the views of property rights that I have articulated and that could be applied to the economically and technologically complex societies in which many people now live.

14. *Market Socialism: The Current Debate*, eds. Pranab K. Bardhan and John E. Roemer (New York: Oxford University Press, 1993), p.7.

15. John E. Roemer, "A Future for Socialism," *Politics and Society*, Vol. 22 No. 4 (December 1994): 451–478. I am applying Roemer's scheme to the primary forms of mediated property only. In his theory of market socialism, ownership extends to other forms of mediated property.

16. In this form of corporate financing, firms are organized into groups called *keiretsu*, and are financed for the most part by bank loans. Each *keiretsu* is associ-

ated with a main bank. Banks organize loan packages for the firms in the group with which they are associated, and are largely responsible for monitoring the management of the firm. A bank has an incentive to discipline firms, so that its *keiretsu* can be attractive to new member firms.

17. A constraint on these small firms is that after they reach a certain large size they would become public firms.

18. Thomas E. Weisskopf, "A Democratic Enterprise-Based Market Socialism," in *Market Socialism*, Bardhan and Roemer.

19. Overall economic productivity could be understood here as measured by Gross Domestic Product, which includes the total sum of all of the goods and services transacted in a year in a given economy.

20. Note that a market system with nonuniversal private property rights that prioritized wealth redistribution and provision of welfare needs (such as the systems found in Sweden and Norway) would not protect the fundamental ownership claims and economic interests we have discussed. Since their particular systems of taxation and wealth redistribution would be subject to political renegotiation, such economic systems would not provide the stability of protection offered by the market socialist systems we have briefly examined.

21. The satisfaction of basic needs and the attainment of material self-determination are in turn necessary for the exercise of agency and autonomy. Remember that dilemmas concerning the fair distribution of essential natural property and the protection of the universal interest in the autonomy-enhancing primary forms of mediated property lead us to advocate a delimited market socialist model. This model, in addition to resolving these dilemmas better than free-market systems (recall the impossibility of solving the fair distribution problem using only market mechanisms) does not saddle us with the inefficiency and lack of productivity associated with conventional socialist models which eschew market mechanisms.

22. For an example of the problems with full-scale market socialism, see Janos Kornai, "Market Socialism Revisited," and Gerard Roland and Khalid Sekkat, "Market Socialism and the Managerial Labor Market," in *Market Socialism*, Bardhan and Roemer.

23. Discrimination is here defined as systematic practices in which decisions that negatively affect individuals in important ways are made on the basis of involuntary characteristics, such as ethnic or racial heritage. Oppression involves systematic practices which significantly hinder the individual and collective social, economic, and political development of the members of a cultural group.

24. Christopher H. Lutz and W. George Lovell, "K'iche' Maya of Guatemala," in *State of the Peoples: A Global Human Rights Report on Societies in Danger*, ed. Marc S. Miller (Boston: Beacon Press, 1993), p. 227.

25. Christopher H. Lutz, "Maya of Guatemala and Education," in *State of the Peoples*, Miller, p. 230.

26. George A. Collier and Elizabeth Lowery Quaratiello, *Basta! Land and the Zapatista Rebellion in Chiapas* (Oakland, CA: The Institute for Food and Development Policy, 1994), p. 16.

27. Ibid., p. 85.

28. Actually, the existing disfranchised communities would not even exist were it not for the unjust past actions of the state, because the individuals now com-

prising these communities would most likely not exist if the state had treated their predecessors in a just manner. So how is it possible for a group of individuals who owe their very existence to an unjust state to claim rectification for past state actions? This question forces us to rephrase our claim more precisely: The state has the obligation to rectify past injustices by compensating those groups of individuals now existing, whoever they happen to be, who are connected by ancestral lineage to the communities originally wronged by state-sponsored or tolerated discrimination and oppression. From a metaphysical-ethical standpoint, the state owes compensation to all of the possible sets of individuals ancestrally connected (and adversely affected by the past injustices) to the communities it wronged in the past. Since only one such set of individuals inhabit the actual world, however, it owes compensation to this specific set of individuals.

29. This quote from section 6 of the Civil Rights Enforcement Act is cited in Rayford W. Logan, *The Betrayal of the Negro: From Rutherford B. Hayes to Woodrow Wilson* (New York: Da Capo Press, 1997), p. 101.

30. Lerone Bennett, Jr., *Before the Mayflower: A History of Black America* (New York: Penguin Books, 1993), p. 262.

31. Ibid., p. 256–257.

32. William Z. Foster, *The Negro People in American History* (New York: International Publishers, 1954), p. 357.

33. Ibid., p. 360.

34. Limitations of space do not allow me to develop the details of the systematic discrimination and oppression experienced by Mexican-Americans in Texas and other parts of the Southwest at the end of the nineteenth and well into the twentieth century, but persuasive historical evidence exists to substantiate this legacy of domination. See, for example, David Montejano, *Anglos and Mexicans in the Making of Texas 1836–1986* (Austin, TX: University of Texas Press, 1987) and Rodolfo Acuña, *Occupied America* 2nd ed. (New York: Harper and Row, 1981).

35. By individual-centered rectificatory policies I mean social policies in which some form of preferential treatment is given to individual members of cultural minorities when they compete with majority group members for employment, educational, or training opportunities. These policies rectify differences in mediated property ownership between cultural group members to the extent that, by enhancing economic status, they facilitate the acquisition of mediated property and a base of capital-accumulation.

36. Note that the situation is different when compensation is provided to individual cultural group members, or their descendants, who have suffered state-sponsored injustices. Compensation to individual Japanese-Americans who were unjustly interned in concentration camps during World War II or compensation owed to individual Jews whose wealth was expropriated by the Nazis and deposited in Swiss banks are cases in point. In contrast to cases like these, here I am concerned with compensation applied on a *group-wide* basis.

37. A base of capital accumulation is important because in complex economies it facilitates the development of human potential by, for example, providing access to a good education and enhancing opportunities for socioeconomic advancement.

38. Lynn Paine, "Trade Secrets and the Justification of Intellectual Property: A Comment on Hettinger," in *Intellectual Property*, Moore, p. 42.

39. This is certainly true of inventions protected by patents, is perhaps less true of artistic creations such as paintings and literature, and is probably not true of certain rare kinds of trade secrets, such as customer lists. I will discuss trade secrets in what follows.

40. As we noted above, due to its nonexclusive metaphysical character intellectual property can be used by different people simultaneously and is not consumed or worn out from multiple uses. Unlike concrete forms of property, the author could have access and individual control of that intellectual property without denying others similar rights. The focus of intellectual property rights thus shifts to justifying restricting others from having such rights.

41. The state can also legitimately impose other restrictions on intellectual property rights, such as temporal limitations. With regard to technological innovations, for example, it is reasonable to suppose that in technological societies most innovations would be eventually arrived at by others if the inventor had not hit upon them. Thus, Nozick's suggestion that it is justifiable to place temporal limitations on patents corresponding to the time it would have likely taken others to have made the patented inventions appears reasonable.

42. Surendra J. Patel, "Can the Intellectual Property Rights System Serve the Interests of Indigenous Knowledge?" in *Valuing Local Knowledge: Indigenous People and Intellectual Property Rights*, eds. Stephen B. Brush and Doreen Stabinsky (Washington, D.C.: Island Press, 1996).

43. Hettinger, "Justifying Intellectual Property," in *Intellectual Property*, Moore, p. 30.

44. David Noble, *America by Design* (New York: Knopf, 1982), chapter 6, cited in *Intellectual Property*, Moore, p. 32.

45. Russell B. Stevenson, Jr., *Corporations and Information* (Baltimore: John Hopkins University Press, 1980), chapter 5.

46. This is not to say that copyright laws are ideal as they stand. Whether authors should be given greater control over their works (which now typically lies with corporate entities) merits careful consideration.

47. Indigenous groups are not the only groups who have cultivated and maintained nature. Throughout the world, peasant farmers and various ethnic groups have also fulfilled important stewardship functions. However, indigenous groups have been the primary actors in this regard, and so here I will focus on indigenous communities (even though the lines of demarcation between indigenous and nonindigenous are sometimes blurred).

48. Stephen B. Brush, "Whose Knowledge, Whose Genes, Whose Rights?," in *Valuing Local Knowledge*, Brush and Stabinsky, p. 7.

49. Ibid., p. 9.

50. See, for example, Brush.

51. Of course, merely because emphasis is placed on these features in market economies does not imply that these economies are truly efficient or competitive.

52. The characterizations we have made of community and market economies are, needless to say, approximations of empirical reality. In practice both community and market economies include features of each other. Nevertheless, there are important and substantive differences between the two kinds of economic systems, and the contrasts we have made are on the whole sufficiently accurate to allow us to speak about significant incommensurabilities between them.

53. For a discussion of the need to conceptualize indigenous rights in a broad way that goes beyond conventional intellectual property rights, see Thomas Greaves, "Tribal Rights," in *Valuing Local Knowledge*, Brush and Stabinsky, pp. 25–40.

54. These and other features of the Convention are discussed in Francesca T. Grifo and David R. Downes, "Agreements to Collect Biodiversity for Pharmaceutical Research: Major Issues and Proposed Principles," in *Valuing Local Knowledge*, Brush and Stabinsky, pp. 283–285.

10

Developing Democratic Citizenship in Multicultural Societies

I have maintained that the conception of democracy most appropriate for multicultural societies is one that grants pride of place to public deliberation, intercultural understanding and cooperation, and communal self-determination. Initiating the process of reasoned public deliberation will in itself have salutary effects on democratic citizenship, as members of the polity learn to appreciate the merits of dialogue aimed at mutual understanding and fair consideration of diverse viewpoints. But establishing forums of public deliberation can only go so far in the absence of public-spiritedness, social trust, and a willingness among the citizenry to engage in mutual compromise. Thus we are faced with the important question: How are the civic virtues and skills necessary to achieve fruitful civic engagement and successful self-governance developed? That is, how do we systematically cultivate the character traits necessary for democratic citizenship, such as the willingness for deliberation and mutual compromise, the capacity to understand the needs and rights of others, and the commitment to civic reciprocity and social solidarity?

To be sure, civic virtue is crucial for any democratic society, given that moral diversity exists even in culturally homogeneous democracies. But the qualities of character associated with democratic citizenship are particularly important in culturally pluralistic societies, where diverse cultural identities and competing loyalties can fragment the polity. Democratic virtues and capacities are certainly essential in multicultural societies with accommodationist groups, since they seek to coexist with the dominant society in a common political and social community. Likewise, democratic citizenship is important for culturally pluralistic societies with autonomist and even secessionist groups, since the latter need to resolve a variety of political issues with the majority society. And, at the most general level, democratic citizenship is conducive to the development of the transnational civil society in which cosmopolitan democracy can take root.

The need for civic virtue is greater given the decline of community and social solidarity in contemporary democracies. As many authors have noted, in recent decades the traditional sources of social capital, such as the family, residential communities, regional identities, and civic associations, have eroded to the point where it can no longer be taken for granted that the qualities of character necessary for well functioning democracies will be routinely cultivated and reinforced. Although commentators sometimes disagree regarding the factors responsible for the decline in community, there is general concurrence that this decline exists and that it represents a real threat to democratic governance.

As the influence of traditional seedbeds of civic virtue has declined, the morality of self-interest and the influence of commercial culture have attained increasing prominence in contemporary life. As commercial culture and the ethos of the competitive market have permeated individual consciousness and societal institutions, members of the polity have lost an understanding of the common good and a sense of participation in a common life. Policy options are gauged in terms of narrowly conceived individual interests rather than on the contributions they may make to the strengthening of community, the attainment of long-term societal needs, or the improvement of the well-being of the neediest and most vulnerable members of society. The imperatives of ever greater consumption displace the priority to participate in the shared life of the community. Participation in civic affairs is dismissed as futile since the realm of politics is perceived as corrupt and corrupting of individuals, who would be wise to turn to the delimited but safe haven of family and friends.

This turning away from civic engagement is exacerbated by the lack of public spaces in which groups from different socioeconomic and ethnic backgrounds can interact to cultivate a sense of community. Likewise, the privatization of recreation cuts off the members of diverse groups from one another, as individuals retreat into their own socioeconomically circumscribed spaces. Even some well-established means for developing civic virtue have been compromised by recent developments. For instance, the greater reliance of advocacy organizations on monetary contributions rather than traditional face-to-face interactions in which their members learned and practiced civic skills diminishes the chances for developing community and democratic citizenship. That is, as participation in advocacy organizations such as environmental groups, ethnic associations, church groups, and trade unions is reduced to making financial contributions rather than donating time and energy in meetings and organizational activities, opportunities to learn and practice the arts of self-governance are lost.

What are the factors that contribute to democratic citizenship, and how do these factors promote democratic self-governance? And, more important at the practical level, by what means can a multicultural society cultivate the civic virtues and skills necessary for democratic citizenship?

In his groundbreaking work, *Making Democracy Work*,[1] Robert Putnam maintains that a civic community is crucial for the efficient functioning of democratic institutions. He defines a civic community as one that is committed to such values and practices as political equality, interpersonal trust, social solidarity, tolerance, and active participation in public affairs. To appreciate the importance of these features of a civic community, as well as the qualities of character on which they are grounded, we need to see how they promote successful self-governance. A commitment to political equality, for example, entails that citizens relate to one another on the basis of horizontal relations of mutual respect and collaboration, rather than by vertical, hierarchical relations of authority and dependence.[2] In a community that embodies the value of political equality, citizens deal with one another as equals engaged in the project of self-governance in a common political community, rather than as patrons and clients or as adversaries trying to prevail over one another in the political sphere.

The members of a civic community are interested in issues of public concern, and this interest manifests itself through participation in civic affairs. Citizen devotion to public causes, however, need not be based on a high level of altruism and a ready willingness to sacrifice one's interests for the sake of the common good. Rather, civic consciousness is based on a recognition that the self-interests of citizens are best served when broader public concerns are taken into account. That is, self-interest in a civic community is informed and moderated by the realization that the general well-being of a community is a crucial component of the self-interest of its individual members. This enlightened self-interest is aware of and responsive to the needs and interests of others.[3]

In a civic community, members also exhibit social solidarity, trust, and tolerance. These civic traits represent strong interpersonal bonds that go beyond mutual recognition of political equality in a common political community. When citizens exhibit these traits, a civic environment is created which facilitates cooperative political interaction aimed at resolving common problems in a way that respects differences and takes the interests of others into account. But though these traits are not reducible to a mutual recognition of formal equality, neither do they entail ideological homogeneity. As Putnam states, "Virtuous citizens are helpful, respectful, and trustful toward one another, even when they differ on matters of substance. The civic community is not likely to be blandly conflict-free, for its citizens have strong views on public issues, but they are tolerant of their opponents."[4] Social solidarity, trust, and tolerance create a civic environment in which citizens can disagree while respecting the prerogative of other citizens to hold political and moral commitments that may be profoundly different from their own. These civic bonds approximate the conception of generalized friendship that Aristotle believed should hold between the members of the same political community.

When the civic qualities of solidarity, trust, and tolerance are properly understood, they do not presuppose a political community comprised of altruistic, selfless, homogeneous individuals. Even though the members of a civic community do express altruism in their beliefs and practices, this altruism arises from a combination of cognitive capacities and moral orientations that result in a balancing of individual and communal interests. In a civic community individuals appreciate the interconnections between private preferences and public concerns, and they understand that the political sphere is not merely a means for furthering their own private interests. Public-spirited citizens know that as trust and tolerance within the polity decline, it becomes more difficult for citizens to moderate their demands, maintain social cohesion, and arrive at social policies that take everyone's interests into account. Rather than personalizing and privatizing political views so that ideological disagreements become personal attacks, civic citizens are prone to consider the public domain as a space for the mutual articulation and understanding of the diverse needs and interests of the members of the polity.

What social structures and practices engender and reinforce civic virtue, and how do they cultivate democratic citizenship? Of primary importance for creating a civic community are networks of civic engagement. As Putnam points out, civil and political associations promote successful democratic self-governance at two levels: at the "internal" or individual level they instill orientations for cooperation, solidarity, and public-spiritedness, and at the "external" or social-structural level they promote the articulation of interests and facilitate the aggregation or confluence of individual interests.[5]

The internal effects of civic associations on the individual members of the polity have been empirically confirmed by the extensive surveys of citizens in five countries that were conducted by the authors of *The Civic Culture*.[6] The authors of this work discovered that individuals who participated in civic organizations were more politically sophisticated, exhibited greater social trust and general civic competence, and were more politically involved than individuals who were not members of such organizations. Their study also revealed that participants in civic associations developed collaborative skills and a sense of collective responsibility. Other studies have shown that when individuals participate in groups with varied goals and a diverse membership, they tend to moderate their attitudes and perspectives as a result of their interactions with other group members.[7] The salutary effects of membership in civic associations were evident even when people joined organizations whose ostensible goals were not political. Civic skills and orientations were developed in sports clubs and choral societies as well as in political advocacy organizations.[8]

At the external, social-structural level, civic associations contribute to the articulation and aggregation of interests. That is, to the extent that associations adopt or promote a particular perspective, the latter must be more clearly articulated and focused than if it was held by an isolated individual.[9] When individuals come together in an organized fashion to promote a particular view or goal, their different understandings must coalesce and become more precise in order for collective action geared toward promulgating that view or attaining that goal to be successful. The need to coordinate efforts and understandings for the sake of collective objectives contributes not only to the clarification of these objectives, but also to the enthusiasm which drives members to achieve them. This process of interest articulation and aggregation inculcates skills and attitudes which facilitate fruitful civic engagement and which are useful for attaining other goals in the public domain.

Other research has underscored the importance of civic associations for attaining the wherewithal for successful social and economic development. Milton Esman and Norman Uphoff point out that in developing countries, voluntary organizations play a crucial role in rural development.[10] These authors indicate that the most successful organizations contributing to social development are those that have a grassroots foundation, and not those that are "imported" from outside local communities. In other words, the most efficacious civic organizations are those that are based on the cultural resources of local communities and that are initiated by members of local populations, and not those that are designed with a different, exogenous set of values and assumptions.

Democratic Institutions and Social Capital

In order to function effectively, any democratic society must rely on factors such as norms and social networks to coordinate the actions of members of the polity to accomplish collective goals. These factors could be understood as social capital, because they enable a society to produce desired objectives that it would otherwise not be able to achieve. In the absence of social capital, a society will find it difficult to resolve certain dilemmas of collective action. For example, it is crucial for a smoothly functioning society that its members deal honestly and fairly with one another, that they hold their government to high standards, and that they comply with rules and regulations. By contrast, in a society with an absence of social trust individuals will not be able to assume that other individuals will obey the law or keep their agreements. If each person assumes that others will shirk their obligations, it will actually be rational for each person to shirk their obligations themselves, assuming that they do not get caught or pay prohibitively high costs in doing so. In a social environment in which it is understood that laws are made to be broken and commitments are made to be breached, a person would be a naïve fool to be the only one to obey rules and agreements. In a social milieu of mutual distrust, individuals will try to get away with as much as they can unless coercive means are introduced to dissuade them from acting in this manner.

Coercive or authoritarian mechanisms for enforcing social statutes and agreements, however, are costly both in terms of efficiency and in terms of their negative impact on the quality of life in a society. Aside from the fact that the costs of complex regulatory bureaucracies and punitive institutions that compel individuals to act appropriately can be quite high, there is another perhaps more basic problem that emerges when coercive means are employed. This problem arises because there is a need to oversee the people in charge of using the mechanisms of coercion to ensure compliance.[11] In other words, if strong authoritarian institutions are put in place to oversee peoples' behavior, who controls the overseers? If the ethos of the society as a whole is based on narrowly construed self-interest, why should we suppose that those in charge of the most authoritarian and powerful policing institutions will not act like those they oversee? In authoritarian societies with an absence of social trust, interactions between the citizenry and those that control the levers of power, rather than being based on equality of treatment and the rule of law, are likely to take the form of personalism, favoritism, and patron-client relationships.

Putnam points out that two of the most important sources of social trust in contemporary societies are norms of reciprocity and networks of civic engagement. Generalized reciprocity is probably the most basic norm in a civic community. This form of reciprocity, according to Putnam, "refers to a continuing relationship of exchange that is at any given time unrequited or imbalanced, but that involves mutual expectations that a benefit granted now should be repaid in the future."[12] In other words, generalized reciprocity entails the performance of actions which benefit one's fellow citizens even though the precise way in which those actions will be reciprocated is not clear. This norm embodies the civic trust or faith that a beneficial action will be returned at an uncertain future in a yet unspecified way. Generalized reciprocity involves short-term altruistic actions that have the effect of typically benefiting everyone in the long run. By providing long-term advantages that benefit the society as a whole, the norm of generalized reciprocity conciliates social solidarity and self-interest. Like many other norms in a civic community, generalized reciprocity is self-reinforcing, in the sense that repeated episodes of reciprocity increase the likelihood that more members of society will adopt this norm to guide their own behavior.

Networks of civic engagement are another source of democratic virtue. Neighborhood associations, teacher-parent groups, labor unions, sports clubs, environmental groups, and ethnic organizations, for instance, are social environments in which people develop, *inter alia,* a sense of collective responsibility and skills of cooperation to achieve predetermined goals. As Putnam points out, an important feature of such voluntary associations is that their members relate to one another on the basis of "horizontal" relations in which their equality is recognized, rather than on the basis of "vertical" relations of authority and dependence. In general, the more closely knit these associations are, the more effectively their members will be able to cooperate to achieve their goals. By participating in horizontally structured networks of civic engagement, citizens are able to experience and understand the concrete implementation of the civic ideals of equality and inclusion.

Putnam maintains that networks of civic engagement are also able to develop character traits that are important for a democratic society because they reduce opportunism and noncompliance of rules and social agreements. Individuals will be aware that failure to comply with their responsibilities and agreements will be costly, because it will jeopardize future benefits that they expect from their relationships and social interactions. Since individuals who take part in these networks are involved in a number of different interactions and activities over time, it is not to their advantage to shirk their obligations. The high degree of interaction within these networks facilitates the exchange of information regarding the trustworthiness of participants, and makes possible the development of mutual trust. The latter in turn lays the basis for better cooperation among the members of voluntary associations.

Finally, networks of civic engagement provide a "culturally-defined template" that can be used to initiate future collaborative projects.[13] In other words, these networks serve to create a social environment in which collective practices based on cooperation, social trust, mutual responsibility, and other civic traits can be routinely recreated. By promoting civic patterns of interaction, these networks reinforce orientations within the citizenry that are conducive to effective collective action. In networks of civic engagement, citizens internalize attitudes and practice skills that carry over into the political sphere. Unlike kinship ties which are stronger and more enduring, the bonds developed in networks of civic engagement are weaker but more inclusive. Because ties of shared membership in civic associations can range over a broader social spectrum, they are more conducive than kinship ties to creating community cohesion and to promoting general cooperative behavior. Since the relatively weaker bonds created in civic networks can cut across social differences, and are not restricted to small, specific groups based on kinship, they can play a crucial role in the development of general social solidarity.[14]

In addition to instilling within the polity qualities of democratic citizenship, civic associations also serve a mediating function between society and formal governmental institutions. By providing citizens with a forum for the collective articulation and public expression of community problems and concerns, civic associations can inform governments of issues they have inadvertently or intentionally failed to address. The independent and grassroots character of civic associations enable them to introduce a variety of otherwise excluded perspectives into public discourse and, if necessary, challenge the government's position on issues of concern to substate communities. By broadening the range of voices on public issues, they heighten civic awareness of the diversity of needs and perspectives that should be taken into account in arriving at communally adequate solutions to social problems. Their capacity to respond quickly to local, regional, national, and even international problems makes them valuable alternative bases for civic action. While governmental institutions typically react slowly to changing needs and are always in danger of losing touch with their original social functions, civic associations are often grassroots movements that remain closely connected to the communities whose problems they intend to address. Civic associations can also be adept at challenging ossified governmental institutions that are unduly influenced by powerful interest groups or entrenched bureaucracies.

The mediating and mutual aid roles of civic organizations are particularly important in multicultural societies in which ethnocultural communities may be disadvantaged by inequitable political representation and socioeconomic inequalities. Such organizations serve as mechanisms of self-help for ethnocultural groups, whose problems may not be adequately addressed or understood by official governmental institutions. It is significant to note that the number of civic organizations throughout the world that address environmental, economic, cultural, and political issues has increased dramatically in recent years. In Brazil, for instance, the participation of 2.8 million people in the enormously successful Citizenship Action Against Misery and For Life made a significant impact on the level of hunger. In Peru, 300,000 indigenous people have joined forces through local and regional organizations to defend indigenous land rights and protect the ecological integrity of their homelands. Native American civic associations in North Dakota succeeded in blocking a plan by Honeywell corporation to build a nuclear weapons testing site on their land. Global Action Plan International facilitates information exchange and mutual support among more than 7,500 households in Europe and North America that want to develop environmentally sustainable lifestyles.

For the reasons enumerated above, we can appreciate the importance of civic associations for the development of the capacities and the qualities of character relevant for democratic citizenship. Moreover, we have seen that civic associations can play an important role in responding to the vital needs of communities, and that they can be a major source of self-empowerment and mutual aid for ethnocultural and other groups. The support of associational life is one of the most important steps a society can take to cultivate democratic citizenship and to provide communities with the wherewithal to address and resolve problems using their cultural and material resources. There are, however, certain considerations regarding associational activities that Putnam does not take into account, and that must be addressed before civil associations can have a full positive impact on democratic societies. Michael Walzer, who also argues that supporting civil society is crucial for democratic societies, points out that voluntary associations are beset by problems that hinder their effectiveness. He identifies three obstacles that stand in the way of restoring civil society: inequality, fitfulness, and fragmentation.

Walzer contends that the major forms of inequality that exist in the general society are reproduced in civic associations. Inequalities in education, economic power, political access, and professional competence plague civil society. Those groups that are better organized, whose members have a higher level of education, that have access to sources of political power, and that can draw from more wealthy contributors, will be more effective in achieving their goals and implementing their political agendas than groups that are relatively disadvantaged in these areas. Walzer points out that in the U.S., approximately 60 percent of the money spent by Jewish foundations and Catholic charities is derived from public funds. Unlike weaker groups, such as black Baptist organizations, the former use their greater access to political power and their institutional and material advantages to obtain a proportionately greater share of tax money to fund their activities. These inequalities can have detrimental effects in multicultural democracies in which socioeconomic and political differences between cultural groups already exist, because they can reinforce intercultural inequalities. If the revitalization of civil society is to serve the purpose of creating just multicultural societies characterized by social trust and solidarity, the potential of civic associations to magnify existing intercultural group differences cannot be overlooked.

A second problem that afflicts civil organizations is the "fitful" or unsystematic character of associational activity. Walzer points out that participation in civic associations is generally intermittent, part-time, and undisciplined. Most people, even when they are intensely concerned about a particular social cause, do not have the time or resources to devote themselves full-time to associational activities. Their participation is likely to occur after-hours, when the work at home or the office or factory has been done. Further, more urgent obligations sometimes interfere with voluntary commitments, and many people find themselves drifting in and out of intensive participation in associational activities. The absence of continuity that results from the fitful nature of work in associational participation diminishes the efficiency of civic organizations. The lack of material rewards and social recognition for associational activities does not help matters. For the ordinary volunteer who takes care of the everyday, mundane details in civic organizations, such work has to be self-rewarding, because there are no pensions, expense accounts, health insurance, recognition, or other benefits granted in exchange for their work.

The third obstacle to the revitalization of civil society that Walzer discusses is fragmentation. He contends that by their very nature many civic organizations are particularistic. That is, they advance the particular interests and objectives of specific groups. Indeed, an important reason why these organizations can inspire such strong commitments and intense solidarities is due to the fact that they address the needs of particular and enclosed groups. The problem thus arises that by strengthening these groups, we can intensify the divisions within civil society. Ironically, even though participation in voluntary organizations develops democratic capacities and promotes political participation, supporting the revitalization of associational life will most likely come with a price, namely, the fragmentation of society. The danger of fragmentation is exacerbated in societies permeated by the ethos of individualism, competitiveness, and parochialism. Professional organizations, labor unions, ethnic advocacy associations, and even religious organizations can become so narrowly focused on their own agendas that they lose sight of the need to balance and moderate their interests in relation to those of the greater society. And of course, the most extreme examples of voluntary associations with detrimental effects on the building of community are groups such as the Ku Klux Klan and Minutemen organizations.

To contravene the obstacles of inequality, fitfulness, and fragmentation that limit the beneficial impact that civic organizations have on democratic governance, Walzer advocates public funding of associational life. He recommends providing subsistence pay and benefits for individuals willing to spend part or all of their working lives in civil society. A real commitment on the part of these workers would still be needed, because at least some of them would have to forego higher pay in other forms of employment. But at least the monetary compensation would make it possible for them to make a commitment to civic associations that they would not otherwise be able to make, and it would send a strong symbolic and tangible social message that their work is valuable and worthy of public support. The payments would also prevent some of the problems caused by volunteers being forced to stop their associational work due to financial reasons. Knowing that their work would provide a steady source of income would allow them to make long-term commitments to civic organizations. The continuity of employment would reduce the fitfulness of associational activity, and it would strengthen the organizational structure and overall effectiveness of civic associations. In addition, because the payments would be the same for volunteers in different organizations, they would help to equalize existing differences in resources and effectiveness of different civic associations. This would be a particularly important consequence for the weaker ethnocultural group organizations. Finally, since the nominal salaries would come from public funds, it would reinforce in volunteers the idea that their work in civil society, rather than serving particular interests only, should be understood within the context of the needs and interests of the greater society.

Walzer's recommendation regarding the public funding of associational work is a useful and interesting suggestion, one that I believe could be highly beneficial and is worthy of careful consideration. To be sure, the citizenry in most democratic societies would have to be educated regarding the importance of civic associations before they would go along with the idea of payments for work in voluntary organizations. On the other hand, the ideas of self-help and mutual aid have broad political appeal in many democratic countries, and civic associations have been shown to promote these social ideals. The widespread recognition that civil society in many contemporary democracies has significantly deteriorated should also help in making a case for public support of the revitalization of associational life. But despite the fact that some work has to be done before the idea of public funding for volunteering in civic organizations can be accepted, an important question remains unanswered, namely, whether state support of associational activities can successfully deal with the problem of fragmentation. Even though Walzer recognizes the potential dangers of social fragmentation resulting from the strengthening of certain civic associations, he does not provide any recommendations for dealing with this problem. He merely indicates that there must be general solidarity among the citizenry to balance the particularistic identities based on religion, ethnicity, region, class, and other specific characteristics.

Ecological Consciousness and Social Solidarity

I agree that multicultural societies should cultivate a broad sense of solidarity among the citizenry, the question is how to do this. How can we create a broad moral and cognitive vision that enables all of the members of a culturally diverse political community to see themselves as having a shared destiny and a collective responsibility for the fate of their community? How does a political community cultivate in its citizens moral commitments and sentiments that transcend their self-interests and group loyalties? In the second part of this chapter I will argue that ecological consciousness can be a useful vehicle for developing the moral, cognitive, and affective character traits conducive to social solidarity in multicultural societies. I begin by considering the revival of religious tradition as a way of developing social solidarity in a pluralistic democracy.

A straightforward way in which a stronger commitment to moral convictions and sentiments could be developed is through a revitalization of religious traditions. In *Habits of the Heart*,[15] Robert Bellah and his associates advocate the revival of the biblical tradition to stem the rise of individualism and the deterioration of community in the U.S. They argue that contemporary American society has lost a broad normative vision that can be the basis for building communal solidarity and counteracting the morality of self-interest. They discuss how in earlier times the biblical tradition provided a moral language to articulate communal commitments and served as the foundation for a shared consensus of values. Bellah and his colleagues believe that religion can provide a morally compelling and comprehensive perspective that can go a long way to remedy the existing fragmentation of contemporary life in America.

There is little doubt that religion can serve as a powerful force for building community and group solidarity. Religion has served throughout history as a great source of devotion to socially beneficial causes, and has provided communities with a sense of historical memory and narrative unity. By providing individuals with a sense of connection with something that transcends their existence, religion makes it possible for people to attain a sense of meaning and cosmic integration in their lives. The power of religion is that it can very effectively integrate the moral, cognitive, and affective dimensions of the self into a cohesive unity that in turn serves as a basis for communal identity. The problem with relying on a religious tradition to build social solidarity, however, is that in a multicultural society the members of those groups who do not adhere to that particular religious tradition will feel marginalized. By emphasizing a specific religious tradition, a culturally pluralistic society runs the risk of undermining the capacity of some members of the polity to flourish in accordance with their different religious orientation. The more a political community reinforces a specific religious tradition, the easier it becomes for attitudes of exclusion to take root within the majority society. On the other hand, if an effort is made to reinforce all of the religious traditions in a multicultural society, divisiveness and conflict are distinct possibilities. Some of the most hateful and intractable intercultural conflicts occur in countries with strong religious fervor. Religious conflicts in India, Northern Ireland, and the Middle East are a clear testament to the problems that can arise in political communities that are strongly divided along religious fault lines. By strengthening all of the religious traditions in a multicultural political community, we would not fare much better than by selecting one religious tradition to the exclusion of all the others.

What we need is a moral, conceptual, and affective framework or orientation that approaches creating the kind of solidarity that religion engenders without the divisiveness that religion can bring about. This framework should be capable of commanding general assent, and should not exacerbate divisions that already exist within pluralistic societies. It must unify without excluding, and must be substantive enough to make a real difference in the way people see themselves and relate to one another. Ideally this framework would be capable of transforming our cognitive and moral orientations in a direction that is beneficial and useful for living in a multicultural society. Finally, it must create solidarity in particular political communities without the negative effects of nationalistic fervor—which can be as detrimental as those of religious fervor—and contribute to the global solidarity necessary for creating the desirable cosmopolitan democratic institutions we discussed earlier. I believe that ecological consciousness is the only framework that even approaches satisfying all of these conditions.

Before discussing the crucial salutary effects of ecological consciousness on multicultural societies, it is important to recognize that there are compelling independent reasons for adopting an ecological perspective. The stress on the biosphere from human consumption of food, potable water, and fossil fuels, and the use of arable land and other natural resources, is greater than at any point in history. With an ever growing global population, this rising level of consumption (and the waste products created as a result) will create greater stress on the earth's ecosystems. Consider the effects of global warming on the biosphere. There has been a long-term global warming trend in the last century, and it has been particularly pronounced in the final quarter of the 20th century. The rate of warming in the last 25 years has been more than twice that of the 20th century average. If this rate of increase continues, in the next 100 years the global temperature will increase by about 3.5 degrees Fahrenheit. If this figure seems insignificant, consider that the global temperature increase since the last ice age 18,000 to 20,000 years ago has been only 5 to 9 degrees. An increase of the magnitude of 3.5 degrees Fahrenheit in the next century would cause significant and widespread climatic and environmental disruptions, including the rising of sea levels, more extreme weather, and disruptive changes in precipitation patterns in agricultural areas. The evidence of global warming and its causes is sufficiently compelling that now the dominant scientific position is that global warming is at least partly caused by fossil fuel emissions trapped in the atmosphere. Fuel emissions are created by human use of oil, coal, and natural gas. Moreover, there are other environmental issues besides global warming that are a cause for serious concern, such as the loss of biodiversity (plant and animal species) and the world-wide deterioration and insufficiency of fisheries, arable land, and fresh water sources, which are the natural resource bases for sustaining human life.

The point in mentioning the seriousness of ecological issues is that political communities must at some point come to terms with the fact that human political and economic decisions exacerbate or alleviate environmental dilemmas. This is true regardless of the broader implications that the development of ecological consciousness may have on social solidarity in multicultural societies. If the human species is to survive, environmental pollution, destruction of biodiversity, deterioration of natural resource bases, and uncontrolled population growth cannot continue unabated. Sooner or later, political communities must address the ecological dilemmas that we collectively face. Environmental problems will not go away, and the longer we neglect them, the worse they will get. Reckoning with environmental problems can be postponed temporarily, but not indefinitely, and at some point in human history all sustainable political communities will have to be ecological communities. In other words, if the integrity of the biosphere that is necessary for sustaining human life is to be protected, facing ecological dilemmas is inevitable. Regardless of how skeptical or cynical we may be concerning the beneficial effects of ecological consciousness for multicultural democracies, the latter is a perspective that, if we are to survive, we have in any case powerful independent reasons for adopting.

The Moral Implications of Ecological Consciousness

In order to identify the ways in which ecological consciousness can help multicultural political communities develop social solidarity by instilling a sense of collective moral responsibility and common purpose, it is important to first understand the interconnectedness and interdependence that characterize the natural world. Aldo Leopold provides a succinct description of the interconnectedness of ecosystems in the following passage.

> Plants absorb energy from the sun. This energy flows through a circuit called the biota, which may be represented by a pyramid consisting of layers. The bottom layer is the soil. A plant layer rests on the soil, an insect layer on the plants, a bird and rodent layer on the insects, and so on up through various animal groups to the apex layer, which consists of the large carnivores. Proceeding upward, each successive layer decreases in numerical abundance, thus, for every carnivore there are hundreds of his prey, thousands of their prey, millions of insects, uncountable plants. The lines of dependency for food and other services are called food chains. Thus soil-corn-

cow-farmer. Each species, including ourselves, is a link in many chains. The deer eats a hundred plants other than oak, and the cow a hundred plants other than corn. Both, then, are links in a hundred chains. The pyramid is a tangle of chains so complex as to seem disorderly, yet the stability of the system proves it to be a highly organized structure.[16]

One of the consequences of the pervasive connections between natural entities is that alterations to some components of an ecosystem will affect its other components. This is readily observed when changes in links in the food chain, such as the decimation of a species, affect the survival potential of other species, or when loss of vegetation changes the climatic conditions of an ecosystem so that it is no longer a suitable habitat for some species. Change in ecosystems tends to occur slowly and, in general, to produce greater biological diversity. Human generated environmental degradation, however, often takes place with great rapidity and on a very large scale, and instead of leading to greater biological diversification, diminishes the number of plant and animal species. The rate of destruction of numerous species is occurring at a rate much greater than would normally occur in many of the world's ecosystems. It is estimated that approximately "140 species of invertebrate animals and at least one species of plant, reptile, bird, mammal or fish are exterminated *every day.*"[17]

By disseminating ecological knowledge among the citizenry, a political community can help its members recognize the potentially devastating effects that human actions can have on the biological integrity of ecosystems that are vital to our well-being. Acknowledging the impact of human decisions and actions on the environment can in turn serve as a basis for fostering a sense of collective responsibility and a sense of a shared destiny. Since we all share the same biosphere on which we depend for survival, ecological responsibility can be a powerful force in developing a communal perspective that transcends individual and group interests. Everyone has a fundamental interest in ecological survival; it does not matter whether one is a Christian, Jew, Muslim, or Buddhist, or whether one is of Asian, Western European, Latin American, Middle Eastern, or African ancestry. A common concern for survival can unify a multicultural community despite the divergent interests and values of its members. The common concern for ecological survival can be greatly reinforced by the knowledge that the world's ecosystems are interconnected, so that environmental devastation in one area will have an impact on the rest of the globe. The clearing of rain forests a continent away exacerbates global warming, the use of chlorofluorocarbons anywhere in the world harms the ozone layer, and acid rain does not respect the borders of political communities. Even when it is possible to transfer industrial hazardous wastes, such as toxic chemicals, to other communities, this simply postpones the inevitable, since eventually the world as a whole must face up to environmental damage. In an interconnected, interdependent world, ecological harm to any bioregion represents a loss to all.

If using ecological awareness to create a sense of collective responsibility seems too utopian, consider that at the global environment conference in Cairo in 1993, more heads of state congregated to discuss ecological problems than had met to examine any other issue at any time in world history. There was almost universal agreement on a wide variety of environmental issues and on the policies that would alleviate ecological degradation. Even though there were differences between countries concerning enforcement of policies and timelines for their implementation— the U.S. in particular raised objections against some policies that every other country agreed to because of their potentially negative impact on corporate profits—this conference provides an example of an emerging national and global solidarity and cooperation regarding ecological problems. Greater cooperation and solidarity within and between countries could be further generated by making ecological education a priority of political communities.

Ecological consciousness can also expand the moral vision of a multicultural society by broadening the range of beings who should be granted moral consideration. According to most conventional ethical perspectives, only existing persons merit moral consideration. Merely possible human beings are denied status as moral selves. Thus the needs and interests of nonexisting persons are not taken into account in conventional ethical theories. A community that is ecologically conscious, however, would be acutely aware of the ways in which its economic and political decisions might affect future generations. The members of ecological communities are cognizant and morally respectful of the needs that future beings will have for the earth's resources. They would realize that by living in an environmentally unsound way, they would compromise the capacity of the life-sustaining ecosystems on which future generations will depend for their material needs. Patterns of over-consumption and ecologically destructive practices will at some point in time cause very real harm to those human beings who will be our descendants. Simply because this harm will occur in the future does not lessen its morally detrimental impact.

A multicultural society that aspires to achieve ecological consciousness could draw from the richness of its cultural resources to educate its members. Examining the worldview of some indigenous groups would be helpful for this purpose. The Native American Iroquois nation, for example, has traditionally followed the principle that no major decisions should be taken by the community until their implications for the seventh generation are carefully considered. It would be highly beneficial for contemporary societies to examine and adopt this kind of profound moral consideration for the well-being of future human beings.[18]

By educating the citizenry concerning the ways in which environmentally harmful practices negatively affect the viability of the natural resource bases on which future generations will depend, a political community can cultivate in its members an expanded sense of moral responsibility which transcends individual and group interests. A multicultural society could rely on the sense of group solidarity that exists between the members of ethnocultural groups to instill this broader moral vision. Since one of the characteristics of ethnocultural group solidarity is concern for the well-being of fellow members, and since future generations of these cultural communities will depend on the biosphere for their survival, it stands to reason that present members should be concerned about the potentially harmful effects of unsound environmental practices on future members of their communities. A salutary result of this regard for group members is that its beneficial consequences would, even if inadvertently, extend to everyone in the society. If every group in a multicultural society was seriously concerned about the impact of environmental policies on future members of their cultural community, the society as a whole would benefit, since it would be more likely that ecologically sound practices would be adopted by that society.

This last point underscores an important feature of environmental dilemmas, namely, that by their very nature their impact is inclusive and diffused; that is, they cannot be understood as being simply the concern of isolated individuals or groups, since they affect local, regional, national, and international political communities. Clean air, clean water, biodiversity of plants and animals, stable ecosystems, an intact ozone layer, uncontaminated soil, the absence of acid rain, and a stable global climate do not merely benefit one individual or group, but whole communities. While it is true that in some cases a political community can "export" its hazardous wastes—as when technologically advanced countries make contracts with Third World countries to deposit tons of toxic wastes in their territory—these practices merely postpone the day of reckoning with ecological damage to the biosphere we all share. Environmental issues can be ultimately resolved only by a coordinated effort of all political communities. The recognition that everyone has a fundamental interest in resolving ecological problems that affect every community can serve as a basis for creating social solidarity and a sense of common responsibility in multicultural societies.

The Cognitive Implications of Ecological Consciousness

Adopting an ecological perspective, besides promoting an expanded social moral vision, would also have theoretical implications conducive for engendering social solidarity. Consider the epistemological implications of an ecological perspective. The entities constituting an ecosystem are related internally to one another insofar as their nature is largely determined by their relations to the other entities, and to the properties, of their ecosystem. For instance, the structures for the assimilation of nutrients of an organism are strongly affected by the nature of its environment. The members of a species are what they are largely because of the particular niche they have found within their ecosystem. The interconnections and symbiotic relationships between natural entities are as important for understanding their constitution as their internal properties and physiological structures. This shift of focus from the substantive to the relational in understanding the nature of organisms represents a radical departure from the traditional epistemological and metaphysical orientations of Western philosophy.

Despite the great diversity of the Western philosophical and scientific tradition, it is an accurate generalization to claim that this tradition is cognitively oriented toward the substantive rather than the relational. In economics the primary loci of analyses are the decisions of a hypothetical rational, self-maximizing individual rather than the person-in-community; in medicine the dominant paradigm for curing illness is intervention in the internal physiology of the individual rather than the holistic examination of the person's physical and emotional way of life; in metaphysics the focus for 2,000 years has been on the internal constitution of substances rather than on relational or process ontologies; and in ethics the emphasis has been on the rights of individuals rather than the rights of groups or communities. Even that great repository of knowledge, the academy, is structured along compartmentalized, often rigidly segregated lines, with the occasional team-taught course or interdisciplinary program of study being the exceptions that prove the rule.

I emphasize the substance, rather than relational, orientation of Western culture in order to underscore the fundamental transformation that would occur if the holistic perspective implicit in ecological consciousness were to take hold in contemporary technological societies. Whether a conceptual scheme has a holistic or a fragmentary orientation will determine the way many aspects of the world are understood. The way we understand ourselves, our communities, our relation to nature, and our social and political institutions, for example, will all be deeply affected by our cognitive orientation. Adopting the holistic perspective of ecological consciousness would, I believe, have significant salutary social consequences. One of the first lessons that a student of natural ecologies learns is to appreciate the complexity of the interconnections that exist within ecosystems. A holistic cognitive orientation would facilitate the collective recognition that human societies have affinities with natural ecologies, and that, just as the components of the latter exhibit numerous connections and interdependencies, so the institutions and individuals comprising the former are connected and interdependent in far-reaching and important ways. It would make us more aware of how transformations in some social practices may affect other spheres of our lives. We would more readily appreciate the ways in which, for example, the privatization of recreation (e.g., watching television) has diminished the opportunities for interacting with our neighbors and building community, or the ways in which the social isolation of the family has made it harder to raise children in an environment where the moral lessons taught by parents are reinforced by the extended family, neighbors, and friends, or, finally, the ways in which our economic priorities have made it more difficult to spend the time with our children that is necessary for their proper upbringing. Furthermore, cognizance of interconnections within social ecologies would help us see that progress in one area, such as an increase in the Gross Domestic Product, might be accompanied by consequences that are not so positive, such as a sense of uprootedness caused by increased mobility or an increase in fierce economic competition with a corresponding decline in social solidarity and trust.

Being cognizant of the affinities between social and natural ecosystems would also help us see the need to care for and revitalize the practices, institutions, and values on which our society depends. Just as natural ecosystems are susceptible to disequilibrium by harmful patterns of behavior, so our social ecologies are vulnerable to deterioration as a result of socially inimical actions. We cannot continue to draw resources from natural ecosystems without being mindful of the ways in which resource depletion and the carrying capacity of bioregions can be diminished or destroyed altogether. Likewise, contemporary societies have been drawing from inherited social capital for a long time without realizing that social trust, solidarity, and reciprocity do not arise from inexhaustible sources but must be protected and cultivated. We have been assuming that we can structure our social policies on the basis of such priorities as economic growth, efficiency, and the maximizing of profit without being aware of how these priorities may negatively affect the manner in which we design our communities, achieve self-validation, or measure social progress. Recognizing the frailty of natural ecologies would make us more sensitive to the deterioration of the taken for granted cultural practices and values which are the sources of social capital.

In short, adopting the holistic perspective inherent in ecological consciousness would provide us with a better understanding of what we need to do to nurture the civic environment in which democracies can flourish. Learning to think holistically would help counteract the tendency of people in many contemporary societies to dichotomize, to withdraw, to believe that healthy democracies can survive and thrive simply by letting each individual pursue and maximize her own self-interest. If the deterioration of community and civic virtue is to be stemmed, we first need the conceptual means for adequately assessing the dilemmas that we face. While the cognitive consequences of developing ecological awareness are by no means a panacea for the weakening of civic culture, they do provide greatly needed conceptual resources and orientations for counteracting the tendency in many societies to neglect the cultivation of social solidarity.

The Affective Dimensions of Ecological Consciousness

In order for a moral perspective to take hold, it must be accompanied by a set of attitudes and sentiments that reinforce its practice. An individual may be cognizant of moral responsibilities that she is obligated to fulfill, but if she is not effectively disposed or otherwise motivated to act on them, they will likely go unfulfilled. If a moral orientation is to be actually practiced and move beyond the realm of the theoretical, it must be supported by an existing set of values and practices or else generate endogenously those attitudes and sentiments that will promote its implementation. Even though indigenous cultural groups generally hold values and follow practices that conform to the tenets of an ecological perspective, most people in contemporary societies are neither accustomed or predisposed to adopt environmentally sound patterns of behavior. As we have observed, however, the interest in ecological survival can be a powerful factor in transforming social values and practices, so that even if people are presently not interested in following ecologically sound behavior, they can be persuaded to do so. But in addition to appealing to self-preservation, the development of ecological consciousness can in itself generate attitudes and sentiments that will predispose people to follow environmentally appropriate practices. That is, in the process of acquiring an ecological perspective, individuals can also develop the affective character traits that would reinforce its practice.

One of the central features of an ecological worldview is the concept of stewardship of nature. Stewardship involves a relationship of care and nurturance between the steward and what is cared for. Rather than involving relations of manipulation and control, stewardship properly understood entails a comprehension of what is cared for and a respect for its structural integrity. A good steward would not debase that which she cares for, or disrupt its functional capacities. On the contrary, good stewardship means that one is mindful of the ways in which one's actions, as well as the actions of others, affect what one has been entrusted with. In the case of the stewardship of nature, this mindfulness takes the form of understanding the structural integrity of natural entities and ecosystems, and of paying attention to the ways in which human patterns of behavior, particularly economic behavior, affect them. It is safe to say that in the last two centuries technological progress has to a large extent been understood in terms of harnessing the forces of nature. Indeed, in some contemporary societies human progress is sometimes understood as being synonymous with control and manipulation of nature. Technological progress has brought about important benefits, such as better medical care, lower infant mortality rates, and longer life expectancy. But it has also increased stress on the biosphere as a result of population growth, greater levels of consumption, and pollution from the increased use of fossil fuels and other natural resources.

The disruption and deterioration of the earth's ecosystems and natural resource bases (such as fisheries, arable land, and rain forests) represents a collective failure of stewardship of nature. Our willingness to engage, sometimes knowingly, in environmental degradation indicates that we have not been good stewards of nature. Most contemporary societies have not fully understood the ramifications of disrupting the functional integrity of natural ecosystems. One of the reasons for this is the absence of ecological literacy among the general population and another reason has to do with the fact that the areas that experience the greatest environmental devastation are often indigent and ethnocultural minority communities. Of course, there are specialists and organizations who are knowledgeable about environmental issues and who have fought for policies to protect the environment, but in general too many people do not have an adequate comprehension of the ways in which ecological damage occurs or of its consequences. In addition, those who have the power to make decisions concerning environmental policies typically do not have to face directly the consequences of ecological devastation. Incinerators, toxic waste storage areas, polluted water canals, and factories that manufacture highly toxic chemicals, for example, are often located far from middle and upper-class neighborhoods.

An ecologically educated citizenry would know how important it is to protect and, if necessary, support the structural integrity of natural ecosystems. They would be respectful of nature's structural integrity, and would know that it has a status that is independent of human agency. Indeed, an ecologically conscious citizenry would know that human agency is itself a product of natural evolution. But most important, stewardship would involve an attitude of nurturance and care for the health of natural ecosystems. Integral, healthy ecosystems are capable of maintaining their diversity and stability, and can respond successfully to disruptive exogenous influences. Good stewardship involves protecting the functional capacity of ecosystems to maintain the complex web of interrelationships between their plants, animals, and natural properties.

The other-regarding moral sentiments of nurturance, care, and respect are essential parts of any form of stewardship that is not reducible to instrumentalist motivations. That is, any stewardship in which the natural world is valued for its own sake and not merely because it provides resources that are beneficial to human beings is likely to include moral sentiments such as concern and care. It is a complex philosophical question whether non-human animals, natural entities, and ecosystems should be regarded as having intrinsic and not merely instrumental value. Here is not the place to consider this complex issue, even though I think that a plausible case can be made for acknowledging that some natural entities have intrinsic value. The point I want to make is that, to the extent that nature is seen as having value independently of its usefulness to humans, a form of stewardship that is accompanied by the moral sentiments of respect, care, nurturance, and even affection, can be developed. It is significant to note that, practically without exception, all of those cultural groups that have a strong ecological orientation also have strong attitudes of respect, care, and love for the earth. It is as if being immersed within the natural world necessarily engenders other-regarding attitudes and sentiments toward nature.

If a form of stewardship can be developed that involves other-regarding moral sentiments, it would be beneficial for cultivating an expanded moral vision. Having respect and care for the earth is likely to enlarge our capacities for empathy. If we learn to see natural entities such as animals and ecosystems as having intrinsic value, and if we learn to respect and care for them, our conception of the beings worthy of moral considerability would be broadened. We would see ourselves as part of a larger interrelated and interdependent community of beings, whose functional integrity should be protected for the good of all. Moreover, it is reasonable to believe that, if a society adopted such a conception of stewardship, the possibilities for implementing the practices corresponding to an ecological perspective would be enhanced. The concrete implementation of an ecological perspective would, in turn, create a social setting that would foster an appreciation for the interconnections between complex systems, including natural and social ecologies.

Needless to say, it will be harder to develop this more morally encompassing conception of stewardship than one based on human self-interest. It would probably be wise to begin by developing a conception of stewardship based on the importance of protecting the environment for the sake of human interests, and gradually enrich this notion of stewardship as people deepened their understanding of the natural world and their place in it. It is significant to note, however, that even a morally truncated conception of stewardship based on self-interest would engender sentiments of care and nurturance. Given the nature of human moral psychology, it would be difficult for people to embrace a conception of stewardship that involves ongoing care and nurturance of the natural world without also developing moral sentiments that go beyond purely egocentric interests.

Ecological Literacy

None of the suggestions I have made are likely to be realized without a strong commitment by contemporary societies to ecological education. Such a commitment would involve cultivating ecologically conscious citizens from an early age through their later years. It would be particularly important during their early formative years for students to attain an understanding of the importance of protecting the integrity of the natural world. An effective pedagogical approach to ecological literacy would involve not merely the acquisition of information concerning the environment, it would also include field work where students perceive firsthand the effects of environmental degradation. Students also need to achieve an understanding of the many serious ways in which ecological damage can disrupt and in some cases destroy the lives of those affected by it. Ecological literacy should not only inform the mind, it should also cultivate an appreciation for the real human suffering created by environmental degradation.

Above all, effective ecological education should be grounded on a scientific basis capable of commanding general assent. There are many ways in which the meaning of ecological consciousness could be construed, including some based on mystical or scientifically dubious tenets. The authority of science needs to be brought to bear in the service of ecological literacy if a perspective on the environment is to have sufficient credibility to create general agreement that environmentally sound policies should be adopted. But Western science should not be the only source of knowledge used in ecological education. The vast repository of ecological wisdom of indigenous cultures should also play a prominent role in educating people about how to relate to nature in a way that respects the functional integrity of natural ecosystems. Through centuries of close observation of their environment, indigenous groups have collected a vast amount of ecological knowledge, the value and reliability of which has only recently been recognized. But perhaps more important, indigenous cultures have a great deal to teach technological societies about values and practices that are conducive to environmentally sound living. Their views of nature, of self-validation, and of sustainable living, for example, would be important for contemporary societies to know and appreciate. People in technological societies need to reflect more deeply on the connection between materialism and their views of self-validation. The influence of commercial culture on the prevailing conceptions of self-worth and unfettered consumption needs to be critically examined by the members of highly technological societies.

*   *   *

Most of this work has dealt with the normative principles and institutional arrangements that would make possible the development of just multicultural democracies in which all cultural groups would be able to flourish and coexist peacefully. I would like to end with a reminder that all theories and ideologies can be undermined by the failure of human conviction and good faith. Regardless of how theoretically compelling and cohesive a philosophical perspective may be, unless people have the moral and intellectual integrity to deal with others fairly, they will find ways to distort and circumvent, and thereby ultimately subvert, that perspective. The philosophical perspective I have articulated here is also susceptible to being thwarted in this way, and that is why I decided to end this work with a discussion of the need to engender the moral, cognitive, and affective qualities of character necessary for creating just multicultural democracies. In facing the great challenge that the creation of such societies represents, we should not lose sight of the fact that responding successfully to this challenge is not merely a matter of developing the appropriate democratic institutions, but also of properly cultivating the human soul.

Notes

1. Robert D. Putnam, *Making Democracy Work: Civic Traditions in Modern Italy* (Princeton: Princeton University Press, 1993).

2. Ibid., p. 88.

3. Ibid., p. 88.

4. Ibid., pp. 88–89.

5. Ibid., p. 89–90.

6. Gabriel A. Almond and Sidney Verba, *The Civic Culture: Political Attitudes and Democracy in Five Nations* (Princeton: Princeton University Press, 1963), chapter 11.

7. Arend Lijphart, *Democracy in Plural Societies* (New Haven: Yale University Press, 1977), pp. 10–11, Seymour Martin Lipset, *Political Man* (New York: Doubleday, 1960), and David Truman, *The Governmental Process: Political Interests and Public Opinion* (New York: Knopf, 1951). Cited in Putnam, *Making Democracy Work*, p. 90.

8. Ibid., p. 90.

9. Putnam, *Making Democracy Work*, p. 90.

10. Milton J. Esman and Norman T. Uphoff, *Local Organizations: Intermediaries in Rural Development* (Ithaca: Cornell University Press, 1984), p. 40.

11. Putnam, *Making Democracy Work*, p. 165.

12. Ibid., p. 172.

13. Ibid., p. 174.

14. Ibid., p. 175.

15. Robert Bellah, et al., *Habits of the Heart: Individualism and Commitment in American Life* (Berkeley: University of California Press, 1985).

16. Aldo Leopold, *A Sand Almanac, with Essays on Conservation from Round River* (New York: Ballantine Books, 1970), p. 252.

17. J. C. Ray, "Conserving Biological Diversity," *State of the World—1992* (London: W.W. Norton and Co., 1992), chap. 2, cited in Errol E. Harris *One World or None: Prescription for Survival* (Atlantic Highlands, NJ: Humanities Press, 1993), p. 18.

18. There is a natural convergence of interest between the self-determination claims of indigenous groups and some environmental groups. Some environmentalists are recognizing that indigenous groups are long-time stewards of the ecosystems that have among the greatest ranges of biodiversity in the world. In addition, other ethnocultural groups are mobilizing politically on the basis of environmental concerns. See, for example, *Chicano Culture, Ecology, Politics: Subversive Kin*, ed. Devon Pena (Tucson, AZ: The University of Arizona Press, 1998).

Bibliography

Acuña, Rodolfo. 1981. *Occupied America*. 2nd ed. New York: Harper and Row.

Almond, Gabriel A., and Sidney Verba. 1963. *The Civic Culture: Political Attitudes and Democracy in Five Nations*. Princeton: Princeton University Press.

Amy, Douglas J. 1993. *Real Choices/New Voices*. New York: Columbia University Press.

Anaya, James. 1996. *Indigenous Peoples in International Law*. Oxford: Oxford University Press.

Anderson, Benedict.1983. *Imagined Communities: Reflections on the Origin and Spread of Nationalism*. London: Verso.

Archibugi, Daniele, and David Held. eds. 1995. *Cosmopolitan Democracy: An Agenda for a New World Order*. Cambridge, U.K.: Polity Press.

Arthur, John, and Amy Shapiro. 1995. *Campus Wars: Multiculturalism and the Politics of Difference*. Boulder, CO: Westview Press.

Bardhan, Pranab K., and John E. Roemer. eds. 1993. *Market Socialism: The Current Debate*. New York: Oxford University Press.

Becker, Lawrence C. 1977. *Property Rights*. London: Routledge and Kegan Paul.

Beetham, David. 1999. *Democracy and Human Rights*. Malden, MA: Polity Press.

Bellah, Robert, et al. 1985. *Habits of the Heart: Individualism and Commitment in American Life*. Berkeley: University of California Press.

Bennett, Lerone Jr. 1993. *Before the Mayflower: A History of Black America*. New York: Penguin Books.

Bohman, James. 1996. *Public Deliberation: Pluralism, Complexity, and Democracy*. Cambridge, MA: MIT Press.

Bohman, James, and Wiilliam Rehg. 1997. *Deliberative Democracy: Essays on Reason and Politics*. Cambridge, MA: MIT Press.

Bookchin, Murray. 1991. *The Ecology of Freedom: The Emergence and Dissolution of Hierarchy*. Montreal: Black Rose Books.

Boucher, David, and Paul Kelly. eds. 1994. *The Social Contract From Hobbes to Rawls*. London: Routledge.

Brecher, Jeremy, and Tim Costello. 1994. *Global Village or Global Pillage: Economic Reconstruction From the Bottom Up*. Boston: Sound End Press.

Brush, Stephen B. 1996. "Whose Knowledge, Whose Genes, Whose Rights?" In Stephen B. Brush and Doreen Stabinsky, eds., *Valuing Local Knowledge: Indigenous People and Intellectual Property Rights*. Washington, DC: Island Press.

Buchanan, Allen. 1991. *Secession: The Morality of Political Divorce From Fort Sumter to Lithuania and Quebec*. Boulder, CO: Westview Press.

_____. 1995. "The Morality of Secession." In Will Kymlicka, ed., *The Rights of Minority Cultures*. Oxford: Oxford University Press.

_____. 1998. "Democracy and Secession." In Margaret Moore, ed., *National Self-Determination and Secession*. New York: Oxford University Press.

Buchheit, Lee C. 1978. *Seccession: The Legitimacy of Self-Determination*. New Haven: Yale University Press.

Canovan, Margaret. 1996. *Nationhood and Political Theory*. Cheltenhan, UK: Edward Elgar Publishing limited.

Cohen, Joshua. 1989."Deliberation and Democratic Legitimacy." In Alan Hamlin and Philip Pettit, eds., *The Good Polity: Normative Analysis of the State*. Oxford: Basil Blackwell.

Cohen, Michell. ed. 1996. "Embattled Minorities Around the Globe: Rights, Hopes, Threats." *Dissent*, special issue, 43, no. 3.

Cole, Richard L., and Delbert A. Taebel, and Richard L. Engstrom. 1990. "Cumulative Voting in a Municipal Election: A Note on Voter Reaction and Electoral Consequences." *Western Political Quarterly*. 43 (1) pp. 191–199.

Collier, George A., and Elizabeth Lowery Quaratiello. 1994. *Basta! Land and the Zapatista Rebellion in Chiapas*. Oakland, CA: The Institute for Food and Development Policy.

Copp, David. 1999. "The Idea of a Legitimate State." *Philosophy and Public Affairs*. 28, no.1, pp. 1–45.

Cristman, John. 1996. *The Myth of Property: Toward an Egalitarian Theory of Ownership*. New York: Oxford University Press.

Daly, Herman, and John Cobb. 1994. *For the Common Good* 2nd. ed. Boston: Beacon Press.

Davidson, Donald. 1984. "On the Very Idea of a Conceptual Scheme." In Donald Davidson, ed., *Inquiries into Truth and Interpretation*. Oxford: Clarendon Press.

DePalma, Anthony. 1998. "Canada Pact Gives Tribe Self-Rule for First Time." *New York Times*, August 5, p. A2.

Dryzek, John S. 1990. *Discursive Democracy*. Cambridge, MA: Cambridge University Press.

Dworkin, Gerald. 1988. *The Theory and Practice of Autonomy*. Cambridge, U.K.: Cambridge University Press.

Dworkin, Ronald. 1990. "Foundations of Liberal Equality." In Grethe B. Peterson, ed., *The Tanner Lectures on Human Values*. Vol. XI. Salt Lake City: University of Utah Press.

Engstrom, Richard L., Delbert A. Taebel, and Richard L. Cole. 1989. "Cumulative Voting as a Remedy for Minority Vote Dilution: The Case of Alamogordo, New Mexico." *Journal of Law and Politics*. 5(3). pp. 469–97.

Engstrom, Richard L., and Charles J. Barilleaux. 1991. "Native Americans and Cumulative Voting." *Social Science Quarterly*. 72 (2). pp. 388–93.

Esman, Milton J., and Norman T. Uphoff. 1984. *Local Organizations: Intermediaries in Rural Development*. Ithaca: Cornell University Press.

Falk, Richard. 1998. "The United Nations and Cosmopolitan Democracy: Bad Dream, Utopian Fantasy, Political Project." In Daniele Archibugi, David Held, and Martin Kohler, eds. *Re-imagining Political Community: Studies in Cosmopolitan Democracy*. Stanford: Stanford University Press.

Foster, William Z. 1954. *The Negro People in American History*. New York: International Publishers.

Friedman, Milton. 1962. *Capitalism and Freedom*. Chicago: University of Chicago Press.

Gauthier, David. 1986. *Morals by Agreement*. Oxford: Oxford University Press.

Glendon, Mary Ann, and David Blankenhorn. eds. 1995. *Seedbeds of Virtue: Sources of Competence, Character, and Citizenship in American Society*. Lanham, MA: Madison Books.

Goldberg, David Theo. ed. 1994. *Multiculturalism: A Critical Reader*. Cambridge, MA: Blackwell Publishers.

Gracia, Jorge. 1986. ed. *Latin American Philosophy in the Twentieth Century*. Buffalo, NY: Prometheus Books.

Grand Council of the Crees. 1995. *Sovereign Injustice: Forcible Inclusion of the James Bay Crees and Cree Territory Into a Sovereign Quebec*.

Gray, John. 1992. *The Moral Foundations of Market Institutions*. London: IEA.

Greaves, Thomas. 1996. "Tribal Rights." In Stephen B. Brush and Doreen Stabinsky, eds., *Valuing Local Knowledge: Indigenous People and Intellectual Property Rights*. Washington, D.C.: Island Press.

Grifo, Francesca T., and David R. Downes. "Agreements to Collect Biodiversity for Pharmaceutical Research: Major Issues and Proposed Principles." In Stephen B. Brush and Doreen Stabinsky, eds., *Valuing Local Knowledge: Indigenous People and Intellectual Property Rights*. Washington, DC: Island Press.

Guatemala Health Rights Support Project. 1987. Washington, DC: Guatemala Health Rights Support Project.

Gudeman, Stephen. 1996. "Sketches, Qualms, and Other Thoughts on Intellectual Property Rights." In Stephen B. Brush and Doreen Stabinsky, eds., *Valuing Local Knowledge: Indigenous People and Intellectual Property*. Washington, DC: Island Press.

Guinier, Lani. 1994. *The Tyranny of the Majority: Fundamental Fairness in Representative Democracy*. New York: The Free Press.

Gurr, Ted Robert. 1993. *Minorities at Risk: A Global View of Ethnopolitical Conflicts*. Washington, D.C.: United States Institute of Peace Press.

Gutmann, Amy, and Dennis Thompson. 1996. *Democracy and Disagreement*. Cambridge, MA: Harvard University Press.

Habermas, Jurgen. 1993. *Moral Consciousness and Communicative Action*. trans. Christian Lenhardt and Shierry Weber Nicholsen. Cambridge, MA: MIT Press.

_____. 1992. *Faktizitat und Geltung*. Suhrkamp.

Hannum, Hurst. 1996. *Autonomy, Sovereignty, and Self-Determination: The Accommodation of Conflicting Rights*. rev. ed. Philadelphia: University of Pennsylvania Press.

Harris, Errol E. 1993. *One World or None: Prescription for Survival*. Atlantic Highlands, NJ: Humanities Press.

Hawken, Paul. 1993. *The Ecology of Commerce: A Declaration of Sustainability*. New York: HarperCollins Publishers.

Hayek, F. 1990. *The Fatal Conceit*. London: Routledge and Kegan Paul.

Haynes, Jeff. 1997. *Democracy and Civil Society in the Third World: Politics and New Political Movements*. Malden, MA: Polity Press.

Held, David. 1995. *Democracy and the Global Order*. Stanford, CA: Stanford University Press.

_____. 1998. "Democracy and Globalization." In Daniele Archibugi, David Held, and Martin Köhler, eds., *Re-imagining Political Community: Studies in Cosmopolitan Democracy*. Stanford: Stanford University Press.

Hettinger, Edwin C. 1997. "Justifying Intellectual Property." In Adam D. Moore, ed., *Intellectual Property: Moral, Legal, and International Dilemmas*. Lanham, MD: Rowman and Littlefield.

Hirschman, Albert O. 1970. *Exit, Voice, and Loyalty*. Cambridge, MA: Harvard University Press.

Hobbes, Thomas. 1991. *Leviathan*. Richard Tuck. ed. Cambridge, U.K.: Cambridge University Press.

Hollinger, David. 1995. *Postethnic America: Beyond Multiculturalism*. New York: Basic Books.

Huntington, Samuel P. 1996. *The Clash of Civilizations and the Remaking of World Order*. New York: Simon and Schuster.

Jamies, Annette. ed. 1992. *The State of Native America: Genocide, Colonization, and Resistance*. Boston: South End Press.

Kant, Immanuel. 1983. *Perpetual Peace and other Essays*. trans. Ted Humphrey. Indianapolis, IN: Hackett Publishing Co.

Keating, Michael. 1996. *Nations Against the State: The New Politics of Nationalism in Quebec, Catalonia, and Scotland*. New York: St. Martin's Press, Inc.

Klosko, George. 1992. *The Principle of Fairness and Political Obligation*. Savage, MD: Rowman and Littlefield.

Knight, Jack, and James Johnson. 1997. "What Sort of Equality does Deliberative Democracy Require?" In James Bohman and William Rehg, eds., *Deliberative Democracy: Essays on Reason and Politics*. Cambridge, MA: MIT Press.

Köhler, Martin. 1998. "From the National to the Cosmopolitan Public Sphere." In Daniele Archibugi, David Held, and Martin Köhler, eds., *Re-imagining Political Community: Studies in Cosmopolitan Democracy*. Stanford: Stanford University Press.

Kornblith, Hilary. ed. 1994. *Naturalizing Epistemology*. 2nd ed. Cambridge, MA: MIT Press.

Korten, David C. 1995. *When Corporations Rule the World*. Hartford, CT: Kumarian Press and San Francisco, CA: Berret-Koehler Publ.

Krausz, Michael. ed. 1989. *Relativism: Interpretation and Confrontation*. Notre Dame, IN: University of Notre Dame Press.

Kunjufu, Jawanza. 1988. *To Be Popular or Smart: The Black Peer Group*. Chicago: African American Images.

Kymlicka, Will. 1995. *Multicultural Citizenship: A Liberal Theory of Minority Rights*. Oxford: Oxford University Press.

_____.1995. *Multicultural Citizenship: A Liberal Theory of Minority Rights*. Oxford: Oxford University Press.

_____.1996. "The Good, the Bad, and the Intolerable: Minority Group Rights." *Dissent* 43, no. 3, pp. 22–30.

_____.1997. "The Social Contract Tradition." In Peter Singer, ed., *A Companion to Ethics*. Oxford: Blackwell Publishers.

_____.1998. "American Multiculturalism in the International Arena." *Dissent* 45, no. 4.

Kymlicka, Will. ed. 1995. *The Rights of Minority Cultures.* Oxford: New York: Oxford University Press.

Lakoff, George. 1987. *Women, Fire, and Dangerous Things: What Categories Reveal about the Mind.* Chicago: University of Chicago Press.

Le Grand, Julian, and Saul Estrin. eds. 1989. *Market Socialism.* Oxford: Clarendon Press.

Leopold, Aldo. 1970. *A Sand Almanac, with Essays on Conservation from Round River.* New York: Ballantine Books.

Lijphart, Arend. 1996. "Self-Determination versus Pre-Determination of Ethnic Minorities in Power-Sharing Systems." In Will Kymlicka, ed., *The Rights of Minority Cultures.* Oxford: Oxford University Press.

_____.1977. *Democracy in Plural Societies: A Comparative Exploration.* New Haven: Yale University Press.

Lipset, Seymour Martin. 1960. *Political Man.* New York: Doubleday.

Locke, John. 1960. *Two Treatises of Government.* Peter Laslett. ed. Cambridge, U.K.: Cambridge University Press.

Logan, Rayford W. 1997. *The Betrayal of the Negro: From Rutherford B. Hayes to Woodrow Wilson.* New York: Da Capo Press.

Lomansky, L. E. 1987. *Persons, Rights, and the Moral Community.* Oxford: Oxford University Press.

Lutz, Christopher H., and W. George Lovell. 1993. "K'iche' Maya of Guatemala." In Marc S. Miller, ed., *State of the People: A Global Human Rights Report on Societies in Danger.* Boston: Beacon Press.

_____. 1993. "Maya of Guatemala and Education." In Marc S. Miller, ed., *State of the Peoples: A Global Human Rights Report on Societies in Danger.* Boston: Beacon Press.

MacIntyre, Alasdair. 1981. *After Virtue.* Notre Dame, IN: University of Notre Dame Press.

_____.1989. "Relativism, Power, and Philosophy." In Michael Krausz, ed., *Relativism: Interpretation and Confrontation.* Notre Dame, IN: University of Notre Dame Press.

Mansbridge, Jane. 1996. "In Defense of 'Descriptive' Representation." Paper presented at the annual meeting of the American Political Science Association. San Francisco, 29 August-1 September.

Marglin, Stephen. 1996. "Farmers, Seedsmen and Scientists: Systems of Agriculture and Systems of Knowledge." In Frederique Apffel-Marglin and Stephen A. Marglin, eds., *Decolonizing Knowledge: From Development to Dialogue.* Oxford: Clarendon Press.

McGarry, John. 1998. "Orphans of Secession." In Margaret Moore, ed., *National Self-Determination.* New York: Oxford University Press.

Miller, David. 1980. "Justice and Property." *Ratio.* 22.

_____.1995. *On Nationality.* Oxford: Clarendon Press.

Miller, Marc S. ed. 1993. *State of the Peoples: A Global Human Rights Report on Societies in Danger.* Boston: Beacon Press.

Mills, Charles. 1997. *The Racial Contract.* Ithaca: Cornell University Press.

Montejano, David. 1987. *Anglos and Mexicans in the Making of Texas 1836–1986*. Austin, TX: University of Texas Press.

Nader, Ralph, and Lori Wallach. 1997. "GATT, NAFTA, and the Subversion of the Democratic Process." In Jerry Mander and Edward Goldsmith, eds., *The Case Against the Global Economy and for a Turn Toward the Local*. San Francisco: Sierra Club Books.

Nino, Carlos.1991. *The Ethics of Human Rights*. Oxford: Oxford University Press.

_____. 1996. *The Constitution of Deliberative Democracy*. New Haven: Yale University Press.

Noble, David. 1982. *America by Design*. New York: Knopf.

Nozick, Robert. 1974. *Anarchy, State, and Utopia*. Oxford: Basil Blackwell.

_____. 1986. "Distributive Justice." In Robert M. Stewart, ed., *Readings in Social and Political Philosophy*. New York: Oxford University Press.

Nussbaum, Martha, and Amartya Sen. 1989. "Internal Criticism and Indian Rationalist Traditions." In Michael Krausz, ed., *Relativism: Interpretation and Confrontation*. Notre Dame, IN: University of Notre Dame Press.

Pacari, Nina. 1996. "Taking on the Neoliberal Agenda." *NACLA: Report on the Americas*. Vol. XXIX No. 5 March/April. pp. 23–29.

Paine, Lynn. "Trade Secrets and the Justification of Intellectual Property: A Comment on Hettinger." In Adam Moore, ed., *Intellectual Property: Moral, Legal, and International Dilemmas*. Lanham, MD: Rowman and Littlefield.

Palley, Claire. 1979. "The Role of Law in Relation to Minority Groups." In Antony E. Alcock, Brian K. Taylor, and John M. Welton, eds., *The Future of Cultural Minorities*. London: Macmillan Press, LTD.

Patel, Surendra J. 1996. "Can the Intellectual Property Rights System Serve the Interests of Indigenous Knowledge?" In Stephen B. Brush and Doreen Stabinsky, eds., *Valuing Local Knowledge: Indigenous People and Intellectual Property Rights*. Washington, D.C.: Island Press.

Peet, Richard. 1987. *International Capitalism and Industrial Restructuring*. Boston: Allen and Unwin.

Pena, Devon. 1998. *Chicano Culture, Ecology, Politics: Subversive Kin*. Tucson, AZ: The University of Arizona Press.

Phillips, Kevin. 1994. *Arrogant Capital: Washington, Wall Street, and the Frustration of American Politics*. Boston: Little, Brown, and Co.

Pierson, Christopher. 1995. *Socialism After Communism: The New Market Socialism*. University Park, PA: The Pennsylvania State University Press.

Pitkin, Hanna. F. 1986. "Obligation and Consent, II." In Robert Steward, ed., *Readings in Social and Political Philosophy*. New York: Oxford University Press.

Putnam, Robert D. 1993. *Making Democracy Work: Civic Traditions in Modern Italy*. Princeton: Princeton University Press.

Rawls, John. 1971. *A Theory of Justice*. Cambridge, MA: Harvard University Press.

_____. 1996. *Political Liberalism*. New York: Columbia University Press.

Ray, J. C. 1992. "Conserving Biological Diversity." *State of the World—1992*. London: W. W. Norton and Co.

'oemer, John E. 1994. "A Future for Socialism." *Politics and Society*. Vol. 22 No. 4 December.

Rorty, Richard. 1989. "Solidarity or Objectivity?" In Michael Krausz , ed., *Relativism: Interpretation and Confrontation*. Notre Dame, IN: University of Notre Dame Press.

Rule, Wilma, and Joseph F. Zimmerman. eds. 1992. *United States Electoral Systems: Their Impact on Women and Minorities*. New York: Greenwood Press.

Schlesinger, Arthur M. 1992. *The Disuniting of America*. New York: W. W. Norton and Company.

Schlosser, Eric. 1998. "The Prison Industrial Complex." *Atlantic Monthly*. Vol. 282 no. 6 December. pp. 51–77.

Selucky, R. 1979. *Marxism, Socialism, and Freedom: Towards a General Democratic Theory of Labour-Managed Systems*. London: Macmillan Publishing Co.

Sen, Amartya. 1992. *Inequality Reexamined*. Cambridge, MA: Harvard University Press.

Sreenivasan, Gopal. 1995. *The Limits of Lockean Rights in Property*. New York: Oxford University Press.

Steinhorn, Leonard, and Barbara Diggs-Brown. 1999. *By the Color of Our Skin: The Illusion of Integration and the Reality of Race*. New York: Dutton.

Stevenson, Russell B. Jr. 1980. *Corporations and Information*. Baltimore: John Hopkins University Press.

Sumner, L. W. 1987. *The Moral Foundation of Rights*. Oxford: Clarendon Press.

Sunstein, Cass R. 1991. "Preferences and Politics." *Philosophy and Public Affairs*. 20.
_____. 1993. "Democracy and Shifting Preferences." In *The Idea of Democracy*. Cambridge, U.K.: Cambridge University Press.

Tamir, Yael. 1993. *Liberal Nationalism*. Princeton: Princeton University Press.

Taylor, Charles. 1992. "The Politics of Recognition." In Amy Gutmann, ed., *Multiculturalism and the "Politics of Recognition."* Princeton: Princeton University Press.

Taylor, Paul W. 1986. *Respect for Nature: A Theory of Environmental Ethics*. Princeton: Princeton University Press.

Truman, David. 1951. *The Governmental Process: Political Interests and Public Opinion*. New York: Knopf.

Tully, James. 1980. *A Discourse on Property: John Locke and His Adversaries*. Cambridge, U.K.: Cambridge University Press.

United Nations, 1986/7. *Study of the Problem of Discrimination Against Indigenous Populations*. UN Doc. E/CN.4/Sub.2/and Adds. 1-4.

Valadez, Jorge M. 1993. "Pre-Columbian and Modern Philosophical Perspectives in Latin America." In Robert C. Solomon and Kathleen M. Higgins, eds., *From Africa to Zen: An Invitation to World Philosophy*. Lapham, MD: Rowman and Littlefield.

Valleley, Paul. 1990. *Bad Samaritans: First World Ethics and Third World Debt*. Maryknoll, NY: Orbis Books.

Verba, Sidney, Norman H. Nie, and Jae-on Kim. 1978. *Participation and Political Equality: A Seven Nation Comparison*. Cambridge, U.K.: Cambridge University Press.

Verba, Sidney, Kay Lehman Schlozman, and Henry E. Brady. 1995. *Voice and Equality: Civic Voluntarism in American Politics*. Cambridge, MA: Harvard University Press.

Waldron, Jeremy. 1988. *The Right to Private Property*. Oxford: Clarendon Press.

_____. 1992. "Superseding Historic Injustice." *Ethics*. 103 , no. 1 October. pp. 4–28.

_____. 1993. "Special Ties and Natural Duties." *Philosophy and Public Affairs*. Volume 22. No. 1 Winter. pp. 3–30.

Walzer, Michael. 1983. *Spheres of Justice: A Defense of Pluralism and Equality*. New York: Basic Books.

_____. 1997. *On Toleration*. New Haven: Yale University Press.

Weisskopf, Thomas E. 1993. "A Democratic Enterprise-Based Market Socialism." In Pranab K. Bardhan and John E. Roemer, eds., *Market Socialism: The Current Debate*. New York: Oxford University Press.

Werther, Guntram F. A. 1992. *Self-Determination in Western Democracies: Aboriginal Politics in a Comparative Perspective*. Westport, CT: Greenwood Press.

Willett, Cynthia. ed. 1998. *Theorizing Multiculturalism: A Guide to the Current Debate*. Malden, MA: Blackwell Publishers Inc.

Williams Melissa S. 1998. *Voice, Trust, and Memory: Marginalized Groups and the Failings of Liberal Representation*. Princeton: Princeton University Press.

Wolfe, Eric R. 1982. *Europe and the People Without History*. Berkeley: University of California Press.

Wong, David. 1989. "Three Kinds of Incommensurability." In Michael Krausz, ed., *Relativism: Interpretation and Confrontation*. Notre Dame, IN: University of Notre Dame Press.

Young, Iris Marion. 1994. "Justice and Communicative Discourse." In R. Gottlieb, ed., *Tradition, Counter-Tradition, Politics: Dimensions of Radical Philosophy*. Philadelphia, PA: Temple University Press.

_____. 1996. "Communication and the Other: Beyond Deliberative Democracy." In Seyla Benhabib, ed., *Democracy and Difference: Contesting the Boundaries of the Political*. Princeton: Princeton University Press.

Zakaria, Fareed. 1997. "The Rise of Illiberal Democracy." *Foreign Affairs* 76, no. 6. pp. 22–43.

Zimmerman, Michael E., J. Baird Callicott, George Sessions, Karen J. Warren, and John Clark. eds. 1993. *Environmental Philosophy: From Animal Rights to Radical Ecology*. Englewood Cliffs, NJ: Prentice-Hall, Inc.

Index